T0305487

Visitor Attractions and Events

Both visitor attractions and events play pivotal roles in the appeal of tourism destination regions to visitors by virtue of being the main motivator of tourist trips and determining consumers' choices. However, more recently visitor attractions have become multifaceted, have proliferated and fragmented in terms of form, location, scale and style, and their role is undergoing major changes in a post-modern world as a result of consumer demands and innovations.

Visitor Attractions and Events for the first time theoretically and empirically explores the relations between events and attractions to offer new thinking of the role of space and place in shaping development, management practices and strategies in the sector as well as future implications. This book reveals how location is pivotal in the development, planning and management of visitor attractions and events. Whereas the location of natural attractions is relatively fixed in space and they can not be predetermined or relocated, human-made or contrived attractions are more influenced by the planning process in the context of the locational decision-making process. Competition and cooperation between visitor attractions and the aspects which shape these relations, including complementarities, compatibility, knowledge spillovers and diffusion of innovations, product similarities and spatial proximity, remain largely ignored in the sector and thus are major elements in the focus of this book. Comparative examples ranging from small to major attractions in a wide variety of locations are included.

This significant volume will appeal to all those interested in the visitor sector, such as tourism, events, leisure studies, destination management, geography, marketing and economics and sociology.

Adi Weidenfeld is a senior lecturer in tourism management at the Business School, Middlesex University, London, UK, and a visiting researcher at Hanken School of Economics in Vaasa, Finland. Adi has worked on his two-year Marie Curie Intra-European postdoctoral Fellowship at Hanken School of Economics, Finland, and completed his PhD in Geography at the University of Exeter, UK, after graduating a Masters in European Property and Development Planning at University College London, UK. His main interests include visitor attraction management, tourism development planning and policies, tourism clusters, knowledge transfer and innovation in tourism and tourism cross border region.

Richard Butler is an Emeritus Professor of Tourism, Strathclyde Business School, University of Strathclyde, Glasgow, UK, and Visiting Professor, Tourism Academy, NHTV University, Breda, Holland. He has degrees in Geography from the University of Nottingham (B.A.) and the University of Glasgow (PhD), and has been engaged in tourism research from 1964. He taught at the University of Western Ontario, Canada, from 1967 to 1997, and then joined the University of Surrey, UK, where he was Deputy Head of Research in the School of Management Studies for the Service Sector. He then took a part time position as Professor of Tourism at the University of Strathclyde in 2005. He has also taught and conducted research at James Cook University in Australia, CISET in Venice, Klaipeda College in Lithuania and Hong Kong Polytechnic University. His main research interests are in the development process of tourist destinations, island studies and the impacts of tourism, the latter particularly in the context of sustainability and resilience.

Allan M. Williams is a Professor of Tourism and Mobility Studies, School of Hospitality and Tourism Management, University of Surrey, UK. Allan Williams studied economics and geography as an undergraduate, before completing his PhD at the London School of Economics, UK. Subsequently he has worked at the Universities of Durham, Exeter, London Metropolitan and Surrey. His research focuses on the relationship between mobility and economic development, encompassing both tourism and migration. Recent books include *Tourism and Innovation* (with Michael Hall), *Wiley-Blackwell Companion to Tourism* (edited with Lew and Hall) and *Migration Risk and Uncertainty* (with Vladimir Baláž). He is co-editor of *Tourism Geographies*, and a fellow of the Academy of Social Science.

Routledge advances in event research series
Edited by Warwick Frost and Jennifer Laing
Department of Marketing, Tourism and Hospitality,
La Trobe University, Australia

For a complete list of titles in this series, please visit www.routledge.com.

Events, Society and Sustainability
Critical and contemporary approaches
Edited by Tomas Pernecky and Michael Lück

Exploring the Social Impacts of Events
Edited by Greg Richards, Maria deBrito and Linda Wilks

Commemorative Events
Memory, identities, conflict
Warwick Frost and Jennifer Laing

Power, Politics and International Events
Socio-cultural analyses of festivals and spectacles
Edited by Udo Merkel

Event Audiences and Expectations
Jo Mackellar

Event Portfolio Planning and Management
A holistic approach
Vassilios Ziakas

Conferences and Conventions
A research perspective
Judith Mair

Fashion, Design and Events
Edited by Kim M. Williams, Jennifer Laing and Warwick Frost

Food and Wine Events in Europe
A stakeholder approach
Edited by Alessio Cavicchi and Cristina Santini

Event Volunteering
International perspectives on the event volunteering experience
Edited by Karen Smith, Leonie Lockstone-Binney, Kirsten Holmes and Tom Baum

Visitor Attractions and Events

Locations and linkages

Adi Weidenfeld, Richard Butler and Allan M. Williams

Routledge
Taylor & Francis Group

LONDON AND NEW YORK

First published 2016
by Routledge
2 Park Square, Milton Park, Abingdon, Oxon OX14 4RN

and by Routledge
605 Third Avenue, New York, NY 10017

First issued in paperback 2021

Routledge is an imprint of the Taylor & Francis Group, an informa business

British Library Cataloguing in Publication Data
A catalogue record for this book is available from the British Library

Library of Congress Cataloging in Publication Data
Names: Weidenfeld, Adi, author. | Butler, Richard, 1943– author. |
Williams, Allan M., author.
Title: Visitor attractions and events: locations and linkages / Adi Weidenfeld,
Richard Butler and Allan M Williams.
Description: New York, NY: Routledge, 2016. |
Series: Routledge advances in event research series |
Includes bibliographical references and index.
Identifiers: LCCN 2015047048| ISBN 9781138824713 (hbk) |
ISBN 9781315740492 (ebk)
Subjects: LCSH: Amusement rides—Planning. | Amusement parks—Planning. |
Tourism.Classification: LCC GV1859 .W45 2016 | DDC 791.06/8—dc23
LC record available at http://lccn.loc.gov/2015047048

ISBN 13: 978-1-03-224250-7 (pbk)
ISBN 13: 978-1-138-82471-3 (hbk)

DOI: 10.4324/9781315740492

Typeset in Times New Roman
by Keystroke, Station Road, Codsall, Wolverhampton

Contents

Figures

Tables

Boxes

Contributors

Peter Björk is Professor of Marketing at HANKEN School of Economics, Vaasa, Finland. His research focus is in the field of tourism marketing, sustainable tourism, ecotourism and destination development. He has a special interest in destination branding and tourism innovations. Peter Björk is Associate Editor for Scandinavian *Journal of Hospitality and Tourism* and *Finnish Journal of Tourism Research*, and a Board Member of the Finnish University Network for Tourism Studies (FUNTS)

Richard Butler is an Emeritus Professor of Tourism, Strathclyde Business School, University of Strathclyde, Glasgow, UK, and Visiting Professor, Tourism Academy, NHTV University, Breda, Holland. He has degrees in Geography from the University of Nottingham (B.A.) and the University of Glasgow (PhD), and has been engaged in tourism research from 1964. He taught at the University of Western Ontario, Canada, from 1967 to 1997, and then joined the University of Surrey, UK, where he was Deputy Head of Research in the School of Management Studies for the Service Sector. He then took a part time position as Professor of Tourism at the University of Strathclyde in 2005. He has also taught and conducted research at James Cook University in Australia, CISET in Venice, Klaipeda College in Lithuania and Hong Kong Polytechnic University. His main research interests are in the development process of tourist destinations, island studies and the impacts of tourism, the latter particularly in the context of sustainability and resilience.

Anna Leask, PhD, is Professor of Tourism Management at Edinburgh Napier University, UK. Her teaching and research interests combine and lie principally in the areas of visitor attraction management, heritage tourism and destination management. Anna has co-edited several textbooks including *Managing Visitor Attractions* (2008) and *Managing World Heritage Sites* (2006) and contributed to several key tourism textbooks. She is on the Editorial Board for four international tourism journals and has been actively involved in the Scientific Committees for many international conferences in Europe and the US. She has published in key academic journals such as *Tourism Management, International Journal of Tourism Research* and *Current Issues in Tourism*, in addition to publishing a range of case studies, articles and practitioner papers.

Recent research has focused on how visitor attractions and hotels can engage with Generation Y visitors and employees, with primary research being conducted in the UK, Hong Kong, Macau and Singapore.

Ken Robinson, CBE, is an independent tourism adviser who specialises in visitor attractions. With a background in the management of commercial charitable and public sector visitor attractions he led consultancies advising on tourism and visitor attractions worldwide. He chaired the national Visitor Attractions Forum in England, and started the annual National Conference for Visitor Attractions. He describes himself as 'a tourism enthusiast'. His goal is to be a pragmatic pioneer of new initiatives, strategies and solutions to optimise the economic, cultural and social benefits of tourism, for rapidly evolving and developed destinations. Ken is a Board Member of the Tourism Society and Chair of its Think Tank, and a former Board Member and Chair of the Tourism Alliance in the UK, chair of Tourism South East, a member of VisitBritain's British Tourism Development Committee and of VisitEngland's Strategic Industry Group. He has been an adviser to the UN's International Trade Centre on national and destination Tourism strategy development, and is a member of the World Travel Market Advisory Council. He is a Board Member and Trustee of several other Tourism bodies. Ken was awarded the CBE for services to tourism in 1997, and an Honorary Doctorate in 2014.

Adi Weidenfeld is a senior lecturer in tourism management at the Business School, Middlesex University, London, UK, and a visiting researcher at Hanken School of Economics in Vaasa, Finland. Adi has worked on his two-year Marie Curie Intra-European postdoctoral Fellowship at Hanken School of Economics, Finland, and completed his PhD in Geography at the University of Exeter, UK, after graduating a Masters in European Property and Development Planning at University College London, UK. His main interests include visitor attraction management, tourism development planning and policies, tourism clusters, knowledge transfer and innovation in tourism and tourism cross border region.

Allan M. Williams is a Professor of Tourism and Mobility Studies, School of Hospitality and Tourism Management, University of Surrey, UK. Allan Williams studied economics and geography as an undergraduate, before completing his PhD at the London School of Economics, UK. Subsequently he has worked at the Universities of Durham, Exeter, London Metropolitan and Surrey. His research focuses on the relationship between mobility and economic development, encompassing both tourism and migration. Recent books include *Tourism and Innovation* (with Michael Hall), *Wiley-Blackwell Companion to Tourism* (edited with Lew and Hall) and *Migration Risk and Uncertainty* (with Vladimir Baláž). He is co-editor of *Tourism Geographies*, and a fellow of the Academy of Social Science.

Acknowledgements

We would like to thank Mr Ken Robinson CBE for his insight on the visitor attraction sector from an experienced practitioner's perspective and sharing his views on the most recent and future trends in the sector. We are grateful to Professor Peter Björk for adding a marketing perspective to the book in relation to visitor attractions marketing and destination branding, and to Professor Anna Leask for her contribution to defining and examining the complex relationships between visitor attractions and events. Finally, we appreciate very much the support and assistance of Philippa Mullins and Emma Travis and their patience and encouragement during the completion of this volume.

Part I

Introduction

The visitor attraction and event sectors

1   Introduction

Tourism is concerned with people travelling to and from destinations, and in most examples of academic research this is for leisure purposes (including enjoyment, relaxation, excitement, socialising and exercise). The destinations tourists visit are in themselves attractions, in the sense that such places draw or attract visitors, normally to see and experience particular features or ensembles of features, some of which may be uniquely found in specific locations. A destination is regarded by Buhalis and Cooper (1998:325) as 'the raison d'être for tourism, providing an amalgam of tourism products such as facilities, attractions, and activities, which respond to the needs and wants of tourists'. Thus locations with the only, the largest, the smallest or the oldest examples of phenomena tend to become popular with visitors, although that is greatly influenced by the development of accessibility and the provision of necessary facilities and services for tourism. For example, Latvia has become a tourist destination in the last decade, with Riga, its capital city, the prime attraction for tourists to that country. The old town of Riga is a UNESCO World Heritage Site and has a number of impressive and visually appealing buildings within the boundaries of its historic walls. Each of these buildings is a minor attraction in its own right, and worth seeing, although, like the Giant's Causeway in Northern Ireland, probably not worth going to see on its own (Boswell, 1952). Rather it is the combination of so many heritage attractions in a small area that makes Riga an important tourism destination, allied with relatively recent substantial improvements in accessibility from international tourist markets resulting from budget airlines services, and the establishment of a considerable number of hotels offering good quality accommodation at prices below those prevalent in most western European capitals. Riga, therefore, illustrates the complexity of attractions in the tourism context; the need for a large enough set of individual attractions (or a truly unique or distinctive feature with massive drawing power), good mass transport facilities, a positive destination image, the provision of associated services such as accommodation and places of entertainment, and an atmosphere and image of security and hospitality. In short, attractions and events represent major elements in the tourism system, but are features that are dependent on other elements within that system to generate visitation and operate successfully.

Attractions and events come in a variety of forms and scales and, as Lew (1987) notes, much depends on the perceptions and tastes of tourists, with some attractions being seen as one of many attractions in a place, while others are destinations in their own right. In other words, some attractions appeal to visitors and residents because they are inextricably linked to a system of attractions, while others are the raison d'etre of a visit to that destination. They reflect not only the present but also the past tastes and preferences of tourists, because the latter have become articulated and locked into both images and investments in the built environment. Moreover, some are well known and popular at the international level while others will only be known and visited at the local level.

Law (2002) notes that, based on surveys of the relative importance of attractions in drawing visitors to a destination, attractions can be categorised as the sole reason for visiting a destination, one among a range of reasons, and/or one of (virtually) no importance in attracting visitors. Some serve roles as protectors of heritage while others pose threats to heritage, some remain highly popular for decades or longer, while others have short lives as viable economic enterprises. Above all, they are dynamic, reflecting and being modified to meet the changing tastes of tourists, the evolving nature of the destinations in which they are located, and structural changes in societies, as well as continually competing with other attractions for visitors.

This volume endeavours to portray this complexity by exploring the nature of attractions and events and the differences between them, how they affect their host destinations and how they are modified through redevelopment, competition, cooperation, knowledge transfer, innovation and interaction with other elements in their destinations and further afield. This introductory chapter begins with a discussion of what we understand by attractions and events, and their various forms and roles, in order to provide a context for the subsequent chapters, which are then briefly introduced.

Despite their importance in being akin to 'the jewels in a crown', that is, the features which draw tourists to a location, there has been comparatively less written on attractions and events compared to many other aspects of tourism in general (Watson and McCracken, 2002, Weidenfeld and Leask, 2013). Whether this is because their importance and contribution tend to be taken for granted, or because these sectors lack the sub-disciplinary focus that hospitality provides for the accommodation sector is not clear, but there are significant theoretical and empirical gaps in our understanding of attractions, gaps which this book seeks to address.

Recent research has made significant advances in addressing some of the gaps in the literature on attractions. Lew (1987) proposed a useful framework for research on visitor attractions involving three perspectives: ideographic, organisational and cognitive. Subsequently, Swarbrooke (2002) and Walsh-Heron (1990) focused on the nature of visitor attractions and events as businesses and related micro-management issues, such as marketing, human resources and design. A more recent volume by Fyall et al. (2008) added to our knowledge of the development of the sector and addressed specific topics, including marketing and aspects of different types of attractions. An even more current book on visitor attractions by Edelheim (2015) focuses on the nature of identity, memory, narrative and performance in the context of managing the tourist experience offered by visitor attractions. However, none of these books addresses issues related to working relations among visitor attractions and events in general, and between them and the destinations they are located within in particular. This volume takes a more geographical approach to studying visitor attractions and events by considering the spatial relationships amongst them, and with other businesses, in the context of their regional distribution and location.

Spatial relationships

Spatial relationships can be expressed by distance, topography, travel/walking distance, compactness, different spatial patterns of settlements and roadways, zoning, land-use and also in terms of their impact on the business environment. Spatial configuration (or organisation) of a tourism space such as destination regions refers to where attractions (as places) are situated. Every aspect that is influenced directly by spatial factors such as unique location within a certain environmental setting, proximity, clustering, relative distance and spatial organisation (or spatial pattern) can be regarded as a spatial relationship. There are 'no rigid deterministic [spatial] relationships between a particular form of sector organization, inter-company relations, and a particular geography of the supply chain' (Hudson, 2001:201), and even in networked just-in-time systems, component supplier companies can be situated in adjacent locations or literally on the other side of the world (Sadler, cited in Hudson, 2001).

This book views spatial relationships from a broader geographic angle, considering environmental and locational aspects as well as social relations between actors. Spatial relations affect mobilities, whether they are economic, cultural, political or environmental, in production and consumption spaces including the interrelated mobilities of goods, information, services and financial transactions (Shaw and Williams, 2004). Spatial relationships underlie planning tools, which influence strategic spatial planning such as for determining optimal locations. They are a key part of understanding relationships in the world economy (Venables, 2005) and are pivotal in economic geography, which is about 'the geographical variation in what firms produce, how they produce it, their linkages with other firms, labour relations and access to finance' (Sheppard, 2000:176).

In other industries production depends on material interchanges between spatially adjacent processes such as bulk chemicals and steel. In tourism, supply and demand sit together in the same locations, where the customers come to the suppliers and not vice versa. Therefore, as far as the production of tourism is concerned, the location is often an inextricable part of the tourism product (Bærenholdt and Haldrup, 2006). Tourism destinations are, in most cases, networked ubiquitous just-in-time systems, where suppliers operate simultaneously, e.g. transporting tourists to and within a destination and accommodating, catering and entertaining them, which makes spatial proximity between them essential. Thus, spatial relationships within and between tourism spaces, which form one of the foundations of tourism (McKercher and Lew, 2004), are given further attention in this volume.

Understanding attractions and events

Definitions

Part of the reason for the relative neglect of attractions and events centres on definitional difficulties, a problem which has longed affected tourism in its entirety (Butler, 2015). Finding a definition that is widely accepted throughout the academic literature has proved difficult as Leask (2010), Leask and Fyall (2006) and Swarbrooke (2002) have pointed out. This is in part because what may be viewed as a visitor or tourist attraction can take a wide variety of forms depending on context and viewpoint, while also being influenced by scale and size.

An 'official' definition of a visitor attraction is provided by VisitEngland (2013, 2015):

> an attraction where it is feasible to charge admission for the sole purpose of sightseeing. The attraction must be a permanently established excursion destination, a primary purpose of which is to allow access for entertainment, interest, or education; rather than being primarily a retail outlet or a venue for sporting, theatrical, or film performances. It must be open to the public ... attracting day visitors or tourists as well as local residents.

As Robinson notes (Chapter 13) there are good reasons for such a specific definition, including issues of quality control and commonality of purpose amongst members of an industry association, but in the context of tourism and leisure in general, some of the limitations of that definition present problems. While some aspects of the above description are appropriate, such as including a wide range of visitors from local residents and day visitors to tourists, other elements would appear to be misappropriate or too limited. To visitors to London or New York, retail stores such as Harrods in London and Macy's in New York are truly significant attractions and very much part of the appeal of those cities respectively. Furthermore, in many cities leading museums and art galleries charge no admission fees, except for specific exhibitions, a situation which undoubtedly accounts for high visitor numbers in some circumstances (especially when there is bad weather!). The 'permanent' nature of an attraction is also a dubious element of a definition, given the socially constructed, as opposed to objective, nature of attractions. For example, Dismaland in Weston-super-Mare, in the UK, which opened for a limited period in 2015, was most certainly a visitor attraction, drawing over 150,000 people to the site (Harvey, 2015). However, it was never intended to be a permanent exhibition and has since been disassembled and the contents moved to Calais. Another problem with the above definition relates to a feature not being primarily a venue for sporting or theatrical performances. Sporting arenas such as Old Trafford (Manchester), Camp Nou (Barcelona) and Lords Cricket Ground in London (Cardwell and Ali, 2014) are now major visitor attractions even when games are not being played at the grounds concerned, as is the Olympic Games site in East London. Similarly the theatres on Broadway or in central London are major tourist and local attractions, contributing greatly to the visitor appeal of such cities. There is also a growing tendency for other types of tourism and non-tourism businesses to become visitor attractions to varying degrees. Some hotels, such as the Mirage and the Venetian hotels in Las Vegas, Nevada, in the US are visited by many tourists who are not staying guests at those hotels. Others may be a hybrid of a visitor attraction and another business, such as the Ice hotel in Jukkasjärvi, Sweden, which is both a provider of hotel services and a visitor attraction.

Finally, many attractions are free of charge for entry, certainly for visitors to see, and in many cases, to visit. Some of the great religious buildings of the world, military and other cemeteries, battlefield sites, and the historic parts of cities such as Bruges, Jerusalem, Venice and Hong Kong are open to visitors at no charge. Above all, many visitor attractions are natural features. This includes: beaches and geological structures: for example, the Giant's Causeway in Northern Ireland; the Grand Canyon in the US; living features such as the Great Barrier Reef in Australia and the wildlife of Africa; and water features including lakes (e.g. Titicaca, Como), waterfalls (e.g. Iguacu, Victoria, Niagara) and rivers (e.g. Amazon, Nile, Thames, Seine). While considerable cost may be involved in travelling to such features, they can be enjoyed free of charge on site, although additional elements and facilities or activities, for which fees are charged (such as boat trips, restaurants and sightseeing towers), often adorn or mar their vicinities. Some of these features are of such a size, in such locations or are locked into such complex relationships with their surroundings that management is limited if not impossible, and in many cases is related more to restrictions on development and visitor access and behaviour than to pro-active management of the feature itself.

Types of attractions

Given the challenges outlined above, it is tempting to define a visitor attraction in the widest and simplest terms as 'a feature which draws visitors to it', reflecting the enormous variety of features which are truly visitor attractions. The ownership and control of visitor attractions vary as widely as the type of feature involved; many are privately, and in some cases exclusively, owned and controlled, while others are public property with little or no control exerted on visitors or the feature. Some are managed and maintained by public bodies under direct government (at various levels) control, while others are managed and maintained by quasi-public bodies including National Park authorities and other conservation agencies such as the National Trust (UK) and similar organisations. Other charitable bodies operate many smaller and often more specialised attractions such as former residences of famous authors or painters. Yet other attractions are operated by single purpose organisations, sometimes family run and associated directly with the feature involved and not always operated as predominantly commercial enterprises. Many others are privately owned, including theme parks, and operate entirely as commercial enterprises, subject to the discipline of market forces, with little if any sentimentality and limited heritage considerations. The functions and roles of attractions are equally diverse and sometimes conflicting, including entertainment and amusement, heritage preservation, interpretation, education, physical activity and culture (Watson and McCracken, 2002). As tastes in the markets change, so too do expectations about the features and attributes offered at and by visitor attractions. Many have changed from passive viewing to active experience through technological innovations (Benckendorff, 2006), a trend particularly noticeable in heritage and cultural attractions, where attractions previously kept separate from visitors now encourage close contact and inter-action (National Trust for Scotland 2014).

Swarbrooke (2002) classified visitor attractions as being of four types: natural, (hu)man-made purpose-built, (hu)man-made non-tourist purpose-built, and events and festivals. The first category included beaches, mountains, lakes and forests, the second theme parks and rides, the third cathedrals and other historic buildings, and the fourth happenings which were not physical or permanent. Morrison and Mill (1992) produced a similar list with five categories, based on: the attraction of the landscape, urban and cultural attractions, rural historical and cultural attractions, sporting events and artificially created attractions. The first group included not only different forms of landscapes, but also hunting, fishing, spas and health resorts; the second included not only buildings but also religious pilgrimage; the third included ethnic attractions such as native customs as well as physical features, and the last group included theme parks.

A somewhat wider group of features are included in Figure 1.1, which illustrates thematic links between the different elements. Cultural attractions include art galleries, museums and concert halls, thus involving both active performance and passive viewing, as well as ethnic attractions such as indigenous peoples' customs and displays (Butler and Hinch, 2007).

These may be located in both rural and urban settings and in some cases are in the form of events rather than permanent features. In some cities, cultural features are found in specific districts, for example Broadway in New York. Cultural attractions can also include what are known, sometimes inappropriately, as 'dark tourism' attractions, namely battlefields, cemeteries, death camps and sites of horror, torture and death (Butler and Suntikul, 2013). Some of these features, in reality, may be sites of inspiration and homage to past heroics to some visitors, such as Thermopylae, Rorke's Drift, Massada and Gallipoli. Much depends on the interpretation provided at such sites (Laderman, 2013) and the image pre-established in visitors' minds.

Natural attractions involve two main types; first are natural features such as mountains, water bodies, beaches and geological features, some 'visited' only in the sense of being seen, sometimes from a distance, such as the glaciers of Alaska viewed from a cruise liner. The second type relates to living phenomena, parti-cularly animals and birds, but also including marine mammals such as whales, that are normally viewed in the wild, but also in reserves, game parks, zoos and aquaria. This category also includes natural phenomena such as the Aurora Borealis, eclipses and weather conditions (as in storm watching on Vancouver Island, Canada).

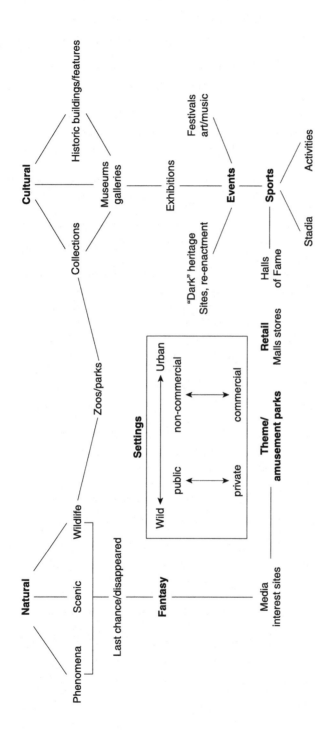

Figure 1.1 Types of attractions and events and their settings

Sporting attractions include events such as the Olympic Games, World Cups and Championships and also the stadia and locations in which such events are held. Thus, famous football, baseball and cricket stadia are popular visitor attractions, and so too are features such as the Old (golf) Course in St Andrews, Scotland, the 'Home of Golf'. This is an iconic attraction, which allows the public to actually play the course on which championships take place, as well as to visit and walk on the course. Winter sports areas where the public may ski on the same slopes as world champions are similar attractions. Enterprises such as 'Halls of Fame' fall between cultural attractions and sporting attractions depending on their focus (e.g. sporting or music).

Retail attractions include iconic stores such as Harrods and Macy's mentioned earlier. They also include collections of retail outlets in shopping malls such as West Edmonton Mall (Butler, 1991) (featuring a beach and wave attraction, an ice rink and a theme hotel as well as shops), and Dubai's Mall of the Emirates (with a ski slope, DUCTAC theatre complex and Magic Planet games attractions) as well as outlet stores and villages and specialist shops for items such as used books. Health attractions include spas which offer more than beauty treatment alone, wellness establishments and health farms (and the features surrounding them such as paths and water based features), as well as hospitals catering specifically to tourists, such as for dental care in Hungary. Rural attractions are somewhat different, tending to be categorised primarily on the setting of the attraction as well as its characteristics. They also include farm based attractions, wineries, distilleries and other attractions focused on rural themes and activities such as museums of agricultural life and events such as farm and game (as in wildlife) shows.

There is one group of visitor attractions which may best be termed 'fantasy' attractions, which are visited purely because of images that have been created, for which there is little or no claim that they bear any relation to local realities. One such example is the Sherlock Holmes Museum in Baker Street in London, which is a twentieth century creation of the home of a fictional literary character, Conan Doyle's famous detective, and while the artefacts within may be genuine antiques, they can have no authentic link to a fictitious figure. Similarly, Platform 9 3/4 at Kings Cross Station (in London) or Hogwarts Theme Park are fantasy attractions based on the Harry Potter books. Ghost tours, sites of movie productions such as *Star Wars* in Tunisia, *Popeye* in Malta and *Lord of the Rings* in New Zealand have all become popular visitor attractions. The last named has been used effectively by the national tourist board of New Zealand to create an image of the whole country. Movie studios themselves, locations of television settings, real buildings portrayed in films and television programmes, and the homes of movie stars in Los Angeles are also popular with visitors, although their real motivations for visiting are not clear (see special issue of the journal WHATT 2011 Vol 3, Issue 2 on Film Tourism).

Finally, there are attractions which do not clearly fall into any specific group. One example is that of attractions which no longer exist, as discussed by Weaver and Lawton (2007), places to which visitors come, even though the attraction is no longer there. Another is collections of unusual or freak phenomena, such as the Ripley's Believe It Or Not attraction at Niagara Falls, or Elvis Presley's Cars in the same location, which have no relation to the primary attraction (the waterfalls) of the destination. An example of a lapsed attraction is the garbage dump in Banff village in Banff National Park in Canada: in the years before the day's garbage was buried each night, and the surrounding fence strengthened, this was a popular site for visitors to see black bears in the evening when the dump was closed. Related to this category of attractions are what are known as 'Last Chance Tourism' attractions (Lemelin et al., 2011), namely features and phenomena that are disappearing and will no longer exist in the foreseeable future: examples include glaciers, wildlife and historic features under threat of erosion or destruction.

Types of events

Events, which although certainly not fitting the VisitEngland definition of visitor attractions noted earlier, are clearly a sub-sector of visitor attractions although they can also be considered as a separate sector (Chapter 2). They are often on a large scale involving thousands of visitors, many travelling considerable distances to witness a specific event, for example, the 'Barmy Army' of English cricket supporters who travel worldwide to watch cricket test matches (Emery et al., 2014). They include sporting events, as already mentioned, of varying duration: a football Cup Final is a one day event attracting up to or even exceeding 100,000 spectators, an Open Golf tournament lasts four days and attracts around a quarter of a million admissions, while the Olympic Games last around two to three weeks and attract several million spectators. Music festivals range in length from one day to several days: the most famous was probably that held at Woodstock in 1969, which was three days long and attracted in excess of 400,000 people. Wider cultural festivals range from evening events such as Halloween, Guy Fawkes Night and Hogmanay (New Year) of less than a day's duration, to mammoth events such as the Edinburgh Festival which lasts a full month and includes many smaller events under its umbrella, from the nightly military tattoo to the 'Fringe' series of 400 specific acts and performances of variable length and audience attendance. The primary role of many events is as a supplementary attraction for a destination, although a few, the aforementioned Edinburgh Festival, the Venice Film Festival and the New Orleans and Rio de Janiero's Mardi Gras festivals, are major attractions in their own right.

Generally events are of short duration and are often established to boost attendance and visitation at established visitor attractions and destinations, and they may or may not have a strong relationship to the location, nature and focus of the destination (Butler and Smale, 1991). Indeed, the fact that the content of an annual or regular event normally changes from year to year is part of its ongoing appeal, providing as it does a 'new' element on each occasion, hence the use of different famous and often iconic groups or individuals as the closing act at the Glastonbury Music Festival and others each year. That three day event, and others elsewhere, generally features a complete change of performers from one year to the next.

This widens and increases their potential audience by attracting new visitors while maintaining a significant proportion of regular repeat visitors, for whom the event itself is almost as important as the headline acts that appear at the festival. Increasingly 'circuits' of events have been created, such as the case with Formula 1 car racing grand prix, with their requirements of a racetrack, associated servicing areas (pits) and spectator stands for up to 200,000 visitors. Golf, tennis, skiing, athletics, horse racing, sailing and surfing all have annual international competitions, generally lasting a few days, also mostly using the same locations at approximately the same time of year. The numbers attending these event attractions are generally large, have specific requirements in terms of event location and facilities and are highly organised and publicised far beyond the host location. The impacts of such events are discussed in more detail in Chapter 10 and in some instances the negative effects may outweigh the benefits gained by the host because of the nature and scale of requirements, including meeting the demands of international media.

Other types of events tend to be smaller in number of participants, if not in duration, and include battlefield tours and battle re-enactments (Daniels et al., 2013), educational courses and tours, anniversary celebrations (for example, the bi-centenary of the Battle of Waterloo in 2015) and commemorations of many First World War events (Jansen-Verbeke and George, 2013) and other military campaigns (including the 70th anniversaries of the Second World War D-Day landings, and 75th anniversary of the Battle of Britain). Attendance at these events is often lower in number than at commercial events and many participants will have specific personal links to the events, ranging from individual actual participation in the original event or family member participation, to official involvement in the ceremonies. Individual attractions often hold their own specific events as part of the tourism marketing and promotion of their destination, commemorating events from the destination's past and celebrating the opening or new or restored facilities and attractions, such as the re-opening of Dreamland in Margate (Chapter 4).

There remains one other feature which is both an attraction and an event, and that is the cruise ship and its journey. To many tourists the cruise ship is both the attraction and the destination, and while it may visit several destinations on its cruise, representing a series of individual events to the passengers, it is the ship rather than the places visited which is the main focus. Over the past three decades, cruise tourism has grown rapidly and the ports of call and home ports involved have changed in location, and the facilities and services provided (Barron and Greenwood, 2006; Lawton and Butler, 1989). Although ships generally remain in an individual port for a matter of hours at the most, even if overnight, and the estimates of their impacts remain unclear although certainly significant (Brida and Zapata, 2010), they have resulted in major development in the ports involved and strong competition amongst them to maintain cruise ship visitation (Hasche, 2015). The ocean-going ships themselves have continually grown in size from a few hundred passengers to over 4,000 in the case of the newest vessels. Much smaller boats (from a few score to a couple of hundred passengers in size) have also begun to offer river cruises on major waterways in Europe, Asia and the Americas. In some cases, cruise itineraries are organised to arrive in specific ports during major events, such as the Carnival in Rio de Janiero, or concerts at towns on major rivers such as Vienna, Austria. The cruise ships in ports do not normally allow access to the ships by non-passengers, thus while they may be a visual attraction (or blight) to other visitors in a destination, unlike other attractions they do not directly engage with the general tourist market. Their passengers, however, often disperse widely through the ports and their hinterlands (Jaakson, 2004).

Attractions and events are complex and varied in nature and function, and encompass many aspects of tourism, recreation and leisure in general. The same attraction or event may serve as a local facility and also as an international attraction. Surf in Australia, e.g. at Manly (New South Wales), is not only a local phenomenon that is used daily by local residents but also at the same time an international feature drawing tourists to that location, and also serving briefly but regularly as the setting for international competitions. Attractions and events are often coordinated in their establishment and marketing, and as Weidenfeld and Leask note (Chapter 2), may become part of the branding of a destination, and they may become indistinguishable from each other. Attractions often contain events as part of their operation, and there is always a possibility that such events may be viewed as less essential than the attractions and in due course may be replaced or removed by the owners/organisers of the event (Walker, 2015). The relationships between attractions and events have not been examined in depth and thus remain an important aspect of the role and function of these phenomena to be studied in more detail. Inevitably the differences and relations between attractions and events are sometimes difficult to disentangle, and analysing these relationships involves understanding the dynamic nature of both phenomena. This topic is discussed briefly below in the context of the subsequent chapters of this volume.

The dynamic relationships of attractions and events

It has been emphasised above that both attractions and events are highly dynamic and it is clear that the relationships between individual attractions and events and their competitors and partners are equally dynamic. As attractions and events represent different elements within a destination's overall package of opportunities for its residents and visitors, it is appropriate to follow this introductory chapter with a discussion of the differences and similarities between attractions and events. This is done by Weidenfeld and Leask in the context of a continuum which serves as a framework for exploring these elements in more detail. That chapter is followed by an examination of the way in which attractions, in particular, cluster and agglomerate. The literature on tourism destinations (Swarbrooke, 2002) reveals clearly how destinations develop and how many begin with only one or a very few attractions, and it is the assembling of a group or cluster of attractions that enables a destination to compete successfully in the tourist market. Clustering is a process common to many economic activities and just as applicable to tourism as to manufacturing. The agglomeration of similar attractions (or producers of goods) can raise the image and visibility of a specific location above its competitors and gives rise to a series of processes (horizontal, vertical and diagonal clustering) which are discussed in the third chapter. Following from this, discussion in the fourth chapter examines how relationships between attractions and events occur in destinations and the relationship of such a process to the theory of the tourism area life cycle of destinations (Butler 1980). The chapter suggests that there are a number of potential life cycles for attractions depending on their nature, function and role within specific destinations, but that all attractions develop and change in their appearance, scale and relationships with each other through their own and their destination's development cycle.

The second part of the book deals with the economic and management processes affecting visitor attractions. First, there is discussion of the compatibility of types of attractions with each other within destinations, followed by examination of the issue of complementarity between attractions. In some cases the existence of a number of attractions that are similar in terms of themes and elements presents potential advantages to destinations where these elements are compatible and complementary with each other, and positive relationships can develop that enable the destination to develop successfully. This aspect is explored further in the next chapter that reviews the issue of cooperation in the attraction sector and the forms that this process can take. Again there are appropriate models and examples in the generic business literature that are suitable for elaborating on some of the issues involved.

In many destinations, however, there remains strong competition between individual attractions for visitors, a process which does not necessarily benefit either the destination as a whole or the individual attractions themselves. Following on from this chapter is the topic of knowledge transfer in this sector. Within the attraction field there is frequent imitation of ideas and features, particularly among attractions that are purpose-built, and the knowledge utilised comes from both within and outside of the host destinations. Different types of attractions and those at different scales approach the gaining and exchanging of knowledge in different ways, using different techniques in efforts to make their specific enterprise more successful in attracting visitors. Part of the knowledge transfer process involves innovation, the subject of the final chapter in this part. Innovation is a key ingredient in determining success or failure in the attraction and event sector, with few attractions able to continue successfully in business without engaging in innovation and change during their existence or life cycle. New knowledge, new attitudes and policies, new arrangements and new products and technologies are all part of the innovation process experienced by attractions and events. Even those features based on heritage and culture can benefit from innovation in terms of providing information and opportunities for deeper and alternative forms of engagement by the visitors.

The final part of the book begins with a discussion of the impacts of attractions and events upon their host destinations. As parts of the tourism industry in general, the specific impacts are mostly those well known from the generic tourism literature (see for example Mathieson and Wall, 1982, Hall and Lew, 2009), but the scale and duration of some of these impacts vary considerably in terms of the effects of attractions and events. The benefits and costs of the operation of attractions and the holding of events need to be examined explicitly to appreciate them fully and they often vary widely from destination to destination with regards to type of attraction and event. Much of their impact depends on the scale of the attraction, and whether it is regarded as iconic or flagship. Iconic attractions draw visitors based on more than the specific features of the enterprise, involving image, authenticity and appropriateness, while flagship attractions are somewhat more straightforward in their appeal and effects (Chapter 11). These elements feature again in the chapter on marketing and branding of destinations and how attractions and events relate to these activities (Chapter 12). In some cases, a specific attraction or specific type of attraction is the brand and image of a destination (theme parks in Central Florida for example), while historic and cultural features in some European cities are another example. Issues such as authenticity and place attachment play major roles in determining how successful and appropriate particular branding and marketing efforts may be.

The penultimate chapter focuses on the future of the visitor attraction and events sectors from the private sector viewpoint. Anticipated innovations, the changing tastes and preferences of the markets, the changing markets themselves and greater cooperation within the sector and between the sector and destinations will all affect the success of this sector in the future. The final chapter summarises the discussions and analysis in the volume and suggests some key areas for future research and policy consideration.

References

Bærenholdt, J. O. and Haldrup, M. (2006). Mobile networks and place making in cultural tourism – Staging viking ships and rock music in Roskilde. *European Urban and Regional Studies*, *13*(3), 209–224.

Barron, P. and Greenwood, A. B. (2006). Issues determining the development of cruise itineraries: A focus on the luxury market. *Tourism Marine Environments*, *3*(2), 89–99.

Benckendorff, P. (2006). An exploratory analysis of travellers' preferences for airline website content. *Information Technology and Tourism*, *8*(3–4), 149–159.

Boswell, J. (1952). *Life of Johnson*. Entry for 12 October 1779. New York: Random House.

Buhalis, D. and Cooper, C. (1998) Competition or co-operation? Small and medium sized enterprises at the destination. In B. Faulkner, E. Laws and G. Moscardo (Eds), *Embracing and Managing Change in Tourism: International Case Studies* (pp. 324–346). London: Routledge.

Butler, R. W. (1980). The concept of a tourist area cycle of evolution and implications for management of resources. *The Canadian Geographer*, *XXIV*(1), Spring 5–12.

Butler, R. W. (1991). Mega malls as tourist attractions. *The Canadian Geographer*, *XXXV*(3), 287–294.

Butler, R. W. (2015). Sustainable tourism: Paradoxes, inconsistencies and a way forward? In M. Hughes, D. Weaver and C. Pforr (Eds), *The Practice of Sustainable Tourism Resolving the Paradox* (pp. 66–80). London: Routledge.

Butler, R. W. and Smale, B. J. (1991). Geographical perspectives on festivals. *Ontario Journal of Applied Recreation Research, 16*(1), 3–23.

Butler, R. W. and Hinch, T. (2007). *Tourism and Indigenous Peoples: Issues and Implications.* Clevedon: Channel View Publications.

Butler, R. W. and Suntikul, W. (2013). *Tourism and War: A Complex Relationship.* London: Routledge.

Cardwell, D. and Ali, N. (2014). Nostalgia at the boundary: A study at Lord's cricket ground. In T. G. Baum and R. W. Butler (Eds), *Tourism and Cricket Travels to the Boundary* (pp. 52–72). Clevedon: Channel View Publications.

Daniels, M., Dieke, P. and Barrow, M. (2013). Civil war tourism: Perspectives from Manassas National Battlefield Park. In R. W. Butler and W. Suntikul (Eds), *Tourism and War* (pp. 232–244). London: Routledge.

Edelheim, J. R. (2015). *Tourist Attractions: From Object to Narrative.* Clevedon: Channel View Publications.

Emery, P., Frost, W. and Kerr, A. (2014). On the march with the Barmy Army. In T. G. Baum and R. W. Butler (Eds), *Tourism and Cricket Travels to the Boundary* (pp. 136–152). Clevedon: Channel View Publications.

Fyall, A., Garrod, B., Leask, A. and Wanhill, S. (2008). *Managing Visitor Attractions: New Directions* (2nd edition). Oxford: Elsevier.

Hall, C.M. and Lew, A.A. (2009). *Understanding and Managiing Tourism Impacts: An Integrated Approach.* London: Routledge.

Harvey, D. (2015, 25 September). Banksy's Dismaland 'Gave Weston-super-Mare a £20m Boost', *BBC.* Retrieved from www.bbc.co.uk/news/uk-england-bristol-34347681 (accessed 26 September 2015).

Hasche, L. (2015). *Hamburg – "The Red Carpet for Cruising"* Unpublished Masters thesis, NHTV University, Breda, Netherlands.

Hudson, R. (2001). *Producing Places.* New York: Guilford Press.

Jaakson, R. (2004). Beyond the tourist bubble? Cruise ship passengers in port. *Annals of Tourism Management, 31*(1), 44–60.

Jansen-Verbeke, M. and George, W. (2013). Reflections on the Great War Centenary. In R. W. Butler and W. Suntikul (Eds), *Tourism and War* (pp. 273–287). London: Routledge.

Laderman, S. (2013). From the Vietnam War to the "War on Terror": Tourism and the martial Fascination. In R. W. Butler and W. Suntikul (Eds), *Tourism and War* (pp. 26–36). London: Routledge.

Law, C. M. (2002). *Urban Tourism: The Visitor Economy and the Growth of Large Cities* (2nd edition). London: Continuum.

Lawton, L. J. and Butler, R. W. (1989). Cruise ship industry: Patterns in the Caribbean 1800–1986. *Tourism Management, 8*(4), 329–343.

Leask, A. (2010). Progress in visitor attraction research: Towards more effective management. *Tourism Management, 31,* 155–166.

Leask, A. and Fyall, A. (2006). *Managing World Heritage Sites.* London: Routledge.

Lemelin H., Dawson, J. and Stewart E. J. (2011). *Last Chance Tourism: Adapting Tourism Opportunities in a Changing World.* London: Routledge.

Lew, A. A. (1987). A framework of tourist attraction research. *Annals of Tourism Research, 14*(4), 553–575.

McKercher, B. and Lew, A. (2004). Tourist flows and the spatial distribution of tourists. In A. Lew, C. H. Michael and M. W. Allan (Eds), *A Companion to Tourism* (pp. 36–48). Malden, MA; Oxford: Blackwell.

Mathieson, A. and Wall, G. (1982). *Tourism: Economic, Physical and Social Impacts.* Harlow: Longman.

Morrison, A. M. and Mill, R. C. (1992). *The Tourism System, An Introduction Text* (2nd edition). New Jersey: Prentice-Hall International Editors.

National Trust for Scotland (2014). *Annual Report*. Edinburgh: NTS.

Shaw, G. and Williams, A. (2004). *Tourism and Tourism Spaces*. London: Sage Publications.

Sheppard, E. (2000). Geography or economics? Conceptions of space, time, interdependence, and agency. In G. L. Clark, M. P. Feldman and M. S. Gertler (Eds.), *Oxford Handbook of Economic Geography* (pp. 99–199). Oxford: Oxford University Press.

Swarbrooke, J. (2002). *The Development and Management of Visitor Attractions*. Oxford: Butterworth-Heinemann.

Venables, A. J. (2005). Economic Geography; Spatial Interactions in the World Economy. Retrieved 2 February 2006, from London School of Economics, Paper written for the Oxford Handbook of Political Economy and CEPR, January 2005 www.econ.ox.ac.uk/members/tony.venables/polec3.pdf (accessed 3 October 2015).

VisitEngland (2013). Visitor attraction trends in England 2013, full report. Retrieved from www.visitengland.com/sites/default/files/downloads/va_2013_trends_in_england-full_report_final_version_for_publication.pdf (accessed 3 October 2015).

VisitEngland (2015). The annual survey of visits to visitor attractions. Retrieved from www.visitengland.com/sites/default/files/annual_visitor_attractions_surveys_-_update_2014.pdf (accessed 3 October 2015).

Walker, T. (2015). Disneyland band given marching orders after 60 years of entertaining theme park guests. Retrieved from www.independent.news.co.uk/world/america/disneyland-band-given-maching-orders-after-60-years-of-entertaining-theme-park-guests-10166999-html (accessed 8 October 2015).

Walsh-Heron, J. (1990). *The Management of Visitor Attractions and Events*. Englewood Cliffs, NJ: Prentice Hall.

Watson, S. and McCracken, M. (2002). No attraction in strategic thinking: Perceptions on current and future skills needs for visitor attraction managers. *International Journal of Tourism Research*, *4*, 367–378.

Weaver, D. B. and Lawton L. J. (2007). 'Just because it's gone doesn't mean it isn't there anymore': Planning for attraction residuality (disaster/crisis management/tourist attractions/teaching case study). *Tourism Management*, *28*(1), 108–117.

Weidenfeld, A. and Leask, A. (2013). Exploring the relationship between visitor attractions and events: Definitions and management factors. *Current Issues in Tourism*, *16*(6), 552–569.

2 Events, visitor attractions and the event–attraction continuum

Adi Weidenfeld and Anna Leask

Introduction

This chapter compares the characteristics of events and visitor attractions, and determines which enterprises, phenomena and places can be defined as visitor attractions, events and/or event attractions. Distinguishing between events and attractions can be a challenging task, particularly when the physical and thematic boundaries are blurred, and there are broad similarities in the managerial and organisational aspects of different types of tourism facilities. This chapter begins by reflecting on the need for greater conceptual clarity in respect of the definitional confusions in this area, in order to provide a baseline for examining the differences and similarities between events and attractions. The chapter then uses a comparison of the criteria employed for measuring their effective and successful management as a means of exploring their similarities and differences.

The complex nature of tourism businesses requires managers to take account of the influences of key determinants and management factors, and how these vary inter-sectorally. A comparison between events and visitor attractions is particularly germane given that these appear to be broadly similar; types of businesses and where there is considerable debate about whether and how management strategies, development planning policies and evaluation criteria differ between the two. The apparent similarities and inter-dependences between businesses in the tourism sector can lead to employing similar management strategies and forming similar development policies even when businesses belong to different sub-sectors, which actually face significant differences in operating and external business environments. The sections examine events as one type of visitor attraction and as one component of the visitor attraction.

Events as a visitor attraction

Visitor attractions and events are usually defined as separate entities (see Chapter 1). Events in the tourism context have the following characteristics – they are a one time or recurring event of limited duration, held no more frequently than once a year and potentially in differing locations. An event has a programme, an organising body, a number of participants and it is open to the public. It is developed primarily to enhance the awareness, appeal and profitability of the host city/region/country as a tourist destination, in addition to intrinsic objectives, such as religion, sports and culture (Mossberg, 2000). Such events may vary from centennial military celebrations (for example, the Battle of Waterloo) to annual festivals, such as that at Glastonbury. In contrast, visitor attractions are permanent natural or man-made features that have been developed and managed for visitor use for multiple purposes such as entertainment, education and wellbeing (Hu and Wall, 2005). Classic examples include some of the great museums and art galleries of Europe such as the Louvre, the Tate, the Prado, the Uffizi and the Rijksmuseum. Some visitor attractions charge for entry while some are free or constitute a mix of both, usually determined by their ownership and associated objectives (see Chapter 1). Usually involving some aspect of interpretation to explain the significance of their particular resource(s), visitor attractions often have a broad but variable mix of visitor audiences including tourists, local residents and day visitors.

Events can be understood as one type of visitor attractions (Weidenfeld and Leask, 2013). In this case, they have similarity to other attractions in several aspects including elements of their structures and their role in the tourism industry as motivators for trips and forming part of the overall destination experience. The programme or the content of the event is similar to the visitor attraction's nucleus and may include both tangible and intangible elements such as spectacle, exhibition, ritual and celebration, trade/sales, performance, competition, and a person and an object, responsible for the Unique Selling Preposition (USP) (Carlsen et al., 2001). Events and visitor attractions can have different markers for their promotion such as road signs and advertisements and/or as a tool to lead customers to the venue of the event within the premises (Weidenfeld and Leask, 2013). Markers in small scale sport events in Kenyir, Malaysia, the largest man-made lake in south east Asia, for example, included advertisements about visitors' involvement, and live broadcasts of sporting events (Yusof et al., 2012).

Planned events can be perceived as temporary visitor attractions, being developed primarily to enhance the appeal and awareness of the host region/city/destination and to draw visitors from outside the local area (Weidenfeld and Leask, 2013). Since each event is unique in some way, whether in respect of size, programme, nature and geographic scale, so are its economic, social and environmental impacts. Events also impact differently on particular groups including residents, domestic visitors, international tourists and different stakeholders (Quinn, 2013, Tyrrell and Johnston, 2011). Social and economic impacts often include community identity, wellbeing, cohesion, image, quality of life, participation, community, costs, breaking routines, over crowdedness, overuse of facilities and social capacity (see Tyrell and Johnston, 2011). Environmental impacts can be negative, with the literature focusing on the need to minimise negative impacts on the natural environment, and the lack of opportunities for natural attractions to capture revenue from visitors that can be used to manage those areas (Banerjee, 2012). However, there are also examples of positive impacts in terms of the opportunities for tourism activity to support forest management (Tyrväinen et al., 2014), or the retention of indigenous community skills, or active engagement of local communities as critical contributions to the successful implementation of environmentally sound practices (Sharpley and Telfer, 2014). Similar to other attractions, events in general, and festivals in particular, can be used in urban renewal strategies for increasing regional appeal, encouraging external economic contributions towards the improvement of infrastructure and business, and developing a sense of community.

Festivals are differentiated from other major types of event settings in not necessarily requiring special-purpose facilities, and this makes them an attractive and flexible tool for generating substantial economic benefits and positive image for specific places. Their contribution to the tourism industry brings them conceptually closer to the perception of visitor attractions by practitioners, policy makers and researchers (Felsenstein and Fleischer, 2003, McKercher et al., 2006, Quinn, 2006). They can be a major motivator for visitors' selections of destinations, form an intrinsic part of a trip (McKercher et al., 2006), and – similar to other attractions – they can draw a broad spectrum of visitors; the latter range from being the main travel motive to an ancillary or complementary activity (Prentice and Andersen, 2003).

Events as a component of visitor attractions

Events can be perceived as one of the integral components of visitor attractions including the marker, the nucleus and/or an additional or complementary activity to the existing nucleus or even as a substitutional USP if the nucleus' appeal is in decline (Weidenfeld and Leask, 2013). Events can become a temporary nucleus in seasonal visitor attractions by replacing the permanent one in the low season. This is particularly typical in attractions which offer complementary services such as retail stores and food outlets. In the UK, Europe and North America, Christmas celebrations help to keep seasonal attractions open in December, particularly where attractions offer shops, cafes and restaurants. Some National Trust houses in the UK, for example, offer limited opening with a Christmas theme activity event, such as 'dressing the house for Christmas' (Connell et al., 2015). The premises of some visitor attractions are occasionally used as a venue for special events, particularly if they share the same thematic context with the visitor attraction, which creates a unique inspiring selling point. For example, Cambo House and Estate, a country estate near St Andrews, Scotland, hosts an annual 'Snowdrop Festival' and 'Snowdrops by Starlight' event each night for one week (http://snowdropsbystarlight.com/) each February in order to boost off-peak business to both the estate and the destination as a whole (Cambo Estate, 2015). This festival builds on a key feature of the visitor attraction, the Royal Horticultural Society National Collection of the Snowdrop, a flower that is the first to appear in Scotland in the Spring, via the creation of a nighttime woodland experience involving local artists to create light and sound effects.

Planned events can also be used to shape or manage the flow of visitors within visitor attractions, particularly to food and retail outlets at specific times, such as a puppet show or a clown, to draw the attention of young children (Whitfield, 2009, Weidenfeld and Leask, 2013). For example, the timing of the daily Penguin Parade at Edinburgh Zoo, conveniently located near to the catering outlets and taking place just after lunchtime. Markers can be used as a marketing tool to draw the attention of tourists and encourage them to visit its premises, such as the daily enactment of the century-old City Open Parade (仿古开城仪式) at Diaoqiao Square, located at the South Gate the City Wall Gate attraction in Xian, China that takes place around its opening time. Other daily performances such as dancing and music are thematically related to the Wall's heritage. Some events are used as a means to increase marginal profits or as a way to overcome seasonality (Connell et al., 2015), and as elements which contribute to visitor attractions' appeal, such as catalysts, animators, place marketers, and image-makers. Events can also be used to form an additional product aspect at specific times of the year: these may be dictated more by season or natural phenomenon than by management. For example, the availability of tours based on natural events such as seabird boat trips to watch nesting birds is only possible at specific times of the year (Scottish Seabird Centre, 2015). Other examples include whale watching or viewing the Northern Lights from the Thingvellir National Park in Iceland.

The integration of events within the nucleus of the visitor attraction depends on the following aspects: its thematic association, functional contribution to the visitor attraction's nucleus, thematic product similarity, physical proximity to the nucleus and to other facilities, duration, the number of participants, levels of involvement of staff and visitors, and contribution to innovation (Weidenfeld and Leask, 2013). Events can be entirely separate from other neighbouring visitor attractions or can be integral key components of the nucleus or one of its markers (Figure 2.1).

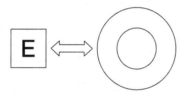

Events and visitor attractions as separate entities

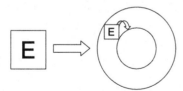

Events as a transit or an internal marker

Events as the nucleus (permanent or seasonal)

Figure 2.1 Events as a key component of visitor attractions

Distinguishing between events and visitor attractions: management factors and effective management criteria

In order to further explore and understand the similarities and differences between events and visitor attractions, this section offers a comparative assessment of the management factors and the criteria that can be used to measure the effective management of events and visitor attractions. As previously discussed by Leask (2010), Hughes and Carlsen (2010) and du Cros and McKercher (2015), there exists a broad range of factors, or influencers, that may determine the effective or successful management of visitor attractions. Weidenfeld and Leask (2013) further developed this research into consideration of the similarity, or otherwise, of these factors with the events sector. Hughes and Carlsen (2010) and du Cros and McKercher (2015) focused specifically on the successful operation of cultural heritage attractions and their increased need to develop commercially. Leask (2010) considered the full range of visitor attractions including those firmly established in commercial operations, such as theme parks, and those in a period of transition between more curatorial and commercial environments, such as museums. Similarly, Catibog-Sinha (2011) and Weaver and Lawton (2011) discuss how the use of nature based resources by visitors to natural attractions is often unpredictable and highly dependent upon local environmental conditions such as the weather, concerns regarding visitor safety and the impact of the visitors on the natural resource feature of visitor attractions, where achieving a balance of appropriate visitor access and revenue generating activity can be difficult.

Leask (2010) identified that a range of diverse factors determine the effective management of visitor attractions: the ownership category; the type and size of the visitor attraction; the range of stakeholders involved; the profile of the visitors; the employee skills within the visitor attraction; the opportunities for product innovation; the individual nature of the resource; and the age and stage in the life cycle of the visitor attraction. See Table 2.1 for a comparison of the similarities and distinctions between the management factors influencing the management of events and visitor attractions. Leask's argument is that each visitor attraction operates within a distinctive, individual situation that is determined by the factors that relate to that individual location. These include, for example, the differences between private sector and public sector owned attractions in respect of decision-making, priorities and measures of effectiveness.

Prebensen (2012) explored the use of benchmarking as a tool to improve the service experience in businesses such as visitor attractions and identified it as being useful in the development of foundations for change and improvement of management processes and performance in experience based businesses. Hughes and Carlsen (2010) focused on more commercial aspects, listing nine business success factors derived from the previous literature, relating mostly to the commercial aspects relevant to managing a cultural heritage attraction. These included aspects such as agreed objectives, effective human resource management and the extent to which interpretation was an integral part of the visitor experience. As might be expected, Hughes and Carlsen's (2010:26) research concluded that

Table 2.1 A comparison of management factors in events and visitor attractions

Management factors	Similar and distinct aspects of the event and visitor attraction sectors
Ownership	Similar between both sectors as these will dictate the key measures of effectiveness and context within which they operate.
Type of visitor attractions/events and diversity of facilities	Distinct differences with typologies of visitor attractions are well developed, while these remain underdeveloped within the event sector. Both sectors offer a diverse range of facilities – increasingly orientated towards financial measures.
Size	Similar, with visitor attraction and events' size being measured in terms of volume and value via figures on occurrence, visitor/attendee numbers and budget size.
Range of stakeholders	Some similarities between both sectors in terms of breadth of potential stakeholders though less regarding variety of potential conflicting stakeholder needs, more likely in the visitor attraction sector where the condition of the resource is significant.
Visitor markets profile and behaviour	Similar, though characteristics, perceptions of value and experience of visitors in the event sector may be harder to communicate than for the visitor attraction experience.
Management and staff skills and nature of employment	Distinct differences in requirements due to need for professional training and mainly temporary staff in events. Importance of need for management skills highlighted for visitor attractions.
Product/process innovation and development opportunities	Similar, though greater concerns regarding achieving a balance between authenticity and commercial activities within the visitor attraction sector than the events, presumably due to resource management issues. Similar in terms of the significance of the experiential aspects.
Individual nature of resource	Similarity between cultural and heritage attractions and the events sector in terms of the basis and authenticity of a fixed aspect or resource associated with an event or location, though potentially more critical for cultural heritage sites due to their very individuality and inability to be replicated.
Age and life cycle	Distinct as an event's "age" is calculated from the year of birth in a country/region while a visitor attraction's age is conceptually vague, with life cycle research remaining under-studied in both.

Source: Adapted from Leask 2010 and Weidenfeld and Leask 2013.

the more 'successful cultural heritage' attractions met the more commercially focused critical success factors than the less commercially focused ones. With particular reference to cultural and natural heritage, it was seen that public funding support was necessary for most visitor attractions due to the limited potential for tourism revenue generation, and the high capital costs associated with the types of resources.

Approaching the topic of success factors, du Cros and McKercher (2015) developed a framework for understanding the key features of a successful cultural tourism attraction in relation to balancing income and expenditure with the development of high quality experiences. They considered the following to be the keys: *tell a story; make the asset come alive; make the experience participatory; focus on quality; make experience relevant to the tourist; and make it relevant to the tourist.* They contend that each of these should be considered in the creation of memorable experiences for visitors to cultural heritage attractions to enable visitors to have a reason to visit and also for the delivery of a quality experience. This is explored in a similar vein by Kang and Gretzel (2012) in their study of the use of podcast tours to increase visitors' social presence and mindfulness in visits to natural parks that, in turn, lead to enhanced tourist experiences and improved environmental stewardship. Their study, conducted at Padre Island National Seashore, Texas, the US, identified the value of mindfulness and the use of the human voice in constructing and affecting the quality of the visitors' experiences during their visits.

Moving on to the criteria that might be used to measure successful or effective management of events and visitor attractions, Table 2.2 presents a comparison of the key measures in relation to each sector. The first point in relation to the condition of the resource refers to the need to achieve a balance between public access to a heritage feature (or resource) that forms the basis of the visitor attraction and the condition of that resource. The very act of enabling visitor access can compromise the conservation of the resource via deliberate or unconscious behaviour (Leask, 2010). Issues raised by Hughes and Carlsen (2010) in relation to achieving a balance between authenticity and conservation and commercial activities were considered to be manageable where education and entertainment were combined within the visitor experience and the wider tourism arena. Considerable dilemmas relating to authenticity and conservation were raised where allowing visitor access to a fragile resource feature is considered to be simply too damaging, and where a decision is taken to protect the resource. This could be by limiting the volume of visitor access (see Sistine Chapel, Italy) to fixed levels or by stopping visitor access to the original feature and offering a replica or substitute visitor experience instead (see La Grotte Chauvet-Pont d'Arc in the Ardèche, France).

In considering the variety of objectives that visitor attractions and events might aim to achieve, du Cros and McKercher (2015) discuss the different factors that could be used by commercial and non-commercial visitor attractions. They establish that the adoption of more commercial measures of success could be of value in the less-commercial attractions, even if they are not expected to generate revenue. In an environment of decreasing public funding sources, there is an increased need to demonstrate the achievement of a broader range of objectives, including social inclusion, community involvement and economic benefits across a destination. These measures are common to both the event and visitor attraction sectors, where demonstration of value for funds invested has become more prominent.

There exists a range of literature that investigates the critical success factors and measures in visitor attractions. Many of these specifically relate to cultural heritage attractions, which could be argued to have more in common with the

Table 2.2 A comparison of key measures of successful and effective management in events and visitor attractions

Success and effectiveness management factors	Similarities and differences
Condition and authenticity of the resource	Different as considerably more dependency on the resource (main feature e.g. historic building or artefact) in visitor attractions, which makes them more vulnerable. If the resource is damaged then the motivation for visiting can be compromised, particularly in relation to the difference in high capital costs associated with maintaining heritage resources.
	Events are less vulnerable as they can relocate or develop new features to attract attendees.
Funder, educational and community objectives	Strong similarity between festivals and cultural and heritage attractions in terms of considering social, educational and cultural objectives of local communities, considerably less similarity with private, purpose built visitor attractions.
	Similar in terms of necessity to demonstrate value for money and broader economic/social benefit for public funding and return on investment for both sectors within their broader destinations; not the case for private ventures in each sector.
Management and planning functions including marketing strategies	Similar functions needed in terms of marketing, financial management and strategic development functions but significant differences in terms of availability of staff expertise (seasonal for many events, permanent for visitor attractions) and the need to stimulate visitor engagement year round (visitor attraction needs to sustain visits year round while events only for short duration of event). Particular emphasis on examination and evaluation of event managers' success records in bidding processes for organising new events. For visitor attractions the emphasis is more on visitor numbers (volume, value and range) and broadening visitor engagement to encourage funding support.
Visitor satisfaction and experience	Similar, notably between festivals and cultural and heritage visitor attractions in terms of the importance of visitors' and attendees' perceptions to their satisfaction, linking in turn to repeat visitation and recommendation. Different for visitor attractions which may have more opportunity to engage visitors due to permanency.

successful management of festivals and events than the more general visitor attraction sector. This is because cultural heritage attractions tend to operate in a similar environment to many events, having multiple stakeholders, a greater variety of measures of success and reliance on public sector support for ongoing sustainability. In contrast, visitor attractions such as theme parks are more likely to have commonality with established mainstream events linked to private, commercial companies, for example popular music festivals. While some authors argue that the success factors relate to very practical aspects such as cleanliness and safety (Prebensen, 2012), and the quality of facilities as well as services (Milman, 2009), others have argued the success relates to far broader aspects such as the interaction and synergy between the visitor attraction and other tourism activities and associated infrastructure (Jansen-Verbeke and Lievois, 1999). Calver and Page (2013:25) observe changes in the approach of visitor attraction managers to the role of service within the attraction, 'from pragmatic regard to being more experientially motivated' and contributing to a greater understanding of visitor needs in relation to experiences and achieving successful outcomes. Seen in relation to visitor satisfaction and experience, both events and visitor attractions need to recognise the importance of enhancing positive visitor and attendee perceptions, since these are linked to personal recommendations via both word of mouth and digital form, and repeat visitation (Leask et al., 2013, Jaffry and Apostolakis, 2011).

The event–attraction continuum

As the previous section argues, consideration of management factors and measures of effectiveness can be used to structure and differentiate between events and visitor attractions and to contribute to a clearer understanding of the sector. The event–visitor attraction nexus is shaped by various factors including ownership, structure, size (annual visitor markets), location and appeal to local versus international markets (Connell et al., 2015). It is related to the need to consider whether businesses, enterprises and places are defined as visitor attractions or events or in-between hybrids (i.e. event attractions). It is important for policy makers, protagonists and practitioners to distinguish between events and attractions because each of these is a distinctive sector and requires different development planning policies and management strategies. The event–attraction nexus is influenced by the relationship between events and the nucleus of visitor attractions. These relationships are shaped by their spatio-temporality, their premises and their physical and organisational structures.

The event–attraction continuum (see Figure 2.2) is suggested as a mechanism to further develop the understanding of this area. It is determined by the levels of thematic and functional integration of the visitor attraction's nucleus to the event's programme, as well as by their spatio-temporality, i.e. levels of occurrence and permanence of location. This variety of combinations on the continuum is divided into five groups; three of these fall under the term event attractions. Event attractions are visitor attractions (enterprises, places or phenomena), which host events within their premises (the 'hosting visitor attraction'). They are more likely to be held more frequently than events (which by definition are usually organised once a year) and their organising and management bodies are likely to be the same or strongly associated with their hosting visitor attraction management, rather than an independent management and organising team. In other words, some of their spatio-temporal features and management aspects are shared between the

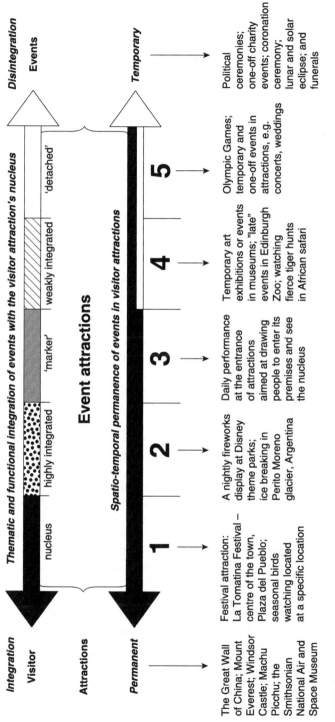

Figure 2.2 The event–attraction continuum

Source: Adapted from Weidenfeld and Leask (2013).

Figure content

Integration → **Disintegration**

Visitor ← → **Events**

Thematic and functional integration of events with the visitor attraction's nucleus

Spatio-temporal permanence of events in visitor attractions

Event attractions

Attractions — **Permanent** ← → **Temporary**

Integration levels along the continuum:

nucleus | highly integrated | 'marker' | weakly integrated | 'detached'

1 — Festival attraction: La Tomatina Festival – centre of the town, Plaza del Pueblo; seasonal birds watching located at a specific location

2 — A nightly fireworks display at Disney theme parks; ice breaking in Perito Moreno glacier, Argentina

3 — Daily performance at the entrance of attractions aimed at drawing people to enter its premises and see the nucleus

4 — Temporary art exhibitions or events in museums; "late" events in Edinburgh Zoo; watching fierce tiger hunts in African safari

5 — Olympic Games; temporary and one-off events in attractions, e.g. concerts, weddings

Events → Political ceremonies; one-off charity events; coronation ceremony; lunar and solar eclipse; and funerals

Attractions → The Great Wall of China; Mount Everest; Windsor Castle; Machu Picchu; the Smithsonian National Air and Space Museum

Legend:
- ■ Spatio-temporal permanence or full integration of the events in the tourist attractions' nucleus
- □ Permanent location or temporality
- ▨ Varying levels of integration of events to the tourist attraction's nucleus

visitor attraction and the event it contains within its boundaries. Event attractions aim to enhance the awareness, appeal and profitability of the hosting visitor attraction rather than the tourism destination. They have to cater for the needs of the hosting attraction's visitors, rather than being open to the public, and contribute to the appeal of the entire destination region (Weidenfeld and Leask, 2013).

The event–attraction continuum provides a conceptual framework for all types of tourism events with different levels of seasonality, temporality and permanence in space including human-made and natural phenomena (Weidenfeld and Leask, 2013). It also includes examples from across the globe (Figure 2.2). At the two ends of the of the visitor event–attraction continuum are visitor attractions (left) and events (right). Visitor attractions are characterised by full permanence in space and time and include all year attractions, which are inextricably linked to their location. The Great Wall in China and the Taj Mahal in India, in common with many other heritage constructions, cannot be replicated or rebuilt elsewhere while maintaining their authentic architecture and heritage value. Others, such as the Eiffel Tower, are inextricably linked to their original location as a unique icon, e.g. the Palace of Culture in Warsaw, Poland (see Chapter 11).

In-between the two ends (or groups) of the continuum (groups 1–5), enterprises, places and phenomena fall under the definition event attractions with elements of appeal to visitors (man-made or natural). They consist of events with differing levels of spatio-temporality and integration with the visitor attraction's nucleus or USP. The black colour of the continuum indicates high levels of spatio-temporal permanence (bottom arrow) and the nature and levels of integration with the nucleus (top arrow). Spatio-temporal permanence indicating a fixed location and occurrence is typical of visitor attractions and events, which have fixed locations with permanent seasonality (groups 1–3). Greater spatial and temporal permanence and integration with the visitor attraction's nucleus being reflected in higher proximity to the 'visitor attraction' end of the continuum and vice versa. Groups 4 and 5 are characterised by a permanent location or temporality of occurrence but not by both.

The continuum suggests a typology which is more schematic than dichotomist. Enterprises, places or phenomena can fall into more than one category and move along the continuum if they change, innovate, relocate or decline. For example, the Tower of London is a designated World Heritage Site and established visitor attraction operated by Historic Royal Palaces, with over 2 million visitors paying entrance fees to access the buildings, tours and exhibitions within its fixed location each year. In 2014 the Tower hosted the art installation 'Blood Swept Lands and Seas of Red' to mark the centenary of the First World War. A display, eventually comprising 888,246 ceramic poppies, representing the number of British and Commonwealth personnel killed in the First World War, was built up over a period of three months, with the poppies then being sold to raise money for the Royal British Legion (Historic Royal Palaces, 2014). This one-off event attracted a distinct type of visitor to the Tower during the period of the installation, those visiting purely to see the event without necessarily any intention to, or interest in, paying for access to the Tower. Thus, the Tower of London could be seen to temporarily move along the continuum as the focus of the motivation and behaviour of the visitors varied with the products on offer.

Events as the most important component of the visitor attraction are inextricably linked to the nucleus and included in the admission fees (Group 1). In this case the event will be attended by all of its visitors. This group includes two sub-groups of event attractions. The first consists of events which are the sole nucleus (or the USP) of a seasonal attraction, such as La Tomatina Festival, centre of the town, Plaza del Pueblo, where a certain area within the centre is closed and an entrance admission fee is introduced at the time of the festival. The other sub-group includes events which are integrated to the permanent nucleus of the attraction but do not add any surcharges to the entrance admission fees, such as performances in the Drum Towers in Beijing and Xi'an, China. In ancient China, the drums were used to signal the running of time and/or as an alarm in emergency situations. In Xi'an, China, the biggest drum in the country is located in the heart of the tower ('the drum tower') and is used for hourly performances, which are already included in the admission price. The Old Faithful Geyser in Yellowstone Park, Wyoming, the US, is a natural event, which takes place on an hourly basis and is considered to be the most important USP of the park. Exceptionally, this natural phenomenon is fixed in time and space and provides the visitor with a guaranteed experience compared to other geysers in the park at no additional cost.

Other events can be highly (but not inextricably) linked to the nucleus both functionally and thematically with relatively high levels of occurrence and may not necessarily incur extra costs to the visitor (Group 2). A nightly fireworks display at Disney theme parks is a complementary experience aimed at providing an additional excitement to the thrill of a theme park, and to extend the length of stay of visitor groups. Natural phenomena, which are inextricably linked to the nucleus, permanent in their time and duration, can also fall in this group, such as the ice breaking event at the Perito Moreno, which is one in a group of 48 glaciers located in the Andes, Argentina. The glacier breaking into large chunks of ice on the lake where it is located is a periodic event caused by the glacier's advance, which normally happens every summer and attracts around 200,000 per year. The Last Post Ceremony, Ieper (Ypres), Belgium, takes place every night under the Menin Gate in Ieper (Ypres) to pay tribute to the courage and self-sacrifice of those who fell in defence of the town during the First World War. The Ceremony has become part of the daily life in Ieper (Ypres) and local pride amongst the local residents. Events can be a marker to the nucleus of the visitor attraction (Group 3). They are normally free and can be thematically and functionally linked highly or weakly to the nucleus with relatively moderate to high levels of occurrence (daily to weekly) inside or outside the premises of the attraction. These may include music and dance shows in proximity to food and retail outlets in the attraction's premises or in the destination region.

Group 4 may include events which have little degree of thematic or functional attachment to the visitor attraction's nucleus and some degree of permanence in their location and/or temporality or both. Examples include events aimed at excitement through staged events or even euphoria in heritage attractions, whose property has a religious or spiritual dimension (Calver and Page, 2013). If visitor attractions are human-made, they are often aimed at increasing demand in general and repeat visitors in particular. For example, temporary art exhibitions or events in museums can be thematically related to permanent exhibitions. In natural attractions, watching tiger hunts in African safari is possible but incidental to the visit. Group 5 is entirely detached from the nucleus with low levels of occurrence and low levels of probability of being repeated in the same location. For example, visitor attractions which are used for the sole purpose of providing physical settings for occasional exhibitions and events (such as weddings, ceremonies and concerts).

'Pure' events on the right end of the continuum, which are neither events nor event attractions, are characterised by neither temporal nor spatial permanence. The EU enlargement's ceremonies in Eastern Europe on 1 May 2004, Peace Treaty's between countries (though mainly for politicians, diplomats and journalists), funerals and coronation ceremonies of Royalty and celebrities, and one-off charity events fall into the classification of events. For example, the Moonwalk, a nighttime charity marathon walking event held annually in several major cities. Similarly lunar and solar eclipses can be predicted or planned in advance and therefore draw tourists to the destination but their temporality and locational permanence are extremely low. In summary, the event–attraction continuum provides a conceptual model which disentangles the definitional complexity and suggests a new typology which clarifies why events and visitor attractions can be perceived as different sectors rather than the same.

Conclusions

Events and visitor attractions have been shown to be two separate sub-sectors in tourism which, while sharing some similarities, are more different than similar in terms of structures (in terms of elements that constitute them as well as size ownership), content (thematic context) and spatio-temporality (permanence in location and seasonality). This chapter contributed to the understanding of the differences and similarities between them and provides some theoretical insights to help scholars and practitioners to address associated management issues, and to optimise effective management criteria in the visitor attraction and event sub-sectors. There are a number of management factors and measures of effective management common to both events and visitor attractions, for example, the implications of ownership category and the broad range of stakeholder objectives. However, significant differences can be seen in some of the management factors, such as the limited supply of management and staff skills.

Events suffer from an exacerbated management and human capital situation due to the temporary nature of the experience, and the very individualised nature of the experiences offered at different events and visitor attractions. Another example of where they differ relates to the condition of the resource feature on which a visitor attraction is based. This is critical in visitor attractions where the resource feature (natural, built or artefact) cannot be replaced and so its sustainable management is very important. This is not necessarily the case for events, where the experience is rarely based on a fixed, permanent resource feature and could be replaced relatively easily.

The main operational and structural differences whereby a business, an enterprise, a place or a natural phenomenon can be considered a visitor attraction or a planned event is the spatio-temporality of its nucleus or programme. Whereas, in the case of visitor attractions, the permanent physical presence and prolonged (between seasonal daily) opening of the nucleus to visitors are clear evidence of being visitor attractions rather than events which are characterised by episodic and a temporary (or even coincidental or circumstantial) location. However, there are also hybrid cases of events, where seasonality and temporary locations, as well as the thematic and functional integration of events' programmes with the visitor attraction's nucleus, vary and they are defined as event attractions. These different factors underlie the classification of enterprises, places and phenomena on the event–attraction continuum and determine what can be classified as an event or attraction. It is notable that the dichotomy is not rigid and static, but has to be understood as dynamic because businesses may move on the continuum temporarily or permanently through their life cycle.

This chapter suggested the need for conceptual clarity for distinguishing between business, enterprises and phenomena, which are visitor attractions and events, and those which can be classified as having features of both events and attractions, i.e. event attractions. An understanding of the differences and similarities between events and visitor attractions, in terms of their management and effective management criteria, can help scholars and practitioners to adopt a more informed and effective approach to managing and studying these sub-sectors.

References

Banerjee, A. (2012). Is wildlife tourism benefiting Indian protected areas? A survey. *Current Issues in Tourism, 15*(3), 211–227.

Cambo Estate (2015). Snowdrops by starlight. Retrieved from http://snowdropsbystarlight.com/index.html (accessed 12 February 2015).

Calver, S. J. and Page, S. J. (2013). Enlightened hedonism: Exploring the relationship of service value, visitor knowledge and interest, to visitor enjoyment at heritage attractions. *Tourism Management, 39*, 23–36.

Carlsen, J., Getz, D. and Souta, G. (2001). Event evaluation research. *Event Management, 6*, 247–257.

Catibog-Sinha, C. (2011). Sustainable forest management: Heritage tourism, biodiversity, and upland communities in the Philippines. *Journal of Heritage Tourism, 6*(4), 341–352.

Connell, J., Page, S. J. and Meyer, D. (2015). Visitor attractions and events: Responding to seasonality. *Tourism Management, 46*, 283 298.

du Cros, H. and McKercher, B. (2015). *Cultural Tourism* (2nd edition). Oxon: Routledge.

Felsenstein, D. and Fleischer, A. (2003). Local festivals and tourism promotion: The role of public assistance and visitor expenditure. *Journal of Travel Research, 41*, 385–392.

Historic Royal Palaces (2014). Tower of London – About the charities. Retrieved from www.hrp.org.uk/tower-of-london/history-and-stories/tower-of-london-remembers/about-the-charities/ (accessed 12 January 2016).

Hu, W. and Wall, G. (2005). Environmental management, environmental image and the competitive tourist attraction. *Journal of Sustainable Tourism, 13*, 617–635.

Hughes, M. and Carlsen, J. (2010). The business of cultural heritage tourism: Critical success factors. *Journal of Heritage Tourism, 5*, 17–32.

Jaffry, S. and Apostolakis, A. (2011). Evaluating individual preferences for the British Museum. *Journal of Cultural Economics, 35*, 49–75.

Jansen-Verbeke, M. and Lievois, E. (1999). Analysing heritage resource for urban tourism in European cities. In D. Pearce and R. W. Butler (Eds), *Cultural Issues in Tourism Development* (pp. 81–107). London: CABI.

Kang, M. and Gretzel, U. (2012). Effects of podcast tours on tourist experiences in a national park. *Tourism Management, 33*, 440–455.

Leask, A. (2010). Progress in visitor attraction research: Towards more effective management. *Tourism Management, 31*, 155–166.

Leask, A., Fyall, A. and Barron, P. (2013). Generation Y: Opportunity or challenge – strategies to engage generation Y in the UK attractions' sector. *Current Issues in Tourism, 16*, 17–46.

McKercher, B., Mei, W. S. and Tse, T. S. M. (2006). Are short duration cultural festivals tourist attractions? *Journal of Sustainable Tourism, 14*, 55–66.

Milman, A. (2009). Evaluating the guest experience at theme parks: An empirical investigation of key attributes. *International Journal of Tourism Research, 11*, 373–387.

Mossberg, L. (2000). Event evaluation. In L. Mossberg (Ed.), *Evaluation of Events: Scandinavian Experiences* (pp. 30–46). New York: Cognizant Communication Corporation.

Prebensen, N. K. (2012). Benchmarking tourist attractions in Northern Norway. *Advances in Hospitality and Leisure*. Bingley, UK: Emerald Group Publishing Limited.

Prentice, R. and Andersen, V. (2003). Festival as creative destination. *Annals of Tourism Research Policy, 30*, 7–30.

Quinn, B. (2006). Problematising 'festival tourism': Arts festivals and sustainable development in Ireland. *Journal of Sustainable Tourism, 14*, 288–306.

Quinn, B. (2013). *Key Concepts in Event Management. Key Concepts in Event Management.* London: Sage Publications.

Scottish Seabird Centre (2015) Seabird boat trips. Retrieved from www.seabird.org/book/boat-trips/16/54 (accessed 20 January 2016).

Sharpley, R. and Telfer, D. J. (2014). *Tourism and Development: Concepts and Issues.* Bristol: Channel View Publication.

Tyrrell, T. J. A. and Johnston, R. (2011). A spatial extension to a framework for assessing direct economic impacts of tourist events. In S. J. Page and J. Connell (Eds), *The Routledge Handbook of Events* (pp. 329–346). Oxon: Routledge.

Tyrväinen, L., Mäntymaa, E. and Ovaskainen, V. (2014). Demand for enhanced forest amenities in private lands: The case of the Ruka-Kuusamo tourism area, Finland. *Forest Policy and Economics, 47*, 4–13.

Weaver, D. B. and Lawton, L. J. (2011). Visitor loyalty at a private South Carolina protected area. *Journal of Travel Research, 50*(3), 335–346.

Weidenfeld, A. and Leask, A. (2013). Exploring the relationship between visitor attractions and events: Definitions and management factors. *Current Issues in Tourism, 16*, 552–569.

Whitfield, J. E. (2009). Why and how UK visitor attractions diversify their product to offer conference and event facilities. *Journal of Convention and Event Tourism, 10*, 72–88.

Yusof, A., Shah, P. M. and Geok, S. K. (2012). Application of Leiper's tourist attraction system to small-scale sport event tourism in Malaysia. *World Applied Sciences Journal, 18*, 896–900.

3   Clustering and agglomeration of visitor attractions

Introduction

Co-location of firms is a necessary condition for agglomeration economies to emerge, but the mere co-location of firms does not guarantee the process of optimising gains from economies of scale and of scope, which is the rationale for clustering (e.g. joint marketing, training of staff, buying groups, etc.). Rather, it is a process in the form of a continuum, by which firms enhance their ability to cluster effectively and increase the chances of external economies. As the cluster grows, so does the impact of agglomeration economies but the potential to expand is shared among the cluster firms even if the outcomes fall asymmetrically between cluster members. The traditional cluster theory approach sees a production process as a series of links in a chain, where as in a value chain, each link adds a value in a sequence of steps to produce a final product. Even co-location of complementary firms does not guarantee the generation of synergies or cost efficiencies between them. Co-location offers an opportunity for firms to establish mechanisms and strategies, especially in marketing, leading to common business practices or tactics (Michael, 2007b). Clustering produces a range of synergies which may enhance the growth of market size and employment and is more typical of urban areas, where a variety of businesses and services co-locate (Paül Agustí, 2013, Michael, 2007a).

This chapter begins by examining how the business cluster approach and cluster theory apply to concentrations of visitor attractions in tourism clusters. It also emphasises the conceptual differences between the simple co-location of visitor attractions as businesses and different types of clustering, and discusses different types of clusters and clustering and their relevance to visitor attractions. Then, it explores the relevance of agglomeration economies for tourism in general and concentrations of visitor attractions in particular.

Tourism clusters and clustering of visitor attractions

The two concepts, which are grounded and used in the theory of economic geography for the phenomena related to agglomeration economies, comparative advantage and central place distribution, are the cluster model and the industrial district model. The cluster model refers to 'concentrations of interrelated but different industries [and] ... industrial districts are usually local clusters of single product industries e.g. fashion district of Manhattan and the leather footwear clusters of Italy' (Jackson and Murphy, 2002:38). Whereas the theory of industrial districts refers to a homogenous product, the Porterian cluster theory refers to a heterogeneous product involving different industry segments. Therefore, they argue that the cluster model provides a broader analytical framework to assist in understanding success factors in tourism destinations by demonstrating its applicability in two case studies. Consistent with Jackson and Murphy's cluster approach, the outcome of agglomeration of tourism businesses in a tourism space is perceived as industrial clusters (Porter, 1998, Porter, 1990) rather than an industrial district. In the next sections, the cluster model, its applicability to tourism clusters in general and to clusters of visitor attractions in particular will be discussed.

Tourism as industrial clusters

Industrial (or business) clusters are a form of complex spatial relationships and a result of a process of co-location and spatial clustering. Porter defines clusters from a regional economic approach as 'geographic concentrations of inter-connected companies specialised suppliers, service providers, firms in related industries and associated institutions', such as universities, standard agencies and trade associations (Porter cited by Jackson and Murphy, 2002:38). He captures the reality of interacting business concentration in combining both demand and supply side within a cluster, where companies do not only collaborate but also compete (Jackson and Murphy, 2002).

The competitive nature of clusters is attributed to their fostering innovations, productivity and sustained rates of employment growth which enhance a firm's strategic position within or beyond their local context (Bennett and Smith, 2002, Leibovitz, 2004). 'Through cluster development, factor endowments could be better packaged to develop a region's competitive advantage' (Jackson and Murphy, 2006:1033). There is a common perception that co-location of similar industries can produce economic multiplier effects and imply a change in economic well-being, and consequent social externalities especially due to the co-location of symbiotic industries. This is particularly germane to non-metropolitan environments, when the activities of the co-located industries are based on visitation like tourism, where clustering increases demand and the need for support industries and complementary attributes that serve customer needs (Michael, 2007b).

The definition of a cluster can be used to describe a destination 'with its conglomeration of competing and collaborating businesses, generally working together in associations and through partnership marketing to put their location on the map' (Jackson and Murphy, 2006:1022). The definition of a tourism cluster in this study is an array of linked industries and other entities in competition, which provide complementary products and services as a holistic tourism experience such as accommodations, attractions and retail outlets (Wang and Fesenmaier, 2007). These businesses come from a range of different types of enterprise, meaning that each has its own agenda and priorities (Jackson and Murphy, 2002). Tourism clusters include all elements of the tourism mix including accommodation providers, food and beverage, travel and tours, attraction coordinators, event promoters, education and research institutions (Jackson and Murphy, 2006).

The quality of the destination experience product is even more based on interdependency between firms than in other production chains of manufacturing clusters (Nordin, 2003) and collaboration and synergy between tourism clusters are even more crucial than in other clusters. They include synergetic relationships of production of a comprehensive tourism product comprised of a few sub-products (economies of scope), where each visitor attraction adds a product to a chain of products 'manufacturing' the overall tourism product. Cooperation between neighbouring attractions, particularly in marketing, results in economies of scale, and minimising transportation costs and distance, i.e. gains attributed to the cluster's formation captured as a result of reductions in the average costs of the member firms.

These are the cost advantages that may arise when performing two or more activities together within a single firm rather than performing them separately. When economies of scope exist, firms have an incentive to internalise the production of goods and services that otherwise would be acquired through transactions with external suppliers. Such internalisation often generates reductions in production costs. Economies of scope can exist when an organisation extends its horizontal or vertical line of production. Economies of scope occur where additional products share common inputs, e.g. in advertising new products, suppliers can draw on existing resources such as travel agents and tour operators, and serve new market segments using existing reservation systems and staff (Shaw and Williams, 2004).

Most important is the realisation that the success of clustering is not simply co-location, but the structure that generates the synthesis and synergies in their production processes (Michael, 2003, Michael, 2007b); in other words, the ability of firms to identify potential externalities of scale and of scope, establish strategies and employ clustering tactics. Porter's theory has its limitations in relation to tourism as it ignores spatial relationships within the cluster as well as governments' interests and involvement, which are often highly influential in the tourism and travel industry (Nordin, 2003). It is also noteworthy that without appropriate communicative relationships between partners, and a cluster champion accompanied by formal and informal strategies, co-location may lead to rivalry (Hall, 2004). The extent to which visitor attractions see themselves as a part of a production chain of a comprehensive tourism destination region product is questionable; the cooperative relationships between visitor attractions, cooperation with other businesses in tourism clusters and different forms of clustering including horizontal, vertical and diagonal clustering which they create, will be discussed later in this chapter.

The cluster model of visitor attractions

Based on the elaboration of Porter's (1998) Diamond model to tourism clusters by Weidenfeld et al. 2011, a suggested model of clusters of visitor attractions

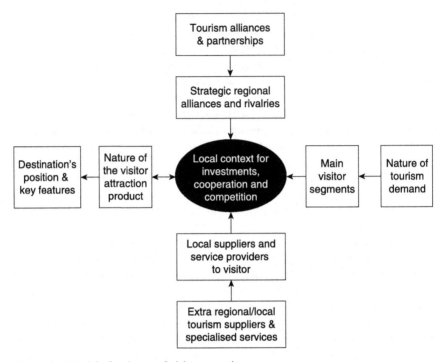

Figure 3.1 Model of a cluster of visitor attractions

Source: After Weidenfeld et al. (2011).

emphasises the most relevant factors affecting visitor attractions within tourism clusters (Figure 3.1):

a.   Destination's position and features – the nature of the visitor attraction product includes their relative competitive position in terms of the production of the visitor attraction experiences, related to the main motivational factors of a holiday, e.g. a country's natural and human factors (mainly cultural, heritage, archaeological, technological, trained human resources, access to natural resources, suitable capital markets to finance long-term investments).

b.   The nature of tourism demand for products and services includes the types of visitor segments and their special preferences, which are often addressed by regional or local (neighbouring) groups of visitor attractions determined by their spatial proximity and product similarities (see Chapter 6).

c.   Tourism alliances and partnerships: strategic regional alliances of and rivalries between visitor attractions – strategies that improve the competitive and comparative advantages of visitor attractions, supported by both public and private sectors, such as public–private partnerships and strategic alliances.

d. Tourism suppliers and specialised services – the presence or absence of local actors with whom there could be a closer collaboration, communication and constant learning. These actors provide visitor attractions with custom-made high quality inputs, components and services often at lower prices. In tourism clusters, the quality, diversity and specialisation of the suppliers and the operating networks – e.g. providers of food at hotels and restaurants, good personnel training schools, engineers and technicians – define a tourism area's competitive position and have a direct impact on the quality and efficiency of the visitor attraction experience.

Forms of clustering

Production linkages between clustered firms can be categorised as horizontal, vertical and diagonal, although this classification is not rigid and clusters can fall into more than one category in respect to their production link. Horizontal clustering refers to co-location of competitors selling similar products and using similar productive processes from the same stage in the value chain, while their co-location attracts the potential customer base and increases externalities, mainly external economies of agglomeration. In tourism, museum clusters around the world are a common example of horizontal clusters, which have been developed and redeveloped in city centres, such as the Museum Mile in New York, museum quarters or parks in Vienna, Utrecht, Amsterdam, a museum park in Rotterdam, a museum island in Berlin, as well as Museum Island and a museum bank in Frankfurt.

Horizontal clusters consist of those complementary firms that produce similar goods and compete with one another but are inter-linked through a network of suppliers, service and customer relations (Bathelt et al., 2004), which are common amongst attractions in destination regions. Vertical clustering refers to the co-location of firms operating at different stages of the production chain, which minimises logistics and distributional costs and enhances specialisation (Michael, 2003, Michael, 2007b). The visitor attraction cluster in Lolland Foster was initially a horizontal cluster of visitor attractions, which collaborated in staff training and marketing. Gradually, other types of tourism businesses joined the cluster, which has moved gradually from mostly horizontal to also vertical clustering with hotels, transport services, etc. (Sørensen and Fuglsang, 2014).

Diagonal clustering refers to an increasing concentration of complementary (or symbiotic) firms, where:

> each firm adds to the activities of the others, even though their products may be quite distinct and clearly belong to other industry classifications. Diagonal clustering occurs where firms working together create a bundle of separate products and services that the consumer effectively purchases as a single item.
> (Michael, 2007a:26)

In the visitor attraction sector, many amusement parks work as diagonal clusters of different facilities (e.g. rides), which can be purchased as a bundle of services or separately as different individual visits. Other attractions such as Disney theme parks cluster diagonally with hotels and other services, which are sold as a package deal. Santa Claus Village and neighbouring attractions and activities in Rovaniemi, Finland, are sold as a weekend tour, particularly around Christmas time, which includes flights, accommodation, transfers to/from Rovaniemi Airport, northern lights tour with reindeer, visit to Ranua Wildlife Park and Fazer candy shop, lunch and a visit to a reindeer farm and Santa Claus Village.

Horizontal and vertical clustering are found in tourism clusters, but Michael (2007a) argues that diagonal clustering is common in many tourism destinations, where separate firms with separate production processes supply activities such as transport, hospitality and accommodation.

Complementary relationships between firms in a cluster are a pivotal element for diagonal clustering in general and for tourism clusters in particular (Michael, 2003, 2007a). Since a competitor is defined as a 'firm that seeks to sell a substitute product or whose activities detract from the value of the original product in some way', and complementary firms 'are neither the providers of complements nor substitutes to them' (Michael, 2007a:26), the latter are not considered competitors. Competition, therefore, 'is confined to specific market segments where only the activities of some firms can affect the outcomes of other similar producers ... [Moreover], business growth is more about expanding complementary activities than it is about competition' (Michael, 2007a:28).

Diagonal clustering (and/or integration) is more about economies of scope internal to the firm, whereas horizontal and vertical clustering are more about external economies of scale including interdependencies, trust in sustained collaboration and cooperative competition. External economies of scale as well as synergies between products enhance collaboration between visitor attractions at the local and regional scales and will be discussed in Chapter 6. Diagonal clustering widens production possibilities, i.e. the maximum combination of goods and services that can be produced when the available productive resources are used efficiently (Michael, 2007a). Complementary firms in diagonal clusters are typical of tourism micro clusters and small scale regional tourism development. It is noteworthy that these are idealised models and not all businesses or firms have to be diagonally clustered. Some within the same cluster are expected to be clustered diagonally with other businesses, but vertically and horizontally with others.

Various forms of clustering reflect different relationships of production between visitor attractions. It is argued that the more attractions are competitors selling similar products and using similar productive processes from the same stage in the value chain, the more they are horizontally integrated than any other form of clustering. Horizontal clustering is aimed at achieving economies of scale and agglomeration among visitor attractions. The more attractions are less perceived by the others as competitors and offer complementary products, the more they are diagonally clustered. Since attractions are not firms operating at different stages of the production chain, they are not argued to be vertically clustered.

Agglomeration economies in visitor attractions

Agglomeration economies underlie the very rationale of the co-location of visitor attractions and other tourism and non-tourism facilities and services, such as the Penn Quarter in Washington, where a combination of museums, theatres, galleries, spectator sports, restaurants, retail shops, offices and residences illustrates the agglomeration economies that can be generated by the concentration of interdependent activities. When external economies of scale are a result of agglomeration and are caused by factors beyond the actions or responsibilities of a firm, they are called agglomeration economies (Cohen and Morrison, 2005). Benefits to firms in the form of external economies of scale, which can be attributed to spatial concentration of firms, are called external economies of agglomeration. These spillovers act as shift factors that affect cost-output relationships, and thus economic performance and competitiveness (Cohen and Morrison, 2005). Agglomeration economies are external economies of spatial concentration, and are also called positive spatial spillovers or thick market effects. Proximate specialised inputs, transport, infrastructure and possible information or knowledge spillovers tend to generate more efficient or cost effective production processes. They include the economic utilities and benefits including costs reductions, efficiency gains, a local pool of specialised labour, the provision of shared inputs and the maximisation of flows of information and ideas that accrue from the geographical concentration of firms (Gordon and McCann, 2000). Spatial concentration also allows for minimising transaction costs, as well as the improvement of communication (Leibovitz, 2004). 'These are the ways in which the external benefit to firms of a location in an industrial district manifests itself. Unit production costs will be lower within the industrial district than outwith it' (Newlands, 2003:522). Standard agglomeration theory provides an explanation of why firms might co-locate, sharing services, infrastructure and a diversified labour force, and forming extensive local linkages with other firms.

Proximity does not necessarily result in all kinds of positive externalities related to agglomeration of tourism production. It also depends on complementarities in terms of the production of tourism services, and trust between actors as well as other external economies of scale explored in Chapter 6. The following four aspects of agglomeration economies derive directly from co-location of firms within an industrial cluster identified in the literature (Krugman, 1991, Cohen and Morrison, 2005, Hjalager, 2000, Santagata, 2002, Jackson and Murphy, 2002):

i. Pool of labour;
ii. Flexible division of labour;
iii. Shared inputs, infrastructure and services (particularly transport);
iv. Diffusion of knowledge and technology.

The way each of these addresses agglomeration of visitor attractions is discussed below.

Pool of labour

Not all tourism occupations or sub-sectors belong to one single labour market, but all labour markets 'share the structure of the industry and are therefore open to its influence' (Riley et al., 2002:50). Such influence involves two related components: size of operating units and spatial dispersion (or density) of tourism business units, which constitute a dual structure where high employment density prevails, e.g. resorts, airport and large organisations, as opposed to small employment densities in smaller fragmented concentrations such as hotels, restaurants, visitor attraction centres and car hire offices (Riley et al., 2002).

A pool of labour is a pooled market for workers with industry-specific skills, ensuring both a lower probability of unemployment and of labour shortage (Krugman, 1991). Every agglomeration economy can have a pool of labour, especially skilled workers, in a system which maximises the job-matching opportunities between the individual worker and the individual firm and minimises the search costs for both (Gordon and McCann, 2000). Skills of qualified workers can be localised and opportunities outside the *milieu* can be limited for the local labour, which keep their mobility between local firms (Capello, 1999). At high levels of agglomeration of visitor attractions, high levels of labour turnover and competition and low barriers to labour mobility can be disadvantageous in terms of loss of skills and recruitment costs, but there is an advantage in terms of the diffusions of skills within the cluster.

In the conduct of visitor attractions and other tourism businesses, most jobs require unskilled and low-paid labour and mandate long, non-traditional working hours, coupled with monotonous tasks associated with high turnover (Milman, 2001). Fyall et al. (2001) imply that joint-training of staff prevents 'free-riding' and poaching of staff, given that 'the quality of the entire pool of staff is being improved for the benefit of the sector as a whole' (p. 221). In terms of level of agglomeration of visitor attractions, a pool of labour is advantageous in over-coming seasonality, encouraging innovations and information spillovers, as well as in developing specialised niche products for niche markets employing specialised labour (post-Fordism), but might lead to poaching workers between attractions and rising wages.

Visitor attractions in low levels of agglomeration, which do not enjoy a pool of labour, may find more permanent long-term loyal workers but suffer from fixed products, absence of innovations and information, spillovers, skills shortages and barriers to seasonality. A direct implication of this aspect is a flexible division of labour between firms within clusters. Spatial proximity or density of visitor attrac-tions in Weidenfeld's (2008) UK study comparing two clusters of visitor attractions in Newquay (more agglomerated) and the Lizard (less agglomerated) was important in terms of difficulty in recruitment and attractions' appeal for employees in general. However, there was no direct evidence of any impact of a pool of labour on the production or profitability of visitor attractions. There was evidence of the disadvantage of the lower agglomerated cluster, the Lizard Peninsula, among attractions in terms of competition for labour, compared to the more agglomerated Newquay cluster. In Newquay, visitor attraction managers did not complain of such competition. Attractions at a lower level of agglomeration and those located in edge-of-cluster locations were disadvantaged in terms of competition for labour with other attractions and other businesses.

Flexible division of labour

Flexible division of labour is typical of industrial clusters, where workers and firms have much more choice in selecting their workplace and workers (Hjalager, 2000, Jackson and Murphy, 2002, Shaw and Williams, 2004). Openness to external labour markets and migration by the large number of job opportunities offered by cluster members and the ability to change workplaces in a relatively flexible manner may also be associated with this aspect. The more an industry has a fragmented division of labour, the more there will be necessary transactions between firms in the production process (Storper, 2000). This flexibility in the tourism and leisure labour markets is attributed to both permanent and temporary (or secondary) workers where the formalisation of dual labour markets within companies occurs and 'stems from the particular nature of the demand for tourism and leisure services' (Shaw and Williams, 2002:174). Dual labour markets within companies include two groups; one is a group of core workers who are full-time, permanent employees performing a wide range of tasks, and are functionally flexible, i.e. managerial and professional staff. The other group is peripheral workers, grouped around the core group. This group can be full-timers, part-timers or temporary workers whose jobs are less secure and are often semi-skilled workers, trainee scheme placements and those working at home (Atkinson, 1984, cited by Shaw and Williams, 2002, 2004). The former are considered skilled workers, who are often in short supply in the external labour market and therefore employers are keen on retaining their services. The former has functional flexibility to employers by being able to move easily between tasks but are less likely to have numerical flexibility. The latter are more likely to be numerous but functionally inflexible.

Hjalager (2000) exemplifies this functional and temporal flexibility in clusters as 'more shifts and overtime can be introduced, and the employment of peripheral workers accounts for the expansion [or reduction] of time resources available for production'. Moreover, 'part of the temporal flexibility is due to the fact that production tasks can be smoothly re-allocated among the firms in a group' (p. 203). For example, flexibility in employing students, seasonal or immigrant labourers (Hjalager, 2002) can encourage businesses like hotels to cluster and to incorporate with educational institutions offering courses in tourism and hospitality in an attempt to overcome labour shortage in high seasons. Thus such incorporation and the effect of the supply of labour may affect the locational decisions of businesses, and they may tend to locate close to such institutions, whose holidays usually correspond with tourism high seasons (Jackson and Murphy, 2002). Such cooperation can also underlie other flexibilities such as work time, wage and procedural (Rimmer and Zappala, 1988, cited by Shaw and Williams, 2004). These flexibilities are used to reduce costs particularly through de-skilling and re-skilling, depending on the system of remuneration and the social groups undertaking certain types of 'unskilled work', justifying lower wages irrespective of the real skill content of the job or the employees (Shaw and Williams, 2004). This mechanism is particularly germane to flexibility in seasonal workers like students.

Visitor attractions' locations within agglomerations may allow them to function and develop differently than if they were non-agglomerated because of flexibility in recruiting and employing staff in visitor attractions. Fyall et al. (2001:221) note that 'the flexible use of a collective pool of part-time, casual or volunteer workers and the broader enhancement of the overall profile of employment of visitor attractions can benefit from greater collaboration among the latter'. In this context, it is pertinent to highlight that unlike other clusters or districts, a large proportion of the workforce in tourism clusters is temporal and imported from other areas, which reduces the possibility of creating a pool of professional and stable workforces. Likewise, given that many tourism clusters are situated in peripheral areas, research and development (R&D), sales and functions and even supply production tend to relocate to head offices and specialised departments such as reservation centres may move to more central areas.

It is assumed that attractions at high levels of agglomeration include more functional and temporal flexibility in skilled workers and numerical flexibility in semi- and unskilled workers, overcoming seasonality and temporal variations in demand, e.g. weekday versus weekend, unexpected peaks, etc. Disadvantages include poaching and high labour turnover. By contrast, low-agglomerated attractions would enjoy a labour market dependency on a few employers resulting in lower pressure on wages and lower turnover, but would have less flexibility in labour and less selection of skilled/unskilled workforce (Table 3.1). In both Newquay and Lizard clusters, there was some supporting evidence of these flexibilities as well as the advantage of cooperation between R&D institutions and educational institutions (Weidenfeld, 2008). The latter potentially provided tourism businesses with a higher skilled staff for their businesses. The study shows that agglomerated attractions enjoy to some extent a more functional and temporal flexibility, especially the numerical flexibility of students as semi-skilled cheap and temporal workers, helping to overcome seasonality. There are some indications that attractions on the Lizard also employ students but mainly for research purposes as part of collaboration with research institutions.

Transport, infrastructure, specialised inputs and services

This aspect can be identified in most industrial clusters and is presumed to exist in every tourism cluster. Such positive externalities include lower transport and freight costs of both inputs and outputs, cost savings and various types of thick market effects, which are solely and directly attributed to the physical dimension of spatial agglomeration (Cohen and Morrison, 2005, Gordon and McCann, 2000). Tourism demand depends on both long and short distance access networks and a transport system, particularly airport facilities (Clavé, 2007). Transport

Table 3.1 Advantages and disadvantages of agglomeration economies in the visitor attraction sector

Agglomeration economies / Advantages/disadvantages for visitor attractions	Tourism spaces of high agglomeration		Tourism spaces of low agglomeration	
	Advantages	Disadvantages	Advantages	Disadvantages
1. Shared inputs, infrastructure and services, e.g. transport	"Thick market effects": more variety allowing a chain of production and complementarities. Competitive advantage: accessibility to more visitors.	Congestion, environmental degradation, rising land prices. More competition between attractions.	Sustaining natural and exclusive environment, reduced local competition, sustaining exclusiveness of the tourism product.	"Thin" market effects: accessible to less visitors, higher costs, less variety in the tourism experience, attracting fewer market segments, less potential for chain of production.
2. Flexible division of labour	Functional flexibility amongst skilled workers. Numerical amongst semi- and unskilled workers as response to overcoming seasonality.	Poaching employees, high labour turnover.	Labour market dependency on a few employers resulting in less pressure on wages and lower turnover.	Less potential flexibility in labour and reduced pool of skilled/unskilled workers to recruit from.
3. Pool of mobile and specialised labour	Larger and more diverse labour pool. Inter-firm skills diffusion via mobile labour.	Poaching of employees, rising wages and a consequent deterrence to building trust amongst firms.	More long-term loyal workers and less poaching.	Fixed products, reduced innovation and information, spillovers, skills shortages and less scope to respond to seasonality challenges.
4. Diffusion of knowledge and innovations	More innovative products and other enhancements which sustain the appeal of the destination region.	More similarity in production, reduced distinctiveness of the product as an attractor, more product imitation.	Less pressure to change the core product contributes to greater retention of long-term loyalty amongst repeat visitors.	Tendency to obsolescence, more vulnerability to competitors.

systems are also important for travel between attractions and between attractions and services within destinations (Swarbrooke, 2002) and sometimes they become elements of attractions in themselves (Clavé, 2007).

Transport may generate opposite tendencies in spatial clusters; for example, the development of different modes of transport can facilitate concentration or accelerate dispersal across tourism spaces (Shaw and Williams, 2004). Transport as a key factor in attracting visitors needs to be examined differently in tourism spaces accessible mainly by car users, e.g. peripheral areas to those more central locations that are accessible by public transport as well. Conversely, some negative externalities may be caused by transport, leading to congestion. Negative external economies of agglomeration might therefore be caused by transport leading to congestion and the preference of tourism businesses to move to peripheral locations (Bale, 1976, Raco, 1999, Newlands, 2003, Cohen and Morrison, 2005). The impact of transport and accessibility depends on the levels of agglomeration between attractions within the same cluster, i.e. between those centrally located in a cluster versus attractions on the edge of a cluster, and also between attractions at low and high levels of agglomeration at the regional cluster scale (Weidenfeld, 2008).

Thick 'market effects' in central locations are expected to allow more complementary relationships to develop, and cost efficiency, as visitor attractions and businesses would tend to use Fordist production, such as joint ticketing schemes encouraging mass visits to visitor attractions in tourism destinations (see Chapter 6). In other words, transport leading to concentration of growing numbers of similar types of visitor segments might result in mass markets, in which more tourism enterprises offer similar products. This can be advantageous in terms of external economies for entrepreneurs, but disadvantageous for maintaining a destination distinctiveness and tourism appeal. Low-agglomerated attractions can also gain from less intense provision of services, infrastructure and transport, thus sustaining a clean, natural and exclusive environment and enjoy a more monopolistic and stable business local environment with less competition and sustaining exclusiveness of their tourism products (Table 3.1).

In Weidenfeld's (2008) study, visitor attractions on the Lizard Peninsula, situated remotely or on the edge of town location, suffered from poor visibility and accessibility to public transport and private vehicles even if they were not that far from other attractions. By contrast, low levels of agglomeration were also perceived by some attractions' managers to be advantageous in terms of less transport access, infrastructure and services, which restrict the number of visitors and therefore endow attractions with a clean, natural and exclusive environment and a more monopolistic and stable business environment. Therefore, they also objected to further tourism development in the Lizard (Table 3.1). At the regional cluster level, the more attractions are central, the more they gain a competitive advantage by being accessible to visitors, but at the same time, they faced some negative external agglomeration economies as a result of congestion and a lack of parking. Negative externalities counter positive externalities and encourage attractions to move to a more peripheral location. The best location appeared to be edge-of-cluster, where attractions enjoy positive externalities of agglomeration and avoid the negative ones. Location in a remote, low-agglomerated destination might result in negative external agglomeration economies such as services, recruitment, transport and infrastructure. Conversely, these 'thin' market effects also contributed to maintaining environmental quality settings and sustaining the uniqueness of the destination cluster (Weidenfeld, 2008).

Diffusion of knowledge, innovations and technology

Knowledge has a variety of overlapping forms (for example, aesthetic, cognitive, scientific, discursive, digital, information, tacit, explicit, emancipatory, embrained, embodied, encultured, embedded and encoded – see Hall and Williams, 2008) and is central to the operation of contemporary advanced economies (Henry and Pinch, 2000, Williams, 2005). In general, to create competitive advantage, there are always strong systemic pressures to find 'new' ways of producing 'old' commodities, making existing products that reduce costs by cutting the labour time needed in production (Hudson, 2005). In tourism, technology is important in enhancing the visitor experience at the attraction location; for example, using virtual reality and interactive media (Watson and McCracken, 2002). The advantages of agglomerated firms could entail more innovative production helping to sustain the regional destination appeal, but greater similarity in the production and less distinctiveness of the product as a result of imitation between neighbouring firms can be disadvantageous as well (see Chapter 9). Among attractions of low levels of agglomeration, less diffusion of innovation and the absence of change might decrease tourist appeal and draw fewer visitors as products become obsolete and vulnerable to competition. However, the same factors could be advantageous for sustaining the original place and maintain repetitive and regular visitors (Table 3.1).

The factors responsible for spatial dispersal/degglomeration

Forces counteracting economies of scale deriving from spatial clustering may also exist. For example, congestion or greater input competition in high-density areas could cause firms to locate in more rural areas (Bale, 1976, Cohen and Morrison, 2005). Negative spillovers or externalities, or insufficient density to facilitate economic production, can conversely be called thin market effects that may be linked to distance – such as limited telecommunications or transportation infrastructure – as well as rising land and wage prices, environmental degradation, congestion, corrosive competition and diseconomies of scale, particularly for small firms (Newlands, 2003, Raco, 1999, Cohen and Morrison, 2005). Bale (1976) refers to the point of critical size of the nucleus of spatial clustering beyond which benefits would be replaced by disbenefits. Michael (2007a:41) argues that:

> tourism generates more than its fair share of externalities. This is largely because it generates visitors to any particular destination, and they bring with

them not just an increase in the demand for goods and services, but also a whole range of social impacts for the host community

It is plausible that different shaped curves of agglomeration and degglomeration exist for different types of visitor attractions within the same cluster (Bale, 1976). Apart from agglomeration economies, external economies of scale emerge when visitor attractions cluster and will be discussed in Chapter 6.

Conclusions

Co-location of visitor attractions may engender agglomeration economies, including pool of labour, flexible division of labour, shared inputs, infrastructure and services (particularly transport), and diffusion of knowledge and technology. However, other external economies, including of scale and of scope, are likely to emerge when visitor attractions cluster horizontally, vertically and/or diagonally. Unlike other tourism clusters, visitor attractions' diagonal clusters can be formed by other businesses from the same sub-sector (i.e. other attractions). They may also be the main reason for forming a diagonal cluster with other types of tourism businesses, which complement the visitor attraction experience. Visitor attractions at high levels of agglomeration may not only enjoy spillovers from the mere spatial concentration, but could potentially gain external economies of scale and scope if they form an industrial cluster. Horizontal clustering between complementary attractions can be formed in tourism destinations at the beginning of the process and later develop vertical and diagonal clustering with other types of businesses such as accommodation and transport facilities. The study of economic externalities as a result of agglomeration and spatial clustering in the visitor attraction sector and the role of visitor attractions in tourism clusters remains rare and requires further studies. These studies should undertake further in-depth analysis including qualitative and quantitative analysis of different types of clustering and agglomeration economies in spatially concentrated visitor attractions.

References

Bale, J. (1976). *The Location of the Manufacturing Industry – Conceptual Frameworks in Geography*. Edinburgh: Oliver and Boyd.

Bathelt, H., Malmberg, A. and Maskell, P. (2004). Clusters and knowledge: Local buzz, global pipelines and the process of knowledge creation. *Progress in Human Geography*, *28*, 31–56.

Bennett, R. J. and Smith, C. (2002). Competitive conditions, competitive advantage and the location of SMEs. *Journal of Small Business and Enterprise Development*, *9*, 73–86.

Capello, R. (1999). Spatial transfer of knowledge in high technology milieux: Learning versus collective learning processes. *Regional Studies*, *33*, 353–365.

Clavé, S. A. (2007). *The Global Theme Park Industry*. Wallingford: CABI.

Cohen, J. P. and Morrison, J. C. P. (2005). Agglomeration economies and industry location decisions: The impacts of spatial and industrial spillovers. *Regional Science and Urban Economics*, *35*, 215–237.

Fyall, A., Leask, A. and Garrod, B. (2001). Scottish visitor attractions: A collaborative future. *International Journal of Tourism Research*, (3), 211–228.

Gordon, I. R. and McCann, P. (2000). Industrial clusters: Complexes, agglomeration and/or social networks? *Urban Studies*, *37*, 513–532.

Hall, M. C. (2004). Small firms and wine and food tourism in New Zealand: Issues of collaboration, clusters and lifestyles. In R. Thomas (Ed.), *Small Firms in Tourism-International Perspectives* (pp. 167–181). London: Elsevier.

Hall, M. C. and Williams, A. M. (2008). *Tourism and Innovation*. London: Routledge.

Henry, N. and Pinch, S. (2000). Spatialising knowledge: Placing the knowledge community of Motor Sport Valley. *Geoforum*, *31*, 191–208.

Hjalager, A. M. (2000). Tourism destinations and the concept of industrial districts. *Tourism and Hospitality Research*, *2*, 199–213.

Hjalager, A.–M. (2002). Repairing innovation defectiveness in tourism. *Tourism Management*, *23*, 465–474.

Hudson, R. (2005). *Economic Geographies, Circuits, Flows and Spaces*. London: Sage Publications.

Jackson, J. and Murphy, P. (2002). Tourism destinations as clusters: Analytical experiences from the New World. *Tourism and Hospitality Research*, *4*, 36–52.

Jackson, J. and Murphy, P. (2006). Clusters in regional tourism – An Australian case. *Annals of Tourism Research*, *33*, 1018–1035.

Krugman, P. (1991). Increasing returns and economic geography. *Journal of Political Economy*, *99*, 483–499.

Leibovitz, J. (2004). Embryonic knowledge-based clusters and cities: The case of biotechnology in Scotland. *Urban Studies*, *41*, 1133–1155.

Michael, E. J. (2003). Tourism micro-clusters. *Tourism Economics*, *9*, 133–145.

Michael, E. J. (Ed.) (2007a). *Micro-Clusters and Networks: The Growth of Tourism*. Oxford: Elsevier.

Michael, E. J. (2007b). *Micro-Clusters: Antiques, Retailing and Business Practice*. Oxford: Elsevier.

Milman, A. (2001). The future of the theme park and attraction industry: A management perspective. *Journal of Travel Research*, *40*, 139–147.

Newlands, D. (2003). Competition and cooperation in industrial clusters: The implications for public policy. *European Planning Studies*, *11*, 521–532.

Nordin, S. (2003). *Tourism Clustering and Innovation – Paths to Economic Growth and Development*. Oestersund, Sweden, European Tourism Research Institute, Mid-Sweden University.

Paül Agustí, D. (2013). Differences in the location of urban museums and their impact on urban areas. *International Journal of Cultural Policy*, *20*, 471–495.

Porter, M. (1990). *The Competitive Advantage of Nations*. New York: The Free Press.

Porter, M. (1998). *On Competition*. Cambridge, MA: Harvard Business School Press.

Raco, M. (1999). Competition, collaboration and the new industrial districts: Examining the institutional turn in local economic development. *Urban Studies*, *36*, 951–968.

Riley, M., Ladkin, A. and Svias, E. (2002). *Tourism Employment Analysis and Planning*. Clevedon: Channel View Publications.

Santagata, W. (2002). Cultural districts, property rights and sustainable economic growth. *International Journal of Urban and Regional Research*, *26*, 9–23.

Shaw, G. and Williams, A. (2002). *Critical Issues in Tourism: A Geographic Perspective* (2nd edition). Oxford: Blackwell.

Shaw, G. and Williams, A. (2004). *Tourism and Tourism Spaces*. London: Sage Publications.

Sørensen, F. and Fuglsang, L. (2014). Social network dynamics and innovation in small tourism companies. In M. McLeod and R. Vaughan (Eds), *Knowledge Networks and Tourism* (pp. 28–44). Abingdon: Routledge.

Storper, M. (2000). Globalization, localisation, and trade. In G. L. Clark, M. P. Feldman and M. S. Gertler (Eds), *Oxford Handbook of Economic Geography* (pp. 146–165). Oxford: Oxford University Press.

Swarbrooke, J. (2002). *The Development and Management of Visitor Attractions*. Oxford: Butterworth-Heinemann.

Wang, Y. and Fesenmaier, D. R. (2007). Collaborative destination marketing: A case study of Elkhart county, Indiana. *Tourism Management, 28*, 863–875.

Watson, S. and McCracken, M. (2002). No attraction in strategic thinking: Perceptions on current and future skills needs for visitor attraction managers. *International Journal of Tourism Research, 4*, 367–378.

Weidenfeld, A. (2008). *'The Destination Story' Cooperation, Competition and Knowledge Transfer Between Tourist Attractions in Cornwall*. PhD, University of Exeter.

Weidenfeld, A., Williams, A. M. and Butler, R. W. (2011). Why cluster? Text and sub-text in the engagement of tourism development policies with the cluster concept. In D. Dredge and J. M. Jenkins (Eds), *Stories of Practice: Tourism Policy and Planning* (pp. 335–338). Surrey: Ashgate Publishing.

Williams, A. M. (2005). Working Paper. No. 17, International Migration and Knowledge. Oxford: Centre on Migration, Policy and Society, University of Oxford.

4   The visitor attraction life cycle

Changing relationships between
attractions in tourism destinations

Introduction

Tourism destinations represent the focus of tourist travel and result in large investments of finance, human capital and promotion. These destinations are major
attractions for tourists and normally consist of a wide range of specific attractions,
varying with the underlying thematic focus of each specific destination. Thus,
beach resorts can be expected to have many attractions primarily focused on
outdoor activities, while urban resorts may have an emphasis on cultural and heritage attractions such as museums and artistic venues. The way in which these
different attractions relate to each other in resorts can be expected to vary both
with the nature and scale of the resort, and also with the stages of its development.
Resorts have been shown to be dynamic, their development over time reflecting
both endogenous and exogenous influences such as changes in tastes of visitors,
in means of access and in markets (Walton, 2015). It is reasonable to assume that,
over the life of a resort, the relationships between attractions within that resort
will alter with changing conditions, and what may be a positive relationship
expressed through cooperation at one point in time, may become competitive at
another stage. Relations may also develop, grow and decline with attractions in
the surrounding region as tourism evolves at the larger scale.

The dynamism and evolution of resorts has been well documented (see for
example Butler, 2006a, 2006b), the most commonly cited model being the tourism
area life cycle (TALC) model (Butler, 1980) which is still being utilised in contemporary research (e.g. Butler, 2015, Chapman and Speake, 2011). In its original
form, the TALC model focused on describing the process of development through
which tourism destinations proceeded, noting a number of stages common to
most resorts. It also described the creation and evolution of what became tourism
clusters in the form of destinations, and the physical, environmental, social and
economic changes that occur throughout this cycle. While the model emphasised
the dynamic nature of destinations, it did not explore relationships between the
stages of development and processes such as competition or cooperation between
individual attractions or destinations. There was a brief discussion in the original
model of the spatial implications of the pattern of development, which focused
primarily on the location of subsequent neighbouring resort developments but
not on the location of attractions within a specific resort or its hinterland.

In more recent research, the TALC model has been applied to evaluate networks and inter-organisation arrangements and their dynamics in tourism destinations through the different stages of development (Caffyn, 2000, Zehrer and Raich, 2010). However, these studies also did not address the interrelationships – such as cooperation and competition – between individual attractions at different spatial scales. There have been a number of studies which have examined the impact of spatial proximity on, and agglomeration between, tourism businesses on cooperation in tourism, generally through a focus on tourism clusters (Brown and Geddes, 2007, Erkus-Öztürk, 2009, Hall, 2004, Jackson and Murphy, 2002, Michael, 2003, Michael and Hall, 2007, Mitchell and Schreiber, 2007, Nordin, 2003, Weidenfeld et al., 2011). A smaller number of researchers (Baum and Mezias, 1992, Tsang and Yip, 2009) have addressed the impact of these spatial parameters on competition between enterprises. It is the nature of the patterns and relationships involving cooperation and competition among attractions within destinations which is the specific focus of this chapter, along with an examination of the spatiality of tourism destinations in general and the process of agglomeration of tourism firms over the development cycle of destinations.

The literature that exists on competition, cooperation and coopetition between businesses includes little specifically on individual tourism enterprises such as visitor attractions (see Chapter 7) and thus the following introduction to relevant studies is drawn primarily from the generic business literature. A similar situation occurs when examining research on the potential significance of the relative proximity or density (agglomeration) of businesses with respect to cooperation or competition between them. Following a very brief review of this literature, a conceptual model is developed to explain the potential behaviour of visitor attractions during the different stages of destination development described in the TALC model, and to show how this is affected by spatial proximity between, and the agglomeration of, visitor attractions.

Context and theoretical aspects

There is more detailed discussion in Chapters 3, 6 and 7 of the primary literature on agglomeration, clustering and cooperation and competition between destinations and attractions. Therefore, this brief discussion is focused on the research most directly relevant to these issues in the context of specific tourist enterprises in the form of attractions. The issues of cooperation and competition between tourism businesses in destinations have attracted research attention for a number of years (Buhalis and Cooper, 1998), along with the wider topic of destination competitiveness (Blanke and Chiesa, 2007, Ritchie and Crouch, 2003). Drawing on this literature, it is contended that over the life cycle of a destination or region there will be changes in the behaviour (group, compete and cooperate) of individual attractions in relation to other attractions as circumstances change.

The creation and development of tourism destinations, through the clustering of attractions at a level sufficient enough to attract tourists, has been discussed in the context of tourism resort models (see for example Butler, 1980, Lade, 2010, Pearce, 1989). Clustering can occur at a number of levels or scales, from the neighbourhood or local level within a community, between small communities themselves, through the regional level up to and including the national and even international levels (Malmberg and Maskell, 2002). In the context of attractions, the patterns and processes at the local and regional levels are the concern here. The local scale refers to relationships between individual tourism businesses (attractions) within the same destination, while at the regional level the focus is on the working relations amongst several small and medium size tourism enterprises (SMTEs) at a larger geographic scale where the relationships are more likely to be constituted through forming groups or associations.

The development of a destination is a necessary condition for effective clustering to occur but the mere co-location of firms does not guarantee either cooperation or optimising gains from economies of scale and of scope. The definition of a cluster can be used to describe a destination 'with its conglomeration of competing and collaborating businesses, generally working together in associations and through partnership marketing to put their location on the map' (Jackson and Murphy, 2006:1022), each with its own agenda and priorities. Potential reductions in costs for attractions may result in production linkages, which can be categorised as horizontal, vertical and diagonal clustering (described earlier in Chapter 3). All forms of clustering are dynamic and can be expected to evolve during the life cycle of any tourist destination, in terms of relationships both among individual visitor attractions and also among resorts in close proximity.

One particularly interesting example of the attempted clustering of visitor attractions has been documented by Tien (2010) in the context of museums in Taiwan. At the local scale Tien suggests clusters of smaller museums are capable of fostering local development. Thus, competitiveness can be increased through cooperation in symbiotic clusters which may also prolong over time the appeal of the individual museums involved through shared promotion and coopetition. The example of the efforts of Glasgow to develop itself as a cultural destination for the tourist market, as noted by Lennon (2003), was driven in part by the opening of the Burrell Collection (1983) and attempts to coordinate other heritage attractions with that iconic element. This initiative was a factor in, and consequently further supported by, Glasgow being named City of Culture in 1990. However, historic restrictions imposed by the donor of the collection made the desired cooperation between museums in Glasgow extremely difficult, illustrating that some barriers to cooperation lie outwith the control of individual attractions, and may stem from decisions made many years previously and which may not be related to the present destination stage of development.

The spatial configuration of destinations is also dynamic in response to changes over time in the popularity of resorts. Traditional models of the spatial development of tourist destination regions (Pearce 1989) suggest that, during the first stages of destination development, an emerging tourism destination casts an agglomeration shadow on other communities in a region, and that a concentration of new resorts subsequently emerges around a successful destination as a result of

its increasing economic success and improvements in means of access, infrastructure and services. A core-periphery configuration and spatial competition
may then occur (Papatheodorou, 2006). At this point, centripetal forces of agglomeration coexist with centrifugal forces of degglomeration: as tourist flows increase,
the pressure on natural and environmental resources can prove detrimental to
the overall quality and appeal of a destination. Land rents, and subsequently the
costs of accommodation and other supporting services in popular resorts, tend to
increase. As these costs are passed on to tourists, the result can be negative in
terms of gaining additional tourists or even maintaining numbers in the face of
increasing competition, particularly in the price sensitive mass tourism market.
When the carrying capacity or balance point is surpassed, however, tourist
flow autocorrelation becomes negative and can result in degglomeration unless
rejuvenation is achieved (Butler, 1980, Papatheodorou, 2004), emphasising the
need for the active management of destination communities and the attractions
within them.

The TALC model is derived from the generic business literature (Butler, 2006a)
and it is not surprising that models in related fields are relevant in the case
of competition and cooperation between individual enterprises. Attractions sell
experiences and therefore can be expected to behave in ways similar to other
retail enterprises. This is a point made by Coles (2006) who notes comparisons
with models used in retailing, particularly in the context of the creation, marketing, selling and modification of a product over its life-span. He discusses, as does
Russell (2006), whether the process is a cycle or a 'wheel', with developments
such as agglomeration and degglomeration being responsive to entrepreneurial
inputs and innovations, and particularly reflective of price considerations at specific periods. The spectacular and rapid rise in popularity of Macau, China, as
a tourist destination reflects both the role played by key individuals and the
expansion of gambling, enabled by legislative changes (McCartney, 2010), with
the result that this destination has become the largest gambling destination in
the world within a decade. While the casinos that provide a major element of the
regional comparative appeal of Macau are highly competitive as individual visitor
attractions, they also cooperate to further the overall appeal of Macao as a major
international gambling destination.

The contributions of entrepreneurs can significantly change, often abruptly,
the relationships between a destination and its markets and the nature of competition and cooperation within a tourism cluster (Butler and Russell, 2010).
Disney's establishment of theme parks in Anaheim and Florida has resulted in
massive changes in the development paths of both locations (Shani and Logan,
2010), requiring cooperation from a variety of other interests, and resulting in
increased competition in areas such as accommodation and other tourism
services. In the initial stages of development of a destination the majority of
entrepreneurs and other agents of change can be expected to be local or endogenous, as most resorts begin by utilising existing attributes and attractions.
As development increases, destinations may attract exogenous agents, sometimes resulting in local opposition when control of the direction, scale and rate of

tourism growth shifts away from local residents, and periods of instability may ensue (Keller, 1987).

All destinations and their attractions are vulnerable to change, some of which is deliberate and/or planned, some incidental, some caused by endogenous forces and some by exogenous ones. Weaver and Oppermann (2000) argue that these triggers of change can be summarised as being intentional or unintentional, and internal (endogenous) or external (exogenous) to the destination itself. Individual attractions can be particularly vulnerable to sudden changes (both endogenous and exogenous) affecting the host destination, and in line with Weaver and Oppermann's model, a shift from local control to exogenous decision-making may expose weaknesses in the viability of attractions. This may bring about changes in behaviour, for example in marketing and promotion, towards both competitors and allies. Such events can sometimes stimulate cooperation to ensure the survival of a destination, and in other cases may shift the balance of intra- or inter-regional competition to favour one location or one type of development over another. Decisions may also be taken to remove or add certain types of attractions in order to engender change in the image of a destination following a major upheaval. This is often done with the intent of 'upgrading' a destination. Sometimes upgrading is promoted as moving towards greater 'sustainability', but such claims are often contentious (Dodds, 2008). A good example of the manner in which attractions come in and go out of fashion and need to receive re-investment and renovation is provided by Dreamland (Box 4.1). This attraction had gone so far into decline that it had closed and was intended to be demolished before a new owner and local support made it possible for it to re-open as part of the general revitalisation of the resort (Margate in south east England) in which it is located.

Box 4.1 Dreamland 'UK's original pleasure park': reimaged

Dreamland is an entertainment attraction in the form of an amusement park located in Margate in south eastern England. Margate is a classic seaside resort which began in the eighteenth century by attracting short-term visitors from London who travelled by steamer down the Thames. It grew with the advent of railway services and was a major resort until after the Second World War, with Dreamland remaining an attraction until the end of the twentieth century. Margate has become synonymous with the old-style declining UK resorts (Shaw and Williams, 1997), experiencing a serious decline in hotels and beds and, inevitably, visitors. It has always had a high proportion of holiday amenities in local ownership. In the case of Dreamland, the local council financially supported this loss-making privately owned major attraction for a number of years.

Margate's 'Hall by the Sea', which opened in the 1860s, was one of the UK's top ten major attractions in its earlier years. It is located on a prime 16 acre site near the centre of the town, very close to the railway station with which it had links. It was purchased by a new owner in 1919 and renamed Dreamland in 1920, and was expanded into an American style amusement park with an investment equivalent to £15 million at current values. At one time it contained a zoo, a miniature railway, many rides, a ballroom with a capacity of over 2,000 which attracted major music acts, restaurants, bars and a cinema seating 2,200. It was claimed to be the oldest entertainment amusement park in the UK. The park continued to attract large numbers of visitors well after the Second World War when it returned as a visitor attraction after being given over to war related services from 1939–45. It remained popular in the 1950s and 1960s and gained additional attractions in the 1970s. New ownership resulted in additional rides being added again in the 1980s and 1990s despite declining numbers of staying visitors in Margate. Falling visitor numbers to the park in the late 1990s, changes in ownership, and rumours of closure and redevelopment for other commercial purposes, however, meant that the park was well in decline by the end of the twentieth century.

The above pattern of establishment, ownership change and major re-development, followed eventually by decline, illustrates the pattern of the TALC, and closely mirrors the pattern of tourism in the host town of Margate. In decline and suffering from lack of reinvestment and consequently customers, Dreamland was closed in the early years of the twenty-first century and plans were made to convert the property to housing. This scheme was opposed by a 'Save Dreamland' campaign and *The Dreamland Trust* was established with the aim of reopening the park. The scenic train ride and the cinema were given 'listed' building status by the national government, and the prospect of losing what was seen as the major attraction of the town for visitors led to some £18 million of public funds being raised, reflecting the long history of public support of such attractions in Margate and elsewhere. The site was acquired using a compulsory purchase order by Thanet District Council in 2013 and measures taken to rebuild the scenic railway and offer 17 'updated, restored upcycled and retrofitted' rides (www.dreamland.co.uk). The site reopened in June 2015 offering a range of mostly traditional seaside-style forms of entertainment.

The redeveloped Dreamland sits close to the Turner Contemporary (art gallery) which opened in 2011 with a goal of rejuvenating the town, along with a number of recently renovated hotels and restaurants. Dreamland is an interesting example of attraction rejuvenation, providing the opportunity to observe whether a restored and somewhat renovated old-style amusement park now over 150 years old can still draw large numbers of visitors to the town and to its own specific attractions. While Dreamland's cycle of growth, decline and rejuvenation is not unusual, the refurbishing of old-style rides and amusements, rather than the replacement of these features by contemporary theme park rides, is probably unique. It will prove an interesting test case revealing whether retrofitting and repairing old attractions can be successful in bringing back the 'lost' tourists who used to visit Margate to the town and to the attraction itself. If it is successful it will identify an alternative approach to attraction regeneration as well as supporting the concept of a Visitor Attraction Life Cycle.

Shaw and Williams (1997); www.dreamland.co.uk; www.turnercontemporary.org

Changing relationships during a resort's life cycle

As noted earlier, little attention has been paid to date to the way in which either attractions or destinations change their internal and external relationships with respect to cooperation or completion over the course of a destination's life cycle.

This reflects, perhaps, the general neglect of both the agents of change and the nature of change relating to attractions and destinations in studies of the TALC, where the emphasis has been on the pattern of change of specific destinations and whether that pattern matches the idealised scenario of the model (Butler, 2015). In recent years some attempts have been made to explain rather than describe the TALC, and to identify the forces of change and the way attractions and destinations respond to these (Gale and Botterill, 2005). Caffyn (2006) is one researcher who has produced a variation of the life cycle model which, in this instance, is applied to partnerships and cooperation between attractions at the destination level. That model comprises six phases closely resembling the original TALC stages of development: pre-partnership, take-off, growth, prime, decelera-tion and several options of 'after life' phases. The stages are differentiated by their characteristics in terms of how specific partnerships in a destination change over time, and whether there are commonalities in their patterns of evolution (e.g. decision-making, leadership, commitment) in relation to a deliberately undefined scale of success.

A second model has been developed by Zehrer and Raich (2010) relating to network development, a factor discussed in the context of one aspect of cooperation between enterprises (Wang, 2011). This model proposes five stages: foundation, configuration, implementation, stabilisation and transformation. These also match the TALC stages of development, consolidation, stagnation and post-stagnation (decline, rejuvenation or stabilisation). Zehrer and Reich's model refers more to the levels of cooperation in terms of size of the network and engagement in network activities rather than the nature of cooperation which is central to Caffyn's model. In both cases changes in the relationships of individual enterprises, such as attractions, are not discussed specifically but their work is important in recognising that changes in such relationships occur throughout the TALC of the host destination.

While the focus of this chapter is on the way that cooperation, competition and coopetition between attractions vary through the life cycle of their respective destinations, it must be borne in mind that the life cycle of a typical destination is comprised of multiple life cycles, representing the elements and attributes (includ-ing attractions) that comprise the overall tourist offering at a destination (Butler, 2009). Thus, the conventional life cycle modelled in the TALC is an amalgam of many cycles which may be at various stages of development. There are, for example, cycles representing different forms of tourism demand (Zimmermann, 2000), as well as cycles of supply factors such as attractions and accommodation.

Swarbrooke (2002) was perhaps the first researcher to produce examples of a life cycle for individual visitor attractions, fusing the argument that attractions, at least human-made ones, are products and therefore likely to follow the traditional product life cycle. He noted that such a cycle was likely to vary from the classic 'S' curve and suggested there could be a range of curves. One cycle that he suggested for major attractions might have the maximum numbers of visitors achieved in the initial years of the attraction, partly because of extensive promotion and the need to achieve large numbers in order to repay high capital costs over a short time period. He argued that other attractions can demonstrate a bi-modal profile reflecting relaunches or major renovations, and the addition of new elements within the attraction after a few years.

This argument is in line with the findings of Cornelis (2011) that major reinvestment in many theme parks takes place every third year or thereabouts. The issue of reinvestment and continuous updating and renovation of attractions in general is central with respect to their competitiveness. The original TALC argued the necessity for destinations to manage and modify their resources through renovation and to adapt to changing market priorities (Butler, 1980). In the context of theme parks, Cornelis (2011:151) found that managers of such attractions viewed investing in new facilities such as rides within their parks as being the most important factor in maintaining visitor numbers. This was true for both the long and short terms: new features (as a result of investment) were the most important factor for maintaining and increasing visitor numbers in the long term, and the second most important action in the short term. Regular reinvestment was viewed as essential, with the majority of theme park attraction operators undertaking major reinvestment approximately every three years in order to retain their competitive position and visitor numbers. Interestingly, the managers ranked competition as only tenth of 12 factors in terms of influencing visitor numbers in the long term and seventh in the short term. The lack of priority given to competition may reflect the situation in central Florida where additional numbers of theme park attractions have resulted in increased numbers of visitors overall to the region, suggesting that tourists attracted to these parks find the presence of multiple parks of major appeal. Clearly not all attractions behave in the same way as theme parks, and not all attractions are able to reinvest on a regular basis, but it is also clear that those attractions, which do not renovate and upgrade their features, run a considerable risk of becoming outdated and less attractive to their existing and potential markets.

Swarbrooke (2002) suggests that new attractions in destinations are likely to face competition almost immediately unless they are highly innovative or unique in some key regard. In the early stages of the TALC, however, there would be few competitors as visitor numbers would be small and tend to be attracted by existing, often natural, attributes rather than by 'manufactured' attractions. In recent decades the traditional form of the destination life cycle has been overtaken in some locations by 'instant' resorts which may well be based on created attractions, and rely on the existence of a critical number of such attractions to draw in tourists, thus ensuring competition from the start. However, while multiple attractions may represent competition, they may also enhance the overall appeal of the destination involved, thus representing a form of coopetition that persists as a feature of such destinations throughout their life cycles.

Swarbrooke notes that some attractions, while charging for admission, are not operated on the conventional business model but as non-commercial or lifestyle attractions. These may be used for primarily non-tourist purposes, of which heritage and cultural properties such as cathedrals are the most common examples. In such cases, their life cycles may be very different, reflecting both their origins and basic functions, with their tourist role being seen as supplementary and supportive to their primary role. He concludes (2002:55) that:

> It is probably true that ... the life cycle of the individual attraction is related to another life cycle. That is, the life cycle of the area as a tourist destination and the stage it has reached in its life cycle as a destination. Attractions may stimulate the onset of the growth stage in the development of the destination but they can also help cause, as well as suffer from, the decline stage of a destination's life cycle.

Law (2002:88) also discusses the idea of a visitor attraction life cycle in his volume on urban tourism, noting that 'the relationship between visitor attractions and the growth of a tourist destination is a difficult one to untangle and is likely to vary from one city to another'. He notes the effect of a large single attraction on a destination, citing the example of the Disney theme park development in central Florida as being large enough to attract other visitor attractions and change the character of the region. In the case of major cities such as London or New York, Law argues that such cities, often possessing iconic attractions, become major attractions in their own right and generate sufficient demand for additional visitor attractions, thus creating a positive feedback loop (see Chapter 11).

Las Vegas, over its lifetime, has operated in the same way with each additional casino making the destination even more attractive to the gambling market. Law goes on to note that in smaller 'second tier' cities, which lack an iconic feature, tourists may only be attracted if there are sufficient numbers of attractions, with quantity replacing iconicity. The addition of further attractions could result in an increase in tourist numbers but, if not, then visits per attraction would decline reflecting the effect of increased competition. Law (2002:89) notes that in specific situations 'a group of allied but complementary attractions could strengthen the marketing of the city. In this case the attractions could be seen to be working collaboratively rather than competitively', as is illustrated by the example of the city of Glasgow. The creation of museum clusters, cited by Tien (2010), is a development in a similar vein (see above and Chapter 3).

Lennon (2003:154) is another author who has argued the case for a visitor attraction cycle and demonstrated that there are multiple forms of such a cycle reflecting the varied forms of visitor attraction. While there are similarities between the life cycles of both paid and free attractions in his examples, he notes considerable variation between those attractions which have a programme of reinvestment and those that do not, with the former experiencing more consistent growth (Lennon 2003:158). He acknowledges that major economic factors (mostly exogenous) and other variables make it extremely difficult to identify the impact of competition on the operation of an attraction over time, with the opening of other attractions in the vicinity 'causing displacement effects on visitation levels' (ibid.). Where attractions are developed which are similar but not outstanding, as has been the case with some theme parks in China, their life cycles have proved to be extremely short. Lewis (2015) suggests that less than a third of the 3,000 or so theme parks in China

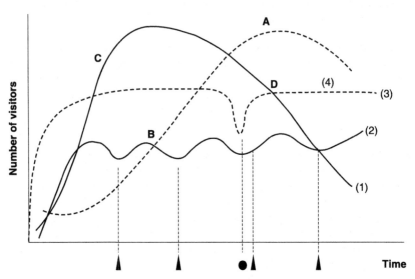

Figure 4.1 Simplified life cycles of visitor attractions
Based on Cornelis (2011), Law (2002), Lennon (2003) and Swarbrooke (2002).

▲ Major re-investment
● Event subjected to negative occurrence

turn a profit, primarily because many are of poor quality and/or were destined to fail so that the site could eventually be used for housing or other development. Oversupply of that form of attraction has meant that only the distinctive ones survive competition, which is particularly fierce in the initial years of operation, while the high failure rate contributes to a short life cycle.

In the light of the above discussion it is possible to suggest a number of variations on a Visitor Attraction Life Cycle reflecting the influences at work in typical destinations (Figure 4.1). Undoubtedly some attractions will follow Butler's 1980 original simple life cycle curve (A), reflecting the fact that many destinations are indeed products, some entirely created by humans, while others may be of natural origins but have been modified and managed by humans. As such they have been established and adapted to meet what are felt to be shifts in demand and market preferences, and by extension they continue to need adjustment and investment to ensure that their appeal does not diminish in a dynamic market (see Lennon 2003:156, for a similar argument). Given the evidence of Cornelis (2011) and Lewis (2015), the curves of attractions with regular periodic major investment and those with little or no such investment are likely to be very different (B and C, respectively, in Figure 4.1). Such curves will inevitably be affected by competition, which if not successfully met, is likely to result in a decline of visitor numbers. Two of the graphs indicate the 'wow factor', which is a sharp incline in the number of visitors during a relatively short period of time, related to an innovative sensational new experience or facility, which draws a large number of visitors to the attraction and is particularly typical of the first period when a new attraction opens to the public (Curves B and D). A new art show on the seafront site in the town of Weston-super-Mare, England (Dismaland), featuring 'entry-level anarchism' and satirising the tourism and theme-park industries, was visited by 150,000 people in the first five weeks after it opened in August 2015, generating a £20m boost to the local economy of the town (Harvey, 2015).

Reflecting generally on destination development, while an increase in the overall number of attractions in a destination may increase the overall appeal of that destination and also total visitor numbers to all of its attractions for a period, it is likely that – sooner or later – some attractions will be more successful in attracting visitors than others. Even major free attractions such as the British Museum periodically offer 'blockbuster' events such as exhibitions which boost awareness of the attraction through media attention and increase attendance in much the same way as reinvestment (B). The effect of such temporary additional features can be seen in the case of the 2011–12 *Leonardo da Vinci – Painter at the Court of Milan* exhibition (which charged entry fees) at the National Gallery (London) which attracted almost a third of a million visitors during its opening, out of a yearly total of over 6 million visitors. This was mirrored by the 2013 exhibition on *Life and Death in Pompeii and Herculaneaum*, which led to record visitor numbers to the British Museum of over 6.7 million in 2013, with almost half a million going to the special exhibition (which also charged entry fees). Numbers of visitors to major attractions such as these are unlikely to decline significantly, even without special exhibitions, as their audience is made up of both London residents and visitors to that city. Many of the latter will be first time visitors and thus the potential market is constantly renewed, reflecting the overall appeal of the destination. Major changes such as the reinstitution of fees for general admission, however, would be likely to result in a decline in visitors from the local area who had already seen the permanent items on display. The appeal of all attractions is likely to diminish over time if new elements and features are not added to the offerings to visitors (A in Figure 4.1).

In the case of event attractions, the situation is somewhat different. Annual or regular sporting events such as international tennis or golf tournaments are 'new' events each time they are staged, in the sense that the outcomes are never identical or easily predicted and may feature new participants. In the case of events such as concerts and festivals, e.g. Glastonbury Music Festival, most feature a different programme with different acts each year, again offering a 'new' event each year. Although not all individual acts have equal appeal, in general visitation can be expected to be maintained or increase rather than decline as a consequence of this change in content. On the other hand, external forces such as bad weather, failure of performers to appear or logistical problems may cause declines in visitation but such occurrences are generally 'one-off' problems and are not necessarily reflected in subsequent years (D in Figure 4.1).

In conclusion, there are pressures on most operators of visitor attractions to regularly renew their attraction and its constituent elements in order to at least maintain, if not increase, its appeal to its existing market and to attract new and replacement markets. Such steps may involve innovative processes including incremental changes to existing facilities and new product development (Chapter 9). Without such reinvestment and re-embellishment, most attractions, even those natural ones that have been subject to relatively little human modification, are likely to experience a decline in growth and perhaps ultimately a decline in overall visitation. While purely 'natural' attractions such as beaches and lakes may remain popular for a long period, they can also benefit, in terms of attendance, from improvements and updating of access and associated services such as parking, maintenance, toilet facilities and security assistance. Few, if any, attractions are so important that they will continue to attract visitors without regular product enhancement and innovation, especially in the face of continually expanding competition from new alternative opportunities.

Modelling competition and cooperation over the life cycle

The potentially changing relations between attractions in a destination, in the context of shifts in competition and cooperation over time, were discussed by Butler and Weidenfeld (2012). A conceptual model for predicting the likely extent and nature of cooperation and competition between attractions at each stage of the TALC model is illustrated in Figure 4.2. Unlike the original TALC figure (Butler, 1980), the vertical scale in Figure 4.2 shows the level of agglomeration as a measure of development instead of the traditional number of visitors, and also levels of clustering and the levels of cooperation and competition between attractions. The horizontal axis shows the time or stage of development of the hypothesised destination.

The stages of development of the TALC are shown above the curves which end in the option of decline or rejuvenation. The nature of the clustering at each stage is shown by boxes above the curves. Line 1 in the figure indicates the levels of

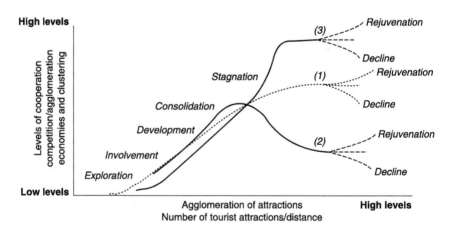

Figure 4.2 Relationships between agglomeration, cooperation and competition for visitors between visitor attractions throughout the TALC
After Butler and Weidenfeld (2012).

(1) Agglomeration; (2) regional (cluster) cooperation/competition; (3) local cooperation/competition between individual neighbouring businesses

agglomeration of attractions within the destination. Lines 2 and 3 illustrate the differing levels of cooperation/competition in relation to increasing agglomeration of businesses at different scales. The bell-shaped line (2) illustrates the suggested levels of *regional* cooperation or *regional* competition between attractions. Line 3 outlines the levels of *local* cooperation or *local* competition between intra-destination individual attractions. The figure shows how levels of agglomeration, cooperation and competition vary through the stages of the life cycle in a theoretical fashion, and the following discussion proceeds through those stages incorporating a comparison between the stages (in italics and in brackets) of the TALC and those of Zehrer and Raich (2010).

As a destination begins to attract tourists it will have few facilities and its attractions will be mostly small scale, locally owned and some may simply be natural amenities such as beaches and natural areas and scenery, or the cultural heritage and lifestyles of the residents. At the *Exploration (foundation)* stage, therefore, there are usually a limited number of operating businesses at low levels of agglomeration (Haywood, 2006, Papatheodorou, 2004). Before the operators and owners of these attractions decide to collaborate and define ground rules regarding interaction and communication, they need to appreciate the potential benefits from cooperation such as economies of scale. They also have to believe that such benefits will outweigh any costs incurred, either directly as financial charges or potential loss of business to competitors. Local and regional cooperation between attractions is likely to evolve but competition will be almost non-existent as business activity would still be at its preliminary stage with few establishments, reflecting the low and irregular numbers of tourists. At this stage, continued and regular visitation will not have been established and the market will not be seen as large enough or reliable enough to encourage multiple similar attractions or services.

As numbers increase and a pattern of regular visitation emerges in the *Involvement (configuration)* stage, one can expect local and regional cooperation and competition to begin to grow. Some forms of vertical clustering are likely to emerge as the destination experience and identity is built from various complementary products and services, and multiple offerings of services and attractions may begin to appear as opportunities are realised. Tourism businesses may still be in the process of building initial trust with their neighbours and establishing regional collaborative mechanisms. Although Zehrer and Raich (2010) suggest that in the initial stage actors become network promoters themselves and might be supported by regional institutions, this is more likely to begin in the *involvement* stage and be followed by symmetric collaborative relationships, including controlling mechanisms and communication, being set. In this stage a primary concern in most destinations will be to increase tourist numbers and capture a regular market. Because of limited resources for cooperation, attractions can be expected to prioritise regional over local cooperation due to the need to increase overall tourist numbers to the destination.

It is in the *Development (implementation)* stage that destinations experience rapid growth in tourist numbers and normally rapid expansion in investment and development of tourist related services and attractions, as well as improved and enlarged infrastructure and transportation services. Agglomeration (clustering) and the levels of regional and local cooperation and competition are likely to increase (Lines 1 and 2 in Figure 4.2), and trust develops between managers/ owners, particularly between local operators. These developments are character- ised by increased vertical clustering, and more trust between neighbours which in turn would encourage businesses to cluster horizontally. As continued growth is emphasised, regional cooperation will be seen as critical for attracting more tour- ists to the area and establishing a regional identity and appeal that will be vital for further development. Barring unforeseen problems, such as crises or exogenous negative influences, it is likely that cooperation will increase and some forms of horizontal clustering are likely to emerge. In this stage, network partners develop their tourism activities, and critical tasks are systematically monitored according to Zehrer and Raich (2010).

As in the original TALC model, growth continues but at a reduced rate in the *Consolidation (stabilisation)* stage. By this time the destination will be well established as a tourist resort with multiple forms of attractions and services in competition with each other for the, by now, established and regular tourist market. Operators are likely to direct their resources at competition with other intra-cluster businesses at the expense of marketing through membership in regional alliances (regional cooperation) (Figure 4.2, Lines 1 and 3) because they will see local competitors as a more serious problem than attracting more tourists at the regional level. The system will be more complex because of the greater number of actors and level of competition in the network. During this stage there are likely to be more clearly defined results of early collaboration, including both successful and unfulfilled outcomes, resulting in further negotiations and compromises (Zehrer and Raich, 2010).

In the TALC model, *consolidation* is followed by *Stagnation (transformation)* at which point visitor numbers cease to grow and investment and further physical development of the destination slows or stops. By this stage agglomeration will have stabilised and individual enterprises will have become more concerned over local issues and less involved with regional cooperation. The growth in local and regional cooperation can be expected to decrease but local cooperation and competition may continue to grow, and vertical and horizontal clustering is likely to continue. Stagnation is always, to some extent, a result of changes in the market and reflects the relative appeal of the destination. Some enterprises may consider moving out of tourism, either partly or completely (Baum, 2006). Others may engage in inter-sectoral collaboration in order to maintain the competitiveness of the tourism destination experience (Zehrer and Raich, 2010). Diagonal clustering and collaboration are likely to emerge as businesses try to minimise costs, reduce risks and survive, sometimes in cooperation with other businesses as, effectively, a single integrated attraction. When attractions close down, relocate or lose their appeal, the remaining businesses will prioritise their own survival and become more likely to revert both to competing with similar local attractions and maintaining existing forms of local cooperation.

The final stages of the traditional TALC process were identified as ranging from *Decline* through *Stability* to *Rejuvenation*. In the *decline* stage it was suggested that some businesses would close, there may be a reversal from external to local ownership of businesses, the destination may seek to restructure itself, some businesses would convert to non-tourism outlets or the destination may exit tourism completely (Baum, 2006). Problems noted earlier such as congestion costs, poor image and environmental degradation may have already caused potential new and existing attractions to relocate to alternative less-developed areas (Figure 4.2, Line 1). In some cases tourism businesses may diversify into other activities, pushing tourism activities into peripheral areas (Gordon, 1994). Degglomeration can occur resulting in a reduction in density as well as in local cooperation between neighbouring individual attractions (Line 2). It is also possible that, in the *decline/rejuvenation* stages of the TALC, exogenous forces might result in cooperation between individual neighbouring businesses remaining at the same level or even increasing as a result of possible governmental incentives, or the availability of other external resources to stimulate regional cooperation and improve the competitiveness of the destination (Line 3). In one of the most successful large scale rejuvenations of a destination (Atlantic City) (Stansfield, 2006), there was intense competition between individual major attractions (casinos) but cooperation in destination marketing and image creation that proved successful for a quarter of a century. As Atlantic City is now facing decline again in the 2010s (Frean, 2014), interest will focus on whether or not cooperation and competition remain at a similar level.

It is likely that as a destination develops in the early stages of the TALC (*exploration, involvement* and *development* stages), the density of businesses increases and local competition between co-located businesses also intensifies (Lines 2 and 3). This would mean that tourists would increasingly have more choice, at least in terms of the number of attractions and service outlets, and businesses would have to adjust to a more competitive business environment. When destinations approach the *consolidation* stage, businesses are more likely to direct their resources to competition with other intra-destination cluster businesses (local competition). This could be at the expense of marketing through membership in regional alliances (regional cooperation) for the purpose of competing with other destinations (regional competition). Therefore, it can be expected that regional competition would level off in the stagnation phase or even begin to decrease. Beyond the *stagnation* stage, decline or rejuvenation may ensue in the TALC, but cooperation between individual neighbouring businesses (Line 3) could remain at the same level as previously since some businesses may try to increase tourist numbers by strengthening linkages and business cooperation in marketing with their neighbours. In the case of *decline*, agglomeration as well as local competition between intra-cluster individual businesses can be expected to decrease, with businesses increasing resources in regional cooperation, in order to bring tourists back to the area by competing directly with other destinations and extra-cluster businesses (regional competition).

Conclusions and agenda for future research

Previous studies (Butler, 2015, Butler and Weidenfeld, 2012, Caffyn, 2000, Swarbrooke, 2002, Wang, 2011, Zehrer and Raich, 2010) have shown that relationships between individual enterprises in a tourism destination vary over time and that specific businesses may follow individual life cycles. In this chapter a general conceptual model has been proposed that suggests the nature of those changing relationships during a generic life cycle of resorts. It emphasises the dynamic nature of both destinations and the individual attractions within them. The model also illustrates how these relationships may vary with the level of agglomeration or clustering within a destination and at different scales (local and regional). Weidenfeld et al. (2011) demonstrated that there is a positive relationship between local behaviour (competition and cooperation) and level of agglomeration, and a similar but negative relationship at the regional scale. One potential area of future research would be to determine if any or all of these relationships are causal and whether they are consistent over most or all tourism destinations and regions.

To what extent links or competition between individual attractions are driven by conventional agglomeration economics also remains to be determined. It is clear (Caffyn, 2000, Gale and Botterill, 2005) that in the later stages of development, i.e. once a destination has established a consistent tourism market, business owners and operators look beyond their own immediate needs and explore the potential benefits of at least coopetition, if not cooperation, with both similar and dissimilar products in their own destination. There has been little study, however, of the role of policy makers and public agencies in encouraging and enabling cooperation between endogenous attractions and whether destinations are specifically encouraging such cooperation internally and supporting either or both cooperation and competition at the regional scale (Farmaki et al., 2015, Newlands, 2003, Vernon et al., 2005). Further in-depth research at the destination level, such as that conducted by Gale and Botterill (2005), is needed to explore this topic in detail in order to identify what are sometimes hidden relationships.

Tourism research in general has paid insufficient attention to the political and governance aspects of the subject (Hall, 2008). At the destination level, there is a substantial lack of information about the level of influence of individual actors such as entrepreneurs (both endogenous and exogenous), political control from higher levels of government, and the impact of exogenous events upon the way individual relationships are formed and modified between attractions in tourism destinations. To understand fully how such relationships react throughout the life cycle of both an attraction and a destination it will be necessary to understand more clearly the forces that shape Visitor Attraction and Destination Life Cycles.

References

Baum, T. G. (2006). Revisiting the TALC: Is there an off-ramp? In Butler, R. W. (Ed.), *The Tourism Area Life Cycle Conceptual and Theoretical Issues* (pp. 219–230). Clevedon: Channel View Publications.

Baum, J. and Mezias, S. (1992). Localized competition and organisational failure in the Manhattan hotel industry. *Administrative Science Quarterly*, *37*(4), 580–604.

Blanke, J. and Chiesa, T. (2007). *The Travel and Tourism Competitiveness Report 2007 Furthering the Process of Economic Development*. Geneva: World Economic Forum.

Brown, K. G. and Geddes, R. (2007). Resorts, culture, and music: The Cape Breton tourism cluster. *Tourism Economics*, *13*(1), 129–141.

Buhalis, D. and Cooper, C. (1998). Competition cooperation? Small and medium sized tourism enterprisese at the destination. In E. Laws, B. Faulkner and G. Moscardo (Eds), *Embracing and Managing Change in Tourism: International Case Studies* (pp. 324–346). London: Routledge.

Butler, R. W. (1980). The concept of a tourist area cycle of evolution: Implications for management of resources. *The Canadian Geographer/Le Géographe Canadien*, *24*(1), 5–12.

Butler, R. W. (2006a). The origins of the tourism area life cycle. In R. W. Butler (Ed.), *The Tourism Area Life Cycle: Applications and Modifications* (pp. 13–26). Clevedon: Channel View Publications.

Butler, R. W. (2006b). *The Tourism Area Life Cycle: Applications and Modifications*. Clevedon: Channel View Publications.

Butler, R. W. (2009). Tourism destination development: Cycles and forces, myths and realities. *Tourism Recreation Research*, *34*(3), 247–254.

Butler, R. W. (2015). Tourism area life cycle. In C. Cooper (Ed.), *Contemporary Tourism Reviews Volume One* (pp. 183–226). Oxford: Goodfellow Publishers.

Butler, R. W. and Russell, R. (2010). *Giants of Tourism Key Individuals in the Development of Tourism*. Wallingford: CABI.

Butler, R. W. and Weidenfeld, A. (2012). Cooperation and competition during the resort lifecycle. *Tourism Recreation Research*, 37(1), 15–26.

Caffyn, A. (2000). Is there a tourism partnership life cycle. In B. Bramwell and B. Lane (Eds), *Tourism Collaboration and Partnerships* (pp. 200–229). Clevedon: Channel View Publications.

Chapman, A. and Speake, J. (2011). Regeneration in a mass-tourism resort: The changing fortunes of Bugibba Malta. *Tourism Management*, *32*(3), 482–491.

Coles, T. (2006). Enigma variations? The TALC, marketing models and the descendants of the product life cycle. In R. W. Butler (Ed.), *The Tourism Area Life Cycle – Conceptual and Theoretical Issues* (Vol. 2, pp. 49–66). Clevedon: Channel View Publications.

Cornelis, P. C. M. (2011). A management perspective on the impact of new attractions. *Journal of Vacation Marketing*, *17*(2), 151–163.

Dodds, R. (2008). Sustainable tourism policy – Rejuvenation or critical strategic initiative. *Anatolia*, *18*(2), 277–298.

Erkus-Öztürk, H. (2009). The role of cluster types and firm size in designing the level of network relations: The experience of the Antalya tourism region. *Tourism Management*, *30*, 589–597.

Farmaki, A., Altinay, L., Botterill, D. and Hilke, S. (2015). Politics and sustainable tourism: The case of Cyprus. *Tourism Management*, *47*, 178–190.

Frean, A. (2014, 6 September). As the wheel stops, Atlantic City's number is up. *The Times*, p. 51.

Gale, T. and Botterill, D. (2005). A realistic agenda for tourist studies, or why destinations areas really rise and fall in popularity. *Tourist Studies*, *5*(1), 151–174.

Gordon, I. (1994). Crowding, competition and externalities in tourism: A model of resort life cycles. *Geographical Systems*, *1*, 289–307.

Hall, M. C. (2004). Small firms and wine and food tourism in New Zealand: Issues of collaboration, clusters and lifestyles. In R. Thomas (Ed.), *Small Firms in Tourism – International Perspectives* (pp. 167–181). London: Elsevier.

Hall, M. C. (2008). *Tourism Planning; Policies, Processes and Relationships.* Harlow: Pearson-Prentice Hall.

Harvey, D. (2015, 25 September). Banksy's Dismaland 'gave Weston-super-Mare a £20m boost', *BBC.* Retrieved from www.bbc.co.uk/news/uk-england-bristol-34347681 (accessed 26 September 2015).

Hayward, K. M. (2006). Legitimising the TALC as a theory of development. In R. W. Butler (Ed.), *The Tourism Area Life Cycle Vol. 2: Conceptual and Theoretical Issues* (pp. 29–44). Clevedon: Channel View Publications.

Jackson, J. and Murphy, P. (2002). Tourism destinations as clusters: Analytical experiences from the new world. *Tourism and Hospitality Research, 4*(1), 36–52.

Jackson, J. and Murphy, P. (2006). Clusters in regional tourism – An Australian case. *Annals of Tourism Research, 33*(4), 1018–1035.

Keller, P. (1987). Stages of peripheral tourism development – Canada's Northwest Territories. *Tourism Management, 8*(1), 20–32.

Lade, C. (2010). Developing tourism clusters and networks: Attitudes to competition along Australia's Murray River. *Tourism Analysis, 15*(6), 649–661.

Law, C. M. (2002). *Urban Tourism: The Visitor Economy and the Growth of Large Cities.* London: Continuum.

Lennon, J. J. (2003). *Tourism Statistics: International Perspectives and Current Issues.* New York: Cengage Learning EMEA, Continuum.

Lewis, L. (2015, 12 January). The game is up for China's cheap and nasty theme parks. *The Times.* Retrieved from www.thetimes.co.uk/tto/business/columnist/leolewis/article4364410.ece (accessed 25 February 2015).

McCartney, G. (2010). Stabley Ho Hung-sun: The 'King of Gambling'. In R. W. Butler and R. Russell (Eds), *Giants of Tourism Key Individuals in the Development of Tourism* (pp. 170–181). Wallingford: CABI.

Malmberg, A. and Maskell, P. (2002). The elusive concept of localisation economies: Towards a knowledge-based theory of spatial clustering. *Environment and Planning A, 34,* 429–449.

Michael, E. J. (2003). Tourism micro-clusters. *Tourism Economics, 9*(2), 133–145.

Michael, E. J. and Hall, C. M. (2007). A path for policy. In E. J. Michael (Ed.), *Micro-Clusters and Networks: The Growth of Tourism* (pp. 127–140). Oxford: Elsevier.

Mitchell, R. and Schreiber, C. (2007). Wine tourism networks and clusters: Operation and barriers in New Zealand. In E. J. Michael (Ed.), *Micro-Clusters and Networks: The Growth of Tourism* (pp. 79–102). Oxford: Elsevier.

Newlands, D. (2003). Competition and cooperation in industrial clusters: The implications for public policy. *European Planning Studies, 11*(5), 521–532.

Nordin, S. (2003). *Tourism Clustering and Innovation – Paths to Economic Growth and Development.* Oestersund, Sweden: European Tourism Research Institute, Mid-Sweden University.

Papatheodorou, A. (2004). Exploring the evolution of tourism resorts. *Annals of Tourism Research, 31*(1), 219–337.

Papatheodorou, A. (2006). Corporate rivalry, market power and competition issues in tourism: an introduction. In A. Papatheodorou (Ed.), *Corporate Rivalry and Market Power, Competition Issues in Tourism: An Introduction* (pp. 1–19). London: Tauris.

Pearce, D. G. (1989). *Tourist Development.* Longman: Harlow.

Ritchie, J. R. B and Crouch, G. I. (2003). *The Competitive Destination: A Sustainable Perspective*. Wallingford: CABI.

Russell, R. (2006). Chaos theory and its application to the TALC model. In R. W. Butler (Ed.), *The Tourism Area Life Cycle – Conceptual and Theoretical Issues* (Vol. 2, pp. 164–180). Clevedon: Channel View Publications.

Shani, A. and Logan, R. (2010). Walt Disney's world of entertainment attractions. In R. W. Butler and R. A. Russell (Eds), *Giants of Tourism* (pp. 155–169). Wallingford: CABI.

Shaw, G. and Williams, A. (1997). *The Rise and Fall of British Coastal Resorts*. London: Mansell.

Stansfield, C. A. (2006). The rejuvenation of Atlantic City: The resort cycle recycles. In R. W. Butler (Ed.), *The Tourism Area Life Cycle Applications and Modifications* (Vol. 1, pp. 287–305). Clevedon: Channel View Publications.

Swarbrooke, J. (2002). *The Development and Management of Visitor Attractions*. Oxford: Butterworth Heinemann.

Tsang, E. W. K. and Yip, P. S. L. (2009). Competition, agglomeration, and performance of Beijing hotels. *The Service Industries Journal*, *29*(2), 155–171.

Tien, C-C. (2010). The formation and impact of museum clusters: Two case studies in Taiwan. *Museum Management and Curatorship*, *25*(1), 69–85.

Vernon, J., Essex, P., Pinder, D. and Curry, K. (2005). Collaborative policymaking. *Annals of Tourism Research*, *32*, 325–345.

Walton, J. K. (2015). Tourism and history. In Cooper, C. (Ed.), *Contemporary Tourism Reviews* (Vol. 1, pp. 31–56). Oxford: Goodfellow Publishers.

Wang, T. (2011). Collaborative destination marketing: Principles and applications. In T. Wang and A. Pizam (Eds.), *Destination Marketing and Management Theories and Applications* (pp. 259–283). Wallingford: CABI.

Weaver, D. and Oppermann, M. (2000). *Tourism Management*. Milton: Miley.

Weidenfeld, A., Butler, R. W. and Williams, A. M. (2011). The role of clustering, cooperation and complementarities in the visitor attraction sector. *Current Issues in Tourism*, *14*(7), 595–629.

Zehrer, A. and Raich, F. (2010). Applying a lifecycle perspective to explain tourism network development. *The Service Industries Journal*, *30*(10), 1683–1705.

Zimmermann, F. (2000). Future perspectives of tourism; Traditional versus new destinations. In M. Oppermannn (Ed.), *Pacific Rim Tourism* (pp. 231–239). Wallingford: CABI.

Part II

Economic and management aspects of the visitor attraction sector

5 The appeal, attractiveness and compatibility of visitor attractions

Introduction

The linkages between the appeal of tourism spaces and their spatial relationships have been discussed theoretically (Miossec, 1976, Kim and Fesenmaier, 1990, Lue et al., 1993, Dredge, 1999, Papatheodorou, 2004, Shoval and Raveh, 2004) and empirically examined (Jansen-Verbeke and Lievois, 2002, Hunt and Crompton, 2008, Weidenfeld et al., 2010, Zoltan and McKercher, 2014). However, the role of visitor attractions, which is central to the appeal of destinations and their growth, remains largely ignored. To some extent this is unsurprising, because the visitor attraction experience is problematic to define and measure due to the complexity in the ontological, methodological and epistemological dimensions, let alone the challenge of analysing such a wide range of different types of visitor attractions. Additional challenges are posed by the subjectivity of expectations and the emotions experienced by visitors before and after the visit (Jensen, 2014).

Drawing on the literature on tourism appeal, marketing, tourism geography and visitor attraction management, this chapter examines how spatial proximity, density of businesses and product similarity are related to tourism appeal and demand. Destinations with different and similar product attractions can evolve (organically and planned) into spatial concentrations (agglomerations) of tourism businesses, thereby generating enhanced appeal to a range of tourism market segments (Swarbrooke, 2002).

The chapter provides a better understanding of the associations between the activities offered by visitor attractions, their spatial organisation, i.e. where and how they are situated, and their attractiveness for tourists. These factors are inextricably linked to the concept of compatibility, which will be explored later. The chapter begins with the theoretical framework of what constitutes the appeal of tourism spaces at the destination region and individual visitor attraction levels. Then, it examines the impact of spatial proximity between neighbouring visitor attractions at the local scale, and the density of a group of attractions at the regional level, on their appeal. The intervening impact of product similarity on these relationships is also explored.

The first section provides some theoretical background for defining the relative attractiveness of tourism spaces to potential visitors and how this is relevant to visitor attractions. Second, the relationships between the attractiveness of tourism spaces and the spatial organisation of visitor attractions are explored. This is followed by a discussion of the relevance of the compatibility between visitor attractions to their appeal, and how spatial proximity and density are relevant factors at the regional and local scales. Finally, the implications for collaboration and competition between visitor attractions in marketing themselves are suggested, followed by exploring the current measures of appeal of visitor attractions.

Attractiveness and 'attraction' of tourism spaces

The attractiveness of tourism spaces, whether they are attractions, resorts or destinations, are the reason for their visitation. According to the Oxford English Dictionary, appeal and attractive (attractiveness) have the same meaning (Trumble and Brown, 2001). The attractiveness of a place includes the surrounding geographical and environmental characteristics which constitute the stage, i.e. the features that make a place draw people to visit or experience the place. It is critically influenced by the degree of distinctiveness of these components of attractiveness. Each element of attractiveness can be viewed as an amenity resource, variously defined as pleasantness, a pleasure, a delight, a pleasant feature or a desirable facility, which becomes relevant to the attractiveness of tourism spaces. An element may appear as an object, culture, climate or tradition, which directly or indirectly draws visitors to experience it (Betz and Perdue, 1993).

Another distinction can be made between the meaning of attractiveness and attraction of a tourism space. Attractiveness is the inventory of touristic attributes, possessed by a tourism space. It is 'closer to some innate quality of a place and need not be directly related to attraction ... it may spring from attributes either natural or [hu]man-made (e.g., mountains, museums)' (Husbands, 1983:292). Therefore, while a place may be considered attractive (because of the effect of a number of touristic attributes), it need not have a large or a thriving tourism industry. Attraction, on the other hand, has more to do with the actual levels and patterns of visitation. The attraction of a tourism space is its attractiveness minus the deterrents or barriers to travel.

Sweeping generalisations about people's preferences for and perceptions of favourable tourist attributes, and the relative importance they place on some but not on others of these attributes, based on studies of specific regions, are inappropriate. Different preferences and perceptions are a function of experiences (good and bad) on previous visits, degree of familiarity with a destination, cultural background, geographic origin and prior expectations (Goodrich, 1978). Hence, attractiveness is personal and difficult to quantify or generalise, via the old adage 'beauty is in the eye of the beholder'. The more the attractiveness outweighs the barriers, the greater will be the overall attraction. Potential barriers include natural features, climate, cultural and social characteristics, infrastructure, services, access and transportation, attitudes to tourists and economic, political and social ties, which are further detailed by Morrison and Mill (1992). All the aforementioned amenities can be considered as deterrents as well as elements of attractiveness.

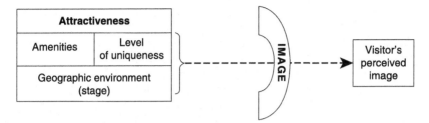

Figure 5.1 The elements of attractiveness and the image of a tourism space

They are also sources of risks and uncertainty, as the resulting experience cannot be known for certain. In this context, the image has a crucial role in the way the attractiveness is perceived among tourists. Consequently, countries which are competing tourism destinations must base their marketing strategy on attractiveness, but take into account their relative attraction (Husbands, 1983).

Attractiveness is refined and goes through the 'prisma' of the image, portrayed to visitors to consider in their decision-making process mainly by marketing campaigns. The extent to which the image reflects the attractiveness to potential visitors determines its impact on their perceived image (Figure 5.1). To increase a place's attractiveness for visitors, tourism spaces attempt to use a well-established image, which, according to the Oxford Dictionary, is an artificial imitation or representation of the external form of any object (Trumble and Brown, 2001). This can be complex, dynamic, multiple in nature, subject to change and often relativistic, involving many different physical and service attributes, along with comparisons and evaluations resulting from promotional messages, and an interaction of visitor experience (Ryan, 2003). Eventually, visitors make a decision to go to a particular destination or an attraction when they perceive that it possesses adequate and desirable facilities and attributes deemed important for their tourist needs (Goodrich, 1978).

Unlike the natural environment, the amenities and uniqueness of a tourism space can highly depend on the human-made built environment, such as man-made visitor attractions, that have a critical role in the attractiveness to visitors. Image is crucial. If an appealing space is incapable of establishing a well-established positive image, it will not appeal to a large number of visitors, and may adopt strong competitive strategies (based upon quality, product differentiation and product innovation) and attract niche markets (see Chapter 7). The overall attraction of a tourism space is also affected by travel barriers or deterrents such as transportation costs. The role of marketing is pivotal and the increasingly competitive nature of the tourism industry requires tourism destinations to develop a successful marketing plan and strategy in order to compete. This should be based on perceived images of the destination relative to the other competitors in the marketplace (Baloglu and Mangaloglu, 2001). Above all, the trip to a visitor attraction or attractions can be presented to potential tourists as an enjoyable experience rather than a challenge.

Ryan (2003) highlights the importance of the dissemination of information about a place and notes that the credibility of that information affects the durability of the image. Visitors receive and perceive images, and these influence destination choice, but image cannot be sustainable if there is no congruence between tourists' experiences of the actual attributes of a place and the portrayed image. Therefore, measuring tourism image has to take into account its levels of attractiveness, i.e. the extent to which features of the human and natural settings draw people to visit or experience the place. Ideally, these levels should be equal to the levels of perceived image, i.e. the extent to which visitors perceive that a destination or an attraction possesses adequate and desirable facilities and attributes deemed important for their tourist needs. Failure to balance the levels of attractiveness with those of perceived image in marketing strategies and promotional policies will result in equal but lower levels of both (Husbands, 1983). The extent to which visitor attractions are used as a part of the tourism destination image is crucial. Tourism destination strategies may use one or more visitor attractions to enhance their image relying on their appeal as being representative of a larger tourism space, e.g. the Opera House is used as a marker to sell Sydney and sometimes Australia (see Chapter 11). Goodrich (1978:12) demonstrated that 'the more favourable the perceptions of a vacation destination [with respect to tourist-attractive attributes], the greater the likelihood of choice of that destination [as a first priority for visiting] over other less favourably perceived destination'.

Attractiveness of visitor attractions

Visitor attractions have broadly similar elements of attractiveness to other tourism spaces such as destination regions. However, more specific elements of attractiveness (Table 5.1) have been identified by three studies: Milman's (2009) study on theme parks in the US, Prebensen's (2012) study on importance–performance analysis to benchmark nature and culture based attractions in visitor attractions in Northern Norway, and a report based on tourist attractions in Queensland, Australia (Ritchie et al., 2008). These studies address issues related to the quality and variety of products and services or refer to aspects of ambience and settings. The generic relevance of these elements from studies in only two countries to the visitor attraction sector as a whole remains questionable and requires further empirical studies.

A better understanding of the associations between the activities offered by visitor attractions, their spatial organisation and their attractiveness is needed to enable development of a predictive planning tool to assist in making anticipatory policies for tourism spatial planning. Pearce (1995:88) calls for more rigorous efforts to be made 'to synthesize the many different types of attractions and to derive a composite measure of tourist attractiveness', but to date this has not been addressed.

In order to avoid confusion between the term 'attraction' and visitor attractions, in the remainder of this book we will use the term 'appeal' when we refer to 'attraction', i.e. levels of actual visitation. The appeal of visitor attractions, among

Table 5.1 Elements of attractiveness of visitor attractions

	Theme parks	*Visitor attractions*
Study and location	Milman (2009)	Queensland, Australia (Ritchie et al., 2008). Importance–performance analysis of nature- and culture-based attractions in northern Norway (Prebensen, 2012)
Ambience and environment	Entertainment variety and quality Safety and security Courtesy and cleanliness	Good impression/welcome Overall atmosphere at the attraction
Products and services	Food variety and value for money Quality of theming and design Availability and variety of family-oriented activities Quality and variety of rides and attractions Pricing and value for money	Electronic displays Interactive displays Appropriateness of displays Quality of service Helpful human guides Front reception information Maps and information available Parking facilities Value for money for retail goods Overall, high-quality facilities/ services

other factors, depends in part on neighbouring attractions at the local scale and its spatial relationships with other attractions at the regional scale.

The appeal and spatial organisation of visitor attractions

Understanding the spatial patterns of visitors' trips is a key to firms' capacity to access the potential market (Lue et al., 1993). Jansen-Verbeke and Lievois's (2002) spatial analysis of urban heritage clusters proposes a model of the time-space use patterns of urban heritage tourists. They consider the morphological characteristics of heritage buildings and their location pattern within a historic city to be vital for structuring and developing attractive tourist zones and trails. These characteristics take into account the distance of buildings in relation to key landmarks (extracted from tourists' mental maps) as part of a process of forming a morphological positioning index of heritage buildings; 'the higher the index the more central (distance wise) the building is situated in a cluster of heritage buildings' (Jansen-Verbeke and Lievois, 2002:94). They are also concerned with the integration of heritage buildings and complexes into the multifunctional structure of the city. Their concept of clustering (similar to agglomeration) is based on the walking distance between different locations and, similar to a gravity model, it includes allocating a weighing factor to measure the relative appeal of specific buildings.

Jansen-Verbeke and Lievois (2002) state that the clustering of urban heritage attractions increases with the degree of centrality, reflected in the number, scale and marker value of heritage buildings in a particular area or a street. This is also the case of centrally located urban museums, which offer more possibilities of generating synergies with other facilities and services such as shopping, leisure and restaurants than museums in peripheral areas (Paül Agustí, 2013). Aside from the location, the importance of purpose-built facilities for tourists is also considered to be important for tourists. For evaluating factors such as accessibility, the tourist function and use of a heritage attraction, they presented a functional index measuring these factors, which indicated that the higher the accessibility and multifunctionality, the higher the index. In other words, core clusters of heritage attractions are more attractive to the average pedestrian tourist than those which are less integrated both spatially and functionally (Jansen-Verbeke and Lievois, 2002).

A combination of the two indices provides a tourist attraction index, which can be used as a planning tool. However, this requires more information 'on the components of the tourist attraction and on the activities and preferences of tourists. In particular the construction of themed trails and the role of intervening opportunities need further fieldwork' (Jansen-Verbeke and Lievois, 2002:100). Another spatial model of the consumption of visitor attractions by Shoval and Raveh (2004) categorises urban tourist attractions according to the consumption and characteristics (i.e. number of visits, relative percentage of tourists and length of stay) of visitors and this constitutes an innovative spatial analysis. However, this model is only valid for large cities with a developed tourism function. These two models (Jansen-Verbeke and Lievois, 2002, Shoval and Raveh, 2004) link tourism spatial organisation of production spaces and tourists' behaviour (consumption), but do not synthesise the different sorts of attractions with different sorts of environments (Morrison and Mill, 1992).

Compatibility or cumulative attraction

Cumulative attraction or attraction compatibility was initially studied in the context of retailing and recreation and then subsequently in the visitor attraction sector (Hunt and Crompton, 2008, Weidenfeld et al., 2010). The central concept of cumulative attraction (Nelson, 1958) is the principle of compatibility (Hunt and Crompton, 2008). This occurs when the same tourists visit more than one visitor attraction on the same holiday trip and, in most cases, at the same destination region. Given that, in general, more than two attractions are visited by tourists during a trip (Xia et al., 2010), compatibility between visitor attractions is an essential element for sustaining their individual appeal.

Tourists can combine several attractions within a single trip, particularly when attractions are in close proximity. This allows them to minimise their time and travel costs. In such cases, pairs of attractions are often packaged by operators in line with tourist interests, and planned according to marketing intelligence and promotion policies, e.g. discounted entrance fees for combined attractions (Xia et al., 2010). The use of joint ticketing offerings such as passport schemes and destination cards, which offer free or highly discounted entry into partner

---

Box 5.1 The destination card of Ticino, Switzerland

Tourist behaviour in the Canton of Ticino Switzerland, a geographically dispersed destination, has been examined by analysing use patterns of a 'destination card'. This has an embedded chip, is sold by the local destination management organization, and offers admission to a series of attractions and other activities within the boundaries of the destination region for a period of 72 hours. The analysis found that concentrated behaviour existed in four discrete markets, defined either spatially or by activity. Three of the markets showed a high degree of spatial concentration in visitor movements, augmented by clearly defined activity preferences. The fourth showed no clear pattern, with visitors travelling widely throughout the Canton and sampling a range of activities. Hence, the combination of transport and attractions appealed to two different user groups, one looking to gain access to attractions and one utilizing ease of transport. The point of sales of the destination cards had an important role in identifying the consumption of activities and the extension of the area visited. Thus, the spatial structure of a destination seems to play a greater influence on behaviour than its product structure. The researchers also identified a number of recommendations especially for destination managers and tourism operators. These include product bundling, regional cooperation and strategic marketing opportunities at sales points in order to further incentivize tourist mobility between attractions.

Source: Zoltan and McKercher (2014).

---

attractions and activities, is sometimes coupled with free public transport access in the area (Box 5.1).

Compatibility can also emerge between visitor attractions at low density if they are visited in the same trip. In peripheral locations, attractions are often more isolated and need to create or stimulate complementary offers that meet the needs of their visitors (Paül Agustí, 2013). This is particularly the case when a location fits within the framework of a popular itinerary that many tourists, individually and/or as a group, choose to take. If an attraction is appealing enough, and provides adequate facilities such as lavatories, shops and a pleasing natural setting, it may develop compatibility with other attractions on the same route. For example, the Alta Museum in Northern Norway (Box 5.2) demonstrates how location is pivotal in shaping compatibility in tourism routes (Johanson and Olsen, 2010).

A visitor attraction's appeal can be measured in terms of its compatibility, i.e. the number of visitors shared by attractions, in relation to their spatial location (intra/extra cluster) and product similarity (including dissimilarity and complementarity). Compatibility levels range from low to high according to the percentage of customers shared (Crompton and Gitelson, 1979). At the local scale compatibility is found in individual neighbouring attractions that affect each other in a positive manner in terms of number of visitors, or volume of sales resulting from the interchange of visitors (synergies of appeal) (Hunt and Crompton, 2008,

---

Box 5.2 The Alta Museum, Northern Norway

The Alta Museum in Finnmark, Northern Norway, which opened in 1991, is situated beside the main road, which traverses the country from north to south. It receives on average approximately 65,000 visitors a year and is considered a successful attraction and one of the 50 most visited attractions in Norway. The main selling point of the museum is the rock carvings, which are between 2000 and 6000 years old and are on UNESCO's World Heritage List. The museum's visitors can view the rock carvings by walking along the paths by the carving area. The museum has a permanent exhibition, which mainly chronicles local history from the earliest settlement in Finnmark to the struggle against the damming of the Alta-Kautokeino River for hydroelectric power in the 1980s.

Customers in the summer are both individual visitors and group visitors, who are predominantly tourists, i.e. a mixture of tourists on package tours and tourists travelling in private cars. The latter segment is likely to increase due to the soaring popularity of cruise tourists along the Norwegian coast. The Alta Museum has both locational and qualitative features which engender computability with other spatially distant attractions. Hammerfest is the world's northernmost town and is a 2 hour drive from Alta. The latter is similarly distant from the Sami settlement, Kautokeino, further east, and to the famous panoramic view from Kvænangsfjellet in the west. North Cape, which is another attractive point, and the Sami (native culture) administrative centre of Karasjok, can be reached within 3 or 4 hours. Alta's location is not near any other attractions, which ensures that a visit is well suited to most tourists whether travelling by private car or bus. Functionally, and from the tour operator's perspective, the museum offers a short stop which can be comfortably integrated into the larger itinerary schedule, and is perceived as the primary attraction in the area. And as there are a couple of hours drive from/to each of the other abovementioned attractions (or points of interest), there is little competition as a convenient place for tourist, guides and drivers to stop and rest. This endows the Alta Museum with high levels of compatibility with the other attractions and makes it an important element in the regional tourism system.

Source: Johanson and Olsen (2010).

Weidenfeld et al., 2010). Lue et al. (1993) suggest that attractions in spatial proximity, located en route to a destination or in a logical thematic similar or complementary sequence to each other, draw more visitors than if they were randomly distributed. Apart from considering alternatives and price competition, visitors' choice is based upon features such as crowd size, types of attractions, admission price and nature of the theme, or other factors, e.g. several theme parks in close spatial proximity presenting different themes (Hunt and Crompton, 2008).

At the regional scale, compatibility includes the sum of the compatibilities between attractions in a destination region or cluster (Weidenfeld et al., 2010). However, some researchers argue that a tourism cluster's appeal as a whole is greater than the sum of the individual attractions (Piperoglou, 1967, Miossec, 1976, Dredge, 1999, Law, 2002). Linked to this, a tourism cluster with a high level of collective compatibility amongst its attractions is likely to benefit in terms of generating visits, and visitor preferences (Lue et al., 1993, Weidenfeld et al., 2010). This is consistent with the argument that agglomeration economies and spatial clustering enhance the perceived critical mass of tourism attractions and the number of visitors (Chapter 3).

Both complementary relationships and compatibility between visitor attractions contribute to a destination's unique character, mediated by their spatial relationships and the regional spatial organisation (Weidenfeld et al., 2010, Weidenfeld et al., 2011). Identifying and collecting information on compatibility and complementarity can be a means for firms and policy makers to enhance cooperative promotion between visitor attractions, resulting in positive impacts on their cumulative attractions (Kim and Fesenmaier, 1990, Hunt and Crompton, 2008, Weidenfeld et al., 2010).

Product similarity, complementarity and compatibility

Tourism products' themes are related to features of the tourism product, such as heritage, wildlife, amusement and gardens (Swarbrooke, 2001). Complementary relationships can exist among dissimilar as well as among similar visitor attractions. Thematic complementarity between attractions refers to 'two similar product attractions, which do not offer an identical product and therefore complement rather than compete for the same market, e.g. two wildlife attractions which exhibit different types of animals and are assumed to be compatible' (Weidenfeld et al., 2010:5). Both thematic complementarity and dissimilar attractions tend to be compatible. This reflects visitor preference for an area with multiple but different types of attractions, e.g. heritage, nature or recreation (Lue et al., 1993). Thus, compatibility between individual neighbouring attractions (at the local scale), and compatibility between a group of attractions at the regional scale, is higher in the case of dissimilar attractions and those with thematic complementarity than it is amongst similar attractions (Weidenfeld et al., 2010). Higher levels of compatibility at the regional scale tend to increase the overall regional appeal as a result of the synergies amongst the attractions (Piperoglou, 1967).

It might be expected that having similar products would be problematic for attractions which are in close spatial proximity. However, Weidenfeld et al.'s (2010) study shows a complex relationship, wherein product similarity between attractions is not always negatively related to tourism appeal (Box 5.3). The findings in Box 5.3 can be summarised in Figure 5.2. Product similarity is positively related to tourism appeal but depends on the nature of the tourism product.

The triangular shape (Figure 5.2) indicates the levels of appeal in relation to the extent and nature of product similarity between attractions. In Weidenfeld et al.'s (2010) study, most neighbouring intra-cluster attractions (at the local scale) were not very similar but rather were more complementary, which is positively related to compatibility. Dissimilar attractions were also found to share visitors with each other but to a lesser extent.

Box 5.3 Compatability between visitor attractions in Cornwall, UK

A study of the differences between the compatibility of visitor attractions in two tourism clusters in Cornwall, south west England, with lower and higher density of visitor attractions, provides insights into the relationship between product similarity, density/spatial proximity and the appeal of visitor attractions. The Newquay cluster contains more visitor attractions at a higher density and also has better accessibility to private and public transport than the Lizard Peninsula. Newquay has a reputation for being the UK capital of water sports and surfing, and its main appeal includes beaches and rural and maritime landscapes. While most of its appeal lies in leisure attractions, tailored for families and water-based recreation, the Lizard Peninsula's main attractiveness lies in its lightly developed coast, heritage and garden attractions and a theme/fun park. The Newquay cluster's visitor attractions have greater product similarity and thematic complementarities among attractions than those in the Lizard cluster. The Newquay area attracts more tourists, particularly families (mass tourism) than the Lizard, where the attractions draw on more similar markets and niche markets (e.g. garden tourists and heritage tourists). The findings of the study include:

1. Similar complementary attractions, and dissimilar attractions, share the same visitors (evidence of high compatibility), while similar product attractions do not.
2. At the local scale, similar complementary neighbouring attractions have the largest positive impact on each other's appeal to visitors, given that they tend to share visitors more than do dissimilar and similar attractions.
3. Dissimilar attractions were also found to share visitors with each other but to a lesser extent.
4. Similar product attractions (except gardens) appear to have no impact or negative impact on each other's appeal, given that most do not share the same visitors.
5. Neighbouring individual attractions were more likely to be visited by the same tourists than distant attractions.

Source: Weidenfeld et al. (2010).

Conclusions

This chapter has examined the notions of the appeal (attraction) and attractiveness of visitor attractions, and the compatability between them. The associations between the themes of visitor attractions, their spatial organisation, i.e. where and how they are situated, and their attractiveness for tourists were examined. These factors are linked to the concept of compatibility, which is influenced by spatial proximity at the local scale and spatial density at the regional scale. These, together with the interevening impact of product thematic similarity, were explored. Several elements constitute the attractiveness of visitor attractions including the quality and variety of products, presentations and services, their

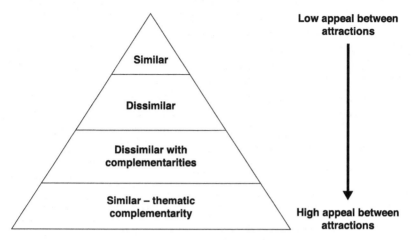

Figure 5.2 Relationships between tourism appeal to visitors and product similarity between attractions

ambience and their wider settings. In particular, design, layout and services associated with the touristic experience are considered to be the most important factors in influencing visitors' attitude, intention to revisit and their involvement in the experience offered.

The relationships between these factors have a substantial impact on the sequence of intra- and inter-attraction visitor movements between visitor attractions. The contribution of visitor attractions to destination appeal and image can be enhanced by investments in appropriate and efficient transport modes, convenient schedules and good signage. Knowledge of tourist movements in time and space is particularly useful for marketing, organising and scheduling individual and group tours. In combination with knowledge of tourist market segmentation, marketers can facilitate tour package designs. These will increase the clarity of the overall destination images and promote experiences better, allowing for the creation of place identities aimed at specific market niches (Xia et al., 2011). Of course, the decision to visit attractions is determined by factors such as the nature and type of attraction, and the nature of its experience, crowd size and admission. Visitor attractions may create a competitive advantage by developing compatibility with their neighbouring businesses, particularly other attractions.

Compatibility, which is a key concept, is defined as the degree to which two businesses interchange customers. It is determined by the percentage of customers shared by the same attractions, which can also be used as a measure of visitor attractions' appeal. At the local scale, it refers to the interchange of each individual visitor attraction with its neighbours, and at the regional scale to the sum of compatibilities between visitor attractions in a destination or region. Synergies between attractions is an important element for sustaining their appeal. These are generated by various complementary relationships between visitor attractions, particularly thematic complementarity (Chapter 6).

Clustering is likely to increase complementarities and compatibility and there-fore the overall appeal of visitor attractions in a destination region. Compatibility between individual neighbouring attractions at the local scale, and among a group of attractions at the regional scale, is often based on dissimilarities and comple-mentarities between visitor attractions, particularly if these are thematic. The com-bination of complementary attractions can create synergies, which increase the overall regional appeal of destination regions. Nevertheless, as noted in Chapter 6, the co-location of complementary firms does not guarantee generation of synergies or cost efficiencies among businesses: rather this represents a source of potential benefits which are only realised if accurately identified and managed effectively.

An effective approach to the development of destination regions could be improved by collecting and analysing data on potential complementarities, with the aim of increasing compatibility between attractions. This would also involve assessment of the spatial organisation of attractions such as their location in clusters and on tourism routes. The management of these factors may influence the movement of tourists in destination regions and could contribute to sustainable development, and the avoidance of overcrowding and exceeding the social and environmental carrying capacities of visitor attractions. At present, our knowledge of these relationships and issues is constrained by a lack of detailed studies of compatibilities. Therefore, there is a need for further studies to examine how these features differ between different types of attractions, and how they can be accurately measured. Furthermore, as previously emphasised, there is a need to take into account the spatial organisation of visitor attractions in tourism destination regions in terms of proximity, density and other spatial characteristics, for example along tourism routes and within core clusters of heritage attractions. These are directly related to spatial patterns of movement of tourists in space and the concepts of clustering, compatibility and product similarity.

The relationships between these various factors can have a major impact on the sequence of intra- and inter-attraction visitor movements, i.e. on the patterns in which tourists move within and between visitor attractions (Xia et al., 2010). Understanding the decision-making processes made by visitors, which underlie such mobilities, can be useful to practitioners including tourism planners, managers and operators in developing new and existing tourism routes and facilities at the macro level. At the micro level, this knowledge can help planners and developers of visitor attractions to make decisions about where signage, food stops, paths and internal transport can be located within and adjacent to the attraction (Xia et al., 2011).

References

Baloglu, S. and Mangaloglu, M. (2001). Tourism destination images of Turkey, Egypt, Greece, and Italy as perceived by US-based tour operators and travel agents. *Tourism Management*, *22*, 1–9.

Betz, C. J. and Perdue, R. R. (1993). The role of amenity resources in rural recreation and tourism development. *Journal of Park and Recreation Administration,*_*11*(4), 15–29.

Crompton, J. L. and Gitelson, R. J. (1979). The theory of cumulative attraction and compatibility: A case study of two major commercial leisure attractions. *Baylor Business Studies*, *10*, 7–16.

Dredge, D. (1999). Destination place planning and design. *Annals of Tourism Research*, *26*(4), 772–991.

Goodrich, J. N. (1978). The relationship between preferences for and perceptions of vacation destinations: Application of a choice model. *Journal of Travel Research*, *17*(2), 8–13.

Hunt, M. A. and Crompton, J. L. (2008). Investigating attraction compatibility in an East Texas City. *International Journal of Tourism research*, *10*, 237–246.

Husbands, W. C. (1983). Tourist space and touristic attraction: An analysis of the destination choices of European travelers. *Leisure Sciences*, *5*(4), 289–306.

Jansen-Verbeke, M. and Lievois, E. (2002). Analaysing heritage resources for urban tourism in European cities. In D. Pearce and R. W. Butler (Eds), *Contemporary Issues in Tourism Development* (pp. 81–108). London: Routledge.

Jensen, Ø. (2014). Approaches for the evaluation of visitor experiences at tourist attractions. In N. K. Prebensen, J. S. Chen and M. Uysal (Eds), *Creating Experience Value in Tourism* (pp. 139–156). Wallingford: CABI.

Johanson, L. B. and Olsen, K. (2010). Alta Museum as a tourist attraction: The importance of location. *Journal of Heritage Tourism*, *5*(1), 1–16.

Kim, S.-I. and Fesenmaier, D. R. (1990). Evaluating spatial structure effects in recreation travel. *Leisure Sciences*, *12*, 367–381.

Law, C. M. (2002). *Urban Tourism: The Visitor Economy and the Growth of Large Cities*. London: Continuum.

Lue, C.-C., Crompton, J. L. and Fesenmaier, D. R. (1993). Conceptualization of multi-destination pleasure trips. *Annals of Tourism Research*, *20*, 289–301.

Milman, A. (2009). Evaluating the guest experience at theme parks: An empirical investigation of key attributes. *International Journal of Tourism Research*, *11*(4), 373–387.

Miossec, J.-M. (1976). Eléments pour une théorie de l'espace touristique, Centre des Hautes Études Touristiques. *Les cahiers du tourisme* Série C(n.36, Aix-en-Provence).

Morrison, A. M. and Mill, R. C. (1992). *The Tourism System, An Introduction Text*. New Jersey: Prentice-Hall International Editors.

Nelson, R. L. (1958). *The Selection of Retail Location*. New York: R.W. Dodge Corporation.

Papatheodorou, A. (2004). Exploring the evolution of tourism resorts. *Annals of Tourism Research*, *31*(1), 219–337.

Paül Agustí, D. (2013). Differences in the location of urban museums and their impact on urban areas. *International Journal of Cultural Policy*, *20*(4), 471–495.

Pearce, D. G. (1995). *Tourism Today – A Geographical Analysis*, 2nd edition. Harlow: Longman Group Limited.

Piperoglou, J. (1967). Identification and definition of regions in Greek tourist planning. *Papers in Regional Science*, *18*(1), 169–176.

Prebensen, N. K. (2012). *Benchmarking Tourist Attractions in Northern Norway Advances in Hospitality and Leisure* (Vol. 8, pp. 85–107). Bingley: Emerald Group Publishing Limited.

Ritchie, B., Mules, T. and Uzabeaga, S. (2008). Visitor attraction satisfaction benchmarking project. National Library of Australia Cataloguing-in-Publication entry. Australia Gold Coast: CRC for Sustainable Tourism Pty Ltd.

Ryan, C. (2003). *Recreational Tourism, Demands and Impacts*. Clevedon: Channel View Publications.

Shoval, N. and Raveh, A. (2004). Categorization of tourist attractions and the modeling of tourist cities: Based on the co-plot method of multivariate analysis. *Tourism Management*, *25*, 741–750.

Swarbrooke, J. (2001). Key challenges for visitor attraction managers in the UK. *Journal of Leisure Property*, *1*(4), 318–336.

Swarbrooke, J. (2002). *The Development and Management of Visitor Attractions*. Oxford: Butterworth-Heinemann.

Trumble, W. and Brown, L. (2001). *Shorter Oxford English Dictionary*. Oxford: Oxford University Press.

Weidenfeld, A., Butler, R. W. and Williams, A. M. (2010). Clustering and compatibility between tourism attractions. *International Journal of Tourism Research*, *12*, 1–16.

Weidenfeld, A., Butler, R. and Williams, A. M. (2011). The role of clustering, cooperation and complementarities in the visitor attraction sector. *Current Issues in Tourism*, *14*(7), 595–629.

Xia, J., Evans, F. H., Spilsbury, K., Ciesielski, V., Arrowsmith, C. and Wright, G. (2010). Market segments based on the dominant movement patterns of tourists. *Tourism Management*, *31*(4), 464–469.

Xia, J., Zeephongsekul, P. and Packer, D. (2011). Spatial and temporal modelling of tourist movements using Semi-Markov processes. *Tourism Management*, *32*(4), 844–851.

Zoltan, J. and McKercher, B. (2014). Analysing intra-destination movements and activity participation of tourists through destination card consumption. *Tourism Geographies*, *17*(1), 19–35.

6 Cooperation in the visitor attraction sector

Introduction

This chapter discusses the nature of cooperation in the visitor attractions sector in terms of its characteristics, determinants and contribution to the tourism destination experience at the local and regional scales. It begins with the broader context of cooperation in tourism followed by the specificities of the visitor attraction sector. Then it describes the benefits and drawbacks of cooperation between visitor attractions and explores how different aspects of economies of scale influence the cooperative behaviour of visitor attractions. In particular, it identifies the specific elements which define cooperation including complementarities and product similarities, and the way spatial proximity and density mediate between these factors at the local and regional scales.

Cooperation between tourism firms

Cooperation in tourism is defined as 'a form of voluntary joint actions in which autonomous stakeholders engage in an interactive process, using shared rules, norms and structures, to act and decide on issues related to tourism development in the region' (Czernek, 2013:84). Collaboration, coordination and networking are all implicated in this definition: they describe different spectra of definitions of cooperation in the literature, with mostly subtle differences. Paradoxically as it may initially seem, many firms cooperate to increase their competitive position. They may also cooperate to create barriers to new entry to their particular markets, or to reduce or eliminate competition as for example by forming a cabal to fix prices and eliminate competition (Shaw and Williams, 2004). Collaboration or cooperation can also be a response to the growth of complexity, fragmentation and turbulence in tourism. Different theories of collaboration provide different explanations of how and why organisations respond to the complex nature of tourism. There are also variations in the terminology used: other terms describing inter-organisational collaboration in the tourism literature include consortia, alliances and partnerships, but there is no universal agreement regarding their use and usage. In tourism, 'exhortations are typically for the development of partnerships, consortia, alliances or co-operative agreements among organisations based in the tourism industry itself' (Fyall et al., 2001:211). However, cooperation is not an automatic response in the face of specific competition and other economic conditions because a large proportion of small to medium-sized enterprises in tourism are family run and reluctant to collaborate with other businesses in the same geographical area or business sector, especially visitor attractions, for reasons such as lack of trust, unhealthy competition, etc. (see Fyall et al., 2001).

The conditions in which collaboration between visitor attractions take place are critical. The determinants of cooperation in tourism include a range of circumstances – situations, events, objects, features, actors' capabilities, etc. – that determine readiness to start cooperation, the process and the results or outcomes. In their role as preconditions, the determinants of cooperation can be understood as certain competitive, technological, socio-cultural, economic, task-related or political forces that work towards cooperative interaction among independent entities (Xia et al., 2010). These determinants have remained understudied in the visitor attraction sector. There are exogenous and endogenous determinants. The exogenous (external) determinants refer to the broader territorial systems beyond the region, such as a country, the EU or the world, where individual stakeholders have little, if any, influence. In contrast, endogenous (internal, regional) determinants within a region result from direct and frequent contacts between actors and are rooted in the internal relations within a tourist region (Xia et al., 2010). Studies of cooperation in the visitor attraction sector remain rare and, to date, have almost entirely focused on endogenous determinants (Butler and Weidenfeld, 2012, Weidenfeld et al., 2011, Fyall et al., 2001, Buhalis and Cooper, 1998).

Cooperation between visitor attractions

There are several forms of collaboration between visitor attraction firms including 'the sharing of resources, searching for areas where mutual benefits can be realised, and achieving economy of effort in maximising the appeal of the generic product' (Fyall et al., 2001:217). Cooperation or collaboration takes place at various geographic scales. There are several international associations of visitor attractions. Some are generic associations and include all types of visitor attractions. The International Association of Amusement Parks Attractions (IAAPA) based in Belgium is the largest international trade association for permanently situated amusement facilities worldwide, and represents more than 4,500 facility, supplier and individual members from more than 97 countries including professionals from amusement parks, theme parks, museums, water parks and wildlife attractions. It is aimed at promoting safe operations, global development, professional growth and the commercial success of its members. The emphasis is on providing reliable data, training, statistical analysis and branding (www.iaapa.org/about-iaapa). Similar emphases have been the focus of the first inaugural attractions management conference held in Cape Town, South Africa, on June 2014, where information on online ticketing, maximising profitability, staff development and making the most of marketing were among the key themes (South African Tourism, 2014).

Marketing varies between visitor attractions of different sizes and ownerships but is similar in terms of issues and deficiencies including product/service offering, lack of suitable marketing information, limited availability of market research and of branding (Sotiriadis and Loedolff, 2015). At the regional scale, collective marketing, buying groups, knowledge transfer and joint political input to local authorities are common. At the local scale, cooperation between individual attractions focuses on marketing, cross-selling and promotion and in some cases joint investment, coordination of activities and knowledge exchange. The most common form of collaboration between attractions is in marketing communications, e.g. collective advertising, joint promotion and the dissemination of shared promotional leaflets. While each attraction retains its own identity and branding in such ventures, they also focus on and utilise their mutual complementarities (Weidenfeld et al., 2011). The aim is to create a collective competitive advantage as a destination while enhancing the competitiveness of each individual attraction.

The closest form of cooperation between attractions was identified by Weidenfeld et al. (2011) as joint financial investments in development and tourism production and/or cross-selling, including vouchers and joined ticketing regardless of, or in addition to, activities managed by existing marketing associations. Even individual neighbouring attractions, which are not members of a marketing alliance, may agree to sell each other's vouchers and/or advertise or promote each other. Inter-firm collaboration and possible economic transactions between tourism firms (production) or between tourism networks are intended not only to have an impact on flows of information but also on flows of tourists (consumptions) (Hall, 2005, Michael and Hall, 2007). This is very much the case in the visitor attraction sector (Weidenfeld et al., 2011) and has been discussed in Chapter 5. The motivation to cooperate can be related to economies of scale and is mediated by the spatial proximity between individual attractions at the local scale, and the spatial density/agglomeration of visitor attractions at the regional scale.

External economies of scale

This section explores some of the main economic and geographical concepts associated with cooperation between firms and their locational patterns in general, and especially in relation to tourism firms and visitor attractions. The question of whether and how spatial proximity is important for establishing contact networks ranging from the local to the international is relevant to any industrial and service sector. This issue is addressed here by drawing on some basic concepts in economics and economic geography relating to the impact of spatial proximity and cooperation on firm operations and strategies.

Economies of scale are 'the cost advantages gained by large scale production, as the average cost of production falls with increasing output' (Johnston et al., 2000:199). They generally arise from conditions internal to the firm's production process such as production being adjusted to the capacity level at which the marginal cost of production is declining, thereby reducing the average unit cost of production. There are a number of reasons for this, one being the benefits from the cost and productivity advantages resulting from a greater internal division of labour (specialisation). Advantages may also relate to reduced unit costs when purchasing inputs in bulk. In short, economies of scale are based on supply costs per unit of production declining as inputs are increased and output expands. Under the assumptions of neo-classical economics, firms will expand production as long as average unit costs are falling, assuming that demand remains constant. There is, of course, the point at which unit costs start to rise, and this represents diminishing economies of scale. Economies of scale can be external as well as internal, and the former may augment (or counteract) internal scale economies. Internal economies of scale are achieved when a business reduces costs and increases production and external economies of scale stem from direct strategic interdependency, collaboration and shared costs of services with other firms. External economies of scale are important also, particularly to small firms such as most tourism businesses, which can't achieve internal economies of scale.

Some external economies derive from purchasing material or service inputs more cheaply from other specialised firms, instead of producing them internally; for example, accountancy, insurance facilities, design, and repair and maintenance services. While these transactions are effectively led in terms of being successfully beneficial to the business, being reliant on individual decision-making, firms of all sizes, but especially small firms, can also benefit from formal collaboration to buy particular goods and services (Johnston et al., 2000), whether this is for energy, marketing or cleaning. A group of firms acting collectively has stronger buying power than individual firms and can negotiate reduced prices and tariffs (Estall and Buchanan, 1980).

Although economies of scale are important, they are not the only determinant of economic outcomes. Although large firms can realise economies of scale that are not available to small firms, the latter – and this particularly applies to tourism businesses – can also succeed in the same market. They can serve specialised smaller markets, not served by large scale operators, or they can benefit from external economies of scale. External economies of scale can exist between firms regardless of the relative spatial distance between them. Leask and Fyall (2006) argue that unlike other tourism components such as transportation and accommodation, visitor attractions do not enjoy the benefits of globalisation in terms of product standardisation and economies of scale to the same extent because of their individualised and differentiated characteristics. Where external economies of scale are a result of spatial concentration, and are caused by factors beyond the actions or responsibilities of firms, they are called agglomeration economies (Cohen and Morrison, 2005). Cost advantages can include reductions in operating costs associated with sources such as local availability of skilled labour, research facilities, the existence of local ancillary industries and specialised services (Johnston et al., 2000).

External economies of scale and agglomeration economies are important drivers of collaboration between firms, including visitor attractions. If they are recognised as mutually beneficial for firms, then potentially they may engage in collaborative mechanisms at both the local and regional scale although these drivers can, in certain circumstances, also inhibit collaboration. The outcome depends on how the spatial conditions of visitor attractions, i.e. density, location, organisation, are juxtaposed with the nature of their tourism product, and how or whether these become drivers for collaboration aimed at achieving external economies of scale and agglomeration economies. It is noteworthy that external economies are not necessarily a result of agglomeration, but often characterise agglomeration economies. The following externalities generate economic benefits for firms cooperating with other firms: interdependence of firms, trust in sustained collaboration and cooperative competition. This is not to say that external economies of scale necessarily generate collaboration between firms, but if there is mutual recognition between firms of potential positive externalities to be generated, then there will be a propensity to cooperate to a certain extent. The effect of spatial proximity and density between visitor attractions on external economies of scale has been studied in the context of the different aspects including interdependence between firms, trust in sustained collaboration and cooperative competition (Weidenfeld et al., 2011).

Interdependence of firms

It would be unlikely for firms to cooperate without seeking to realise traded and/or untraded interdependencies as their main motive. Traded and untraded interdependencies, consisting of a set of practices, rules, routines, agreements and networks, are closely linked to information flows, labour markets, regional conventions and norms (Morgan, 1997, Storper, 1997, Raco, 1999, Newlands, 2003, Storper, 2000, Shaw and Williams, 2004). Traded interdependencies, which are broadly the market transactions between economic actors, are inextricably linked to untraded interdependencies, i.e. to the webs through which information is developed and exchanged (Newlands, 2003). Traded interdependencies involve a series of transactions, including purchasing inputs, contacting and dismissing staff, selling products and financing investment, which imply transaction costs to the organisations concerned (Storper, 2000, Fyall and Garrod, 2005). Frequent contact favours the exchange of specialised inputs, repeated transactions and facilitates the circulation of information. It also makes it easier for firms to find contractors to verify the quality of goods and services and to draw up standardised contracts (Santagata, 2002). Such contracts generate market transactions, which benefit both sides and underpin traded interdependencies. Furthermore, technology is a strong driver of change behind these transactions at the local and international scales (Storper, 2000).

While many forms of external economies are realised informally, strategic alliances are institutionalised arrangements that firms develop among themselves to access complementary resources and skills that reside in other companies. They provide:

> the means for a firm to share any of its information, production or distribution resources with one or more other firms on a cost-effective basis, as long as it does not lead to collusion in the market behaviour of the allied firms.
>
> (Michael, 2007:24)

In other words, alliances offer cooperative frameworks for both traded and untraded interdependencies. For example, firms may cooperate in seeking to get new work, especially on large projects, by forming a consortium to access cheaper finance, by joined procurement of materials or funding research. They may conjointly receive technical financial and other services together (Newlands, 2003).

Previous tourism studies (Mackun, 1998, Hjalager, 2000, Jackson and Murphy, 2002) have examined how providers collaborated in 'pooling financial resources, share questions and concerns, lobby local and regional government agencies, and coordinate marketing and advertising efforts' (Mackun 1998:269), engaging in both traded and untraded interdependencies. Groups of visitor attractions organise joint activities and events, where the time, risk-management and finance involved are often beyond the scope of individual attractions. Traded interdependencies lead to market transactions such as joint-selling and buying or cross-selling (e.g. joint-ticketing and vouchers), joint-advertising, financing investments, allowing institutionalised arrangements to access complementary arrangements, products and specialised services (Fyall et al., 2001, Weidenfeld et al., 2011). In Chicago, for example, 26 dissimilar attractions, such as wildlife attractions and theme parks, jointly sell a discounted price ticket compared to standard ticketing options (Smart Destinations, 2010). Similarly, in other tourism destinations other schemes such as passports, vouchers or destination cards are offered to tourists, such as in the Canton of Ticino, Switzerland, where destination cards 'offer free or highly discounted entry into partner attractions and activities often coupled with free public transport access in the area' (Zoltan and McKercher, 2014:19). These schemes are also used by smaller, secondary, less visited or more peripherally located visitor attractions such as in Victoria, Canada, where seven of its smaller museums and art galleries share a pass which encourages their visitors to get off the beaten track and visit attractions, which they otherwise may miss, in an attempt to draw a larger overall number of visitors (McCulloch, 2014).

Traded and untraded interdependencies

Traded and untraded interdependencies between visitor attractions are inextricably linked. Market transactions allow a more productive and cost efficient production but also encourage information sharing whether between individual attractions or among an alliance's members. 'Retail collectives' or 'buying groups' in tourism destinations aimed at enhancing their bargaining power with other players such as suppliers, tour operators and tourist boards are formed (Fyall et al., 2001, Weidenfeld et al., 2011). For example, visitor attractions in Weidenfeld et al.'s (2011) study in Cornwall used the same suppliers, media, print companies and collective distribution networks, and sometimes specialised services such as maintaining and operating joint internet websites. Likewise, many of these attractions retailed similar products and sourced from the same suppliers, using the same media, print companies and collective leaflet distribution networks. They also enhanced their bargaining power with local, regional and national tourist boards, tour operators and group bookings as well as undertaking research and training staff together.

In tourism, strategic alliances (untraded interdependencies) can emerge between individual competitors or amongst groups of these and may be based on various objectives. These include improving market access (mutual, shared distribution of costs and benefits), market development (especially in the face of risk), reducing competition in key markets, sharing costs of research and development, as well as sharing the costs of the production process, distribution and marketing. Alliances are means by which individual businesses are operationally linked together within their local microenvironment. They are mechanisms for institutional cooperation by which individual actors (typically small and medium size enterprises (SMEs) in tourism) can work together towards shared agendas and common objectives, formalising their mutually beneficial untraded interdependencies.

Spatial proximity and interdependencies

The interrelationships between spatial proximity and interdependencies create both advantages and disadvantages to visitor attractions, which are detailed in Table 6.1 and are assumed to be more intense between attractions with high levels of agglomeration within the same destination. Conversely, attractions with low levels of agglomeration are likely to establish fewer interdependencies with other attractions compared to agglomerated attractions. This might lead to disadvantages such as fewer complementary products, less integration with the overall regional tourism experience product, less cost efficient production and higher production costs as a result of not sharing costs and services with other businesses and attractions (Table 6.1). Possible advantages of low levels of agglomeration are greater stability and easier maintenance of the existing interdependencies, even if there are only a few of them and fewer entrants to the market reducing internal competition.

The relationships between spatial proximity and interdependencies differ between the local and the regional scales. At the regional scale, such as in a destination region, the agglomeration of visitor attractions is positively related to untraded interdependencies in general, including marketing, since visitors are likely to visit more than one neighbouring attraction in the same destination region. In more dispersed destination regions, cooperation in marketing is likely to be stronger as competition for markets with other destinations is also stronger. At the local scale, spatial proximity is positively related to traded and untraded interdependencies (Weidenfeld et al., 2011); in other words, neighbouring attractions are more likely to engage in cooperation, such as buying the same services as cleaning, transporting staff, etc. as well as tending to have more exchange of ideas and information on customers.

Trust in sustained collaboration

Trust in sustained collaboration builds up between businesses as a result of long-term business relationships, and embedded social values rather than through formal contracts (Jackson and Murphy, 2002, Hjalager, 2000). It is important

Table 6.1 External economies of scale in visitor attractions at Newquay and the Lizard tourism clusters in Cornwall, UK

External economies of scale	Tourism spaces of high agglomeration (positive externalities)		Tourism spaces of low agglomeration (negative externalities)	
	Advantages	*Disadvantages*	*Advantages*	*Disadvantages*
Trust in sustainable collaboration	Facilitating a chain of tourism production, joint-ventures, innovations spillovers, innovative products, joint political input to local authorities and activities to improve regional destination competitive advantages.	Less flexibility in the openness to new players, ideas and lock-in effects when adhering to conventional forms of collaborative practices.	None	None
Traded and untraded interdependencies	Complementary relationships, more cost efficient production	Less competitive environment due to more interdependency between individual attractions and less regional competition.	Interdependencies that exist even at low levels are possibly stable and easy to maintain between neighbouring attractions.	Less complementary relationships of production and segregation from the regional tourism experience product, less cost efficient production.
Cooperative competition	Healthy competition, constant imperative to remain cooperative and cooperate for enhancing innovations.	Problems in building and maintaining trust.	More clarity in firms' relationships, easier to build trust.	Less competitive and innovative business environment, hinder development. Unhealthy competition or even fierce competition between neighbours or too much interdependency.

Source: Adapted from Weidenfeld (2008).

because it expedites learning 'because people and organisations are privy to richer and thicker information flows and people divulge more to those they trust' (Hudson, 2005:130). Trust in sustained collaboration is implicit in the social-network model used by Gordon and McCann (2000), who note that 'social networks of certain strong interpersonal relationships can transcend firm boundaries, with the result that many interfirm social interactions may be stronger than their intra-firm counterparts' (Gordon and Mccann, 2000:520). Strong interpersonal relationships are underpinned by interpersonal trust and, according to Gordon and McCann (2000), can be identified as central according to the following three trust based behavioural features of collaboration:

1. Firms within the social network are willing to undertake risky cooperative and joint-ventures without fear of opportunistic behaviour from their collaborators.
2. Firms are willing to re-organise their relationships without fear of reprisals.
3. Firms are willing to act as a group in support of common, mutually beneficial goals.

These are particularly germane in situations where neither price signals nor monitoring are sufficient to ensure the implementation of a particular project or activity. In other words, where knowledge ends, trust is one of the ways to overcome uncertainty (Williams and Baláž, 2015).

The emphasis on development relationships based on trust is underpinned by the argument that physical proximity facilitates trust, which in turn facilitates territorialised knowledge transfers between firms, organisations and individuals (Williams, 2005, 2006). This also constitutes part of the broader debate about whether, and/or the extent to which, social networks are spatially inherent in any industry or whether space is not as important as other factors such as shared values, interests and professional background. 'Due to the existence of mutual trust, trade within the community [or within a cluster of firms] is generally assessed by the enterprises as less risky than trade with outsiders' (Hjalager, 2000:206). Trust assists in how firms approach, and survive, minor crises while the sustainability of a local economy is further enhanced by a geographical and cultural proximity which is nurtured through repeated face-to-face contacts and contracts among firms, in social as well as business connections (Hjalager, 2000, Newlands, 2003). The strength of trust based relationships is described as the level of 'embeddedness' of the social network (Gordon and McCann, 2000:520).

Trust is particularly germane to tourism, given that compared to other industries, networking, social embeddedness, interest group representation and institutionalisation are generally weak in many segments of the tourist industry (Williams and Shaw, 1998). Tourism businesses managers are considered to have weaker trust relations due to barriers such as difficulties around lack of common beliefs, values and goals that are attributed to: variation in firms' size, type and affiliation; rapid turnover of managers and professionals; deliberate disassociation (especially by international large firms) from building ties with the local community; 'free-riding' and attitudes of the local community towards tourists and the tourism industry (Hjalager, 2000).

Trust as the essential glue in sustained collaboration between visitor attractions at high levels of agglomeration can be beneficial in facilitating a chain of tourism production, joint-ventures, innovation spillovers, innovative products, joint political input to local authorities and activities to improve regional destination competitive advantages (Hjalager, 2000, Newlands, 2003, Williams, 2005, 2006). In the family destination of Lolland Foster, on an island in the southern part of Denmark, the development of trust between managers enhanced the development of collaboration between visitor attractions, which generated marketing initiatives, a common webpage, joint special offers and team building courses (Sørensen and Fuglsang, 2014). However, trust can give rise to disadvantages in terms of lack of openness to new players and ideas, whereby firms become locked-in to existing or conventional forms of collaborative practices (Boschma, 2005). Distance alone cannot explain trust and collaboration between visitor attractions in agglomerated and dispersed attractions. However, trust is determined in part by spatial proximity, and also by the very nature of the tourism product as will be further discussed in this chapter.

Cooperative competition

For firms, it is not a simple question of whether or not to compete with or collaborate with other firms in their locality. Instead, firms within a region may compete with each other in some of their activities, on the basis of their individual strengths or comparative advantages, while also cooperating with a view to enhancing their collective inter-regional competition with other regions. The benefit from collaboration in terms of collective inter-regional competition is a particularly important incentive for inter-cluster cooperation (Huybers and Bennett, 2003, Malmberg and Maskell, 2002). As a result, firms, which in other circumstances are direct competitors, find themselves becoming 'cooperative competitors'. They collaborate in some activities such as lobbying, trying to create markets, participation in trade fairs or providing infrastructure, specialised training and market intelligence. Yet they also compete in other areas such as company-specific marketing, production, sales and new product and process development (Enright, cited by Huybers and Bennett, 2003). The number of firms, the frequency and durability of their interactions, the degree of homogeneity among the firms and their learning capacities determine the chances of successful cooperation in a destination region (Huybers and Bennett, 2003). Collaboration provides opportunities for firms to pool resources in purchasing, marketing or training alongside a constant and insistent imperative to withhold competitive advantages from this collaboration so as to remain competitive against the same firms within the same region. Thus, building and maintaining trust can be problematic given the mounting pressures of increasing competition, which may tempt firms to try to appropriate collective assets. Yet there are real benefits in that cooperation may also ensure the continuity of 'healthy' competition within the cluster, and the ensuing market discipline and innovation may increase the competitive advantages of individual firms (Newlands, 2003). This may result in a greater growth rate of business service firms in spatial clusters compared to those in dispersed spaces (Keeble and Nachum, referred to by Newlands, 2003).

Tourism is characterised by a persistent dynamic tension between competitive and collaborative forces (Fyall et al., 2001). Moreover, cooperative competition or vertical and horizontal 'coopetition' within destinations and within value systems is likely to become increasingly important for the survival and profitability of organisations, sharing the same destiny or 'co-destiny' (Buhalis, 2006). It is a means of avoiding 'the cannibalisation of individual attractions through the pursuit of conflicting strategies on the part of local competitors' (Fyall et al., 2001:218). Inevitably, the balance between cooperation and competition between firms involves a strategic trade-off between firms within the same region depending on their spatial distance from one another. Coopetition is particularly germane to small visitor attractions since their ability to compete with major players can be enhanced by being a part of consortia (Weidenfeld et al., 2011, Swarbrooke, 2001). The nature of coopetition also depends on many factors including the spatial distance between individual attractions: there is evidence that the propensity for cooperative competition is negatively related to distance (Weidenfeld et al., 2011, Jensen, 2014). This business environment can be an obstacle to building and maintaining trust if it results in attractions being unclear about when, and in what areas, to cooperate with neighbouring firms that are also their competitors.

Thematic product similarities: complementarities and interdependencies

Product assembly linkages between visitor attractions in destination regions might develop circumstantially or deliberately in order to achieve mutual benefits (Benur and Bramwell, 2015). Product similarity between visitor attractions refers to the thematic nature of that product: whether the attraction is gardens, wildlife, theme parks or heritage sites. At the local scale, thematic-product similarity has a polarising effect. It decreases the level of cooperation in marketing between neighbouring individual attractions but increases the levels of other areas of cooperation. For example, zoos in Cornwall county, south west England, were not collaborating in marketing as much as in buying professional services like a vet and purchasing food for animals. By contrast thematic-product dissimilarity between attractions increases the level of cooperation in marketing (Weidenfeld et al., 2011).

The visitor attraction experience product consists of two phases. The first phase is staging, which includes setting up, arranging and contextualising the attraction, and the second is thematising, which situates attractions by developing particular themes and endows them with dramatic content. When compatible, complementary or contrasting themes emerge in neighbouring attractions, a narrative structure can be built across thematically and complementary interrelated sub-attractions, resulting in an enhanced destination experience, extended length of stay and the creation of more business opportunities (Sternberg, 1997). The narratives and thematic linkages are likely to encourage individuals to visit more than one attraction, particularly if each attraction is well connected thematically and functionally to the other creating a story. Stratford-Upon-Avon, England, is the birth place of William Shakespeare, the famous English poet, playwright and actor. The town includes a cluster of visitor attractions, managed by the Royal Shakespeare Company, which tell his life story and that of his family including Shakespeare's birth place; his wife's, Anne Hathaway's, cottage; his daughter's home, Hall's Croft; his grave; and his mother's farm, Mary Arden's farm, which is situated in Wilmcote just outside Stratford-Upon-Avon.

The narratives and thematic linkages are likely to encourage further cooperation on the basis of other potential interdependencies. The establishment of tourism trails based on prescribed routes where visitor attractions are designed as chapters telling different types of stories based on the historical, cultural, geographic and/or natural story of the destination(s) is a good example of joint marketing, coordination and complementarities. Trails connect tourists to the region, providing a memorable experience and act as place branding often through complementary attractors such as visitor attractions, focal points and accommodation facilities. One of the most recent tourism trails (popular with both tourists and pilgrims), founded in 2007, is northern Israel Jesus Trail in the Galilee. While following Jesus' footsteps and encouraging tourists to visit both paid and unpaid attractions, it is also designed for anyone interested in archaeology, history or nature (Timothy and Boyd, 2014). Similarly, there are current attempts to build complementary relationships between visitor attractions, which constitute a new tourism route along the geographic locations of Che Guevara's life journey in South and Central America (Zeppel, 2006). If thematic complementarities are also strengthened by additional complementarities such as coordinated timetable and matching a variety of different activities offered by neighbouring attractions, cooperation is stronger. In other words, certain historical or chronological stories, such as the life of an iconic figure such as a leader, a poet, a pop star or even a cartoon can be exploited through visits to several connected, complementary and neighbouring attractions. These can be engendered by the following types of product complementarities identified by Weidenfeld et al.'s (2011) study in Cornwall, UK:

a. Market segment complementarity: neighbouring attractions offer different products or services to people, who belong to different market segments and tend to travel together, such as men and women, children and adults. These markets or sub-markets would rather visit attractions which offer the desirable experience to all the members of the group (or travel companions). Therefore, neighbouring visitor attractions or the same attraction can offer complementary products and services to different segments of the same group. Potential cooperation between neighbouring complementary attractions in terms of complementary markets is enabled if spatial proximity exists. If successful, it may create synergies and result in increasing the collective appeal of the visitor attractions and the entire destination. For example, neighbouring attractions may effectively have, or actively seek to achieve, a market divided into sub-markets; some attractions target their experience products to children, while others address their parents' touristic preferences and interests.

b. Indoor/outdoor and passive/active complementarity: outdoor attractions referring (or cross-selling) visitors to a nearby indoor attraction's product on a rainy day or those that would be more suitable for changing weather conditions. For example, there has been a recent trend of European theme parks welcoming the emergence of neighbouring water parks in 2014 which continues through 2015 including Europa-Park in Germany and Liseberg in Sweden considering adding such facilities. This is following the success of introducing Aquaventura Slidepark at Avonturenpark (Looping Group) in Hellendoom, the Netherlands, in 2013, which is a 5,000 square-metre outdoor attraction with 11 water slides and a water playground. A recent attempt to create a nearby complementary attraction based on weather conditions and spatial proximity is the case of Agua Mágica (see Box 6.1). Attractions often find it appropriate to recommend neighbouring attractions to visitors on specific

---

Box 6.1 Agua Mágica

Isla Mágica is a theme park in Seville, Spain, theming the world of the conquistadors, the Spanish conquerors of South America. Since acquiring Isla Mágica in March 2013, Looping Group's goal has been to achieve profitability at the park within one to two years by providing an upgrade feature through investing around €5.7 million (around US$7.6 million) in Agua Mágica, a new mini water park, which covers an additional 35,000 square meters. Its theme is adventure including the discovery of South America, connected with the story of Seville. For example, the water park's lazy river is inspired by the Amazon River. Overall, Agua Mágica's attractions include a 1,800-square-metre (19,375-square-foot) wave pool (one of the largest in Europe), a 600-square-metre (6,458-square-foot) water playground, and a range of slides. The water park is an attempt to create a thematic complementary between the two attractions which is South America and its linkage to the country of the destination, Spain. The theme park is based on historical aspects related to South America and Spain and the water park takes the visitor chronologically and geographically forward to the next 'chapter' of the story of the conquest. According to Arnaud Coste, COO at Looping Group, the success in increasing the number of visitors to 2000 per day in July–August is not only due to the thematic link but also the complementary relationships which were engendered by weather conditions. Seville's sunshine drives theme park visitors to spend the midday heat at the waterpark when temperature rises to around 40C and return to the theme park in the evening. Visitors to the theme park pay an extra charge (Gilling, 2014).

occasions, for example, outdoor attractions might suggest proximal indoor attractions to their visitors on a rainy day. The greater the spatial proximity between attractions, the more likely it is that visitors would follow such a recommendation. Similarly, attractions offering a passive tourist experience, such as a museum, may engage in joint marketing with attractions which offer an active experience such as an adventure centre, as many visitors seek to combine both types of experiences in the same day. In other words, there is a need to think of how tourists combine visits to different attractions over a time period – say a day, a weekend or a week – in order to produce their overall tourism experience and to think of how the spatial organisation of other tourism services influence their decision-making.

c.   Visit time/duration: when two attractions sell a short visit, or when they offer similar price discounts when customers visit more than one of the attractions during the same holiday trip. This complementary relationship is more likely to emerge after earlier mentioned complementarities have managed to attract similar market segments. Attractions in spatial proximity are more likely to cooperate in offering a special price or a discount for visitors who visited the neighbouring attraction. However, pricing strategies are challenging for firms, which have to balance the contribution of volume and price level to their neighbours, because there is less competition and they are more likely to cooperate in joint-selling.

Interdependencies differ according to the different levels of product-thematic similarity amongst visitor attractions: whether they are very similar, similar complementary or dissimilar (Figure 6.1). This mostly reflects cooperation in marketing as an indicator of interdependencies. Product dissimilarity between visitor attractions at the local and regional scales is positively related to interdependencies, so that attractions with dissimilar products are more likely to demonstrate high levels of cooperation among themselves. Moreover, the more that attractions' products are similar complementary, the higher the cooperation, which is correlated with the levels of interdependency. In Newquay, Cornwall, south west England, visitor attractions such as a zoo, an aquarium and a wild life sanctuary had more traded and untraded interdependencies such as joint marketing, purchases of services and more close cooperation between their managers than attractions in the Lizard cluster (Weidenfeld et al., 2011). Thus, co-located similar product attractions are likely to be less cooperative, whereas thematic complementary ones are likely to become the closest cooperators and to achieve the highest levels of interdependency.

Other similarities

Other similarities (non-complementary) affect cooperation including similarities in market segments, market size and product quality. Similar market segments, including visitor type (profile) and market size, are a catalyst for collaboration in marketing regardless of whether or not firms have thematic similarity. Similar

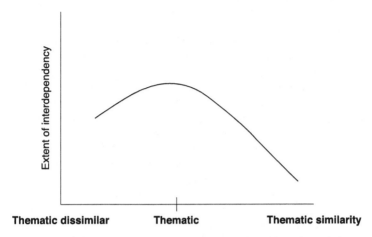

Figure 6.1 Generalised relationships between extent of interdependency and product thematic complementarity of visitor attractions

Source: Adapted from Weidenfeld et al. (2011).

thematic attractions sharing the same markets may find common interests, which drive them to collaborate in marketing and exchange of information about visitors. Therefore, thematic similarity does not always intensify competition, particularly if mediated by other complementarities. These include marketing for the same market such as joint marketing of neighbouring gardens and heritage attractions targeting the same type and visitor profiles. In Cornwall, Weidenfeld et al. (2011) identified two garden attractions, different in size, which were open at different times (visit time complementarity), which created close collaboration between them including joint marketing and cross referencing.

Attractions which have dissimilar market segments are less likely to cooperate in marketing. The same applies to the degree of similarity in market size (visitor numbers) because dissimilarity in market size may cause concerns for the managers of those with larger markets about free-riding by the smaller attractions. Therefore, market size is a significant factor that not only increases cooperation among attractions but also between attractions and other businesses such as restaurants and pubs.

Product quality is also an influential factor as attractions which consider themselves to be of high quality usually prefer to cooperate with similar ones: this offers esteem through association. Joint marketing and cross-reference between similar product quality attractions is crucial to many attraction managers in terms of their creditability in the eyes of their potential customers as a source of high quality tourism experiences, and for maintaining their reputation. Other factors influencing collaboration include the binding restrictions and regulation required by membership in particular tourism associations, different patterns of ownerships (public/private) and personal relationships between managers. A summary of the interrelationships between these factors is illustrated in Figure 6.2.

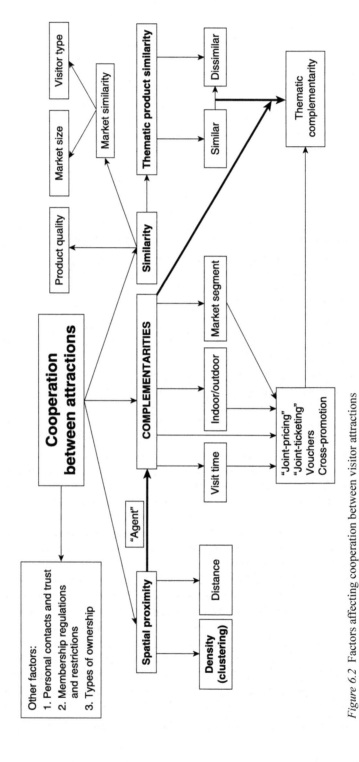

Figure 6.2 Factors affecting cooperation between visitor attractions

Source: Adapted from Weidenfeld et al. (2011).

When attractions have the same owner, they are likely to develop trust and collaboration, and sustain close cooperation, and are less likely to compete and more likely to cooperate. However, to date a clear pattern of attractions collaborating or competing with other attractions of similar or dissimilar ownerships has not been identified (Weidenfeld et al., 2011).

Conclusions

Spatial proximity and product-thematic similarity between visitor attractions both tend to offer opportunities to realise external economies of scale, including traded and untraded interdependencies (Fyall et al., 2001) and cooperative competition (Buhalis, 2006, Huybers and Bennett, 2003, Jackson and Murphy, 2006). In the case of high thematic similarity, strong competition might deter attractions from cooperation aimed at achieving such external economies. Very similar product attractions are likely to cooperate only if they are distant enough not to compete directly for the same visitors. By contrast, high levels of thematic complementarity may sometimes encourage collaboration, especially in marketing. Complementary product attractions are likely to cooperate most intensively and dissimilar product attractions are likely to cooperate if they are spatially proximate. However, other complementarities, including visit time, indoor/outdoor and duration as well as market segment, can positively encourage different forms of collaboration, such as 'joint-pricing', 'joint-ticketing' and vouchers, and cross-promotion. These complementarities are facilitated by spatial proximity, which is 'an agency' or a facilitator of collaboration (Weidenfeld et al., 2011). There is no evidence that visitor attraction managers tend to gain more trust in sustained collaboration if the spatial proximity between their attractions is higher.

Thematic similarity also encourages cooperation among attractions regardless of geographical scale, leading to the formation of networks and collaboration such as learning and training (see more in Chapter 8). The relationships between spatial proximity and interdependencies differ between the local and the regional scales. At the regional scale, the agglomeration of visitor attractions is positively related to untraded interdependencies in general, including marketing. However, in more dispersed destinations, cooperation in marketing is stronger and competition for markets within the destination is weaker. At the local scale, spatial proximity is positively related to traded and untraded interdependencies. Most visitor attractions are interlinked in what is defined as 'coopetitive' relationships (Buhalis, 2006, Wang and Krakover, 2008). Other product similarities, including market segments, market size and product quality, have a positive influence on cooperation and external economies of scale among tourist attractions. Other influential factors on collaboration, including binding restrictions and regulations due to membership in tourism associations, different patterns of ownerships (public/private) and personal relationships, have both positive and negative influences. However, there has been very little evidence (or indeed of research on) the role of trust in sustained collaboration between managers, and this externality needs to be further studied.

The factors affecting cooperation between tourist attractions, including product similarities, complementarities and spatial proximity, and the relationships between them are summarised in Figure 6.2, which clearly shows their complexity. These factors, and their interrelationships, should be considered by practitioners, policy- and decision-makers in the creation of tourism development policies, and by entrepreneurs and managers considering new development projects.

Product complementarities between neighbouring visitor attractions are pivotal in their success. Creating new complementarities needs to consider the nature and type of the product and activities, facilities, duration of visit, opening time, seasonality, access, spatial structure and market demand against spatial proximity. If different types of product complementarities between attractions are established, synergies among visitor attractions potentially could lead to success in terms of increasing tourist numbers and market segments by providing a more appealing destination experience. At the regional level, visitor attractions are vertically integrated with other producers (e.g. accommodation providers) by virtue of specialising in one stage of the tourism production chain, as well as being horizontally integrated in complementary relationships with other attractions at the same stage of production (Michael, 2003).

The study of complementarities, synergies and collaboration remains rare. Further studies are required to identify other types of complementarities amongst attractions and between attractions and other businesses in other geographical contexts, such as national and cross-border. The behaviour of tourists and tour operators in cruises may reveal some other complementarities between different destinations, which shape the selection of destinations where ships dock allowing passengers to make the most of their limited time. Visitor attractions can be metaphorical of book chapters, which tell a story. Like book chapters, visitor attractions need to be linked and complement each other to build a successful destination which would appeal to the reader (or visitor) and keep him/her involved, and staying more days within the same destination story. It is imperative to consider that while economic factors and a simple calculation of costs and benefits are essential at the beginning of any cooperative initiative in tourism, other determinants – such as social and cultural factors – are pivotal in the willingness of actors to cooperate in order to realise these. This means that it is important to view collaboration in a broader context, which includes the specificities of national culture, the economic and political history of a country, and social capital (Xia et al., 2010). These issues require far more attention than they have been given to date in the dominantly neo-classical economic literature in this field.

References

Benur, A. M. and Bramwell, B. (2015). Tourism product development and product diversification in destinations. *Tourism Management, 50*, 213–224.

Boschma, R. A. (2005). Proximity and innovation: A critical assessment. *Regional Studies, 39*, 61–74.

Buhalis, D. (2006). The impact of information technology on tourism competition. In A. Papatheodorou (Ed.), *Corporate Rivalry and Market Power, Competition Issues in Tourism: An Introduction* (pp. 143–171). London: I.B. Tauris.

Buhalis, D. and Cooper, C. (1998). Competition or co-operation? Small and medium sized enterprises at the destination. In B. Faulkner, E. Laws and G. Moscardo (Eds), *Embracing and Managing Change in Tourism: International Case Studies* (pp. 324–346). London: Routledge.

Butler, R. and Weidenfeld, A. (2012). Cooperation and competition during the resort lifecycle. *Tourism Recreation Research, 37,* 15–26.

Cohen, J. P. and Morrison, J. C. P. (2005). Agglomeration economies and industry location decisions: The impacts of spatial and industrial spillovers. *Regional Science and Urban Economics, 35,* 215–237.

Czernek, K. (2013). Determinants of cooperation in a tourist region. *Annals of Tourism Research, 40,* 83–104.

Estall, R. C. and Buchanan, R. O. (1980). *Industrial Activity and Economic Geography: A Study of the Forces Behind the Geographical Location of Productive Activity in Manufacturing Industry,* 4th edition. London: Hutchinson.

Fyall, A. and Garrod, B. (2005). *Tourism Marketing: A Collaborative Approach.* Clevedon: Channel View Publication.

Fyall, A., Leask, A. and Garrod, B. (2001). Scottish visitor attractions: A collaborative future. *International Journal of Tourism Research, 3*(3), 211–228.

Gilling, J. (2014). Water park wave – Europe's theme parks are finding success by introducing water parks, News Articles – Water Park. Retrieved from www.iaapa.org/news/newsroom/news-articles/water-park-wave—-october-2014 (accessed 20 January 2016).

Gordon, I. R. and McCann, P. (2000). Industrial clusters: Complexes, agglomeration and/or social networks? *Urban Studies, 37,* 513–532.

Hall, M. C. (2005). Rural wine and food tourism cluster and network development. In D. Hall, I. Kirkpatrick and M. Mitchell (Eds), *Rural Tourism and Sustainable Business* (pp. 149–164). Clevedon: Channel View Publications.

Hjalager, A. M. (2000). Tourism destinations and the concept of industrial districts. *Tourism and Hospitality Research, 2,* 199–213.

Hudson, R. (2005). *Economic Geographies, Circuits, Flows and Spaces.* London: Sage.

Huybers, T. and Bennett, J. (2003). Inter-firm cooperation at nature-based tourism destinations. *Journal of Socio-Economics, 32,* 571–587.

Jackson, J. and Murphy, P. (2002). Tourism destinations as clusters: Analytical experiences from the New World. *Tourism and Hospitality Research, 4,* 36–52.

Jackson, J. and Murphy, P. (2006). Clusters in regional tourism – An Australian case. *Annals of Tourism Research, 33*(4), 1018–1035.

Jensen, Ø. (2014). Approaches for the evaluation of visitor experiences at tourist attractions. In N. K. Prebensen, J. S. Chen and M. Uysal (Eds), *Creating Experience Value in Tourism* (pp. 139–156). Wallingford: CABI.

Johnston, R. J., Gregory, D., Pratt, G. and Watts, M. (2000). *The Dictionary of Human Geography.* Oxford: Blackwell.

Leask, A. and Fyall, A. (2006). Researching international visitor attractions. *Tourism Recreation Research, 31*(2), 23–32.

McCulloch, S. (2014). See seven attractions with Pass It Around Victoria, *Times Colonist.* Retrieved from www.timescolonist.com/see-seven-attractions-with-pass-it-around-victoria-1.1256415 (accessed 10 February 2015).

Mackun, P. (1998). Tourism in the Third Italy, Labour and social-business networks. In D. Ioannides and G. Debbage (Eds), *The Economic Geography of the Tourist Industry, A Supply-Side Analysis* (pp. 235–256). London: Routledge.

Malmberg, A. and Maskell, P. (2002). The elusive concept of localisation economies: Towards a knowledge-based theory of spatial clustering. *Environment and Planning A*, *34*, 429–449.

Michael, E. J. (2003). Tourism micro-clusters. *Tourism Economics*, *9*, 133–145.

Michael, E. J. (Ed.) (2007). *Micro-Clusters and Networks: The Growth of Tourism*. Oxford: Elsevier.

Michael, E. J. and Hall, C. M. (2007). A path for policy. In E. J. Michael (Ed.), *Micro-Clusters and Networks: The Growth of Tourism* (pp. 127–140). Oxford: Elsevier.

Morgan, K. (1997). The learning region: Institutions, innovation and regional renewal. *Regional Studies*, *31*(5), 491–503.

Newlands, D. (2003). Competition and cooperation in industrial clusters: The implications for public policy. *European Planning Studies*, *11*, 521–532.

Raco, M. (1999). Competition, collaboration and the new industrial districts: Examining the institutional turn in local economic development. *Urban Studies*, *36*(5–6), 951–968.

Santagata, W. (2002). Cultural districts, property rights and sustainable economic growth. *International Journal of Urban and Regional Research*, *26*, 9–23.

Shaw, G. and Williams, A. (2004). *Tourism and Tourism Spaces*. London: Sage.

Smart Destinations (2010). 26 of Chicago's top tourist attractions collaborate on new ticketing option customizable pass to Chicago. Retrieved from www.smartdestinations. com/blog/pressrelease/26-of-chicagos-top-tourist-attractions-collaborate-on-new-ticketing-option-customizable-pass-to-chicago/ (accessed 9 February 2015).

Sørensen, F. and Fuglsang, L. (2014). Social network dynamics and innovation in small tourism companies. In M. McLeod and R. Vaughan (Eds), *Knowledge Networks and Tourism* (pp. 28–44). Abingdon: Routledge.

Sotiriadis, M. and Loedolff, C. (2015). Nature-based visitor attractions and alliances/ partnerships: Suggesting a collaboration framework and the factors determining effectiveness. *Journal of Human Ecology*, *49*, 89–101.

South African Tourism (2014). Inaugural attractions management conference held in Cape Town. Retrieved from www.southafrica.net/trade/en/news/entry/news-inaugural-attractions-management-conference-held-in-cape-town (accessed 9 February 2015).

Sternberg, E. (1997). The iconography of the tourism experience. *Annals of Tourism Research*, *24*, 951–969.

Storper, M. (1997). *The Regional World: Territorial Development in a Global Economy*. New York: Guilford Press.

Storper, M. (2000). Globalization, localisation, and trade. In G. L. Clark, M. P. Feldman and M. S. Gertler (Eds), *Oxford Handbook of Economic Geography* (pp. 146–165). Oxford: Oxford University Press.

Swarbrooke, J. (2001). Key challenges for visitor attraction managers in the UK. *Journal of Leisure Property*, *1*, 318–336.

Timothy, D. J. and Boyd, S. W. (2014). *Tourism and Trails Cultural, Ecological and Management Issues*. Bristol: Channel View Publications.

Wang, Y. and Krakover, S. (2008). Destination marketing: Competition, cooperation, or coopetition? *International Journal of Contemporary Hospitality Management*, *20*, 126–141.

Weidenfeld, A. (2008). *'The Destination Story' Cooperation, Competition and Knowledge Transfer between Tourist Attractions in Cornwall*. PhD thesis, University of Exeter.

Weidenfeld, A., Butler, R. and Williams, A. M. (2011). The role of clustering, cooperation and complementarities in the visitor attraction sector. *Current Issues in Tourism, 14*, 595–629.

Williams, A. (2005). Working Paper. No. 17, International Migration and Knowledge Oxford: Centre on Migration, Policy and Society, University of Oxford.

Williams, A. M. (2006). Lost in translation? International migration, learning and knowledge. *Progress in Human Geography, 30*, 588–607.

Williams, A. M. and Baláž, V. (2015). Tourism risk and uncertainty: Theoretical reflections. *Journal of Travel Research, 54*(3), 271–287.

Williams, A. M. and Shaw, G. (1998). Tourism politics in a changing economic environment. In A. M. Williams and G. Shaw (Eds), *Tourism and Economic Development, European Perspectives* (pp. 375–391). London: Routledge.

Xia, J., Evans, F. H., Spilsbury, K., Ciesielski, V., Arrowsmith, C. and Wright, G. (2010). Market segments based on the dominant movement patterns of tourists. *Tourism Management, 31*, 464–469.

Zeppel, H. (2006). *Indigenous Ecotourism: Sustainable Development and Management*. Wallingford: CABI.

Zoltan, J. and McKercher, B. (2014). Analysing intra-destination movements and activity participation of tourists through destination card consumption. *Tourism Geographies, 17*(1), 19–35.

7 Competition in the visitor attraction sector

Introduction: competition as the driver of change and performance

Competition is strongly entwined with competitiveness, productivity and innovation and can be expressed in the following terms: 'innovation, enterprise and competition are connected through systems of complementary market and non-market instituted frameworks' (Metcalfe, 2005:23). Figure 7.1 presents a summary of the key relationships. There is considerable evidence to corroborate the importance of these relationships between competition and competitiveness at the level of the economy as a whole (Foster et al., 2001), but far less evidence that is specific to the attractions sector. Yet the nature of competition is critical to the performance of visitor attractions.

The relationship between competition and productivity is particularly strong and is seen to operate through two key mechanisms: at the inter-firm and intra-firm scales. The inter-firm scale emphasises that productivity is heterogeneous across the sector and that, over time, the least productive firms will be forced to

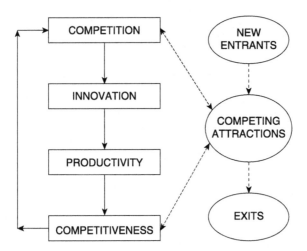

Figure 7.1 Competition as the driving force of change in attractions

exit the market (close, or are bankrupted), while new entrants will tend to have higher than average levels of productivity (Disney et al., 2003). The net effect will be to increase average productivity in the sector over time. Although there is no specific evidence for this effect in the attractions sector, Foster et al. (2006) provide evidence that productivity changes in retailing – another consumer services sector – are largely due to the differential productivity of entrant versus exiting firms. Arguably, the entry of new companies such as Disney World or Legoland have had analogous effects in the attractions sector.

Competition also induces intra-firm productivity increases, driving individual firms to innovate in order to increase their efficiency, whether just to survive or to increase market share. Flambards theme park in Cornwall, south west England, for example, was initially a small attraction based on an aviation museum, but innovated over time, adding reconstructions of period houses and shops, and theme park rides. The increase in scale and diversification contributed to enhanced performance. Although innovation in the face of competition can increase productivity in the individual firm, this also involves risks – innovation requires resources, including the priorities and time of managers. If the innovation fails in either its implementation, or in attracting new or different customers, then the opportunity costs constitute a major risk for that firm (see Figure 7.2). Competition can be an unforgiving driver of change in any market. Moreover, the effects of innovation on competition are not necessarily positive for the performance of the sector as a whole, or for customers. Innovation can inhibit competition, particularly where a firm is able to protect its innovation from imitation or emulation by competitors (Baumol, 2002). Arguably, the enormous investment costs involved in starting up mega theme parks such as Disney World or Legoland deters competition, both because of the scale of the resources involved and their ability

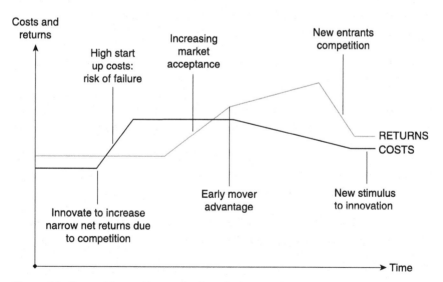

Figure 7.2 Competition and innovation in a single attraction

to protect their core product or identity from imitation by competitors, by the uses of patents, trademarks and other measures.

The relationship between competition and economic performance is complex and certainly cannot be seen as deterministic: but competition – in all its various forms – shapes the economic performance of visitor attractions. Competition is assumed to be endemic to all private sector, or mixed public-private sector economies and therefore many competition features are generic across sectors. However, attractions also have distinctive features, including substitutability, perishability and the blurring of production and consumption. First, substitutability refers to the largely discretionary nature of expenditure on attractions, and the existence of competing alternatives: similar and different types of attractions at the destination; other forms of tourism expenditure at the destination (for example, on different quality levels of accommodation); alternative tourism destinations; home based leisure; and other forms of non-tourism/leisure expenditure. This high level of substitutability generally serves to intensify the competition faced by visitor attractions.

Second, the tourism services provided by attractions are perishable, and unsold services cannot be stock piled or inventoried. This means that there is intense competition to maximise revenue by balancing prices with numbers of visitors, especially in terms of discounting or differential pricing of unsold capacity. As Papatheodorou (2006:7) emphasises, tourism is generally characterised by perishability and non-inventoried services, and by distinctly seasonal patterns of demand. In this context, and in the face of intense competition, firms are likely to indulge in product differentiation and/or in price wars, including reducing prices to the levels of marginal costs.

Third, the experiences provided by attractions are mostly based on the simultaneity of production and consumption: consumers have to be corporeally or physically present at the attraction in order to experience it. This means that competition in the sector is highly spatial, a theme that we return to later in this chapter. Wine tours to vineyards at harvest time in Bordeaux face intense competition. The product is highly substitutable – many intermediary companies offer such tours, and individuals also arrange their own visits to some of the hundreds of vineyards in the region. The product is also highly perishable for the harvest period lasts no more than a few weeks. And the experience has to be produced for the visitor on site, which means that there is intense competition from neighbouring vineyards.

In recent years, the intensity of competition has increased, as evidenced in both the growth in the number of attractions within national spaces, and the trend to increased internationalisation of competition. Even mega parks such as Disney now face strong competition within their original markets and locations in the USA. While varying degrees of competition have always characterised the operations and development of visitor attractions, globalisation tendencies have intensified the competition in large parts of the market. For example, the top 100 theme parks in Europe opened 271 new attractions in just three years in the late 2000s (Cornelis, 2011:42). Yet care should be taken not to exaggerate the competition provided by individual new attractions; for example, a survey by Cornelis (2011:61) of 56 leading European attractions found that only 3 per cent highly ranked changes in competition as the main implication of their investments in the long term.

Additionally, the growth of internet marketing and intermediaries, and of social media – whether commercialised as in the case of TripAdvisor, or social networks as with Facebook – have revolutionised the amounts, diversity and quality of information available to consumers. This increase in the transparency of the market tends to increase competition between attractions, although also creates new market imperfections. Stigler (1961) propounded the concept that, at some point, the marginal utility of additional information may be less than the cost of acquiring it – for example, the hours spent huddled over a laptop or tablet, and the stress induced in evaluating 'too much information' about potential attractions to visit. This is epitomised by the experiences of many visitors at tourist information centres, where they are confronted with a mass of information in various forms about the local visitor attractions. In summary, therefore, there are persistent barriers to full market transparency and theoretical notions of competition.

While competition is generally presented as a driver of change, much of the theoretical discussion around this assumes the existence of perfect competition. In reality, the extent to which competition exists in a particular market is conditional. Papatheodorou (2006:1) comments that the idea of perfect competition represents an 'idealistic market situation where infinitesimal firms produce a homogeneous product and compete freely against each other for the custom of infinitesimal rational, perfectly informed and mobile customers'. Usually there are limited numbers of firms, and some may constitute oligopolies or monopolies either because they own or control highly valued attractions, such as Lands End in the UK, or have proprietary rights over particular technologies, such as Legoland or Disney. In other words, markets are characterised by varying degrees of contestability (Baumol et al., 1982). Contestability is, however, scale-dependent. An attraction may be the only establishment offering a particular type of product in an area, and may be considered to exercise a monopoly in that locality. But it will also be in competition with different attractions in the locality or with similar attractions in other areas. Therefore, the notion of 'local monopolies' seems increasingly problematic in the face of the globalisation of competition. What really matters in respect of contestable markets 'is not whether an industry is actually a monopoly or not, but whether there is a real threat of competition' (Lei, 2006:21).

There has been considerable research on competition in tourism generally, but this has mostly been at the macro scale, typically considering the competition faced by tourism destinations in contexts of changing prices, incomes and other factors. For example, Patsouratis et al. (2005) examined tourism competition amongst Mediterranean destination countries, developing a model which incorporated price indexes and exchange rate differentials. In contrast, there has been far less research on competition between attractions, and at the micro scale of the firm, and this constitutes the focus of the chapter. Competition is in fact shaped by a myriad of interrelated macro and micro factors, and the next section examines some of these issues through the lens of Porter's (1998a) conceptualisation of the five forces that shape competition.

Porter: five forces that shape competition

With a few exceptions (Buhalis, 2006, Wang and Krakover, 2008, Sinclair and Stabler, 1997) competition remains surprisingly under-developed, or at least unevenly developed, in the research literature in tourism, and in the visitor attraction sector in particular (Wanhill, 2006, Butler and Weidenfeld, 2012, Weidenfeld et al., 2014). Porter's conceptualisation of the five forces that shape competition provides a starting point for understanding the complex nature of competition. As Porter (1998a:xii) in his seminal overview of competition stated: 'In understanding competition and value creation [the] aim is to capture the complexity of what actually happens on the ground'. Practices in relation to competition are necessarily complex and difficult to unravel from a host of other business and business-related practices, but Porter's (1998b) thesis of the five competitive forces that shape strategy provides a useful analytical starting point.

Porter (1998a:xiv) argues that 'competition is often defined too narrowly, as if it occurred only between direct rivals'. This brings into question how competition is framed both sectorally and spatially – what, and where, constitute the competition for attractions, whether directly or indirectly. For example, for a nature based tourism attraction is it only other nature based activities within a particular locality, or is it all commercial and non fee charging attractions in a locality, or nationally or internationally, or does it also include spending on retailing while on holiday, or even the competition for spending on leisure activities when at home? In other words, the scaling of competition is crucial.

Porter (1998a:xxvi) argues that five main forces 'have become shorthand for the way in which industry structure shapes the field on which competition unfolds':

- the intensity of rivalry amongst existing firms,
- the power of buyers,
- the power of suppliers,
- the threat of new entry, and
- the threat of substitutability.

Rivalry amongst firms is shaped by the following: the number, size and power of other firms within the industry; industry growth rates; the existence of exit barriers; individualised commitment to an activity; and ability to read signals from competitors. Price rivalry tends to be greatest when products are similar; there are low switching costs for customers, and high levels of perishability. This tends to drive down profits. In contrast, non-price competition, for example via new product development, can increase the total market and raise value.

In tourism, competition amongst firms is related to product similarities, as Baum and Mezias (1992) indicate in relation to the size, room price and physical location of hotels. Competition amongst visitor attractions is more complex because these are multifaceted: for example, whether they appeal to children or adults, offer tranquillity or adventure, and focus on nature or technology. The scale of the sector is also highly variable, ranging from a few mega attractions – major theme parks or museums, for example – to large numbers of relatively small businesses.

The distribution of property rights can also de-intensify competition amongst rival attractions because many are vested not in private ownership but in public or voluntary bodies. An important feature of visitor attractions is that many have grown out of the particular interests and commitments of individuals and volunteer groups (Lew, 1987) and often these are less profit driven and more motivated by individual passions and interests. This can constitute an effective exit barrier which mediates the consequences of competition: the owners may be less inclined to quit the market if their economic returns decline, even to the level of their marginal costs, because they still have a surplus of emotional returns. This applies to many of the large number of small museums, and heritage properties, which are owned and staffed by volunteers in most developed countries.

Most visitors face relatively low switching costs when choosing between 'similar' or even different attractions, and this intensification of competition is a real challenge for all attractions. However, some attractions – perhaps because of their niche positioning or strong local embeddedness – may also have a highly loyal market segment. These market segments may be informed by emotional attachments to a particular attraction, such as a steam train, or a historic house or site. The perishability of the tourism product is also well documented (Shaw and Williams, 2004) and specifically mentioned by Porter (1998a:20): 'services such as hotel accommodations are perishable in the sense that unused capacity can never be recovered.' This adds urgency to competition in the form of rivalries amongst firms.

Other important considerations are that the overall tourism experience is constituted of multiple experiences accumulated across different attractions, and that tourism is a complex of linked industries (Papatheodorou, 2006:4) which 'exhibit demand complementarities'. There are pecuniary externalities (Scitovsky, 1954) resulting from investments in a dynamic economy, so that tourist businesses in a destination have shared interests in increasing total numbers of visitors. In other words, firms that are rivals also recognise there are advantages in competition (see Chapter 7 on cooperation). However, whether visitor attractions can respond to the complex and mixed market signals of competition, as opposed to the immediate direct, short-term interests of the firm, is questionable (Shaw and Williams, 2004), although the widespread existence of formal associations of visitor attractions suggests that they do so, at least in respect of co-marketing.

The power of buyers. Porter argues that competition depends on the number of buyers, whether an industry has undifferentiated products and whether buyers face switching costs. Visitor attractions tend to have very large numbers of individual buyers and varying levels of tour group buyers. Therefore, with the exception of larger intermediaries, individual buyers have relatively modest power – although the growth of social media size does provide a channel for expanding their power. Switching costs for most buyers are also relatively low, which significantly strengthens their collective power to shape competition. Ultimately, however, the power of buyers is shaped by product differentiation and the distinctive appeal of attractions. To what extent do potential customers consider individual visitor attractions to have substitutes and, therefore, how price (or price-quality ratio) elastic is their demand? We return to this question later.

The power of suppliers. As with any firm, how attractions respond to competition is conditional on their relationships with their suppliers, while there is also competition to secure suppliers, such as local ice cream or beer producers. In some instances, the attraction has enticed the producer to locate on site, such as the brewery at the Founders Heritage Park in Nelson, New Zealand. According to Porter, competition depends on the degree of concentration amongst suppliers, their dependence on particular markets, switching costs and whether industry products are differentiated. There is relatively limited concentration of suppliers for many of the routine purchases of attractions – such as standardised food and catering equipment, cleaning materials and security equipment. But there may be relatively few suppliers of specialist products relating to their attraction theme – such as exotic animals or plants, or historic equipment and artefacts. The power of these specialist suppliers may be increased by having national, if not international, markets, and therefore not being dependent on particular attractions. In practice, therefore, attractions often have polarised power relationships with different groups of suppliers. Whether switching costs are likely to be relatively high for suppliers will depend on the alternative customers for their products, that is on the numbers and types of substitute buyers. In such cases, competition may be counterproductive and attractions are likely to collaborate in buying such specialised and expensive services rather than compete. For example, wildlife attractions in Cornwall coordinated the visits of a specialist vet, who travelled from London to provide medical care for the animals (Weidenfeld, 2008).

The threat of new entrants stems from the assumption that they are likely to have higher productivity resulting from having the latest technologies, and are only willing to enter the market if they consider they have a competitive advantage (Foster et al., 2006). However, in practice the threat of new entrants depends on a number of considerations: whether barriers exist in the form of the economies of scale of incumbent firms, customer switching costs (both economic and emotional), capital requirements, incumbency advantages independent of size (e.g. controlling or owning a distinctive natural feature), a preference for firms used by others, unequal access to distribution channels and government regulation (Porter, 1998b). For example, the large scale Ferris wheel was first introduced at the 1893 World Fair in Chicago (Zukin, 1991), but there were only relatively weak barriers to new entrants subsequently imitating this.

Economies of scale effects in supply are, predictably, highly variable amongst visitor attractions, which can range from attracting millions to only a few thousand visitors annually. Capital requirements are similarly variable, ranging from mom and pop type businesses, focused on a particular hobby or inheritance (say a historic site or house), to high-tech mega theme parks, such as Europa-Park (Germany) and Port Aventura (Spain) (Clavé, 2007). Existing popular destinations do, however, enjoy a significant demand side benefit: Porter's notion that there is preference for companies that are used by others resonates with the idea that tourists prefer those sites whose significance is marked by the presence of others (Urry, 1990). However, even taking this into account, customer switching costs in visiting a different attraction are relatively modest, unless they have deeply engrained loyalty. An example of such emotional costs would be the loss of a cherished and long established family tradition of an annual outing to a particular site. Perhaps a more significant barrier is Porter's incumbency advantage independent of size, which could include ownership by private capital of a distinctive historical site or advantageous location: there is only one Lands End (the further west point in Cornwall in the UK) or only one set of caves with prehistoric art in Cantabria, with the reputation of those at Santillana del Mar in Spain.

Government regulation may also restrict entry through licensing, land use planning controls or health and safety requirements – that are sometimes applied only to new entrants and not retrospectively to current owners of attractions. For example, if national park regulations exclude the opening of any new commercial attractions in a park, this inevitably reduces competition for the incumbents. In addition, Papatheodorou (2006:6) argues that sunk costs are a major barrier to entry in many sectors, including tourism. Although he does not specifically mention visitor attractions, his arguments do have broader applicability:

> tourism is characterised by substantial fixed costs in transport, accommodation and in some cases technological infrastructure; airports, hotels and electronic reservation systems are good examples. These costs are largely sunk as they cannot be easily recovered due to their spatial fixity (e.g. a hotel cannot move) and asset specificity (e.g. the functionality of an airport is limited to air transport services). As a result, they may constitute significant barriers to market entry and exit.

The argument about the sunk costs in hotels and airports also applies to some degree to attractions. However, there are exceptions and, for example, collections of artefacts can be relocated relatively easily to a new museum or gallery, and the buildings they were previously housed in may have alternative functionality for other occupiers. For example, the Courtauld art collection in London relocated from Portman Square to Somerset House in 1989.

The threat from substitutes. Porter (1998b) emphasises that competition depends on the existence, or the perception of the existence, of substitutes, on whether the price/performance relationship is attractive and whether switching costs are low. For example, a visitor to Amsterdam who is interested in art and art history can choose to visit one of several excellent art galleries, the house where Rembrandt lived or (at no cost) various sites around the city that feature in particular art works. As already noted, attractions potentially face considerable competition from substitutes including entry-free attractions such as beaches or rural/urban trails, leisure and sports facilities, and even educational activities (Swarbrooke, 2001). Moreover, spending on attractions is ultimately a discretionary expenditure so that, despite the status attached to holiday taking, attractions have to compete against other non-basic expenditures, including leisure activities, retail and catering whether in the local area or in the home. Virtual attractions also pose a significant threat from substitutes, such as video and online games.

The value of Porter's work is that it draws attention to the many different facets of competition. Attractions are competing against rivals in the face of relatively low switching costs for customers, and relatively high but variable degrees of threats from substitutes. However, they are also competing in terms of suppliers, labour and – in a sense – in terms of seeking to exert influence on the policy makers who determine the regulatory environment they operate in, including the ease of entry for new competitors. Their overall competition environment is therefore complex and multi-dimensional, not least because these different forms of competition are enfolded. Moreover, the spatiality of competition adds significantly to the complexity of completion amongst visitor attractions, as discussed in the next section.

Spatial competition

It is important to understand the nature of spatial competition in the case of any firm, but especially in respect of attractions. Three features are important. First, the density of competing producers in an area is significant. If a product is homogenous, then competition will increase as the number of competitors in an area increases. For example, Syverson (2004) demonstrates that in the concrete production industry, which has a very homogeneous product, increasing density of competition makes it very difficult for inefficient firms to survive. Second, and linked to this, attractions do not provide homogeneous products so there are issues about the extent to which there is a threat of substitutability. For example, how similar or different to each other are the many casinos and gaming rooms in Las Vegas? Third, attractions face competition at different scales, both locally and extra-locally, and increasingly there is a need to rethink the idea of competition as being territorially delimited. Does the Picasso museum in Barcelona compete against other art museums, or a range of other visitor attractions in the city, or against Picasso collections elsewhere in Europe?

Buhalis (2006) has addressed the issue of scale in terms of various spatial and organisational levels. These levels provide a generalised framework for studying the spatiality of competition, although his typology is ad hoc and lacks theoretical grounding. The levels are also necessarily more complex than suggested by an idealised typology, but that of course is inherent to idealisations. Despite these limitations, it provides a useful starting point:

- Level 1: Competition from spatially proximate similar products and service providers, which facilitate 'coopetition' strategies and collaboration at the destination scale, e.g. amongst visitor attractions competing but also cooperating with other attractions in the same destination.

- Level 2: Competition from similar or undifferentiated destinations/tourist products, which encourages regional collaboration in establishing their collective brand and 'uniqueness'. Many destinations or firms have an image amongst consumers which is easily substitutable by alternative destinations, e.g. as amongst Mediterranean sun and sea destinations. They may collaborate in order to differentiate themselves and compete more effectively with other destinations.
- Level 3: Competition with differentiated destinations characterises those destinations whose 'uniqueness' (distinctiveness) in terms of natural and/or socio-cultural resources creates value which is not easily substitutable. There are also limitations in the extent to which direct challenge is possible. However, as noted in the work of Porter (1998a), the notion of substitutability is slippery, complex and highly differentiated across market segments.
- Level 4: Competition within the distribution channels reflecting the effort of each channel member to increase its own rent or profits at the expense of the members of other channels. This is based on the assumption that consumers would pay up to a certain price before switching channels.
- Level 5: Competition with alternative leisure activities and other forms of consumption at the place of origin (home). This may reduce the need or capacity for individuals to travel away from home to consume the tourism product.

Although these levels provide a relatively broad framework for studying competition in tourism, the inclusion of different types of tourism entities at different spatial scales is problematic. Tourism destinations and tourism organisations vary enormously in size, and spatial relationships and are far more complex than implied above. However, these levels do provide insights into the nature of the spatiality of competition. Level 1 refers to competition from similar product attractions and service providers which are spatially proximate. They are involved in intense competition but there is also potential to collaborate with or to compete at a different scale, that is with other destinations. Coopetition can be characterised as 'healthy competition' which allows attractions to achieve external economies of scale (Wang and Krakover, 2008), but the tensions between competition and cooperation are difficult to manage in practice.

Competition from spatially distant similar product attractions (Level 2) is less contradictory and drives regional collaboration amongst attractions to establish their brand and develop collective differentiation. Level 3 refers to competition in differentiated regions with dissimilar product attractions, whose distinctive natural and socio-cultural resources are not easily substituted. There are some limits to direct substitutability, and this provides an element of protection from competition from direct rivals, although not from the broader set of alternative targets of consumer expenditure. Level 4 addresses competition with other tourism firms within the distribution channels, as each member of the channel seeks enhanced profit margins; for example, between transport firms, travel agents, tour operators and attractions. The reintermediation of tourism channels in the internet age has challenged the competitive power of these different components of the distribution channel. Level 5 relates to competition in a broader sense, that is with recreational and leisure facilities and activities, both at places of origin and in tourism destinations.

Unsurprisingly, geographers have been especially interested in spatial competition issues. 'Tourism is a geographical phenomenon par excellence and the explicit treatment of space is essential in a supply side analysis' (Papatheodorou, 2006:4). There is a substantial literature on spatial competition, much of it drawing on neo-classical economic analyses of the locational advantages and disadvantages of firms in competition for market share, and in influencing pricing. This includes, for example, neo-classical models of spatial competition, and formal models for a limited range of institutional structures: spatial price, equilibrium, oligopolistic competition and monopolistic competition (Rushton and Thill, 1989, Williams and Kim, 1990, Plummer, 1996). These studies necessarily assume away many of the complexities of competition, which resonates with Porter's (1998a:xiv) comment that research on competition tends to be overly narrowly focused on relationships between rival firms, to the exclusion of suppliers, buyers and new entrants.

In recent years, the conceptualisation of the role of space in economic activities has re-entered mainstream economics in the form of the 'new economic geography' (Krugman, 1991, 1998) or geographical economics (Brakman et al., 2001), understood as the study of spatial relationships between economic actors (Krugman, 1991, 1998). However, economic geographers have mostly rejected the notion of distance as having a pre-ordained meaning. Instead they consider that distance is given meaning by the economic relationships amongst firms (Sheppard, 2000), and their understanding of these in relation to competition. Following Massey (1994) and Sheppard (2000), the spatiality of competition can be understood as being constituted of economic relationships amongst firms at the local, regional and international scales, characterised by sets of interconnections which constitute a socially produced space. This leads to the argument that the position, or activities, of any firm can only be understood in relation to its connectivity to other entities, that is, it is relational. In other words, there is a need to understand the network of economic relationships, at different scales, within which tourism attractions are embedded. Those relationships are not, of course, static, as is evident in the way particular museums and art galleries have repositioned themselves through signing partnership agreements with larger, more famous collections, or acquiring particular highly valued items.

Location is an inextricable part of the tourism experience (Bærenholdt and Haldrup, 2006). At one level, location is about setting or context: for many visitor attractions, the local setting can be as important as the attractions they offer (Lew, 1987). This is linked to the importance of the co-terminality of tourism production and consumption: tourists have to be present at particular tourism sites and this gives a distinctive role to the spatiality of competition. For example, tourists have fixed time-space budgets within a particular holiday (Cooper, 1981, Thornton et al., 1997), so that proximity matters, not only to the individual attractions, but also in terms of the proximity amongst all the attractions and activities that a tourist could potentially visit. There are tempo-spatial limits in terms of how they can combine different activities, including visits to particular sets of attractions while on holiday. Spatial proximity is therefore a significant influence on the forms and intensity of competition amongst attractions.

Spatiality is inherent in all of Porter's (1998b) five competitive advantages, which were discussed in the previous section. Spatiality and proximity play strategic roles in inter-firm rivalry: being spatially isolated, as opposed to clustered, can be crucial in competitive practices. A comparative advantage can be built by developing a strong and differentiated image, and one way to achieve this is to locate in a remote location that endows the attraction with an outstanding and 'unique' environmental setting. In contrast, being located within a cluster of attractions offers advantages in capturing visitors who are en route to other destinations (McKercher and Lew, 2004). Spatiality is also important in terms of the articulation of the power of buyers. Attractions that are more centrally located are more likely to be attractive to tourists with limited time-space budgets who are concerned not just with visiting a particular attraction, but also with how this is related to bundling together other activities within a given spatio-temporal framework (Thornton et al., 1997). The powers of suppliers are also mediated by how space determines the number of firms willing and able to compete to supply an attraction. Substitutability also has a clear spatial dimension with proximity to, say, shopping centres, representing a potentially important source of competition. Finally, the threat of new entrants is not homogeneous across space but is highly spatialised, being determined not only by the supply of production factors, but also by local and national land use and planning controls.

Despite recent developments, spatial competition is still under-researched in tourism, especially for attractions. The proximity of competitors can have negative (reduced market share) or positive (complementarities) consequences, depending in part on visitor preferences and switching costs, and in part on the degree of substitutability of attractions. However, what also matters is how attractions 'make economic sense' of proximity, that is how they develop economic relationships around being located in close spatial proximity to each other. Box 7.1 presents a summary of the authors' study of the spatiality of competition in Cornwall, in the UK.

'Strong' and 'weak' competitive strategies

Firms may face 'strong' or 'disruptive' versus 'weak' or 'repetitive' competition (Schumpeter, 1919), and Porter (1998b) sees this in terms of the competitive forces that shape strategies. Non-price (strong) competition can increase the total market and may raise value. 'Strong' strategies are based upon quality, product differentiation and product innovation, emphasising dynamic disequilibrium and chronic and deliberate market disturbances (Hudson, 2001). Such strategies often require companies to develop new markets. Relocation is one strategy for developing new markets but this can be problematic for those attractions which rely on particular

Box 7.1 Spatial competition in Cornwall

This study used qualitative research methods to analyse how managers understand, and respond to, the spatiality of competition in two contrasting clusters of attractions in Cornwall: a higher density cluster in Newquay and a lower density cluster in the Lizard peninsula.

a) Nature of competition

Competition for visitors was understood to be not only amongst neighbouring similar-product attractions but also with shops, pubs, and supermarkets as alternative targets for tourist spending (Swarbrooke, 2001). However, competition in both clusters was mainly for markets, i.e. for visitors' time and money (Buhalis, 2006), as indicated by an amusement attraction manager in Newquay: '… the biggest one [competition] is sharing your time and money with other attractions. The visitor only has a certain amount of disposable income and a certain amount of time available, so it is time and money'. Attractions not only compete for visitors but also attempt to retain them as long as possible on site so as to maximize spending on ancillary services and products, such as food and souvenirs. However, managers also saw competitors as potential co-operators, and these inter-firm relationships were not only difficult to manage, but were also scale differentiated.

Other forms of competition identified by Porter (1998a) were also important. The importance of competition for low cost or high quality suppliers was part of the response of managers who sought to out-compete rival attractions. Attractions also competed for labour, especially in Newquay where potential employees had relatively large numbers of accessible, alternative employers. There was less indication of competition within distribution channels, but some attraction managers emphasised the important role played by coach operators who effectively channelled visitors around selected attractions in Cornwall. They also hinted at the financial incentives that some of their competitors offered coach drivers in order to influence their itineraries.

b) The spatiality of competition

Some attraction managers claimed they had no, or almost no, competition, particularly those on the Lizard peninsula: they saw their natural and socio-cultural features as 'unique' and non-substitutable. In contrast, other attraction managers saw competition as being inter-regional, including overseas destinations. Regional collaboration in both clusters aimed to establish a brand and develop collective differentiation from other clusters, but this was relatively stronger in the Lizard peninsula as discussed below.

However, most managers also considered there was substantial competition for visitors within the clusters and that this was mainly shaped by access to markets and by travel time. More than half of the 'biggest' competitors, and most of the 'other' competitors, in both the Newquay and Lizard clusters are intra-cluster attractions. The impact of spatial proximity and agglomeration on competition was seen as positive by some managers '… because it keeps them on their toes. They have to stay competitive and they have to look at their product each year. It's the further distance [to competitors] that actually makes people more complacent'. This broadly confirms the expected relationship between competition and productivity at the intra-firm level.

c) Differences between clusters

The more spatially dispersed attraction managers in the Lizard cluster complained more about their remoteness from major urban areas than the Newquay managers. All Newquay attraction managers perceived the other intra-cluster attractions as being competitors. In contrast, only some Lizard managers held this view, indicating a less intensive competitive environment than in the Newquay cluster. Indeed, competition between attractions was perceived to be a major obstacle by some attraction managers in Newquay, but not by any managers in the Lizard cluster. In both clusters, product similarity played a key role in terms of determining which attractions were seen as competitors: the higher level of product similarity in Newquay reinforced the competition-inducing effects of a higher density of attractions in that cluster. While attractions in both clusters recognized the importance of competition from beyond the clusters, this was relatively more important in the Lizard.

Source: Weidenfeld et al. (2014).

place associations, such as Stratford-Upon-Avon, which is Shakespeare's birth place. Sunk costs can also inhibit relocation or (local) market exit (Papatheodorou, 2006). Therefore, strong competition strategies are usually worked out by firms in-situ, albeit the spatiality of relations with buyers or sellers may be realigned, for example, sourcing from new suppliers beyond the local cluster.

'Weak' competition occurs within a given technological-organisational paradigm (Hudson, 2001). Inter-firm price rivalry (Porter, 1998b) tends to be greatest when products are similar, there are low switching costs for customers and high levels of perishability. Costs, and prices, are reduced through attractions accepting lower average returns per unit of service sold and/or by minor reorganisation of the production of tourism services.

The production process occurs within and beyond the boundary of the firm, partly being constituted of networked and unevenly empowered relationships with suppliers and intermediaries. Spatiality is important here. For example, within a cluster of attractions, external economies of scale associated with availability of skilled labour, research and design facilities, and specialised suppliers can reduce costs. In some instances, however, clusters can be associated with higher costs as, for example, when competing for a limited supply of labour (Weidenfeld et al., 2014). Relationships beyond a cluster also inform firms' competitive strategies. For example, if suppliers within the cluster are relatively powerful due to strong competing demands for their goods and services, visitor attractions may seek new 'external' suppliers, in order to reduce costs as part of a weak competition strategy. But if those suppliers can provide distinctive products, then these new relationships offer potential for strong competition strategies. Furthermore, visitor attractions may prefer to collaborate with other attractions outside a cluster, as part of a strong competition strategy, in order to minimise knowledge spillovers to local rivals.

Finally, it must be emphasised that the distinction between 'weak' and 'strong' competition has to be understood as schematic rather than as a strict dichotomy, as firms engage in many different strategies within each of these polar types as well as combining both (Shaw and Williams, 2004). This makes it particularly difficult to unravel the complexity of competition practices. Indeed, in Weidenfeld et al.'s (2014) study of competition in clusters in Cornwall (see Box 7.1), the competitive strategies of attractions inevitably were located on a continuum between these two poles, rather than at either pole.

Conclusions

This chapter has explored the nature of the competition amongst attractions, and the consequences in terms of productivity and competitiveness. Competition is becoming increasingly globalised and intensified, so that it is difficult for attractions to protect themselves through reliance on customers' lack of information, or on the assumption of territorially bounded competition, or on government regulations. Even well-established visitor attractions can face severe consequences if they fail to address effectively the challenge of competition, as is illustrated by the experiences of New York's Coney Island amusement parks (see Box 7.2).

Although competition initially seems to be a relatively straightforward concept, the discussion in this chapter has indicated two important sources of complexity. The first is the nature of the competition, and here the starting point was Porter's (1998a:xiv) assertion that 'competition is often defined too narrowly, as if it occurred only between direct rivals'. Instead, he identified five main forces that provide a shorthand for understanding the broader influences that have shaped competition: the intensity of rivalry amongst existing firms, the power of buyers, the power of suppliers, the threat of new entry and the threat of substitutability. Some of these influences are generic, but others take specific form in the attractions sector due especially to the importance of the co-terminality of production and consumption, the changing power of buyers, the variable degree of substitutability between attractions and the spatiality of competition.

The spatiality of competition is the second important source of complexity. Competition occurs at several different levels, including the international, the inter-regional and the intra-locality. The density of competing attractions within a locality and the substitutability of their products really do matter in terms of how competition is experienced and practiced. Competition is mainly understood in terms of market shares (Middleton and Clarke, 2001), but it is not only for disposable expenditures but also for time (and space) budgets. The competition for labour and suppliers within and extra to the locality is also significant. This is not to say that proximity and spatial competition have absolute or objective meanings. Rather they are constituted as part of the economic relationships amongst firms and are therefore informed by the wider institutional framework. For example, the degree and nature of trust amongst actors significantly shapes how managers work out a relationship which balances cooperation and competition. This is not simply an academic issue of how to conceptualise competition, because the practices that firms adopt, in the face of the spatiality and reality of competition,

Box 7.2 Competition and Coney Island

Coney Island, New York's playground, exemplifies the rise and fall of the amusement park, as a culturally and technologically defined attraction. Coney Island, in fact, is an amalgam of visitor attractions, which began attracting visitors, mainly from New York, from the 1830s. Large new hotels opened to cater for overnight tourists, but improvements in steamship, train and tramcar connections meant that it mainly became a destination for day excursionists.

The golden years of Coney Island's amusement parks – and there were three main ones in this period – were from about 1880 to World War Two. During these years Dreamland, Luna Park and Steeplechase Park were locked into intense competition-cooperation relationships. Together, their critical mass of facilities, and collective reputation, made them a strong magnet to draw visitors not only from New York, but from across the USA. But at the same time, the three spatially proximate, and largely thematically proximate, parks competed fiercely to gain market share amongst the mobile consumers who journeyed out from the city.

Competition drove innovation in an intense battle for market shares and, indeed, for survival. The very first amusement ride was a carousel of carved wooden horses which was installed in 1876 at what became known as the Balmer Pavilion, another of the competing amusement centres at Coney Island. Subsequently, several new, technologically state-of-the-art amusement parks were opened, and these attained an iconic status, that was subsequently recognized when they were listed and protected as major New York landmarks: the Wonder Wheel (opened 1920), the Cyclone roller coaster (1927), and the Parachute (originated at the 1939 New York World Fair).

The Coney Island amusement parks were also locked into competition with a range of other attractions, at different spatial scales. The growth of car ownership meant that many families used their new spatial flexibility to visit the quieter beaches of Long Island, and the amusement parks lost a significant part of their proximate, mobile market who had hitherto depended on public transport from New York. Meanwhile, there was competition from nearer to home attractions such as cinemas and theatres, and eventually there would be strong competition from the more technologically and marketing sophisticated Disney parks in California and Florida. Of the three main amusement parks, Luna Park was the first to close in 1946: although this was precipitated by a series of fires, the reshaping of market conditions by competition deterred new investment to rebuild the park. Steeplechase Park battled on but it eventually closed in 1964. Innovation declined, and there was a gap of more than eighty years before a new roller coaster was again opened at Coney Island.

Coney Island did not, however, just roll over in the face of competition. Instead, a series of innovations sought to refresh the appeal of its multitude of attractions. Dreamland and Luna Park were reinvented, and reopened in 2009–2010, while new amusement parks such as Astroland were opened. Innovation also sought to close the gap with its main competitors. Most spectacularly, a new Thunderbolt roller coaster was opened in 2014, which included a vertical drop and a zero-gravity roll.

Sources: Kasson (1978), Denson (2002).

will determine whether they prosper, survive or die. Those practices include inno-vation, and the next chapter considers knowledge transfer, which is one of the most important of these practices.

References

Bærenholdt, J. O. and Haldrup, M. (2006). Mobile networks and place making in cultural tourism: Staging Viking ships and rock music in Roskilde. *European Urban and Regional Studies*, *13*, 209–224.

Baum, J. and Mezias, S. (1992). Localized competition and organisational failure in the Manhattan hotel industry. *Administrative Science Quarterly*, *37*, 580–604.

Baumol, W. (2002). *The Free Market Innovation Machine: Analyzing the Growth Miracle of Capitalism*. Princeton: Princeton University Press.

Baumol, W., Panzar, J. and Willig, R. (1982). *Contestable Markets and the Theory of Industrial Structure*. New York: Harcourt Brace Jovanovich.

Brakman, S., Garretsen, H. and Marrewijk, C. V. (2001). *An Introduction to Geographical Economics*. Cambridge, UK: Cambridge University Press.

Buhalis, D. (2006). The impact of information technology on tourism competition. In A. Papatheodorou (Ed.), *Corporate Rivalry and Market Power, Competition Issues in Tourism: an Introduction* (pp. 143–171). London: I.B. Tauris.

Butler R. and Weidfenfeld A. (2012). Cooperation and competition during the resort lifecycle. *Tourism Recreation Research*, *37*, 15–26.

Clavé, S. A. (2007). *The Global Theme Park Industry*. Wallingford: CABI.

Cooper, C. (1981). Spatial and temporal patterns of tourist behaviour. *Regional Studies*, *15*, 359–371.

Cornelis, P. C. M. (2011). *Attraction accountability: Predicting the unpredictable?!* Nieuwegein: NRIT Media.

Denson, C. (2002). *Coney Island: Lost and Found*. New York: Ten Speed Press.

Disney, R. Haskel, J. E. and Heden, Y. (2003). Entry, exit and establishment survival in UK manufacturing. *Journal of Industrial Economics*, *51*(1), 91–112.

Foster, L., Haltiwanger, J. and Krizan, C. J. (2001). Aggregate productivity growth: Lessons from microeconomic evidence. In C. R. Hulten, E. R. Dean and M. J. Harper (Eds), *New Developments in Productivity Analysis* (pp. 303–363). Chicago and London: University of Chicago Press.

Foster, L., Haltiwanger, J. and Krizan, C. J. (2006). Market selection, reallocation, and restructuring in the U.S. retail trade sector in the 1990s. *Review of Economics and Statistics*, *88*(4), 748–758.

Hudson, R. (2001). *Producing Places*. New York: Guilford Press.

Kasson, J. F. (1978). *Amusing the Millions*. New York: Hill & Wang.

Krugman, P. (1991). Increasing returns and economic geography. *Journal of Political Economy*, *99*, 483–499.

Krugman, P. (1998). *The Role of Geography in Development*. Paper prepared for the Annual World Bank Conference on Development Economics, Washington, D.C., 20–21 April.

Lei, Z. (2006). The theoretical pillars of industrial organization in tourism. In A. Papatheodorou (Ed.), *Corporate Rivalry and Market Power: Competition Issues in the Tourism Industry* (pp. 20–34). London: I.B. Tauris.

Lew, A. (1987). A framework of tourist attraction research. *Annals of Tourism Research*, *14*, 553–575.

McKercher, B. and Lew, A. (2004). Tourist flows and the spatial distribution of tourists. In A. Lew, M. C. Hall and A. M. Williams (Eds), *A Companion to Tourism* (pp. 36–48). Malden, MA: Blackwell.

Massey, D. (1994). *Space, Place and Gender*. Cambridge, UK: Polity Press.

Metcalfe, J. S. (2005). *Innovation, Competition and Enterprise: Foundations for Economic Evolution in Learning Economies*. Manchester: University of Manchester, Centre for Innovation and Competition, Discussion Paper 71.

Middleton, V. T. C. and Clarke, J. (2001). *Marketing in Travel and Tourism*. Oxford: Utterworth-Heinemann.

Papatheodorou, A. (2006). Corporate rivalry, market power and competition issues in tourism: An introduction. In A. Papatheodorou (Ed.), *Corporate Rivalry and Market Power: Competition Issues in the Tourism Industry* (pp. 1–18). London: I.B. Tauris.

Patsouratis, V., Frangouli, Z. and Anastasopoulos, G. (2005). Competition in tourism among the Mediterranean countries. *Applied Economics, 37*(16), 1865–1870.

Plummer, P. (1996). Spatial competition amongst hierarchically organized corporations: Prices, profits, and shipment patterns. *Environment and Planning A, 28*, 199–222.

Porter, M. (1998a). *On Competition*. Cambridge, MA: Harvard Business School Press.

Porter, M. (1998b). Location, clusters and the 'new' microeconomics of competition. *Business Economics*, 7–13.

Rushton, G. and Thill, J.-C. (1989). The effect of distance metric on the degree of spatial competition between firms. *Environment and Planning A, 21*, 499–507.

Schumpeter, J. (1919). *The Theory of Economic Development*. Cambridge. MA: Harvard University Press.

Scitovsky, T. (1954). Two concepts of external economies. *Journal of Political Economy, LXII*, 143–151.

Shaw, G. and Williams, A. M. (2004). *Tourism and Tourism Spaces*. London: Sage.

Sheppard, E. (2000). Geography or economics? Conceptions of space, time, interdependence, and agency. In G. L. Clark, M. P. Feldman and M. S. Gertler (Eds), *Oxford Handbook of Economic Geography* (pp. 99–199). Oxford: Oxford University Press.

Sinclair, T. M. and Stabler, M. (1997). *The Economics of Tourism*. London and New York: Routledge.

Stigler, G. (1961). Economics of information. *The Journal of Political Economy, 69*(3), 213–225.

Swarbrooke, J. (2001). Key challenges for visitor attraction managers in the UK. *Journal of Leisure Property, 1*, 318–336.

Syverson, C. (2004). Market structure and productivity: A concrete example. *Journal of Political Economy, 112*(6), 1181–1222.

Thornton, P., Williams, A. M. and Shaw, G. (1997). Revisiting time space diaries: An exploratory case study of tourist behaviour in Cornwall, England. *Environment and Planning A, 29*, 1847–1867.

Urry, J. (1990). *The Tourist Gaze: Leisure and Travel in Contemporary Societies*. London: Sage Publications.

Wang, Y. and Krakover, S. (2008). Destination marketing: Competition, cooperation, or coopetition? *International Journal of Contemporary Hospitality Management, 20*, 126–141.

Wanhill, S. (2006). Competition in visitor attractions. In A. Papatheodorou (Ed.), *Corporate Rivalry and Market Power: Competition Issues in the Tourism Industry* (pp. 172–186). Londo: I.B. Tauris.

Weidenfeld A. (2008). *'The Destination Story' Cooperation, Competition and Knowledge Transfer Between Tourist Attractions in Cornwall*. Geography, University of Exeter.

Weidenfeld, A., Williams, A. M. and Butler, R. (2014). Spatial competition and agglomeration in the visitor attraction sector. *Service Industries Journal, 34*(3), 175–195.

Williams, H. C. W. L. and Kim, K. (1990). Location-spatial interaction models: Competition between independent firms. *Environment and Planning A, 22,* 1155–1168.

Zukin, S. (1991). *Landscapes of Power: From Detroit to Disney World.* Berkeley: University of California Press.

8   Knowledge transfer in the visitor attraction sector

Introduction

The importance of knowledge, and its management as a competitive tool, was recognised by practitioners long before its emergence as an academic field in the 1980s. Knowledge management is the practice of capturing, encompassing, identifying, processing, preparing, developing, transferring and applying individual and collective knowledge into practice. While this offers potential advantages to organisations, it also can involve costs (Bathelt et al., 2004, Cooper, 2006, Hallin and Marnburg, 2008). Knowledge management and transfer are key components of constant learning and innovation and are vital for gaining and retaining competitive advantage. Within tourism, research on knowledge management and transfer processes is a growing research theme (Poon, 1993, Nordin and Svensson, 2005, Hjalager, 2002, Hjalager et al., 2008, Cooper, 2006, Brackenbury, 2006, Decelles, 2006, Scheidegger, 2006, Weirmaier, 2006, Keller, 2006a, 2006b, Nieves et al., 2014, Borges et al., 2012). This chapter provides a theoretical background for understanding knowledge transfer processes in the visitor attraction sector by identifying different types of knowledge and exploring their management, transfer and sharing with other businesses as well as the different mechanisms and channels which facilitate these processes.

Knowledge management and innovation

Knowledge is defined broadly as 'the use of skills and experience, to add intelligence to information in order to make decisions or provide reliable grounds for action' (Cooper, 2006:52). It is not simply information related to data, but it constitutes a wider process that involves cognitive structured knowledge that assimilates information, interprets this and puts it into a broader context, thereby allowing actions to be undertaken on that basis (Hall and Williams, 2008:77). Information exists independently of the receiver and transmitter and knowledge is information that has been translated so that humans understand it. One viewpoint is that knowledge cannot be said to 'flow' but can be said to be 'shared' or 'transferred' (Hall and Williams, 2008). Knowledge has a variety of overlapping forms and, for example, can be aesthetic, cognitive, scientific, discursive, digital, information, tacit, explicit, emancipatory, embrained, embodied, encultured, embedded and encoded. Whatever the precise form, it is central to the operations of contemporary advanced economies (Henry and Pinch, 2000, Williams, 2005, 2006). Unlike Hall and Williams (2008), however, Hudson (2005) contends that knowledge transfer involves a variety of flows, within firms, between firms, between producers and consumers, and between private sector and public sector organisations, which characteristically have blurred boundaries (Williams, 2005, 2006). Knowledge has to be transferred but also managed effectively and efficiently within and between organisations and individuals in order to bring about change and innovation.

Knowledge management in the context of tourism can be seen as applying the knowledge assets available to a tourism organisation to create a competitive advantage, such as the application of new technologies which may improve queuing systems and improve the visitor experience of rides in theme parks (Cooper, 2006). Knowledge has to be managed effectively before, during and after being transferred – transfer on its own will not realise the full potential for innovation and competitiveness. Capturing knowledge involves a process of identification (locating and evaluating) and then codifying is usually vital for processing knowledge before being transferred. For example, 'complicated and non-focused research results have to be distilled, codified, and modulated before they flow into tourism to become part of practical operations' (Hjalager, 2002:471). Similarly, Cooper (2006) describes three aspects of knowledge management and transfer: capturing tacit knowledge, codifying tacit and explicit knowledge, and its effective diffusion in society and space. Tacit knowledge is not easily visible and expressible, but is highly personal, hard to formalise, difficult to codify and includes that passed from master to apprentice (Nonaka and Takeuchi, 1995, Cooper, 2006).

The effective capture of tacit knowledge requires the identification of the strategic objectives of the specific knowledge management project and also the knowledge sources to be utilised. It involves the identification of business processes and their associated knowledge centres, such as research, sales and marketing, and also profiling individuals including members of staff and/or customers in order to identify the knowledge required. As knowledge harvesting necessarily involves costs, the intended outcome is that only relevant knowledge is collected. The sources of knowledge to an organisation or destination can be internal (often senior employees) and external (such as customers, suppliers, consultants) (Cooper, 2006). Tourism, in common with most other consumer services, is less likely to acquire knowledge and technology from R&D or from purchasing heavy equipment than from cooperation with customers and suppliers (Tether, 2004). Furthermore, 'the sources of knowledge are constantly changing, and the challenge for the tourism firms is to adapt to new sources of knowledge' (Hall and Williams, 2008:92). Theme parks, for example, need to collect knowledge about their visitors' preferences, about their competitors, about new technologies for both backroom operations and their front of house visitor attractions, and about new suppliers. There is no single best way to collect such knowledge. Instead, tacit and explicit knowledge are organised to be efficiently transferred to the right people at the right time by being codified and assessed using appropriate techniques such as data mining, predictive tools, knowledge maps, storyboards and computer based systems (Cooper, 2006).

Effectiveness of knowledge transfer and diffusion

The goal of knowledge transfer and diffusion is the effective transfer and use of knowledge to contribute to competitiveness, which probably represents the most fundamental challenge in tourism, as in most other sectors. Knowledge transfer involves the process of diffusion in society and space, i.e. between different individuals, and groups of actors. Knowledge transfer tends to be considered mainly in terms of transformation from tacit to explicit knowledge and vice versa (Cooper, 2006). This is particularly germane to the collective knowledge shared between stakeholders through various practices and circulated through frequent and intensive interactions. For example, the joint planning meetings for the development of new major visitor attractions such as large museums, as exemplified by a new Jewish museum in Warsaw. This is a foundation, to which representatives of a range of private, public and non-governmental organisation (NGO) bodies bring codified (in the form of documents, data bases, etc.) and tacit (personal) knowledge to the table, and also apply their tacit knowledge to explain their own codified knowledge and to interrogate the knowledge of other participants.

Tacit knowledge is not easily made visible and expressible: instead, it is highly personal, hard to formalise and difficult to codify (Nonaka and Takeuchi, 1995, Cooper, 2006). From this comes a critical advantage. The key to acquiring tacit knowledge is experience and it is therefore challenging, so that tacit knowledge is likely to remain an important resource of the firm. The most significant implication of knowledge being uncodifiable and not amenable or transferable to others is that it can be a source of competitive advantage (Hudson, 1999) as it is difficult to acquire and use for imitative innovation by competitors. Blackler (2002, cited by Williams, 2006) identified four main types of tacit knowledge:

a. *Embrained* knowledge is dependent on conceptual skills and cognitive abilities, which allow recognition of underlying patterns, and reflection on these. The individual mind-set is a key influence on learning and, for example, an accountant and a creative designer will bring substantially different cognitive abilities to a new visitor attraction's events planning meeting;
b. *Embodied* knowledge results from experiences of physical presence (for example, via project work). This is practical thinking rooted in specific contexts, physical presence, sentient and sensory information and learning by doing. An internal designer, an assembler of displays or an architect all bring specific and contrasting embodied knowledge to the operational side of an attraction;
c. *Encultured* knowledge emphasises that meanings are shared understandings, arising from socialisation and acculturation. Language, stories, sociality and metaphors are mainsprings of knowledge, and visitor attraction developers need to understand the different cultural knowledge held by their staff, customers and local residents; and

d.   *Embedded* knowledge is contained in contextual factors and is not objectively pre-given and is more relevant to event attractions. For example, reproducing a popular exhibition which has been displayed in several museums requires embedded knowledge of regulations and routines.

Creativity is pivotal in tourism innovation. In major visitor attractions, the semi-permanent or temporary teams' role is to think imaginatively and initiate ideas for new attractions (Hall and Williams, 2008). Knowledge creation in tourism includes several dimensions including *socialisation*, which is the conversion of new tacit knowledge into the existing base of tacit knowledge. It is followed by *externalisation*, which is the conversion of tacit knowledge into explicit knowledge through verbalisation and *combination*, which refers to the conversion of explicit knowledge into more systematic and complex forms of explicit knowledge. Finally, explicit knowledge is converted into tacit knowledge which can involve internationalisation (Werner et al., 2015). Destinations create and use knowledge constantly in order to adapt to changing conditions of supply and demand in a competitive environment (Cooper, 2006).

One important element in this is technology. Technology plays a major role in tourism by enhancing the visitor experience at the attraction location; for example, using virtual reality and interactive media (Watson and McCracken, 2002). These are rapidly becoming part of the standard tourism experience. In addition, travel agents essentially trade on the basis of other knowledge advantages. They provide feedback from their customers to the industry, and are also selling their commodified tacit and codified knowledge to the customers in the form of tourism packages. When knowledge is managed effectively, it may yield profitability and customer satisfaction, e.g. hotel chains and airlines use data about their customers to improve services or their marketing (Cooper, 2006). The critical question for any organisation is how best to realise such knowledge transfers. Currently there is contradictory evidence about whether tacit knowledge is transferred more efficiently by relational proximity (i.e. achieved via individuals with shared meanings and understandings) or by spatial proximity (Williams, 2005). The lack of research is hardly surprising given that the processes of knowledge circulation is often untraded, intangible, covert, sometimes immoral and even illegal (Henry and Pinch, 2000).

Explicit knowledge is transferable and easy to codify, and can be found in documents and data bases, with the latter having increased enormously in importance in the digital economy. It represents the knowledge capital of an organisation that is independent of its workers (Cooper, 2006). Explicit knowledge provides the infrastructure that people work with and within. It is formal and systemic, easily communicated and expressed in words and numbers (Nonaka and Takeuchi, 1995, Cooper, 2006). For an attraction or event this is typified by the data bases it holds on visitors and participants. Organisations also need to identify the tacit knowledge held by individuals or collectively by groups of workers, and transfer this to the organisational level, so that it can be: a) redistributed to other workers; and b) becomes part of the organisational resource base (Hall and Williams, 2008). A particular need in attractions is to identify, capture and convert the tacit knowledge of customers and of employees (who are at the heart of the service encounter) to explicit knowledge. There is much less evidence of the contribution of tourists in this regard than of employees and external suppliers. This was the case in Weidenfeld et al.'s (2010) study on visitor attractions in Cornwall, south west England. Many employees in wildlife attractions were 'knowledge transfer agents' and idea makers using the knowledge obtained from working previously in other wildlife attractions. In addition, the same study provided evidence of the importance to attractions of using external suppliers as sources of ideas, particularly on new, and improvements to, facilities.

Knowledge transfers occur within networks at both the micro level and macro level. At the micro level, tacit knowledge is created 'in-house' within organisations, through organisational routines, whereby individual knowledge is converted into organisational knowledge, forming the basis of collective learning within organisations (Eisenhardt and Santos, 2002). At the macro level, inter-organisational networks tend to transfer more explicit knowledge from the supply side, although various forms of tacit knowledge are also important (e.g. observation of rivals, conversations with others in the same sector). Given that explicit knowledge is generally considered easier for competitors to imitate, tacit knowledge is increasingly seen as a key to competitiveness and when it becomes more explicit, it is transferred to others and can result in a boost to competitiveness in a tourism destination (Cooper, 2006). Assuming that 'human knowledge is created and expanded through social interaction between tacit knowledge and explicit knowledge', the latter are both complementary entities; and 'they interact with and interchange into each other in the creative activities of human beings' (Nonaka and Takeuchi, 1995:61). This interaction occurs in four ways:

- Tacit to tacit transfers through socialisation, where ideas are discussed and exchanged, for example at meetings, team discussions among producers and between product developers and customers, both before product development and after market introduction.
- Tacit to explicit or externalisation through brainstorming and the use of professionals such as consultants, discussants and focus groups. In this process, identified personal knowledge held by individuals or groups is codified in reports, manuals or guidelines and disseminated within a company (Hall and Williams, 2008). This is a quintessential knowledge-creation process taking the form of metaphors, analogies, concepts, hypotheses and models; in the development of the Dark Sky Route in the first Starlight Tourism Destination in Portugal, a scheme was prepared in association with the Portuguese Amateur Astronomers Association, aimed at developing professional training to tourism entrepreneurs in order to enhance their guiding skills and develop activities with tourists who have little knowledge of stargazing (Rodrigues et al., 2015).
- Explicit to explicit involves moving knowledge or concepts (systemising concepts) around a network of organisations, or within an organisation, through media such as documents, manuals, data files, film or computers.

For example, middle managers' corporate visions, business models or product concepts.

• Explicit to tacit or internalisation involves generating new ideas from a written document, e.g. a report. This is 'learning by doing' when experience is internalised into individuals' tacit knowledge in the form of technical know-how and mental models (similar to assets). Documents and other written material such as manuals and oral stories where knowledge is verbalised and diagrammed help this process.

In practice, effective knowledge transfer and management involves different combinations of these four types. The combination of different types of knowledge transfers is likely to be variable across attractions and events, but surprisingly little is known about this. When knowledge is transferred, the effectiveness of its absorption is influenced by the willingness of both the knowledge provider and the recipient to collaborate in knowledge sharing. In the case of an attraction, this is partly dependent upon management orientation towards learning and partly on perceived profitability or return from the time and other resources devoted to this task. Learning orientation of an organisation is a set of organisational values that influence the propensity of the firm to create and use knowledge, including open-mindedness, commitment to learning and shared vision (Sinkula et al., 1997) and can be transferred through the hierarchical chains in organisations by authorising other managers to 'open-up' or adopt external knowledge to the firm (Steenkamp et al., 1999, Tajeddini, 2011).

The transfer is influenced by the knowledge gap between the two, and when this is too wide, the recipient will face difficulties assimilating the knowledge transferred (Hall and Williams, 2008). There are also issues relating to the form or the type of knowledge. Explicit knowledge is transferable and codified, and, as noted above, can be found in forms, documents and electronic data bases. It represents the tangible knowledge capital of an organisation, whereas tacit knowledge has been shown to be not easily visible and expressible, but rather highly personal, hard to formalise and difficult to codify (Nonaka and Takeuchi, 1995, Cooper, 2006). Firms usually need to combine different forms of knowledge transfer, incorporating both codified and tacit, if they are to successfully manage and utilise knowledge.

Channels of, and barriers to, knowledge transfer in tourism

Hall and Williams (2008) suggest that there are four main channels or mechanisms of knowledge transfer: learning by observation/imitation/demonstration; labour mobility; inter-firm exchanges; and knowledge brokers. A different perspective is provided by Hjalager (2002) who emphasises the roles of regulation, trade, infrastructural and technological systems in knowledge transfer (discussed later in this chapter).

The relevance and effectiveness of these channels is highly contingent on the internal characteristics of the attractions, and the external operating environment, as discussed below.

Learning by observation/imitation/demonstration

Flows of information and knowledge transfers can take several forms: they can be planned, unplanned and/or uncoordinated knowledge spillovers. These can be enacted in a number of different ways including via observation, by 'espionage' and/or through interchanges within communities of association. We contend, and explore later, the notion that attraction managers and staff pay more attention to unplanned and uncoordinated visits (sometimes, even 'espionage') than planned knowledge transfers. Some forms of knowledge transfer extend across all three categories. For example, an important characteristic of attractions is that planned and unplanned observation is a key form of knowledge transfer given the difficulties of concealing innovations in 'front of house' operations. Planned visits of visitor attractions' managers do play an important role in learning and knowledge transfer, for example as a part of the activities offered to members of tourism associations and also individually to attractions at destinations (Weidenfeld et al., 2010). For example, in 2014, the IAAPA offered facility tours to a number of visitor attractions in the US, guided by professionals from the attractions, such as Epcot at the Walt Disney World Resort, Kennedy Space Centre, the Space Shuttle Atlantis and Fun Spot America Orlando. At Fun Spot, team members led a guided tour including three tracks (operations, maintenance and marketing) and provided extensive time for questions and discussion of their approach to customer service. This was in addition to visiting exhibitions where managers could learn about new facilities and technologies, and discuss innovative ideas at an international forum.

There is also an important spatial dimension to such learning and knowledge transfer, which has significant implications for innovation. Local knowledge, including cultural, natural, identity, etc., is key in regional tourism innovation, such as knowledge about outdoor life, the rural lifestyle and the Sami culture, which were crucial elements for the differentiation of a local tourist offer in Norway (Bertella, 2011). Direct global linkages of SMEs in general, particularly those in peripheral regions (Bathelt et al., 2004), are considered to have a great contribution to knowledge and innovation of tourism businesses. In particular, it is likely that some visitor attractions learn about new ideas from distant attractions (located outside their region or even their country), and this is more likely to be a significant or even radical product innovation in the context of their own regions. In contrast, they are less likely to gain knowledge leading to radical innovation locally, but may acquire knowledge from neighbouring attractions that contributes to incremental innovation (Box 8.1, and see Chapter 9).

Knowledge transfer by labour mobility

Mobile individuals play an important role in flows of knowledge through inter- and extra-firm mobility. Tacit or personalised knowledge is transferred by the physical movement of workers who have been exposed to working in organisations with superior technology and different collective or organisational

---

Box 8.1 Local and global knowledge transfer channels between visitor attractions in Lolland Foster, Denmark

In the family holiday destination of Lolland Foster on an island in the southern part of Denmark, which is assumed to fall in-between the stagnation and decline stages on Butler's (1980) Tourism Area Life Cycle, a group of dissimilar visitor attractions including a zoo, a Go kart, and a theme park developed a collaborative exploratory network in terms of knowledge transfer. Trust has been built over a long time and enabled significant exchange of knowledge and ideas amongst the members. In the case of the amusement park, loose inspirational relations and visits to visitor attractions around the world were the knowledge transfer mechanisms whereby ideas for solutions to new facilities within the park were absorbed, and later exploited in collaboration with both global and local networks with local and global suppliers. Temporary project based innovation networks were constantly developed and became a common practice for the theme park, but the non-local networks were more important for innovation at the individual visitor attraction. This dynamic nature enhanced the innovation process in the provision of different and new knowledge. Even in the case of another wildlife visitor attraction, managed by a lifestyle entrepreneur, whose main interest was breeding crocodiles, strong international networks with other actors specializing in crocodiles and other animals were his main source of knowledge. His network resulted in mainly incremental innovation and no real exchange of knowledge between him and other local actors.

Source: Sørensen and Fuglsang (2014).

---

knowledge bases. In the diffusion of knowledge across space, Henry and Pinch (2000) distinguish between ideas which 'move' in space and the knowledge embodied literally in people travelling across space. The latter constitute 'ideas knowledge transfer agents'. Labour mobility is likely to be particularly important in sectors, such as tourism, that have high levels of labour turnover. Not only do the mobile workers (and entrepreneurs) move across space, but they also move between sectors. For example, the founder of Madame Tussauds waxworks museum learnt wax modelling from the doctor who employed her mother as a housekeeper in Austria, and then came to London to cooperate in a failed pioneering magic lantern business, before setting up the highly successful waxworks exhibition.

Inter-firm exchange: 'collaboration and suppliers'

Collaboration between attractions constitutes planned knowledge spillovers or exchanges, as firms work together at particular stages in the production chain. This collaboration may be either vertical, that is with suppliers, or intermediaries (e.g. attractions with tour operators), or horizontal, that is with other tourism attractions. Horizontal collaboration may include working, and sharing knowledge, with potential competitors, for example engagement in destination wide marketing campaigns. Compared to manufacturing, services generally are thought to rely less on in-house R&D, and more on buying in knowledge and innovations via purchases from suppliers, notably of technology. The new aquarium, Acuario Inbursa in the Nuevo Polanco district in Mexico City, for example, offers an innovative design. The designer was Fernando Romero (and his firm FR-EE) who drew on the knowledge and experience he had acquired in designing Soumaya Museum, and other museums in the US, Asia and Mexico.

Knowledge brokers

Knowledge brokers are influential individuals who operate within and between distinctive knowledge communities (Tushman and Scanlan, 1981) and they can play a key role in knowledge transfer in tourism. They may operate at different levels, national and international, and include both professional consultants and company employees: an example of the latter would be representatives of a multi-national theme park group who have been seconded to work in a different country, thereby acquiring distinctive knowledge as a result (Hall and Williams, 2008), and becoming knowledge brokers who can straddle, or negotiate between, two different knowledge communities.

Communities of practice

Scientific communities and professional practitioners can also act as knowledge brokers amongst visitor attractions; for example, zoologists or other animal specialists may advise a number of zoos and other attractions with animals, and may bridge the scientific and commercial attractions communities. Similarly, consulting engineers play a similar role in relation to amusement parks. Scientific communities, for example, have contributed to knowledge transfer to Icelandic and Norwegian whale watching tour companies. Interactions amongst members of communities of practice, including scientists, tour guides and tourists (who are temporary and constantly changing), also contributed to knowledge and stimulated innovations, particularly through co-creation. Communities of practice are a theoretical framework by Wenger, which refer to groups of actors sharing similar concerns or a passion for something they do and learn how to improve through regular interactions amongst its members including conversations and brainstorming (Wenger, 1998, cited by Hall and Williams, 2008). In Norway, many actors sustain their living on the valorisation of local resources and turning them into tourist attractions via collaboration, such as the programme named 'Kort og Godt' (KoG) coming from a Norwegian slogan denoting 'plain speaking'. This offers financial support to groups of firms that cooperate in order to develop short-stay innovative tourist packages (Bertella, 2011). Such communities of practice, whose members develop common knowledge, overlapping values and a shared identity, interact with tourists and are able to co-create (Hoarau and Kline, 2014).

Systems of knowledge transfers

As noted above, Hjalager (2002:471) provides a different typology of 'systems' of knowledge transfer (Figure 8.1): trade, technological service, infrastructural and regulation systems:

a.   The trade system: Trade in both services and goods provides a means of transferring knowledge, at least explicit knowledge. This can be facilitated by personal relationships, or by trade associations, as well as by the knowledge embedded in the traded goods and services. A simple example would be where an entrepreneur bought a souvenir at one visitor attraction in order to acquire the knowledge which is embedded in this, with a view to producing similar or related souvenirs.

b.   The technological system: knowledge transferred through purchases or leases of technology. The level of such transfers depends in part on the extent to which the production of the visitor attraction technological system is undertaken in-house, or is outsourced. This can be exemplified by the buying in of a range of technologies by developers of a new visitor attraction, such as rides for visitors or audio-visual equipment.

c.   The regulation system: regulation assumes various forms of mandatory actions, prohibitions and penalties. This system contains a substantial body of knowledge, which is disseminated to individual firms, for example relating to safety and health hazards. Such knowledge transfer leads to changes in, for example, the provision of fire escapes, or food hygiene practices in an attraction's café.

d.   The infrastructural system: tourism is often based on 'free goods' such as townscapes, natural resources and cultural attractions, which are often developed and managed by public bodies such as local authorities. Innovation and management in relation to these 'free goods' often depend on, and are executed by, such public bodies. The quality of these innovations depends on the knowledge possessed by the key bodies.

The innovative processes in the tourism industry are characterised more by barriers and constraints than by accelerators. These include low levels of linkages between tourism and R&D; lack of funding and risk taking, lack of trust and cooperation between tourism entrepreneurs, rapid change of ownership, low levels of education and training amongst staff, a high turnover of workforce, low salaries and unconventional working hours, and 'free-riding' (Hjalager, 2002, Nordin, 2003).

Conclusions

Knowledge transfer is a key factor in innovation in visitor attractions and is part of a long chain of relationships which may result in product or process innovation, an aspect which will be explored in the next chapter. The sources of knowledge in an organisation or destination can be internal and/or external. They can provide tacit and explicit knowledge that can be efficiently transferred between individuals and organisations by different types of knowledge channels and mechanisms. Codified knowledge is of course easier to transfer. However, tacit knowledge is a key to innovation and is embedded in different individuals including members of staff and also visitors, who are also knowledge transfer agents at the intra- and inter-regional scales. Tacit knowledge is often invisible, highly personal, hard to formalise and difficult to codify but is considered an important resource of a firm.

Collective knowledge shared between stakeholders through various practices is also circulated through frequent and intensive interactions. Attractions usually need to combine different forms of knowledge transfer, such as the mechanisms or channels. These are used by attractions to convert both codified and tacit knowledge if they are successfully to manage and utilise knowledge while overcoming the barriers to efficient management of knowledge transfer. The channels by which knowledge is transferred between visitor attractions are learning by observation/imitation/demonstration; mobility and inter-firm exchange; and systems of knowledge transfer including trade, technological, regulation and infrastructure.

International links are likely to lead to knowledge transfer with potential for product innovation but so also is local knowledge transfer amongst visitor attractions in the destination. In general, the processes and mechanisms of knowledge transfer between visitor attractions are essentially similar to those in other tourism enterprises, rather than representing specific or unique elements to this particular sub-sector. Individual firms will blend together different forms of knowledge and knowledge transfer, and the most fertile mixes will produce the more effective innovations. The chemistry of knowledge transfer is, however, difficult to micro manage because individual firms will participate in a shifting, part planned, part informal, part serendipitous mix of knowledge acquisition and sharing mechanisms.

References

Bathelt, H., Malmberg, A. and Maskell, P. (2004). Clusters and knowledge: Local buzz, global pipelines and the process of knowledge creation. *Progress in Human Geography*, *28*, 31–56.

Bertella, G. (2011). Communities of practice in tourism: Working and learning together. An illustrative case study from Northern Norway. *Tourism Planning and Development*, *8*, 381–397.

Borges, M. D. R., Eusébio, C. and Carvalho, N. (2012). Knowledge transfer for the development of sustainable tourism: Focus on official Portuguese tourism websites. *International Journal of Tourism Policy*, *4*, 183–205.

Brackenbury, M. (2006). Has innovation become a routine practice that enables companies to stay ahead of the comprtition in the travel industry? *Innovation and Tourism Policy.* Paris, France: OECD Publishing.

Butler, R. W. (1980). The concept of a tourist area cycle of evolution: Implications for management of resources. *The Canadian Geographer/Le Géographe Canadien, 24*(1), 5–12.

Cooper, C. (2006). Knowledge management and tourism. *Annals of Tourism Research, 33,* 47–64.

Decelles, X. (2006). A dynamic conceptual approch to innovation in tourism. *Innovation and Tourism Policy,* 85–105, Paris, France: OECD Publishing.

Eisenhardt, K. M. and Santos, F. M. (2002). Knowledge-based view: A new theory of strategy? In Pettigrew, A., Thomas, H. and Whittington, R. (Eds), *Handbook of Strategy and Management* (pp. 139–164). London: SAGE Publications.

Hall, M. C. and Williams, A. M. (2008). *Tourism and Innovation.* London: Routledge.

Hallin, C. A. and Marnburg, E. (2008). Knowledge management in the hospitality industry: A review of empirical research. *Tourism Management, 29,* 366–381.

Henry, N. and Pinch, S. (2000). Spatialising knowledge: Placing the knowledge community of Motor Sport Valley. *Geoforum, 31,* 191–208.

Hjalager, A.-M. (2002). Repairing innovation defectiveness in tourism. *Tourism Management, 23,* 465–474.

Hjalager, A. M., Huijbens, E. H., Björk, P., Nordin, S., Flagestad, A. and Knútsson, Ö. (2008). *Innovation Systems in Nordic Tourism Advance/1,* Icelandic Tourism Research Centre, Swedish School of Economics and Business Administration, European Tourism Research Institute, Norwegian School of Management BI.

Hoarau, H. and Kline, C. (2014). Science and industry: Sharing knowledge for innovation. *Annals of Tourism Research, 46,* 44–61.

Hudson, R. (1999). 'The learning economy, the learning firm and the learning region': A sympathetic critique of the limits to learning. *European Urban And Regional Studies, 6,* 59–72.

Hudson, R. (2005). *Economic Geographies, Circuits, Flows and Spaces.* London: Sage Publications.

Keller, P. (2006a). Towards an innovation-oriented tourism policy: A new agenda? In B. Walder, K. Weiermair and A. S. Pérez (Eds), *Innovation and Product Development in Tourism: Creating Sustainable Competitive Advantage.* Berlin: Erich Schmidt Verlag.

Keller, P. (2006b). Innovation and tourism policy. In OECD (Ed.), *Innovation and Growth in Tourism* (pp. 17–40). Paris, France: OECD Publishing.

Nieves, J., Quintana, A. and Osorio, J. (2014). Knowledge-based resources and innovation in the hotel industry. *International Journal of Hospitality Management, 38,* 65–73.

Nonaka, I. and Takeuchi, H. (1995). *The Knowledge Creating Company: How the Japanese Companies Create the Dynamics of Innovation.* New York: Oxford University Press.

Nordin, S. (2003). *Tourism Clustering and Innovation – Paths to Economic Growth and Development.* Oestersund, Sweden: European Tourism Research Institute, Mid-Sweden University.

Nordin, S. and Svensson, B. 2005. The significance of governance in innovative tourism destinations. Oestersund, Sweden: European Tourism Research Institute, Mid-Sweden University.

Poon, A. (1993). *Tourism, Technology and Competitive Strategies.* Wallingford: CABI.

Rodrigues, A. L. O., Rodrigues, A. and Peroff, D. M. (2015). The sky and sustainable tourism development: A case study of a dark sky reserve implementation in Alqueva. *International Journal of Tourism Research, 17,* 292–302.

Scheidegger, E. (2006). Can the state promote innovation in tourism? Should it? In OECD (Ed.), *Innovation and Growth in Tourism* (pp. 11–15). Paris, France: OECD Publishing.

Sinkula, J., Baker, W. and Noordewier, T. (1997). A framework for market-based organizational learning: Linking values, knowledge, and behavior. *Journal of the Academy of Marketing Science, 25,* 305–318.

Sørensen, F. and Fuglsang, L. (2014). Social network dynamics and innovation in small tourism companies. In M. McLeod and R. Vaughan (Eds), *Knowledge Networks and Tourism* (pp. 28–44). Abingdon: Routledge.

Steenkamp, J.-B. E. M., Hofstede, F. T. and Wedel, M. (1999). A cross-national investigation into the individual and national cultural antecedents of consumer innovativeness. *Journal of Marketing, 63*, 55–69.

Tajeddini, K. (2011). Customer orientation, learning orientation, and new service development: An empirical investigation of the Swiss hotel industry. *Journal of Hospitality and Tourism Research, 35*, 437–468.

Tether, B. (2004). *Do Services Innovate Differently?* Manchester: Centre for Innovation and Competition. University of Manchester.

Tushman, M. L. and Scanlan, T. J. (1981). Boundary spanning individuals: Their role in information transfer and their antecedents. *The Academy of Management Journal, 24*, 289–305.

Watson, S. and McCracken, M. (2002). No attraction in strategic thinking: Perceptions on current and future skills needs for visitor attraction managers. *International Journal of Tourism Research, 4*, 367–378.

Weidenfeld, A., Williams, A. M. and Butler, R. W. (2010). Knowledge transfer and innovation among attractions. *Annals of Tourism Research, 37*, 604–626.

Weirmaier, K. (2006). Product improvement or innovation: What is the key to success in tourism? In OECD (Ed.), *Innovation and Growth in Tourism* (pp. 53–69). Paris, France: OECD Publishing.

Werner, K., Dickson, G. and Hyde, K. F. (2015). Learning and knowledge transfer processes in a mega-events context: The case of the 2011 Rugby World Cup. *Tourism Management, 48*, 174–187.

Williams, A. M. (2005). Working Paper. No. 17, International Migration and Knowledge Oxford: Centre on Migration, Policy and Society, University of Oxford.

Williams, A. M. (2006). Lost in translation? International migration, learning and knowledge. *Progress in Human Geography, 30*, 588–607.

9   Innovation in the visitor attraction sector

Introduction

Tourism has always been subject to change and innovation which, for example, have allowed tourists to reach remoter locations, seen the emergence of new visitor attractions and resulted in reduced costs or improved experiences for both tourists and suppliers. Some enabling sectors such as transport, banking systems, travel equipment, medical services and the intermediating role of technology have contributed to innovation in tourism. Landmark innovators include American Express, Thomas Cook (UK) and South West Airlines (US) with a major focus on the transport systems, particularly the railway and aviation (Hall and Williams, 2008). Less attention has been given in the research literature to innovation in the core tourism product, specifically to visitor attractions.

The lack of attention is possibly due to popular and policy discourses which suggest that tourism businesses are not considered particularly innovative. This is reinforced by the systems of official data collection about innovation which tend to underestimate the levels in consumer-related services such as tourism (Hall and Williams, 2008). However, it is also true that attractions are considered slightly more innovative than most other types of tourism businesses (Hjalager, 2015).

Given the problematic nature of the definition of both innovations and visitor attractions, it is difficult to delineate the history of innovations in this sub-sector. Religious objects, such as the Shroud of Turin, Italy, or the relics of saints (for example St James at Santiago de Compostella, Spain) have long attracted pilgrims. More recently, a significant development occurred in 1683 when private collections of objects were open to the public in Oxford in the Ashmolean Museum. In 1753, prior to the founding of the British Museum, a legislative initiative institutionalised the concept of preservation, research and interpretation for visitors. As a result museums were 'invented' and developed into 'reasons to go' for travellers, becoming essential elements of the tourism infrastructure (Hjalager, 2015). More than two centuries later, the innovation process continues to shape the tourism industry including the visitor attraction product. This is becoming far more multifaceted, complex and involving other facilities such as shopping malls, hotels and conference venues, which gradually become visitor attractions in their own right.

There has been increasing research on innovation in the service sectors generally and tourism is no exception (Krizaj et al., 2014, Weidenfeld, 2013, Hjalager, 2010b, Jacob et al., 2003, Hjalager and Flagestad, 2011, Hoarau and Kline, 2014, Tether, 2004, Rodríguez et al., 2014, Sørensen and Sundbo, 2014, Sørensen and Fuglsang, 2014). However, there is a dearth of knowledge on the specifics of innovations in the sub-sectors of tourism, such as the attraction sector and, to date, there are more studies on the hospitality industry (Orfila-Sintes et al., 2005, Jacob et al., 2003, Hallin and Marnburg, 2008, Yang, 2007, Siguaw et al., 2000, Jogaratnam and Tse, 2004, Claver-Cortés et al., 2006, Thomas and Wood, 2014, Nicolau and Santa-María, 2013) than tourism. Linked to this, there is also relatively limited understanding of the facilitators of innovation. In particular, the role of different levels of proximity facilitators has been neglected with little evidence as to whether tacit knowledge is transferred more efficiently by relational proximity (i.e. achieved via individuals with shared meanings and understandings) or by spatial proximity (Williams, 2005).

Clustering is one of the key concepts in the literature on spatial proximity. Several authors have commented on the characteristics of spatial clustering and the role of spatial proximity in knowledge transfer and innovation in tourism (Nordin, 2003, Bathelt et al., 2004, Hall, 2005a, 2005b, Shaw and Williams, 2004, Williams, 2005, Jackson and Murphy, 2006, Jackson, 2006, Novelli et al., 2006, Sørensen, 2007). There have also been debates about whether competition and cooperation encourage or discourage innovation (Pérez et al., 2006). It is a question that needs to be addressed in conjunction with the issue of spatial proximity. For example, is there more knowledge transfer between attractions that are in close spatial proximity to each other, or between those that have similar products, such as gardens, wildlife, historical sites or theme parks than those which are distant and dissimilar? This chapter provides a review of innovation in the visitor attraction sector and pays particular attention to the role of spatial agglomeration (or density) in contrast to the role of product similarity (i.e. similarity in product and service offerings, such as wildlife or animal based attractions) in mediating knowledge transfers between attractions, which lead to innovation.

Innovation in visitor attractions

Innovation is a complex process, a key component of which is the sharing of both codified and uncodified informal knowledge (Propris, 2002). This effectively occurs at the level of individual entities, whether these be attractions or destinations, and can include minor and major adaptations of products and services (Hjalager, 2002), as well as of organisational and management systems, and in marketing. It rarely involves entirely new products and/or new markets but rather is likely to focus on differentiation, product line extension via brand policies or changes in the cost (price)/quality ratio of the product (Brackenbury, 2006). Attractions which adopt new processes or products are *incremental innovators* if they improve existing products and/or processes, and *radical innovators* if they introduce new products and/or processes elaborated and developed by the attraction itself.

One of the difficulties involved in discussing innovation is that the measurement of innovation remains problematic. According to the Oslo manual – an international set of guidelines for the collection and use of data on innovation activities in industry, published by the OECD and used by the EU – something has to be at least new or provide significant improvement to a firm in order for it to be defined as innovation. It can also be something new to the region, nation, continent and/or world (Eurostat, 2005). A firm can introduce an innovation which is new to its region and thereby increase its regional competitiveness (Eizenberg and Cohen, 2015), even if such innovations have already been introduced elsewhere. This is exemplified by innovations in product development and market diversification outside the peak season which can help visitor attractions overcome seasonal variation in visitor numbers and product demand (Connell et al., 2015). In 1998, Camelback Ski area in Pennsylvania was the first ski resort in the US to install an outdoor park as an attempt to overcome seasonality and increase its annual visitor numbers. This was followed by Michigan's Boyne Mountain which was the first ski area to open an indoor waterpark in the US in 2005 (Entrikin and Berdoulay, 2005).

Tourism innovations can be difficult to create but at the same time are considered to be relatively easy to imitate (Hjalager, 2002, Decelles, 2006), particularly where the front stage processes are highly visible to external observers, and the level of technology is relatively unsophisticated (Hall and Williams, 2008). However, there are constraints on learning and imitation through observation, as many aspects of service quality innovations, for example, are dependent on tacit knowledge (Hall and Williams, 2008). The observer sees the staff producing high quality experiences for visitors, but does not see the tacit knowledge that underlies this, or the training programmes that helped to produce this knowledge.

Product, process, organisational/managerial and marketing innovations constitute the main types of categories in tourism (Hjalager, 2010a). At the heart of the delivery of experiences at the attraction are product and process innovations, although these are supplemented by marketing and organisational innovations. Product innovations consist of changed or entirely new services or products while process innovations tend to raise the performance of existing operations, e.g. by means of new or improved technology such as virtual reality, animation, newly designed tours, re-enactment and personification of the visitor experience, new interpretations and educational added value facilities (Hjalager, 2002, Scheidegger, 2006, Weiermair, 2006). For example, museums, galleries and similar cultural institutions have been at the forefront of using interactive technologies, particularly various forms of personal computing, e.g. mobile guides, tangible interfaces and augmented reality. These enable visitors to interpret collections of physical artefacts in new ways (see Box 9.1). These technologies create engagement and educational experiences and have proven to be especially appealing due to their potential to intensify the connections between conventional physical artefacts and digital information (Green et al., 2014).

New technologies are seen as being key to the participation of new and younger audiences in visits to museums. There has been a recent trend for institutional

Box 9.1 Use of technology in UK visitor attractions

Visitors' flashlights aim to create magical experiences for participants, using technologies that transform large physical structures, such as wall, into interactive surfaces. This has been utilised in several visitor attractions in the UK. The aim was to enhance the experiences of visitors at attractions, whether an ancient castle or an underground cave system. This included enabling visitors to use flashlights (or searchlights at very large scales) to illuminate a surface, and then to use computer vision software to recognise and track the resulting beams of light, using them as pointing devices. In other words, new technology is used to transform what otherwise appears to be a banal or mundane physical object, the flashlight. It is innovation which brings new life and uses to what had been a traditional technology. The key advantage is its utility and adaptability to a range of settings in different attractions.

Source: Green et al. (2014).

donors to allocate grants and specialised funding streams to initiatives which aim to encourage younger audiences to visit museums. One of these is the Bloomberg Connects programme (formerly known as the Digital Engagement Initiative). This provides funding for the development of technology to increase access to cultural institutions and enhance visitor experiences. In 2014, it announced a donation of $17 million for several museums, including the American Museum of Natural History, the Brooklyn Museum, the Cooper Hewitt Smithsonian Design Museum, the San Francisco Museum of Modern Art, Singapore's Gardens by the Bay and the Science Museum in London (Alton, 2014a, Maloney, 2014).

Process innovations, such as improving standards and appeal to various market segments, e.g. improving accessibility, visual adjustment of labelling and technological solutions to queuing, and ticketing are considered to be particularly influential forms of innovation (Hjalager, 2002, Scheidegger, 2006, Weirmaier, 2006, Connell et al., 2015). Wildlife attractions, for example, have raised their entertainment standards by integrating storytelling, interactive activities and simulations (Milman et al., 2010). Another recent trend is the growing awareness of the need to make adjustments and adaptations of facilities for the special needs of disabled customers. The Philadelphia Zoo has recently launched a new zoo within the zoo, *KidZooU*, the design of which addressed the accessibility requirements of special needs children. It partnered with the St. Joseph's University Kinney Centre for Autism Education and Support to develop a social story to prepare children on the autism spectrum for their visit to the zoo. These adjustments, and added facilities such as dedicated quiet areas, help to eliminate the stress of the unknown, which is crucial for enhancing the social outings of parents with a child with autism (Rachel, 2013).

The development and elaboration of such features are also found in other types of visitor attractions. Storytelling, costumed actors, interactive experiences and the use of 3D technology have been prominent in recent attempts by designers to create a distinctive but also a changing visitor experience. The Evermore Adventure Park, a new $100 million, 45-acre theatrical theme park under development in Utah at the time of writing, which is set to open in 2015, will create an interactive and changing experience by 'transporting' guests back in time to Victorian London. Costumed actors will play out seasonal narratives allowing guests to interact with different storylines around a series of weeklong events, weekend celebrations and weekly activities (Alton, 2014b).

Organisational innovation refers to the introduction of new systems and management methods and new types of work organisation and business models (Camisón and Monfort-Mir, 2012). Some museums, such as the Louvre in Paris, have demonstrated such innovation by setting up international branches, similar to the Guggenheim model, which has effectively created a global museum franchise (Hall and Williams, 2008). They can include new approaches to the 'administrative core' or 'social system' of the organisation, such as new management practices of human resources, work structures and organisation, executive systems, processes and external relationships with customers, markets, suppliers and competitors (Camisón and Monfort-Mir, 2012).

Marketing innovations refer to the introduction of new commercial methods including changes in product design, promotional strategies and price. The introduction of museum sleepovers in the 1990s in America is an example of marketing innovation. It started by targeting children as an attempt to increase the popularity of museums amongst young people and as an educational initiative. Subsequently, this has become a widely imitated global trend among arts and cultural institutions and has spread into adults' sleep-over as a part of a strategy to increase external income (Amirtha, 2015).

Radical innovation and the contribution of the entrepreneur

The contribution of entrepreneurs in the fields of tourism and hospitality is a topic which has received only passing reference in most studies, yet many of the significant changes in destinations which have occurred over the past two centuries have been the result of the efforts of key individuals (Butler and Russell, 2012). Many of the innovations in how tourists travel (from Thomas Cook to Richard Branson), how they overnight (Hilton to De Haan), the destinations they choose (John Muir to Keith Williams) and the specific attractions they visit (Walt Disney to A.J. Hackett) are the result of the work of entrepreneurs (Butler and Russell, 2010).

Schumpeter's typology of incremental versus radical innovations (Schumpeter, 1934) identifies these contributions. Incremental innovation involves day-to-day improvements and relatively small scale modifications to existing knowledge. Radical innovation refers to revolutionary leaps which effectively can redefine the rules of competition, at least in the short term. Schumpeter noted five types of innovation: production of new goods, new methods of production, new markets, new sources of supplies and new types of organisations. An example of all five types of innovation is found in the case of the influence of Walt Disney on visitor attractions, which is both unique and outstanding (Shani and Logan, 2010), incorporating character invention, fictitious worlds and linking theme parks (including accommodation and services) with various forms of media at a scale unknown before.

Russell (2010:xi–xii) categorised different forms of entrepreneurship as *organic* (new destinations at the early stage of development, e.g. Williams on the Gold Coast of Queensland); *phase-changing* (moving a destination from one stage of its life cycle to another); *grand-scale* (changing the tourism landscape on a large scale such as Disney in Central Florida); *serendipitous* (reflecting a fortunate combination of timing and environment as H.G. Smith at Manley, New South Wales) (Butler and McDonnell, 2011); and *revitalising* (seizing an opportunity to rejuvenate an old destination/attraction as in the case of Dreamland in Margate, Box 4.1, Chapter 4). In a number of cases, entrepreneurs having major influences on tourism development have done so with no previous involvement in tourism, e.g. the writer Sir Walter Scott who radically changed the image of the Scottish Highlands, resulting in the establishment of many visitor attractions over the subsequent two centuries (Butler and Russell, 2012).

Other examples of radical innovation include the first ever Ice Hotel in the village of Jukkasjärvi, Northern Sweden, which opened in 1990, and is both a hotel and a visitor attraction, and in effect created a new international tourist destination. Similarly, the new planned 'Mall of the World' in Dubai is a 48 million square-foot, climate-controlled complex under a glass dome that will include an 8 million square-foot shopping mall and a Broadway-style cultural district. It aims to be the largest indoor family theme park in the world. At the time of writing, it was scheduled to be completed by 2020 and was expected to attract 180 million visitors each year (Wainright, 2014).

Sources and channels of knowledge in process and product development

Innovation processes in visitor attractions emerge from the knowledge of internal staff as well as from external sources such as the staff of other attractions and other businesses. The mechanisms facilitating internal knowledge creation usually involve transforming tacit into explicit knowledge (see Chapter 8). All the mechanisms identified in the generic literature (Figure 9.1), apart from 'knowledge brokers', are characteristic of visitor attractions. The most common channel is probably 'learning by observation', which occurs by managers/staff observing practices at other attractions during coordinated or uncoordinated visits, where they are exposed to new ideas/new products. Learning by observation can also be realised by visiting media outlets such as websites. Most knowledge transfers through 'learning by observation' are unplanned and uncoordinated, whereby both tacit and explicit knowledge are transferred between attractions or between attractions and other businesses (Weidenfeld et al., 2010).

At the beginning of the innovation process, knowledge (internal or external) is transferred within and between tacit and explicit forms. As noted in Chapter 8,

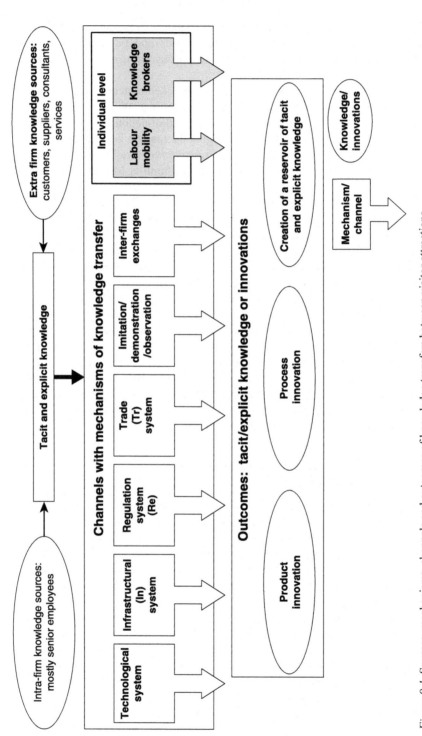

Figure 9.1 Sources, mechanisms, channels and outcomes of knowledge transfers between visitor attractions

Source: Adapted from Weidenfeld et al. (2010).

there are four main types of knowledge transfer: explicit to explicit, explicit to tacit, tacit to tacit, and tacit to explicit, between firms through various channels/ mechanisms (Nonaka and Takeuchi, 1995). At the end of the process, knowledge transfers can result in new product or process innovations, but some remain as knowledge embedded (or encoded) among workers and managers. Most of the innovations by attractions, whether product or process innovations, are classified as incremental innovations. Only a minority constitute radical innovations.

The case study in Box 9.2 shows how different types of intra- (e.g. strategies) and extra-firm knowledge (e.g. observation from geographical positioning systems) are produced, processed and combined through the technological system into product and process innovations. These also serve to improve the company's understanding of their market and users' needs (Sørensen and Sundbo, 2014, Hjalager, 2002, Hjalager et al., 2008, Nordin and Svensson, 2005).

Box 9.2 The use of Geographic Positioning System (GPS) technology in user based innovation processes

A user based innovation process focusing on tourist mobility within a single visitor attraction was facilitated using Geographic Positioning System (GPS) technology in a large Northern European safari Park. The park offers opportunities for visitors to observe animals as well as ancillary services including playgrounds and restaurants, which serve an annual market of 250,000 visitors per year, mainly families with children. GPS data on visitors was collected by lending GPS sports clocks to visitor groups consisting of families with children, a questionnaire survey and semi-structured interviews with some of the tracked visitors. Data interpretation and analysis were integrated with the innovation processes and led to several innovation initiatives, which illustrate how user data can be an important input to innovation in visitor attractions. The innovation process was developed in response to the lack of data available to the Park's management strategies.

The advantage of the GPS system was the generation of information on visitors' itineraries within the park, which was analysed and produced new ideas for process and product innovations. Some new and surprising information, such as that visitors do not tend to spend a long time at the main attractors but more at other areas with different amenities, was provided. The data was combined with other types of knowledge, such as visitor preferences, tourism trends, and the company strategy, to provide an integrated database, which could be interrogated when addressing particular issues. New ideas for development initiatives included a playground area and new facilities including the Monkey Forest and Birds' Paradise. The process has also led to new Smartphone applications, changes to marketing strategies and investments in new activities and facilities such as animal feeding. Management also changed some features in the park such as queuing systems, food outlets, and internet ticket sales. The use of GPS data for innovation may be applied in other visitor attractions, such as amusement parks and museums, where mobility is pivotal in the experience product and service-provision scapes.

Source: Sørensen and Sundbo (2014).

The role of proximity in learning and the diffusion of innovation

A number of different forms of proximity have been identified as facilitating knowledge transfers and learning: cognitive, social, institutional and geographical (Boschma, 2005, Sørensen, 2007). Overall, although Boschma (2005) argues that geographical proximity is not a prerequisite for interactive learning, he attaches more importance to geographical and cognitive proximities than to social, institutional, organisational and size similarities. He argues that geographic proximity (between people or between firms and organizations) – along with minimum levels of cognitive proximity – is sufficient for interactive learning to take place. Although more empirical research is needed to determine the relationships between different dimensions of proximity, these arguments frame our understanding of geographical proximity as being potentially a particularly significant form of proximity. Being geographically closer to other attractions can play a critical role in knowledge transfer and ultimately in innovation and can be seen as being related to clustering and agglomeration (see Chapter 3).

Spatial proximity at the local scale and agglomeration at the regional scale are positively related to knowledge transfer and diffusion of innovations amongst visitor attractions. However, attractions in the same region are more likely to learn from each other about incremental innovations and minor improvements in existing products and services, in part because they already have a shared or common knowledge. In contrast, they may be more likely to adopt or imitate new products and services from more distant, or less spatially proximate, attractions in the same country and internationally. Weidenfeld et al. (2010) found that attractions in Cornwall, south west England, imitated and adopted ideas from other attractions that were considered distant enough not to be in direct competition. Even in the relatively more agglomerated tourism cluster in their study (Newquay), visitor attractions were shown to have imitated or learnt from other UK and overseas attractions rather than from neighbouring local attractions. Furthermore, more imitation and knowledge transfers in the denser Newquay cluster, than in the more dispersed Lizard cluster, were identified (Table 9.1). Coordinated visits of managers to other attractions for the purpose of learning is also more common between distant attractions, whilst uncoordinated learning visits are more common between neighbouring attractions (Weidenfeld et al., 2010).

Visitor attractions are defined as a 'knowledge hub' if they are in a central location in their destination region and are considered by other actors to be the most 'innovative' attractions – and therefore more likely to be imitated. They demonstrate radical and incremental innovations, functioning as knowledge suppliers and knowledge receivers among a relatively large number of other attractions and businesses, and diffusing innovations amongst attractions at the local, regional and national scales (Weidenfeld et al., 2010). Spatial proximity alone cannot explain knowledge transfer and diffusion of innovations amongst firms, which are likely to be very diverse processes. Instead, knowledge gained from enterprises which share product similarity has the potential for more specific learning, and more direct

Table 9.1 Comparison between knowledge transfer and diffusion of innovations between visitor attractions at lower and higher levels of agglomeration

Features of knowledge transfer/innovations	Higher levels of agglomeration	Lower levels of agglomeration
Internal/external sources*	More external	More internal
Product similarity between 'supplier' and 'receiver'	Learning more from similar product attractions	Learning from similar and dissimilar product attractions
Spatial proximity between 'supplier' and 'receiver'	More learning from overseas attractions	More learning at local and regional scales

Source: Adapted from Weidenfeld et al. (2010).

* Internal/external to firm

imitation. Spatial proximity may be less important than the potential to learn from other establishments in the same industry. A key argument is that the wider the knowledge gap between knowledge providers and receivers, the more difficult it is to assimilate the knowledge transferred (Hall and Williams, 2008): firms in the same industry can be assumed to have a relatively high level of shared knowledge.

The issues of proximity are particularly difficult to unravel. Bærenholdt and Haldrup (2006) argue that different types of tourism businesses within a particular locality have little to learn from one another, since their main common interest is attracting tourists into an area (that is, destination marketing). Conversely, it can be argued that firms belonging to different industries are more likely to share information than firms of the same industry, because they are sources of uncommon knowledge (Pérez et al., 2006) and they are not competing directly. On this basis, product-similar attractions do not tend to be spatially proximate in order to avoid duplication of provision in a particular location or region. Therefore, they are more likely to need to undertake coordinated and/or uncoordinated visits to other product-similar but non-proximate attractions. This can be an effective strategy for managing competition issues. In such cases, visits are more likely to be overt and coordinated. In contrast, learning by observation during incidental visits is more likely to be characteristic of dissimilar product attractions which are spatially proximate, or intra-cluster neighbours; that is, they are visited, or observed almost 'in passing' as it were, or through key personnel meeting face-to-face. Hence, agglomeration mechanisms do play a role in knowledge transfer, not least because spatial proximity is conducive to networking at the destination scale (Sørensen, 2007), but also in terms of learning from product dissimilar attractions in destination regions.

However, Sørensen (2007) argues that relations between tourism firms with different products, e.g. accommodation and attractions, are characterised by more general 'explorative' (preliminary, descriptive) information rather than the 'exploitative' knowledge (complex and specific) exchange that leads to innovations. He also argues that different attractions need different types of knowledge inputs and that information networks between tourism firms, including attractions, are influenced by product similarity and firm size. Based on the previous discussion, and drawing particularly on Pérez et al. (2006), Sørensen (2007), Sørensen and Fuglsang (2014) and Weidenfeld et al.'s (2010) work, the relationships between spatial proximity, knowledge transfer and product similarity between visitor attractions in tourism destinations can be summarised in terms of two main points:

a.   Product similarity between attractions is more likely than spatial proximity to generate positive knowledge sharing effects, and is also more likely to increase the level of exploitative knowledge transfers and learning.
b.   Dissimilar product neighbouring attractions share less exploitative and more explorative information that is less likely to result in innovation.

Organisational proximity is another form of proximity (Boschma, 2005), being the degree of similarity between organisational mechanisms, such as tourism networks or associations, that coordinate transactions amongst their members. These networks serve as 'vehicles' that enable exchange of information. Organisational proximity may include similarity in size, which is posited to be positively related to information networks between attractions. Small firms, such as most visitor attractions, benefit less from local networks, and are less involved in these than large firms (Sørensen, 2007). *L'association professionnelle attraction touristique en Wallonie et a Bruxelle* is a Belgian regional association of visitor attractions in Wallonia and Brussels. Similar to many other associations, it is responsible for representing and marketing its members as well as organising colloquiums, seminars and social meetings where exchange of knowledge and information take place (see www.attractions-et-tourisme.be/). Hall (2005b) also argues that spatial clustering of tourism firms does not necessarily increase innovation and knowledge sharing compared to organisational proximity. Another way to approach this is in terms of economic proximity, which refers to 'how economic activities are positioned relative to each other in production systems' (p. 28). In other words, the nature, size, type, variety and impact of different economic activities shape the relationships between them: in particular, it determines the extent to which there is cooperation, competition and complementarity (see Chapters 5–7).

The transfer of knowledge and diffusion of innovations between visitor attractions depends on the impact of both product similarity and spatial proximity. Increased spatial distance between similar attractions means that attractions are less likely to be in direct competition in the same market segment, and this encourages more knowledge transfers. Therefore, the greater the spatial distance between product-similar attractions, the more they are expected to exchange exploitative knowledge and innovations.

Conclusions

This chapter has examined the overall process of knowledge transfer in terms of a sequential order including sources, mechanisms/channels and outcomes in the visitor attraction sector. The process begins with external suppliers and internal sources, which transfer tacit and explicit knowledge within and between attractions through various channels/mechanisms. Some of these result in the creation of a reservoir of tacit and explicit knowledge among staff and managers (Figure 9.2). Others are transformed into product or process innovations, including being 'captured' in new technologies. The chapter has also explored the relationships between spatial proximity/product similarity and knowledge transfers between visitor attractions. Knowledge suppliers in general are both internal and external to attractions. Internal sources include senior managers, attraction staff and internal visitor surveys, while external sources include suppliers, tourism associations, other attractions, businesses in various sectors and visiting professionals.

In line with Cooper's (2006) argument, tacit knowledge is captured and codified 'in-house' within individual attractions whether from employees or customers (Figure 9.2, beginning on the left side). Codifying tacit knowledge into explicit knowledge through simple mechanisms including writing up the outcomes of discussions and brainstorming is the most common mechanism of knowledge transformation. Some explicit knowledge is transformed into new product innovations and later transferred to other attractions in forms, documents and electronic data bases as well as by imitation following visits to other attractions.

Some of the transferred knowledge leads to process and product innovations, whilst some tacit or explicit knowledge is retained with potential for further elaboration (middle part of Figure 9.2). New innovations are sometimes imitated by other attractions, and thereby diffused (right part of Figure 9.2). It is noteworthy that whereas product innovations are relatively easy to imitate, the underlying organisation and process innovations are more difficult to observe and to imitate (Weidenfeld et al., 2010).

In Weidenfeld et al.'s (2010) study, the most common channel of knowledge was 'learning by observation/imitation/demonstrating' followed by 'labour mobility', and 'inter-firm exchanges' through coordinated visits between attractions, tourism associations and exhibitions. Other less common channels were trade, technological, infrastructure and regulation systems. Explicit to explicit knowledge transfers were the most common type of transfer, and included ideas that can be imitated quite easily and implemented by the 'receiver'. Examples include manuals about managing queues, pricing data and food menus.

Innovations and knowledge are diffused through various intra- and extra-national, and intra- and extra-regional, network relations between actors who are embedded in particular regional innovation systems. Within the latter, different forms of mostly explicit knowledge circulate. Identifiable 'knowledge transfer agents' include senior managers, members of staff, professional magazines and journals, intentionally or coincidentally causing knowledge to flow amongst attractions, leading to the diffusion of new products and process innovations. Minor adaptations of existing products and services in tourism are the most common form of innovations that are diffused between attractions. These are more common between similar product attractions than dissimilar ones. At the end of the knowledge transfer process, new products or process innovations

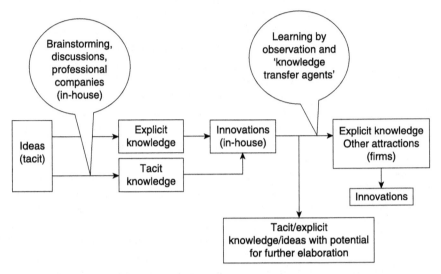

Figure 9.2 Knowledge transfer and ideation within and between visitor attractions

Source: Adapted from Weidenfeld et al. (2010:622).

may be generated, but knowledge can also remain as knowledge embedded (or encoded) among workers, constituting a potential resource for future innovation.

As illustrated in Figure 9.2, tacit knowledge is often captured and codified 'in-house' in tangible forms, whether as investments in products or the production of written reports based on harvesting the informal knowledge held by individuals. Tacit knowledge is often transferred by staff movement between and within firms/attractions and discussions with suppliers. When new knowledge is brought into a company, for example by a new member of staff, that knowledge needs to be shared with and discussed with other staff and perhaps elaborated into more feasible ideas that can be transformed into innovations. Some of the transferred knowledge may lead to process and product innovations; some may remain tacit or explicit knowledge with potential for further elaboration (middle part of Figure 9.2). The new innovations are sometimes imitated by other attractions, and therefore diffuse beyond the originator.

Spatial proximity, product similarity and market similarity all tend to facilitate knowledge transfers, including innovation spillovers at both the local and the regional scales. Product similarity is generally more positively related to effective knowledge transfer and diffusion of innovations than is spatial proximity at both local and regional scales. An additional conclusion is that product similarity is positively related to both exploitative and explorative knowledge transfer between attractions. Tourism destination regions are likely to have centrally located key attractions, which function as 'knowledge hubs'. These diffuse innovations among other intra-and extra-destination attractions, and their managers can be considered lead 'innovators'. These are usually critical to the effectiveness of a local or regional innovation system.

References

Alton, E. (2014a). Bloomberg connects: Betting on mobile apps to bring millennials into museums. *Entertainment Designer*. San Francisco, US.

Alton, E. (2014b). Could evermore change the interactive theme park experience? *Entertainment Designer*. San Francisco, US.

Amirtha, T. (2015). Where do pricey museum sleepovers come from? Weirdly, institutions aren't making tons of money off this global trend. *Fast Company*. Retrieved from www. fastcompany.com/3042603/sleep-week/where-do-pricey-museum-sleepovers-come-from (accessed 14 January 2016).

Bærenholdt, J. O. and Haldrup, M. (2006). Mobile networks and place making in cultural tourism – Staging viking ships and rock music in Roskilde. *European Urban and Regional Studies*, *13*, 209–224.

Bathelt, H., Malmberg, A. and Maskell, P. (2004). Clusters and knowledge: Local buzz, global pipelines and the process of knowledge creation. *Progress in Human Geography*, *28*, 31–56.

Boschma, R. A. (2005). Proximity and innovation: A critical assessment. *Regional Studies*, *39*, 61–74.

Brackenbury, M. (2006). Has innovation become a routine practice that enables companies to stay ahead of the comprtition in the travel industry? *Innovation and Tourism Policy*. Paris, France: OECD Publishing.

Butler, R. W. and Russell, R. A. (2010). *Giants of Tourism*. Wallingford: CABI.

Butler, R. W. and McDonnell, I. G. (2011). One man and his boat (and hotel and pier …): Henry Gilbert Smith and the establishment of Manly, Australia. *Tourism Geographies*, *13*, 343–359.

Butler, R. W. and Russell, R. A. (2012). The role of individuals in the development and popularization of tourist destinations. In C. H. C. Hsu and W. C. Gartner (Eds), *The Routledge Handbook of Tourism Research* (pp. 132–155). London: Routledge.

Camisón, C. and Monfort-Mir, V. M. (2012). Measuring innovation in tourism from the Schumpeterian and the dynamic-capabilities perspectives. *Tourism Management*, *33*, 776–789.

Claver-Cortés, E., Molina-Azorín, J. F. and Pereira-Moliner, J. (2006). Strategic groups in the hospitality industry: Intergroup and intragroup performance differences in Alicante, Spain. *Tourism Management*, *27*, 1101–1116.

Connell, J., Page, S. J. and Meyer, D. (2015). Visitor attractions and events: Responding to seasonality. *Tourism Management*, *46*, 283–298.

Cooper, C. (2006). Knowledge management and tourism. *Annals of Tourism Research*, *33*(1), 47–64.

Decelles, X. (2006). A dynamic conceptual approch to innovation in tourism. *Innovation and Tourism Policy*. OECD (2010). SMEs, Entrepreneurship and Innovation. OECD Studies on SMEs and Entrepreneurship. Paris, France: OECD Publishing.

Eizenberg, E. and Cohen, N. (2015). Reconstructing urban image through cultural flagship events: The case of Bat-Yam. *Cities*, *42*(Part A), 54–62.

Entrikin, J. N. and Berdoulay, V. (2005). The Pyrenees as place: Lefebvre as guide. *Progress in Human Geography*, *29*, 129–147.

Eurostat, O. A. (2005). *The Measurement of Scientific and Technological Activities Oslo Manual, Guidelines for Collecting and Interpreting Innovation Data*, 3rd edition. OECD and Eurostat.

Green, J., Pridmore, T. and Benford, S. (2014). Exploring attractions and exhibits with interactive flashlights. *Personal and Ubiquitous Computing, 18*, 239–251.

Hall, C. M. (2005a). *Tourism: Rethinking the Social Science of Mobility*. Harlow: Prentice-Hall.

Hall, C. M. (2005b). Rural wine and food tourism cluster and network development. In D. Hall, I. Kirkpatrick and M. Mitchell (Eds), *Rural Tourism and Sustainable Business* (pp. 149–164). Clevedon: Channel View Publications.

Hall, M. C. and Williams, A. M. (2008). *Tourism and Innovation*. London: Routledge.

Hallin, C. A. and Marnburg, E. (2008). Knowledge management in the hospitality industry: A review of empirical research. *Tourism Management, 29*, 366–381.

Hjalager, A.-M. (2002). Repairing innovation defectiveness in tourism. *Tourism Management, 23*(5), 465–474.

Hjalager, A. M. (2010a). Progress in tourism management – A review of innovation research in tourism. *Tourism Management, 31*, 1–12.

Hjalager, A. M. (2010b). Regional innovation systems: The case of Angling tourism. *Tourism Geographies, 12*, 192–216.

Hjalager, A.-M. (2015). 100 innovations that transformed tourism. *Journal of Travel Research, 54*, 3–21.

Hjalager, A.-M. and Flagestad, A. (2011). Innovations in well-being tourism in the Nordic countries. *Current Issues in Tourism, 15*, 725–740.

Hjalager, A. M., Huijbens, E. H., Björk, P., Nordin, S., Flagestad, A. and Knútsson, Ö. (2008). *Innovation Systems in Nordic Tourism Advance/1*, Icelandic Tourism Research Centre, Swedish School of Economics and Business Administration, European Tourism Research Institute, Norwegian School of Management BI.

Hoarau, H. and Kline, C. (2014). Science and industry: Sharing knowledge for innovation. *Annals of Tourism Research, 46*, 44–61.

Jackson, J. (2006). Developing regional tourism in China: The potential for activating business clusters in a socialist market economy. *Tourism Management, 27*, 695–706.

Jackson, J. and Murphy, P. (2006). Clusters in regional tourism – An Australian case. *Annals of Tourism Research, 33*, 1018–1035.

Jacob, M., Tintoré, J., Aguiló, E., Bravo, A. and Mulet, J. (2003). Innovation in the tourism sector: Results from a pilot study in the Balearic Islands. *Tourism Economics, 9*, 279–295.

Jogaratnam, G. and Tse, E. C.-Y. (2004). The entrepreneurial approach to hotel operation: Evidence from the Asia-Pacific hotel industry. *Cornell Hotel and Restaurant Administration Quarterly, 45*, 248–259.

Krizaj, D., Brodnik, A. and Bukovec, B. (2014). A tool for measurement of innovation newness and adoption in tourism firms. *International Journal of Tourism Research, 16*(2), 113–125.

Maloney, J. (2014, 8 September). Bloomberg philanthropies gives museums $17 million push toward digital. *The Wall Street Journal*.

Milman, A., Okumus, F. and Dickson, D. (2010). The contribution of theme parks and attractions to the social and economic sustainability of destinations. *Worldwide Hospitality and Tourism Themes, 2*, 338–345.

Nicolau, J. L. and Santa-María, M. J. (2013). The effect of innovation on hotel market value. *International Journal of Hospitality Management, 32*, 71–79.

Nonaka, I. and Takeuchi, H. (1995). *The Knowledge Creating Company: How the Japanese Companies Create the Dynamics of Innovation*. New York: Oxford University Press.

Nordin, S. (2003). *Tourism Clustering and Innovation – Paths to Economic Growth and Development*. Oestersund, Sweden: European Tourism Research Institute, Mid-Sweden University.

Nordin, S. and Svensson, B. (2005). *The Significance of Governance in Innovative Tourism Destinations*. Oestersund, Sweden: European Tourism Research Institute, Mid-Sweden University.

Novelli, M., Schmitz, B. and Spencer, T. (2006). Networks, clusters and innovation in tourism: A UK experience. *Tourism Management, 27*, 1141–1152.

Orfila-Sintes, F., Crespi-Cladera, R. and Martinez-Ros, E. (2005). Innovation activity in the hotel industry: Evidence from Balearic Islands. *Tourism Management, 26*, 851–865.

Pérez, A. S., Borras, B. C. and Belda, P. R. (2006). Technology externalities in the tourism industry. In B. Walder, K. Weirmaier and A. S. Pérez (Eds), *Innovation and Product Development in Tourism: Creating Sustainable Competitive Advantage* (pp. 39–54). Berlin, Germany: Eric Schmidt Verlag.

Propris, L. D. (2002). Types of innovation and inter-firm co-operation. *Entrepreneurship and Regional Development, 14*, 337–353.

Rachel, S. (2013). Animals for all! Philadelphia zoo launches accessibility remodel to meet special needs of all types. *Entertainment Designer*. Retrieved from http://enter tainmentdesigner.com/news/zoos-aquariums/animals-for-all-philadelphia-zoo-launches-accessibility-remodel-to-meet-special-needs-of-all-types/ (accessed 14 January 2016).

Rodríguez, I., Williams, A. M. and Hall, C. M. (2014). Tourism innovation policy: Implementation and outcomes. *Annals of Tourism Research, 49*, 76–93.

Russell, R. A. (2010). Introduction. In R. W. Butler and R. A. Russell (Eds), *Giants of Tourism* (pp. X–XVII). Wallingford: CABI.

Scheidegger, E. (2006). Can the state promote innovation in tourism? Should it? In OECD (Ed.), *Innovation and Growth in Tourism* (pp. 11–15). OECD (2010). SMEs, Entrepreneurship and Innovation. OECD Studies on SMEs and Entrepreneurship. Paris, France: OECD Publishing.

Schumpeter, J. (1934). *The Theory of Economic Development*. Oxford: Oxford University Press.

Shani, A. and Logan, R. (2010). Walt Disney's world of entertainment attractions. In R. W. Butler and R. A. Russell (Eds), *Giants of Tourism* (pp. 155–169). Wallingford: CABI.

Shaw, G. and Williams, A. (2004). *Tourism and Tourism Spaces*. London: Sage.

Siguaw, J. A., Enz, C. A. and Namasivayam, K. (2000). Adoption of information technology in U.S. hotels: Strategically driven objectives. *Journal of Travel Research, 39*, 192–201.

Sørensen, F. (2007). The geographies of social networks and innovation in tourism. *Tourism Geographies, 9*, 22–48.

Sørensen, F. and Fuglsang, L. (2014). Social network dynamics and innovation in small tourism companies. In M. McLeod and R. Vaughan (Eds), *Knowledge Networks and Tourism* (pp. 28–44). Abingdon: Routledge.

Sørensen, F. and Sundbo, J. (2014). Potentials for user-based innovation in tourism: The example of GPS tracking of attraction visitors. In G. A. Alsos, D. Eide and E. L. Madsen (Eds), *Handbook of Research on Innovation in Tourism Industries*, (pp. 132–153). Cheltenham: Edward Elgar Publishing.

Tether, B. (2004). *Do Services Innovate Differently?* Manchester: Centre for Innovation and Competition. University of Manchester.

Thomas, R. and Wood, E. (2014). Innovation in tourism: Re-conceptualising and measuring the absorptive capacity of the hotel sector. *Tourism Management, 45*, 39–48.

Wainright, O. (2014, 9 July). The world's first indoor city: A greatest hits mashup of London and New York. *The Guardian.*

Weidenfeld, A. (2013). Tourism and cross border regional innovation systems. *Annals of Tourism Research, 42*, 191–213.

Weidenfeld, A., Williams, A. M. and Butler, R. W. (2010). Knowledge transfer and innovation among attractions. *Annals of Tourism Research, 37*, 604–626.

Weirmaier, K. (2006). Product improvement or innovation: What is the key to success in tourism? In OECD (Ed.), *Innovation and Growth in Tourism* (pp. 53–67). OECD (2010). SMEs, Entrepreneurship and Innovation. OECD Studies on SMEs and Entrepreneurship. Paris, France: OECD Publishing.

Williams, A. M. (2005). Working Paper. No. 17, International Migration and Knowledge Oxford: Centre on Migration, Policy and Society, University of Oxford.

Yang, J.-T. (2007). Knowledge sharing: Investigating appropriate leadership roles and collaborative culture. *Tourism Management, 28*, 530–543.

Part III

Implications and trends in the visitor attraction sector

10 The impacts of visitor attractions and events

Introduction

The impacts, or rather the effects, of attractions and events are inevitably best seen as part of the overall impact of tourism, since attractions and events represent subsets of tourism itself. (Most dictionaries define impacts in terms of actions, and the results of such actions as effects, and in most cases it is the effects rather than the actions that have been studied in the case of tourism. For the sake of consistency with the general tourism literature, the term *impacts* rather than the more accurate word *effects* will be used here.) Since the publication of the seminal work of Mathieson and Wall (1982) the impacts of tourism have generally been viewed as falling into three areas: economic, environmental (or physical) and social-cultural. While this categorisation is useful in many respects and is followed here, in some ways it has limited the full analysis of the impacts of tourism for two reasons. In the first case there are clearly more than three types of impact. The most obvious category that is missing from the Mathieson and Wall model is that of the political effects of tourism development (and decline).

A second problem is that such a division of impacts tends to encourage researchers to confine their studies to one category only, ignoring one of the key points made by Mathieson and Wall and others (Wall and Wright, 1977, Hall and Lew, 2009, for example), namely that the impacts of tourism are interrelated and complex. By implication, this means that examining only one category of impacts means the important relationships that exist with the other categories of impacts are often not discovered or researched. As with the supposed 'triple bottom line' of sustainable tourism, tourism impacts are better illustrated as a set of four interlinked categories as shown in Figure 10.1 than as three distinct separate elements.

In almost all cases, an economic impact will have social-cultural, environmental and political effects on the destination in which it occurs. Creation of employment opportunities has social and cultural benefits in most cases, while the development creating the jobs will have environmental effects, and there will be political effects, most likely positive to those in power, from such job creation. This pattern holds true generally for the impacts of visitor attractions and events, although different scales and temporal patterns may be involved. While in the case of a single attraction or event we would expect the resulting impacts to be easily

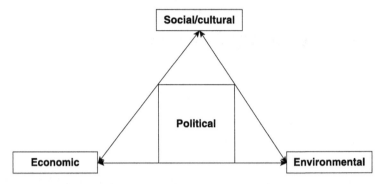

Figure 10.1 Relationships between major areas of impact

identified and even measured, we cannot assume that those impacts remain in their discrete categories and do not affect each other. Traffic generated by visitors to an attraction may result in economic gains to the operators and others from parking charges and economic losses because of space and labour needed for parking provision, but will almost inevitably cause some social, if not cultural, costs in terms of traffic congestion, safety and frustration, as well environmental issues of emission and noise pollution. All of these impacts may have a political dimension in terms of pressure being put on elected and other officials to mitigate or remove any negative and/or unwanted impacts of all types.

Some of the major difficulties in dealing with the impacts of tourism are well recognised (Wall and Mathieson, 2006). One is the fact that the existence of accurate and reliable baselines in terms of conditions before tourism begins rarely exist, thus changes that occur as tourism develops tend to be assigned to or blamed on tourism without firm evidence other than similarity in timing. Another problem is that impacts may take place in one location or at one time, but the effects may not occur in the same place or at the same time and thus some impacts (both positive and negative) of tourism may not be correctly assigned. Most impact studies in the context of tourism have not been longitudinal but instead short term, if not 'one-shot' studies of situations, which make the detection of long-term and cumulative impacts almost impossible to identify. Environmental impacts in particular are often little studied or understood as opportunities to establish control examples and study over long periods rarely occur, and most tourism researchers have not been trained in the physical sciences (Warnken and Buckley, 1998). Finally, because of the inevitable variations in environmental conditions as well great variety in the elements of tourism (tourist characteristics, numbers, timing, purpose of visit and motivation, and pattern and type of activities) comparisons between different destinations are often meaningless if not misleading.

The impacts resulting from specific individual attractions and events, while perhaps being somewhat simpler and potentially easier to correctly identify and assign, are still complex and subject to a range of factors from political interference with studies (and interpretation of results) to changes between the initial proposal for an attraction or event and the actual final result. This situation means that accurate prediction of impacts is extremely difficult and often impossible to achieve. An indication of the nature of impacts of attractions and events is given in Table 10.1, which shows how the characteristics of impacts vary over time, space and their relationships with other elements, and how different types of impact also vary between attractions and events.

Some stakeholders in a destination will have vested interests in achieving identification of certain impacts and concealing the occurrence of other impacts (Hall, 1989b, Hall and Lew, 2009), as discussed below in the context of events. Often legislation that requires impact assessment before projects are approved is limited and does not cover the full range of potential impacts. Environmental assessments that restrict the impacts being examined to those that occur within the 'footprint' of the development, for example, ignore the fact that visitors rarely remain within the physical confines of an attraction or a hotel in which events are held, and thus their impacts are felt far beyond the boundaries of the site itself. Unfortunately, it is rare to find examples of post-hoc evaluation of either impacts or predicted impacts (Nelson et al., 1992).

In summary, therefore, despite the existence of considerable research on the impacts of tourism on host communities and environments (Mathieson and Wall, 1982), the specific impacts of visitor attractions and events have received limited attention. This may be related to limited knowledge of events and visitor attractions in general (Ritchie and Dickson, 2009) and the difficulty in separating the general impacts of tourism from the particular influence of visitor attractions. This gap in our understanding of impacts is surprising and problematic. Considerable public funding has been made available for the development of major attractions in many countries (Dybedal, 1998), and indeed for the organisation of events, sometimes with very thin knowledge of the potential impacts of these attractions at the local and regional scales.

One result of this relative lack of knowledge has been a failure to appreciate the resultant need for ongoing public funding to keep the attractions (and events) operational (Weidenfeld, 2010). In addition, the types of evaluation, feasibility studies and other analyses relating to the impact of visitor attractions and events vary between countries and regions. The diversity in type and size of visitor attractions and events, and in the differing approaches of governments and agencies towards the role of tourism and visitor attractions in urban and regional development, makes it difficult to generalize about such impacts, and to draw lessons about the likely impacts of new initiatives. Hence this chapter provides a rather broad framework for addressing the range of impacts of events and visitor attractions, both as individual business units and as groups of attractions in tourism destinations.

Economic impacts of attractions

All attractions have potential economic impacts, and these vary in geographical range and whether they are directly related to the enterprise itself, or to its impact

Table 10.1 Selected case studies of the economic impact of major visitor attractions

Attraction	Type of attraction/location	Economic impact variables	References
Guggenheim Museum in Bilbao (GMB)	Museum project. Urban area	1. Overnight stays 2. Employment rates and diversity 3. Tax revenue 4. Return on investment (ROI) 5. New establishments in other service sectors 6. Labour productivity	Plaza (2000, 2006, 2008) Rodriguez, Martinez et al. (2001)
Eden Project	Garden project. Peripheral, rural area	*Positive impacts:* 1. Impact of visitors on theattraction and visitor additionality: visitor spending 2. Business turnover 3. Direct employment 4. Leakage (spending on purchases of suppliers and services): reduced via local sourcingstrategy 5. Indirect jobs at suppliers 6. Induced impacts of wage increases 7. Attraction of new investments *Negative impacts:* 1. Negative displacement. 2. Employment leakage	Geoff Broom Associates (2002)

| Iconic attractions in the south west of England | Peripheral | *Positive impacts:*
1. Impact of visitors to the attraction, and visitor additionality: visitor spending
2. Reducing seasonal imbalances
3. Multiplier effects (spending on purchase of supplies and services)
4. Non-market benefits: value of media coverage, enhanced regional profile, improvement of local infrastructure
5. Attracting new businesses, regeneration projects, investments and qualified workforce.

Negative impacts
1. Displacement (negative competition)
2. Reduced availability of funds/capital investments for other local projects
3. Impact on house prices
4. Competition for labour
5. Impact on noise, traffic and local quality of life | South West Regional Development Agency (2005) |

on the region via the generation of tourist flows. In terms of geographical scale, the key point is the distribution of the economic impacts across space (Wall, 1997). In particular, to what extent are the expenditures generated by the enterprise directed to other firms within the region, versus being lost to firms external to the region? It follows that as you increase the spatial scale of analysis, higher and higher proportions of the impacts will be captured within the region. Ultimately, of course, at the global scale, all the expenditures would be captured and none would be lost to other regions. But in practice, of course, most regional analyses work at a far finer spatial scale.

A second important distinction needs to be made between the impacts directly, as opposed to indirectly, related to the visitor attraction. The simplest directly related economic impacts, which are similar to those of other tourism businesses, relate to the direct and indirect expenditures by the attraction itself, as well as what are termed the induced effects related to the expenditures by its employees. In addition to this, however, and signaling their significant role in the economic dynamism of particular destinations and regions, visitor attractions can serve to attract tourists to the region. In effect, it is a key to the generation of external income, that is, of 'exports'. While some of this income will be filtered through the directly related impacts of the attraction, other economic impacts will be more indirect, and will result from the expenditures of visitors on other tourism services – whether attractions, hospitality, retailing or other – within the region. Moreover, the economic impacts of visitor attractions often extend beyond tourism, particularly in the case of iconic attractions such as the Opera House in Sydney (see Chapter 11). In these instances, such iconic attractions may play a significant role in developing, maintaining and enhancing the image of a city, region or even a country.

A good example of the substantial economic impacts of an iconic attraction is provided by the Guggenheim Museum Bilbao (GMB), which is both a successful regeneration project in its own right and in terms of how it shapes the urban economy. Because the cultural attractions of Bilbao are so strongly focused on a single museum, it has provided a valuable laboratory for testing the impact of a major cultural investment. Bilbao, the largest city in the Basque Country and a symbolic site of industrial regeneration, has experienced significant growth in tourism since the opening of the GMB (Plaza, 2006). The aim was not only to secure income and employment effects directly as a result of investments in the Museum, but also to utilise it as a nucleus around which to build a replacement engine of growth for the manufacturing sector in Metropolitan Bilbao (see Box 10.1). The development of the GMB received so much attention that it is claimed to have exercised an iconic role in the revitalisation of Bilbao even before it first opened its doors in October 1997 (Rodríguez, Martínez et al., 2001). The economic impacts of major attractions, such as the Guggenheim, are widely acknowledged in the media, although they have rarely been accurately quantified in academic research.

Investment in an attraction does not automatically generate substantial positive economic impacts because these are contingent on the characteristics of the

---

Box 10.1 Heritage attractions and the urban economy

Investments in cultural and heritage attractions are often seen as a panacea for economic decline and urban revitalization in many cities around the world. However, the effectiveness of a large heritage investment in developing urban economic development depends on four conditions.

A. The main requisite is that the heritage attraction becomes a tourism magnet.
B. A new heritage investment facilitates increased demand in other tourism sectors that spills over to other service industries, creating additional demand for business services, management change and restructuring. However, economic diversity is important and it is important that the city's economy does not become over-dependent on the heritage industry;
C. The level of integration of the redevelopment zone's markets. The new heritage investment should drive demands for new market segments that generate demand for regional products and minimises sources of income leakage. Heritage investments may contribute to balancing seasonal employment fluctuations by adding a complementary product to the hospitality industry in general, and which is attractive to business travellers in particular.
D. That it increases, or at least maintains, its overall productivity and competitiveness, and avoids the negative effects of regeneration, such as an increase in land prices, and other input costs, which may deter other or further development.

Source: Plaza (2008).

---

attraction, its relationships (both competitive and cooperative) with other attractions and businesses, and on the structures and institutions of the local economy. Some of the conditions which determine the intended contribution of major attractions to the urban economy are further outlined in Box 10.1.

The investment in an attraction may simply divert tourists and/or tourism expenditure from existing attractions within the region: in other words, it redistributes demand rather than generating additional demand. There are also opportunity costs – in terms of the opportunities lost for public and/or private investment in other aspects of the regional economy. Furthermore, the demand for attractions and visitors tends to be highly elastic with respect to both income and price (Wall and Mathieson, 2006). Moreover, visitor attractions, and particularly events, in common with other tourism businesses, are vulnerable to both predictable and unpredictable risks from internal and external factors, notably to changing market trends, and the degradation of fixed capital (buildings) over time. This emphasises the need to take a temporal perspective on their development, and to recognise the ways in which their economic impacts are likely to vary over time.

Multiplier effects

There has long been research interest in calculating the economic impacts of tourism, involving bother perceptual (see Apt and Crompton, 1998) and 'objective' estimates. The latter date back to at least the work of Archer (1977) and subsequent modifications by Fletcher (1989) and others. Much of this has been at the level of particular countries or regions, rather than of individual attractions, although the economic modelling follows broadly similar lines, while allowing for scale differences. Three main economic impacts are usually recognised: direct, indirect and induced.

- *Direct impacts* refer to the direct expenditures by visitors and expenditures by the visitor attraction as a business unit. Visitor expenditure includes on-site expenditures and refers to the initial sales to tourists, such as entry tickets, the purchasing of souvenirs and of food and beverage, parking, additional activities and photographs. Some visitor attractions also generate revenues from non-visitors such as corporate or private events and conferencing. The direct impacts can also be measured in terms of employment effects. The employment effect is often relatively small in the context of the overall regional economy because most attractions do not employ a large number of employees and, instead, tend to rely on part-timers, seasonal staff and sometimes volunteers. The temporality or seasonality of the jobs has to be taken into account.
- *The indirect economic impact* is the expenditure by the attractions on goods and services, for example on food, financial services, equipment and marketing. The precise impacts of such expenditures on the destination or region depend on the levels of income leakage to suppliers and other firms outside the destination and region. Leakage can comprise a high proportion of the income generated because many attractions require specific expertise, such as wildlife specialists, artefacts, designers and supplies of materials only found outside their local region. Indirect employment effects can also be calculated, in addition to indirect income effects. One of the major issues in estimating multipliers is the need to decide how far to trace indirect effects: first round effects would only include the direct customers of the attractions, but these in turn would have further indirect effects on their suppliers. For example, the attraction that bought in cakes to sell in its café would have first round effects on the cake producer, and secondary effects on the firms which supplied the flour, sugar and other ingredients to the cake maker.
- *Induced impact*: these are the secondary effects in the economy due to the expenditure of employees' wages, which is spent on a range of products and services.

Multiplier analyses are typically linked to input-output analyses (Tyrrell and Johnston, 2001), which examine the linkages between a sector and the remainder of the economy. The costs of estimating sector specific, let alone firm specific, input-output matrices is prohibitive, so that standardised multipliers are often assumed to apply to particular case studies (Archer and Fletcher, 1996). In recent years, economists have acknowledged the over-simplistic assumptions of most multiplier studies, which tend to overestimate the economic impacts resulting from increased tourism demand. Multipliers assume a perfectly elastic supply of land, capital and labour so that the tourism growth does not impact negatively on the rest of the economy by increasing the costs of factors of production. This weakness has led to the adoption of general equilibrium modelling which recognises that the economy is an integrated economic system (Dwyer et al., 2004). More sophisticated approaches also take into account the costs of the public infrastructures and services which may underpin economic growth (Dwyer and Forsyth, 1997).

In reality, the complexity of such models means that they are rarely used to study the impacts of specific visitor attractions, but rather they deal with regional or national shifts in demand. Smaller visitor attractions in any case are likely to have such a marginal effect on the costs of factors of production that it is not unrealistic to assume away these effects. The same does not apply to major attractions, especially at the more local or sub-regional scale, or to the construction of assemblages of visitor attractions, as at Dubai, the United Arab Emirates or Orlando, Florida. Despite these limitations, the simple multiplier models continue to offer a useful way to conceptualise the economic impacts of individual attractions or events.

The multiplier effects focus on those impacts that directly stem from the increase in demand generated by the visitor attraction itself. However, as noted earlier, there is also a need to estimate the wider *regional effects* of the expenditures resulting from the attraction of tourists to the attraction – that is, to what may be termed 'off-site expenditures'. In other words, those attractions which generate *additional* tourism flows to a destination or region – rather than attracting the expenditures of tourists who would have come to the region anyway – have a net positive additional regional economic impact. It applies particularly to iconic and flagship attractions (Chapter 11), which increase regional appeal and overnight stays (Law, 2002) and therefore generate increased expenditure and income in the region. There may also be inter-regional effects, because spending at the new visitor attraction in one region may displace expenditures in other regions.

Net economic impacts will be influenced by visitor displacement expenditures, that is by the extent to which the expenditures generated by visits to an attraction replace expenditures by the tourists on other services and products in the area, including other visitor attractions. Such displacement effects are likely to be higher where there are clusters of co-located visitor attractions. Evans (2005) emphasises the importance of assessing displacement effects at the local, regional and national levels of flagship projects. However, measuring these effects is problematic because of the hypothetical questions that are posed to tourists in surveys, e.g. 'what would your behaviour and spending have been if you had not visited this attraction?' or 'would you have come here if this attraction was not here?'.

Additionality

More specifically, the visitor additionality factor refers to the additional expenditures generated by an attraction (Fletcher et al., 2013). Therefore, the geographical scale at which additionality is measured, is crucial. Visitor expenditure additionality in an area is divided into on-site expenditures and off-site expenditures. On-site expenditures may include those from visitors who primarily came to the area for reasons other than visiting the attraction (Dybedal, 1998). Since overnight visitors (i.e. tourists) have much higher expenditures at the destination region than other visitors, the existence of local accommodation facilities located alongside attractions are considered a strong indicator of positive additionality impacts (Evans, 2015). Table 10.2 presents the examples of some major visitor attractions (Plaza, 2000, Rodríguez, Martínez et al., 2001, Broom, 2002, South West Regional Development Agency, 2005, Plaza, 2006, Plaza, 2008).

Quantifying these broader regional economic impacts is challenging. While relatively simple questionnaire surveys can estimate the total expenditure generated by an individual tourist trip to a destination, it is much more difficult to calculate whether the visit would have been made, or would have been shorter

Table 10.2 Additionality impacts resulting from visitor attractions and events

	Attractions	Events
Duration	Long-term; proposal to demolition/conversion	Short-term; proposal to termination
Timing	Ongoing for some impacts (visual, costs), primarily when open, maybe seasonal	Occasional, mostly specific event duration
Spatial	Primary in footprint, secondary is access related	Primary in footprint, secondary vicinity- noise, disturbance, access related, otherwise minor
Cultural effects	Minor in most cases	Can be major and positive if local culture related, otherwise minor
Environmental	Primary in construction, secondary related to operation (emissions, noise, drainage, exotics)	Mostly minor, too short for most significant negative effects, may be localised temporary impacts (compaction, wildlife disturbance)
Economic	Often major income and employment generation, can be capable of changing image and market for destination, local, regional, national level effects (taxes), may be high leakage for hardware, franchise fees	Often major income generator, less so for jobs, as often volunteers. Depends greatly on scale, may be high leakage on performers' fees and costs
	Impacts vary with scale of feature; visitor numbers; central or peripheral location; stand-alone or with accommodation and other services provided (e.g. hotel at theme parks, tents at music festivals); nature of ticket sales (single, multiple, combined)	

in duration, in the absence of a specific attraction (Dybedal, 1998). For example, very few tourists would specifically travel to Paris simply to see the Eiffel Tower, but it is part of the assemblage of iconic and flagship attractions that bring millions of visitors to the city. Once they arrive at the city, they generate expenditures in hotels, restaurants, shops and other visitor attractions. Despite these difficulties, measuring a visitor attraction's economic impact, and its contribution to the regional or national economy, is important when lobbying for public investments and subsidies for the sector, or for permission to be granted for developing a new visitor attraction.

At the aggregate scale, there is interesting research sponsored by the International Association of Amusement Parks Attractions (IAAPA), and conducted by Oxford Economics, on the impact of 30,000 attractions in the USA in 2011. These are estimated to have generated $91 billion in direct impacts including attractions' sales, annual capital expenditures, as well as in ancillary spending. The indirect and induced impacts were estimated to have generated a further $127 billion and in total the attractions were considered to have supported more than 2.3 million jobs including full-time and seasonal employment. All such estimates should be approached cautiously, for they depend on the questions posed by the (necessarily self-interested) sponsors, and on the methodologies applied: whether, for example, input-output or general equilibrium models were applied.

Of course, as mentioned earlier, the impacts generated by attractions will be scale specific. The net impacts will be less than the total impacts if the leakage of expenditure is taken into account; that is, the purchases of products from outside the local economy, the wages paid to employees living outside the area, the remittances of migrant workers, the payment of profits or interest to investors and financial intermediaries located outside the region. Travel agents, tour operators and transport companies can also contribute to what are often quite substantial leakages of income from a particular destination. The extent of the leakage decreases as the scale of the regional analysis increases – whereas the impact on a small town or village may be reduced by a very high level of leakages, these may be minimal at the national scale. The net impacts are also highly contingent on the economic characteristics of the destination – whether it has sufficient local capital, labour, knowledge and intermediaries, or whether it has to rely on external sources (Huse et al., 1998). Hence, rural areas tend to be particularly subject to leakage effects.

Temporal issues

Another important aspect of the economic impacts of visitor attractions is their temporality. Their impacts will vary through time, across the construction stage, followed by the various stages in the product (or resort) development. The creation of a new attraction always requires some start up investment costs, which at a minimum include marketing, enhancing or creating the attraction itself, and some adaptation of existing buildings, for example the house of Rembrandt in Amsterdam, to form a museum dedicated to his life and work. However, the development of new attractions may often include major construction projects, which can have a considerable impact (even if temporary) on the local and/or regional economy. For example, the conversion of the Bankside Power Station in London into the Tate Modern art gallery required a major investment and four years of construction work. Investments in five historic sites operated by English Heritage and the National Trust in the UK (Anglesey Abbey, the Great Tower at Dover Castle, Down House, Kenilworth Castle and Elizabethan Gardens and Tyntesfield) also provided an important stimulus for the construction industry. In these instances, local staff were employed and a large proportion of goods and services were procured locally, which resulted in a substantial impact on the local economy (GHK Consulting, 2010). Of course, the effects are dependent on the extent to which the companies are locally based, whether the materials they use are locally sourced and the extent to which labour is local. Larger construction projects are more likely to involve large external firms to source materials externally and to rely on non-local labour.

Environmental impacts of attractions

The impact of visitor attractions on the environment is clear and immediate in some situations and uncertain, delayed and denied in others. Much depends on the environment in which an attraction is located and the impacts are also normally positively related to the physical size and visitor numbers of the attraction involved. Large visitor attractions (in terms of space), such as theme parks, require considerable supplies of energy and water, and may also contribute significantly to air pollution and excess waste produced both by the operation of the attraction itself and by its visitors. Visitor attractions in rural areas may also require the clearing of what were natural habitats with the ensuing potential of endangering species of flora and fauna (Fiecke, 2015). In contrast, some attractions, for example the Eden Project (Kendle, 2003), may market themselves as positive examples of inspired environmental management, suggesting ways of reducing humankind's negative impacts on the environment. Many large natural attractions, and those incorporating natural elements such as wildlife, can serve an environmental conservation purpose, an argument used by zoological attractions which are involved in breeding programmes for endangered species. Thus, the environmental impacts of attractions can vary widely and the nature of the resulting impacts will also vary over the life-span of the attraction itself. The complexity of the interactions between tourism (and related elements of leisure) are well illustrated by Wall and Wright (1977) (see Figure 10.2).

It is not practical to discuss this figure at length; rather its role is to illustrate the interconnectedness of the many elements and processes which exist in any natural or modified environment. Visitor activities have effects upon the various features shown in Figure 10.2, and because of the feedback loops (both positive and negative) that exist in all environments, the results of change in an environment can vary widely in nature, extent and longevity. Thus, an activity such as walking over vegetation has effects not only on that vegetation, but also

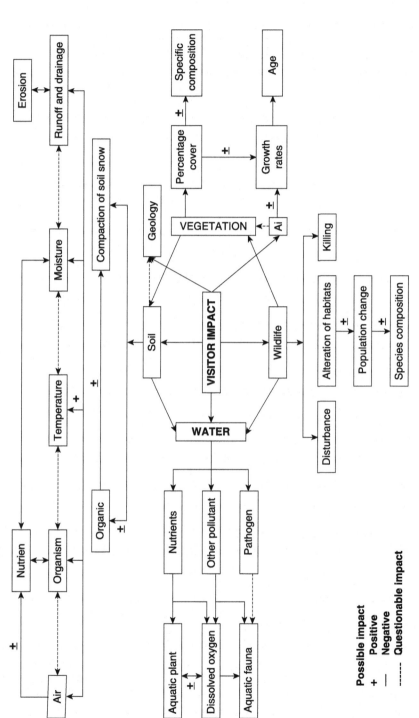

Possible impact

+ Positive
— Negative
----- Questionable impact

Figure 10.2 Visitor-environment impacts and interactions

Based on Wall and Wright (1977).

on soil (and its characteristics), and on species which are dependent on the vegetation and which might be disturbed by human presence. Rather than attempt to identify all impacts stemming from any visitor attraction, it might be more practical and useful to use a process suggested by Speight (1973), namely, to determine the extent or area affected, the uniqueness or irreplaceability of any species or habitat threatened, and the degree of loss of ecosystem diversity involved. Some negative impacts are almost inevitable with each attraction created, and it is the importance and significance of those impacts which needs to be investigated and considered.

During the construction phase of many attractions there are likely to be negative environmental impacts resulting from the physical modification of a site and access routes to it. Alterations in drainage, vegetation and hence wildlife populations, noise and dust pollution, and emission pollution of air and water, are all common side effects of the creation of attractions. In most cases construction of large projects is preceded by environmental impact assessments in order to identify potential impacts and actions which could be taken to mitigate the negative impacts anticipated. However well done and comprehensive these assessments may be, because of the interactions between elements and processes in the natural environment, it is highly likely that unforeseen impacts will be created, although some may not be identified until a considerable time after construction has been completed. Even in attractions such as national parks, management policies may have unforeseen results which may need to be corrected later (Nelson, 2000).

One of the major environmental impacts of attractions relates to disturbance of the surrounding environment and communities. Disturbance is a phenomenon that is extremely difficult to identify and measure, as the researcher more often than not becomes an agent of disturbance. The presence of a changed environment, the resulting noise, smell and other effects on the atmosphere, the presence of large numbers of people and their vehicles, and the associated related developments all ensure that an attraction will have impacts beyond its immediate boundaries. Even in the context of attractions such as the protected environments of national parks, Nelson (2000) listed over 20 sources of stress on Canadian National Parks from activities within and outside of the parks themselves. The effects of disturbance can be reduced by the establishment of buffer zones around attractions that are large sources of disturbance and also around attractions that are particularly sensitive to external influences.

Environmental impacts related to visitor attractions are complex therefore, and it must be remembered that while some attractions create undesirable environmental impacts, in other situations, some attractions may be vulnerable to environmental impacts from external activities and developments. Nelson (2000) noted a third relationship between attractions and their environments, where specific conservation-centred attractions such as national parks had created negative environmental impacts within their own boundaries through the development of specific attractions and facilities. This example serves to emphasise the complicated nature of environmental impacts and visitors and their attractions.

Socio-cultural impacts of attractions

The social and cultural impacts of attractions have received far less attention than have the economic impacts. The impacts generally come in two forms: through the effects of increased visitor numbers on local social and cultural practices and values, and through the potential contribution, positive or negative, of the attraction to the cultural life of the region. In terms of the direct cultural impact of the attraction itself on the cultural life of the region, museums are considered repositories of cultural diversity, education, social cohesion and personal development. They may also promote an integrated approach to cultural heritage and contribute to strengthening or reinforcing community identity (Brida et al., 2012). Other attractions may have a less positive image, draw unwelcome attention to a community and create disagreement over the image, of the community in which it is located. Examples of 'dark tourism' attractions are not always welcomed by host communities and may generate negative reactions from visitors (Laderman, 2013).

The relative lack of research on such impacts is surprising, given that visitor attractions, particularly museums, have long been seen as having an educational function (Swarbrooke, 2002). This may involve visits by individuals or small groups, or larger organised visits from schools and other local institutions. The Eden Project, in Cornwall, UK, for example, offers public education programmes as one of its core charitable activities, including running school programmes, further education and colleges (Kendle, 2003). There is also recognition among museum and gallery owners and trustees of 'the importance of expanding their role and contribution to local education, lifelong learning and combating social exclusion' (Couch and Farr, 2000:161). Museums and other buildings may also be associated with architectural merit, which may come to be seen by local people as a source of pride as well as being a stimulus for tourism, and for the local economy (Couch and Farr, 2000).

Socio-cultural impacts can also be perceived as ambiguous or negative. These include the general socio-cultural impacts of tourism on host populations rather than being specific to the attractions, and relate to the off-site impacts of visitors similar to those noted above in the context of environmental impacts. These relationships change in accordance with shifts in the levels of engagement with destination communities throughout the lives of the attractions. Changes in access arrangements may, for example, suddenly increase the numbers of visitors to a location, causing an undesired greater level of interaction between residents and tourists. An example would be the establishment of air access to St Helena Island in the south Atlantic in September 2015. According to recent media coverage, 'the islanders are hoping that French tourists and Napoleon enthusiasts will arrive in force' (Times, 2015:23) after the newly built airport opens for public service in May 2016. The idea of an air service was first proposed in 1943, and among other reasons given was to 'revive the economy' (Binyon, 2015:40). It remains to be seen if the historic attractions of Napoleon's last residence and his grave do attract large numbers of tourists and if so, whether the attitude of residents remains positive as numbers and interactions grow. The amount and nature of contact between local residents and visitors to attractions appears to be a factor in whether tourism and tourists are perceived to be welcome additions to a community or not (Brougham and Butler, 1981), as well as varying with the personal characteristics and location of the residents themselves (see also Box 10.2 later).

Political attitudes

Ultimately, as Miles (2005:913) argues:

> the success of investment in cultural projects depends, above all, upon people's sense of belonging in a place and the degree to which culture-led regeneration can engage with that sense of belonging, whilst balancing achievements of the past with ambitions for the future.

Of course, these socio-cultural impacts are not homogeneous and are likely to be contested and perceived differently by different segments of the community. Communities may remain divided in their perception of the contribution of visitor attractions to cultural and social life in destination regions (Evans, 2005). McNeill (2000), for example, highlighted contentious identity issues relating to local actors-residents in Bilbao, who were criticised for using the Guggenheim Museum to 'indigenise' dominant cultures for their own Basque political community as a counterpoise to the impact of globalisation on the European city.

Leaders at the national and regional scales may also use visitor attractions as means to glorify their personal reputation or achievements (see Chapter 11). This is particularly relevant for cultural and heritage attractions. The Italian government, for example, has recently caused a debate amongst curators and art critics by hiring foreigners for top museum management jobs. The backlash has been particularly strong after the dismissal of the head of the country's most prestigious gallery, the Uffizi in Florence, followed by the hiring of a German national. This was described by one commentator as 'a slap in the face for Italy' (Day, 2015). The socio-cultural impacts of visitor attractions are also significant for regional and local development. A study on the impact of small museums in rural communities in Sardinia, Italy, suggested that for a museum to act as a stimulus for development, it should build on and celebrate local attributes, providing added value to existing resources and the community's capabilities (Iorio and Wall, 2011).

Of course, not all attractions are cultural in purpose or design. Those which represent the local culture and traditions are generally the ones which create fewer negative impacts in the social-cultural sphere than those which are overtly intrusive and neither authentic nor related to the local community. Casinos often meet with opposition from local communities on a number of grounds (moral, ethical, financial and visual) despite generally having a positive economic impact on communities (Carmichael and Jones, 2007). Where attractions and visitors create strong emotions, political action and change may result (Martin, 2006), sometimes with negative results for further development.

It must be noted, however, that the social and cultural impacts of attractions are not exclusively one way. The concept that it is only local residents that are affected, and then normally in a negative way by the effects of visitor attractions and visitors, is misleading. Visitors are also affected by visiting specific attractions and communities and may well change their behaviour, their appearance and their perceptions as a result of visitation. The process of change resulting from impacts of any kind is never simple and where human emotions, beliefs and perceptions are concerned, the process is extremely complicated.

Impacts of events

One of the key issues in dealing with the impacts of events is that because of the normally short-term nature of events, the impacts often take different forms to the more clearly established impacts of tourism in general. All events require planning, approval, facility development, the actual operation of the event and then closure and often removal of facilities. It is important to acknowledge that impacts occur in each of these stages, and that the nature and dimensions of the impacts will vary considerably throughout the overall time period (Table 10.1). In addition, the nature and features of the impacts are likely to be wider than the traditional three areas of economic, social and environmental, as noted several decades ago by Getz (1977).

Proposal and approval stages of events

The planning period may be as long as several years and for most of this period, the only visible effects will be related to political maneuverings and negotiations. Any firm arrangements resulting from discussions and negotiations are often hidden from the general public until an event moves into the approval stage. It is at this point that the public at large, and particularly residents of the location of an event, generally first hear of the proposed event. There normally follow discussions and arguments, often dominated by economic considerations, with proponents stressing economic gains, along with prestige, rejuvenation and legacy benefits claimed to result from the event, generally despite there being little research supporting such views (Hall, 1989a).

Opponents often base their arguments on social concerns such as removal of permanent residents for temporary events as properties may be demolished to make way for construction of infrastructure (such as stadia, transport, participant housing) if the event is of the scale of a Hallmark event (Syme et al., 1989). Opponents may also cite economic disbenefits such as increased taxes, land and labour costs, as well as disturbance and loss of amenity. If approval is gained from local, regional and national authorities, there may still be a considerable delay before any physical manifestation occurs, as major events such as Olympic Games or football World Cups need to be awarded by international bodies (e.g. FIFA) with all the problems and potential corruption and confusion that procedure may involve.

Ongoing and post event impacts

Impacts during the events generally include increased visitation to the destination involved, but it should be recognised, although it rarely is, that some potential tourists may avoid such destinations while major events are being held. This is because of the knowledge that such places will be more expensive to reach and far more expensive than normal to stay in, if accommodation is even available for non-participants and non-organisers. Organisations such as FIFA and the Olympic Committee require many hundreds of free rooms and transportation for their members from the local organisers which might otherwise have been bought by traditional tourists. It is widely acknowledged that accommodation costs in destinations increase from 100 to 1,000 per cent during major events and transport providers take equal advantage of increased demand. Clearly there are also benefits at the individual level for local residents who offer rooms or houses for rent during such events. In St Andrews, Scotland, local residents can earn £3,000–8,000 for the rental of a house during the ten days when the Open golf tournament is held there, and short-term employment rises significantly. On the negative side, even small events generate garbage, traffic, disturbance and petty crime, best summed up as loss or reduction of amenity or quality of life for local residents, if nothing more permanent or long-lasting. Local attitudes towards events appear to vary widely with circumstance, familiarity with the event, the scale and duration of the event and its appropriateness in its location.

It is clear in recent years that such approval and awarding of events can see the production of blatantly false and both exaggerated benefits and underestimated costs by proponents and sometimes similarly inaccurate forecasts by opponents of events. The then Mayor of London, Ken Livingston, for example, commented on television that the initial forecast of some £4–5 billon cost of the 2012 Olympic Games was not a real figure but simply produced for the bid. The 'real' cost finally being around £12 billion. There has been a universal pattern of gross underestimation of costs of events such as the Olympic Games, and equally gross overestimation of benefits, particularly of what are termed 'legacy' benefits. These normally include the ongoing profitable use of facilities, partly driven by increased participation levels of local and national residents in healthy activities such as sports, improved health of residents and improved cultural relations in the host community/country.

In reality, most hallmark events leave a legacy of underused and overly expensive facilities and have little or no effect upon the diet, fitness or sporting participation levels of host communities. Improved sense of pride may occur during an event but little remains for long afterwards, despite ongoing praise and self-satisfaction of the organisers and politicians involved with the event. While a few events have been credited with major positive benefits lasting beyond the event – the Olympic Games in Barcelona, for example – in many cases post-mortem analyses reveal disappointing results. The Montreal Olympics left the city and the province of Quebec with massive still unpaid debts, while facilities in Athens and to a lesser extent in Sydney are used at levels far below those forecast, and the future for Rio de Janiero is challenging. In all the cases above, the opportunity cost of hosting the events was not openly considered or argued, and only the Los Angeles Olympics appears to have made a profit, or at least not a public loss, in the last 50 years.

The post event impacts of events also vary widely. The two-day appearance of a travelling circus may result in little post event impact and one-day events even less. Some garbage and sanitation problems, parking and other traffic issues, and perhaps scarring of the landscape may occur, which may well disappear in a short time. In the case of major events, there may be deliberate transformation of a neighbourhood or community. Utilisation of participant accommodation for local resident housing post event is common following major events such as the Commonwealth Games in Glasgow in 2014 and the Olympics in London in 2012. Thus, some of the legacy benefits may be only indirectly related to the actual events themselves, and the latter may be seen and used as a successful agent of rejuvenation of areas in urban decline. Legacy benefits of a 'softer' kind are often much less successful, such as predictions of improved health of local residents after major sports events. One year after the Commonwealth Games in Glasgow it was concluded that 'Games fail to boost activity' (Swerling, 2015:4). 'There has been almost no change in levels of physical activity across Scotland since the Commonwealth Games', despite 'one of the key promises made by Games organisers was that Glasgow 2014 would inspire the nation to become more active' (Swerling, 2015:4). The research found that there had been a 1 per cent decline in adults doing the recommended amount of exercise over the intervening period. It is clear that elements of accountability, participation, performance and transparency are important prerequisites to good governance and achievement of legacy benefits from major events (Leopkev and Parent, 2015).

One should not dismiss the argument that there are real benefits as well as costs that accrue from the holding of events. Even when opportunity costs, loss of business because of avoidance by potential visitors, and cost over-runs in construction are taken into account, many mega events do undoubtedly result in increased income and job creation for destinations. Second, there may well be an increase in softer more intangible benefits such as increased civic and national pride, wider awareness and appreciation of the destination from local to global publicity of the destination as well as the event itself. An event may result in future inward investment, and a general 'feel good' factor amongst local residents. Part of the problem with such events is that unreliable forecasts of benefits and costs are rarely corrected or acknowledged, and decisions can often be made in a rush of perceived political and self-serving benefits instead of careful consideration of the full range of costs and benefits.

The impacts of events can also be examined in terms of the impacts on the individual participants of the event, which can be defined as internal impacts. These are personal impacts, the participant's experience of the event; the positive impacts include changes in perceptions, satisfaction, happiness, attitudes, values and personality, while the negative ones are mainly about dissatisfaction and failure to meet value for money expectations. The other impacts are mainly external and address interactions between the event industry, the economy, society and the environment including economic, socio-cultural and environmental impacts (Bladen et al., 2012).

Economic impacts of events

The economic impacts of events are, in many ways, similar to those of visitor attractions, but they have a distinctive temporality. It is therefore particularly important to think of events as having both short-term and long-term economic impacts (Table 10.1). In the short term, the direct impacts include the visitor expenditures at the event, such as entry tickets, programmes, retail products, food and drink, as well as additional off-site expenditures on hospitality services, transport and local taxes (Bowdin et al., 2012). Although the temporality of events can significantly constrain their overall economic impacts, they can be advantageous in terms of overcoming seasonality and supporting key industrial sectors and local businesses, investments in infrastructure and tax revenues (Raj and Musgrav, 2009). Such effects are more likely to be realised when the event generates tourist demand which is complementary to the year-round demand provided by visitor attractions.

There are also longer-term impacts, related to the year-round marketing of an event, advanced sales, programme management and preparation or improvements to the site of the event. While most staff will only be employed during or immediately before and after the event, some labour input will be required at other times of the year. The extent to which there are induced effects stemming from the expenditure of wages is highly dependent on the extent to which the event depends on voluntary as opposed to commodified (paid) workers.

In the UK, the overall impact of different types of events, including those related to businesses and tourism (conferences, exhibitions, sports, etc.), is estimated to be over £22 billion (Bowdin et al., 2012). Such estimates are, of course, dependent on the methodologies used. Moreover, as with attractions, the net economic impacts depend on the scale of analysis and the leakage of income outside the region. Spillovers or leakages, from an event itself to other localities or destination communities, must be taken into account when calculating the regional impacts. For example, revenues generated by the touring performance of a band or an exhibition may flow to its country or region of residence, where the band/exhibition is registered for tax purposes. Such government revenues cannot be taken into consideration in the calculation of the local or regional multiplier effect of the event on the hosting destination, although of course they are part of the inter-regional multiplier, and could be included in the multiplier at a higher level of regional aggregation, or the national scale if applicable.

Where events are infrequent (perhaps one-day or weekend every year) they are likely to be subject to higher levels of external leakages, compared to permanent attractions, because they do not provide year-round demand for the products and services provided by local firms. In these instances, there is a compelling economies of scale logic to the provision of specialist facilities – whether tents, stages, lighting, mobile toilets or food outlets – by small numbers of firms operating at the regional or inter-regional, rather than the local, level.

Long-term impacts

The longer-term positive economic effects of events have a broader dimension, beyond the direct income generated by the planning and delivery of the event. Successful events can make a significant contribution to the regional image, which is in the period before but especially after the event. Positive and sometimes substantial media attention may enhance the destination image (Bowdin et al., 2012). For example, the New Orleans World's Fair stimulated a development boom, founded on positive imagery and longer-term investments, which created a legacy of tourism facilities (Dimanche, 1996). Such long-term economic impacts are often claimed for mega events such as Olympic Games, the World Cup and World Fairs and Exhibitions.

Critics contend that in most cases the legacy of these events is at best over-estimated, and at worst fanciful (Syme et al., 1989). Many of the benefits or 'legacies' quickly fade, if they happen at all. Many events like the Athens and Montreal Olympic have a legacy of games stadia which are unused or underused, and represent a persistent drain on public budgets. There are also displacement effects, with locals (and their daily expenditures) perhaps departing the city during the event. Another displacement effect results from a proportion of the visitors to the event substituting this trip for a visit they would have made anyway. There can also be negative impacts on the destination image if prices for local hospitality services are significantly inflated during the event.

Probably the major concern about long-term significant negative effects centres on the fact that large scale and mega events often require the facilitation of new and sometimes dedicated or exclusive infrastructure. Since they create the need for new and improved infrastructure, they require large investments in temporary construction projects increasing demand for labour over a relatively short period. However, new projects, such as large venues, stadia, roads or even water and electricity infrastructure, require ongoing maintenance, which in the long term may prove to be costlier than their construction. These costs are rarely funded by the event entrepreneurs and funders, and may incur additional ongoing costs for the hosting communities (Bowdin et al., 2012).

The Olympic Games have probably been subject to more economic impact analyses than most events, perhaps because of their almost unrivalled global prominence. In a study of the 2000 Sydney Olympics, Madden (2002), using general equilibrium based modelling, estimated that over the longer period (1993/4 to 2005/6) the Olympics increased the gross state product of New South Wales state by an average of $490 million per year, which equates to an increase of some 0.12 per cent per annum in Australian GDP. However, the impacts on household incomes were far more modest and the author estimated that most of the increased state or national income was allocated either to investment or to payment for external (non-Australian) capital equipment. On the positive side, New South Wales and Australian employment increased by an estimated 5,300 and 7,500 jobs respectively. But there were displacement effects – for example, an estimated $685 million of state expenditure were diverted to the Olympics. Although the overall results were positive, they were also relatively modest compared to the size of the state and national economies. The peak year for positive impacts was of course the year of the event, 2000/1, but there were substantial positive impacts, mainly through construction, in the previous three years. The post-Games impacts were estimated to be low and negative due to ongoing debt.

Social and cultural impacts of events

There has been a surge in recent years in the attention given to the social role of events by policy makers, organisers and communities linked to the perception of events as instruments for cultural regeneration, enhancing identities, as catalysts of social cohesion and for building social capital. Given that the importance of spatial proximity is challenged by digital communication, events can provide new spaces for socialisation and coordination mechanisms, whereby individualised agendas interact, particularly in the contemporary network society (Richards and Brito, 2014).

The social impacts of events are often examined in terms of perceptions of local residents, which are linked to how economic and environmental impacts are perceived by local communities. Positive impacts include a better sense of community and community pride, obtaining new skills, financial contribution to charities, economic benefits and new contacts with different, perhaps foreign, populations. The latter may contribute to socio-cultural change in terms of fashion, norms and values (Reid, 2007, Raj and Musgrav, 2009, Getz, 2012, Kim, Jun et al., 2015). The Notting Hill Carnival (London, UK), for example, is a festival which is aimed at improving relations between communities and strengthening minority communities. Negative socio-cultural impacts include local residents' alienation when events take place, commercialisation, loss of authenticity, social conflict, crime and concerns regarding traffic congestions and environmental consequences such as pollution, as well as the economic costs to the local or regional authority (Shone and Perry, 2004).

The impacts of events can be differentiated between the collective (community) and individual levels. Festivals as a type of event have been identified as having a significant impact both at the community and the individual levels. At the community level, they provide an opportunity to gather, socialise and enhance relationship networks and social capital (Elizabeth, 2007). Greater social capital building is positively related to the levels of active participation, commitment to meet their objectives and the positive perceptions of their outcomes (Richards and Brito, 2014). At the individual level, potential benefits include increasing self-esteem, a sense of contribution, self-worth and personal and life satisfaction. Furthermore, the perception of socio-cultural impacts may vary between different groups in destination communities as shown in Box 10.2.

Box 10.2 Perceived social impacts of festivals – it depends on whom you are asking …

The perceptions of two community festivals, one in Western Australia and the other in Victoria, Australia were examined using qualitative and quantitative methods. Six types of positive and negative impact dimensions were identified: inconvenience, community identity and cohesion, personal frustration, entertainment and socialisation opportunities, community growth and development, and behavioural consequences.

These dimensions were perceived differently by five subgroups identified by a cluster analysis, labelled as tolerators, economically connected (who worked in tourism and who undertook paid work on the weekend of the festival), attendees, avoiders (avoided it by either not attending or leaving town) and volunteers. Volunteers or attendees tended to be the most positive about the festival and its impacts. The avoiders were the most negative in their perceptions and the volunteers were the most positive. In between, closer to the negative end of the scale were the economically connected, who were less negative than the avoiders, given that they also recognised some positive impacts. Attendees and tolerators recognised both positive and negative impacts and had similar perceptions.

At the community level, participation in events provided opportunities for social transactions, relationship building and the development of social networks, which in turn have positive outcomes for community wellbeing and the development of social capital. This study also showed that when studying the impacts of events, it is important to take into account the heterogeneity of communities by identifying groups which have different feelings, and perceptions and needs which should be addressed by event organisers, managers and policy makers.

Source: Elizabeth (2007).

Environmental impacts of events

Because of their temporary nature and varying locations, the environmental impacts of many events are not of major significance and since the majority of events are small in scale, impacts are also generally limited and non-extensive. Even where visitor numbers may be large, the fact that the space used by an event for activites and services such as parking is only temporary means that the space may be available for local use for the remainder of the year, and therefore, impacts will be mostly temporary (Bladen et al., 2012). Negative impacts include air pollution emitted by transport and emissions from catering and accommodation facilities in and around an event venue, as well as noise pollution from the event itself. These impacts tend to be directly related to the size of the event in terms of space, and the number of facilities and attendees.

Other issues include water pollution in or around an event venue, and impacts on the sewage system and depletion of natural resources including as a result of waste disposal (Raj and Musgrav, 2009). Only in rare cases are there significant impacts on wildlife. In Scotland, the largest music festival, 'T in the Park', had to change its regular rural location owing to the presence of an underground pipeline and resulting security issues. The new site a few kilometres away was controversial as a pair of ospreys (a rare and highly protected species) was deemed to be threatened by the relocation of the festival close to their nest. Eventually the relocation took place without apparent harm to the birds. Generally such issues are resolved early in the selection of a site for any large event and negative environmental impacts avoided or mitigated. Short-term compaction of vegetation and disturbance of wildlife (unless in breeding season) cause little permanent damage or change except in the most sensitive of ecosystems, and visitors to most festivals congregate on site to experience the events and acts being offered, thus containing any potential impacts.

Conclusions

The impacts of visitor attractions and events are difficult to generalise and have to be examined in the context of internal and external factors, such as size, type, content and location. In many cases this has not been done and predictions of impacts are often generalised from those resulting from tourism at large and thus are prone to error in specific cases. This can be problematical as major visitor attractions and events are portrayed and used as tools for economic development and as catalysts of urban regeneration, social change and rebranding in urban and rural settings. This is because they can increase a community's appeal to visitors and may improve the quality of life for residents (Weidenfeld, 2010). Their impacts can be considerable; indeed, in many cases they are intended to be so, which makes their planning and management, as well as their design, construction, promotion and post-operation handling, of critical importance. Pre-assessment of likely impacts, cooperation, transparency and involvement of local communities, and acknowledgement and protection of important habitats, processes and patterns of behaviour are essential if impacts are to be positive and mitigated. While generalising potential impacts from single case studies is of debatable value, generalising potential impacts from overall tourism studies to specific attractions or events is equally problematic. Much greater attention must be paid to specific conditions and characteristics of both the setting and the attraction or event under consideration if realistic and accurate predictions of impacts are to be achieved.

References

Apt, J. and Crompton, J. L. (1998). Developing and testing a tourism impact scale. *Journal of Travel Research*, *37*(2), 120–130

Archer, B. (1977). *Tourism Multipliers: The State of the Art.* (Vol. 11). Bangor: University of Wales Press.

Archer, B. and Fletcher, J. (1996). The economic impact of tourism in the Seychelles. *Annals of Tourism Research*, *23*(1), 32–47.

Binyon, M. (2015, 16 September). First aircraft lands on St Helena. *The Times*, p. 40.

Bladen, C., Kennell, J., Abson, E. and Wilde, N. (2012). *Events Management: An Introduction*. Abingdon: Routledge.

Bowdin, G., O'Toole, W., Allen, J., Harris, R. and McDonnell, I. (2012). *Events Management*. London: Routledge.

Brida, J. G., Meleddu, M. and Pulina, M. (2012). Factors influencing the intention to revisit a cultural attraction: The case study of the Museum of Modern and Contemporary Art in Rovereto. *Journal of Cultural Heritage*, *13*(2), 167–174.

Broom, A. G. (2002). *The Economic Impact of the Eden Project*. Totnes, Devon: Geoff Broom Associates.

Brougham, J. E. and Butler, R. W. (1981). The application of segregation analysis to explain resident attitudes to social impacts of tourism. *Annals of Tourism Research*, *8*(IV), 569–590.

Carmichael, B. A. and Jones, J. L (2007). Indigenous owned casinos and perceived local community impacts: Mohegan Sun in South East Connecticut, USA. In R. W. Butler and T. Hinch (Eds), *Indigenous Tourism* (pp. 95–109). London: Butterworth Heinemann.

Couch, C. and Farr, S.-J. (2000). Museums, galleries, tourism and regeneration: Some experiences from Liverpool. *Built Environment*, *26*(2), 152–163.

Day, M. (2015). Appointment of foreign museum directors labelled a 'slap in the face for Italy' by curators and art critics. *The Independent*.

Dimanche, F. (1996). Special events legacy: The 1984 Louisiana world's fair in New Orleans. *Festival Management and Event Tourism*, *4*(1–2), 49–54.

Dwyer, L., and Forsyth, P. (1997). Measuring the benefits and yield from foreign tourism. *International Journal of Social Economics*, *24*, 223–236.

Dwyer, L, Forsyth, B. and Spurr, R. (2004). Evaluating tourism's economic effects: New and old approaches. *Tourism Management*, *25*, 307–317.

Dybedal, P. (1998). *Theme Parks as Flagship Attractions in Peripheral Areas Bronholm, Denmark Bornholms Forskningscenter* (Stenbrudsvej 55, DK-3730, Denmark).

Elizabeth, K. (2007). *Understanding the Social Impacts of Festivals on Communities*. Doctorate of Philosophy, University of Western Sydney.

Evans, G. (2005). Measure for measure: Evaluating the evidence of culture's contribution to regeneration. *Urban Studies*, *42*(5–6), 959–983.

Evans, N. (2015). *Strategic Management for Tourism, Hospitality and Events*. Abingdon: Routledge.

Fiecke, K. (2015). What environmental problems come with making a theme park? *eHow Contributor*.

Fletcher, J. (1989). Input-output analyses and tourism impact studies. *Annals of Tourism Research*, *16*(4), 514–529.

Fletcher, J., Fyall, A., Gilbert, D. and Wanhill, S. (2013). *Tourism: Principles and Practice*. 5th edition. Harlow: Pearson.

Geoff Broom Associates (2002). *The Economic Impact of the Eden Project*. Totnes, Devon: Geoff Broom Associates.

Getz, D. (1977). The impact of tourism on host communities: A research approach. In B. S. Duffield (Ed.), *Tourism A Tool for Regional Development* (pp. 1–9). Edinburgh: Tourism and Recreation Research Unit, University of Edinburgh.

Getz, D. (2012). *Event Studies: Theory, Research and Policy for Planned Events*. London: Routledge.

GHK Consulting, G. (2010). *The Impact of Historic Visitor Attractions London, UK*. English Heritage and the National Trust. Retrieved from http://hc.historicengland.org.uk/content/pub/Impact-of-Historic-Visitor-Attractions (accessed 25 February 2016).

Hall, C. M. (1989a). Hallmark events and the planning process. In G. J. Syme, B. J. Shaw, D. M. Fenton and W. S. Mueller (Eds), *The Planning and Evaluation of Hallmark Events* (pp. 20–39). Aldershot: Avebury.

Hall, C. M. (1989b). The politics of hallmark events. In G. J. Syme, B. J. Shaw, D. M. Fenton and W. S. Mueller (Eds), *The Planning and Evaluation of Hallmark Events* (pp. 219–241). Aldershot: Avebury.

Hall, C. M. and Lew, A. A. (2009). *Understanding and Managing Tourism Impacts: An Integrated Approach*. Londo: Routledge.

Huse, M., Gustaven, T. and Almedal, S. (1998). Tourism impact comparisons amongst Norwegian towns. *Annals of Tourism Research, 25*(3), 721–738.

Iorio, M. and Wall, G. (2011). Local museums as catalysts for development: Mamoiada, Sardinia, Italy. *Journal of Heritage Tourism, 6*(1), 1–15.

Kendle, A. D. (2003). The Eden Project and regional regeneration. *Journal of the Royal Agricultural Society of England, 164*, 1–8.

Kim, W., Jun, H. M. et al. (2015). Evaluating the perceived social impacts of hosting large-scale sport tourism events: Scale development and validation. *Tourism Management, 48*, 21–32.

Laderman, S. (2013). From the Vietnam War to the 'War on Terror': Tourism and the martial fascination. In R. Butler and W. Suntikul (Eds), *Tourism and War* (pp. 26–35). Oxon: Routledge.

Law, C. M. (2002). *Urban Tourism: The Visitor Economy and the Growth of Large Cities*. London: Continuum.

Leopkev, B. and Parent, M. M. (2015). Stakeholder perspectives regarding the governance of legacy at the Olympic Games. *Annals of Leisure Research*.

McNeill, D. (2000). McGuggenisation? National identity and globalisation in the Basque country. *Political Geography, 19*, 473–494.

Madden R. (2002). The economic consequences of the Sydney Olympics: The CREA/Arthur Andersen Study. *Current Issues in Tourism, 5*(1), 7–21,

Martin, B. (2006). The TALC model and politics. In R. W. Butler (Ed.) *The Tourism Area Life Cycle Volume 1 Applications and Modifications* (pp. 237–249). Clevedon: Channel View Publications.

Mathieson, A. and Wall, G. (1982). *Tourism: Economic, Physical and Social Impacts*. London: Longman.

Miles, S. (2005). 'Our Tyne': Iconic regeneration and the revitalisation of identity in NewcastleGateshead. *Urban Studies, 42*(5–6), 913–926.

Nelson, J. G. (2000). Tourism and national parks in North America: An overview. In R. W. Butler and S. W. Boyd (Eds), *Tourism in National Parks: Issues and Implications* (pp. 301–321). Chichester: John Wiley and Sons.

Nelson, J. G., Butler, R. W. and Serafin, R. (1992). Post hoc assessment in resource management. *Environmental Impact Assessment Review, 12*(3), 271–294.

Plaza, B. (2000). Guggenheim museums effectiveness to attract tourism. *Annals of Tourism Research, 27*(4), 1055–1058.

Plaza, B. (2006). The return on investment of the Guggenheim Museum Bilbao. *International Journal of Urban and Regional Research, 30*(2), 452–467.

Plaza, B. (2008). On some challenges and conditions for the Guggenheim Museum Bilbao to be an effective economic re-activator. *International Journal of Urban and Regional Research, 32*(2), 506–517.

Raj, R. and Musgrav, J. (2009). *Event Management and Sustainability*. Wallingford: CABI.

Reid, S. (2007). Identifying social consequences of rural events. *Event Management, 11*(1–2), 89–98.

Richards, G. and Brito, M. d. (2014). Conclusions – The future of events as a social phenomenon. In G. Richards, M. d. Brito and L. Wilks (Eds), *Exploring the Social Impacts of Events* (pp. 219–238). London and New York: Routledge.

Ritchie, B. W. and Dickson, T. J. (2009). *ACT Attractions: Direct Visitor Expenditure and Visitations Patterns Study*. The Sustainable Tourism Cooperative Research Centre.

Rodríguez, A., Martínez, E. et al. (2001). Uneven redevelopment: New urban policies and socio-spatial fragmentation in metropolitan Bilbao. *European Urban and Regional Studies,* 8(2), 161–178.

Shone, A. and Perry, B. (2004). *Successful Event Management: A Practical Handbook*. London: Continuum.

South West Regional Development Agency (2005). *Iconic Tourism Projects in the South West of England*, Final Report v4.0. Bristol, UK: DTZ Pieda Consulting.

Speight, M. C. D. (1973). *Outdoor Recreation and Its Ecological Effects: A Bibliography and Review* Discussion Papers in Conservation. London: University College.

Swarbrooke, J. (2002). *The Development and Management of Visitor Attractions*. Oxford: Butterworth-Heinemann.

Swerling, G. (2015, 23 September). Games fail to boost activity. *The Times*.

Syme, G. J., Shaw, B. J., Fenton, D. M. and Mueller, W. S. (1989). *The Planning and Evaluation of Hallmark Events*. Aldershot: Avebury.

Times (2015, 23 October). Napoleon back on streets of St Helena. *The Times*, p. 23.

Tyrrell, T. and Johnston, R. (2001). A framework for assessing direct economic impacts of tourist events: Distinguishing origins, destinations, and causes of expenditures. *Journal of Travel Research*, *40*(1), 94–100.

Wall, G. (1997). Scale effects on tourism multipliers. *Annals of Tourism Research*, *24*(2), 446–450

Wall, G. and Wright, C. (1977). *The Environmental Impact of Outdoor Recreation*. Department of Geography Publication Series No. 11, Waterloo: University of Waterloo.

Wall, G. and Mathieson, A. (2006). *Tourism: Change, Impacts and Opportunities*. Harlow: Pearson Education Limited.

Warnken, J. and Buckley, R. (1998). Monitoring diffuse impacts: Australian tourism developments. Scientific quality of environmental impact assessment. *Journal of Applied Ecology*, *35*(1), 1–8.

Weidenfeld, A. (2010). Iconicity and 'flagshipness' of tourist attractions. *Annals of Tourism Research*, *37*(3), 851–854.

11 Visitor attractions as flagships and icons

Introduction

Major visitor attractions (e.g. museums, cultural centres, theme parks, shopping malls, galleries) are considered regional catalysts of social change, urban regeneration and economic development and can contribute to increasing both tourist appeal and the quality of life for residents (Hoarau and Kline, 2014, Miles and Paddison, 2005, Plaza, 2008, Miles, 2005). Cultural attractions, for example, can be the objects of urban development schemes as well as active promoters of revitalisation and place marketing: their institutional goals include facilitating positive economic, social and cultural impacts on their surrounding locality or region (Law, 2002). This is particularly germane to cultural buildings, such as the Municipal Theatre, Santiago, Chile, and the Museum of the Revolution, Havana, Cuba, which were constructed as symbols of regional/national identity, engagement and/or economic development. Such development can help cities gain or regain economic dynamism, and stimulate a rejuvenation phase for destinations previously characterised by a mature or declining phase in the economic life cycle. These processes have been often described as 'effects', one of the best known examples of which is the 'Guggenheim effect' (after the Guggenheim Museum Bilbao, Spain). The Guggenheim effect in Bilbao is 'one of the most transformative symbols of city place-making of the last decades' (Evans, 2003:432), being a catalyst of cultural, social and economic enhancements in a post-industrial city, in addition to being a successful museum (Evans, 2003). It is also germane to recent debates about the impacts of other iconic buildings (Hoarau and Kline, 2014, Sklair and Gherardi, 2012, Sklair, 2010).

The urban and regional planning academic literature has marginalised, and often ignored, the fact that many of what are defined as flagship or iconic projects are actually visitor attractions (e.g. museums, galleries) used for tourism activities rather than for cultural and commercial activities, such as shopping. The relationships between the nature of major visitor attractions and the nature and extent of their impacts have also been overlooked in both the regional studies and tourism literatures. This is surprising, particularly given that they are often partly, or even largely, underpinned by public investment. One of the shortcomings of the literature is a failure to differentiate between different types of major visitor attractions (often defined as development projects), linked to the loose and seemingly

interchangeable use of the terms iconic and flagship. Iconic and flagship developments are often largely or partly underpinned by public investments. However,
many new attractions, which are designed to be iconic, are rarely perceived as such
by tourists and residents alike. Many fail to attract visitors and generate revenues,
resulting in sub-optimal allocation of public resources (e.g. the Millennium Dome
in London in its initial years and the recently cancelled Tokyo Olympic Stadium).

The first section of this chapter will define the concepts of iconicity and flagshipness in general, and the terms 'iconic' and 'flagship'. The following section
examines the iconisation processes (including possible de-iconisation and
re-iconisation) and their importance in determining the contribution of major
attractions to destination image. This is followed by a discussion of events as
icons and flagships, identifying the relationship between the event–attraction
continuum and levels of iconicity of visitor attractions, as well as the role of
museums as flagship and iconic attractions. The chapter concludes by discussing
the policy implications of the differences between major attractions.

Flagshipness and flagship attractions

The use of the term 'flagship' as a non-scientific metaphor implicitly assumes the
existence of some defining criteria. It stems from naval terminology, in which a
flagship was usually the largest vessel, which would carry the commander and his
flag and be followed by other ships (Andersson, 2014). It has been mainly used in
the marketing literature for branding retail stores, and in the urban and regional
development literature in the context of major urban development projects. The
term *flagshipness* has been used to describe the use of architecture to endow
renowned premium brand stores with a unique status (Kent and Reva, 2009).

In the urban context, a flagship project is a significant, high profile development
that plays an influential and catalytic role in urban regeneration, and is intended to
stimulate additional investment (Smyth, 1994). It is often enabled and implemented
through a combination of public and private investment, usually involving a
property-led mechanism but stands 'in its own right, which may or may not be
self-sustaining, a marshalling point for further investment; a marketing tool for an
area or city' (Smyth, 1994:5). In this context, self-sustaining means 'covering the
costs of implementation, project management and construction, and could include
operational costs' (ibid.:21). Flagship projects may stimulate further investment,
which could take one of two functional forms: catalytic generation of further
capital investment in administration, services and production; or acting as poles
of attraction and consumption, including household formation and providing
living accommodation. Some post 2012 Olympics developments, including the
stadium itself as well as other existing attractions such as the Millennium Dome,
represent an example of an attempt to build flagship attractions in East London,
which will continue the regeneration processes and encourage further investment
in the built environment.

The flagship, in the form of the physical presence of a development, functions
as a major advertising or promotional feature for an area that is seeking to attract

investment. Development projects are often labelled as flagships, after their conception, in order to harness their development to a policy initiative and attract resources (Smyth, 1994). A flagship project is a:

> large scheme that will attract attention by its scale and architecture and provide a good basis for the regeneration of a zone by attracting further investment in the sites round about ..., e.g. a convention centre, theatres, galleries, museums, art galleries, arenas, concert halls, sports stadiums, and shopping centre. These facilities are often part of the public sector or part of the non profit-making sector which often depends on grants from the public sector.
>
> (Law, 2002:41–42)

Flagship attractions

In tourism, a 'flagship' project is often used to describe major visitor attractions in the context of their outstanding scale, size and significant regional socio-economic impacts (Law, 2002, Wanhill, 2005). In the visitor attraction sector, flagshipness is defined as the ability of visitor attractions to attract a relatively larger number of visitors compared to their neighbouring attractions, and to generate positive economic development contributions for their destination area (Weidenfeld, 2010). The greater the relative attractiveness of visitor attractions, compared to other visitor attractions in their region, then the more likely they are to be defined as flagships.

The wide appeal of flagship attractions can be attributed to their distinct qualities, uniqueness, scale, location, being internationally known and receiving high levels of media attention, which makes them 'must-see' attractions (Law, 2002:79), such as Euro Disney in France and Legoland in Denmark. In urban areas, there may be several flagship attractions but, by contrast, in rural areas, often only one major attraction has such appeal and uniqueness (Dybedal, 1998). The stand-alone Eden project in Cornwall, UK, for example, is the largest 'greenhouse' in the world, and has dramatically increased the number of visitors to Cornwall, strengthening the regional rural economy and attracting investment (South West Regional Development Agency, 2005).

Additionality is a key characteristic of flagships. In particular, a flagship attraction 'should be observed to attract a certain number of visitors [by setting up some absolute number criterion] who otherwise would not have come to the area' (Dybedal, 1998:19). The term 'flagship' is associated by Dybedal (1998) with the *primary nucleus* (major pull-factor) of a destination for the majority of tourists. Accordingly, attractions receive flagship status if they meet the following criteria:

a.   The majority of tourists to the destination or tourism region are attributable to the attraction and would otherwise not have visited the region.
b.   They attract a certain number of visitors in absolute terms, which is not only greater than for other attractions, but also must appeal to multiple segments (Dybedal, 1998).

A flagship attraction can also be perceived as a brand in its own right and, therefore, can be marketed individually regardless of its region, such as Legoland and Euro Disney, Legoland Deutschland or Shanghai Disneyland. The themes and nature of these attractions have little or limited association with the regional culture.

Events can also be seen as flagship, especially mega events. A 'mega' event is a relative term and refers to the largest event in scale or most significant in impact in terms of tourism, media coverage, prestige or economic impact for the host community (Getz, 2012, Anttiroiko, 2014) and can be defined as a flagship event attraction. These are internationally recognised and are used as promotional tools, which enhance place image. They usually involve a bidding process, e.g. Olympic Games, World cups, UEFA champion League games, Eurovision Song Contests and European capitals of culture (Getz, 2012, Anttiroiko, 2014). However, they neither represent the regional image nor have direct connection to the characteristics of their temporary location or regional image – or, if they do, then this is not long term.

The use of the term flagship in the academic literature and in policy jargon and discourses does not differentiate between those flagship attractions which may only draw a large number of visitors to their own premises and those which also draw a large number of visitors to other attractions in their region. Such attractions may not only be defined as flagship but also iconic as will be explained in the next sections.

Iconicity and iconic attractions

The term *iconic visitor attraction* can be understood in the context of the terms iconic, iconicity and iconisation in tourism phenomena. Iconic structures or features in tourism are often described as projects, institutions, monuments, land-marks (used synonymously in the literature) or simply as icons, rather than as visitor attractions. In tourism, an iconic feature is perceived as being similar to a significant something else or representing another object, phenomenon, an important figure or ideas. Perception of the icon is based on the pre-existing knowledge or expectations of the observer, residents and/or visitors (Grayson and Martinec, 2004). According to Alexander (2008), an icon is a symbolic condensation, with roots in generic social meanings in a specific and 'material' form through aesthetic shape.

Communicating and perceiving icons is pivotal in the 'dialogue' between mar-keters and consumers over what is authentic (Grayson and Martinec, 2004). An icon consists of an idea (a signifier), which is made material (a thing) and the signified is not only in people's minds but experienced and felt. The material thing (or the idea) becomes semiotic to the meaning in time and space (Alexander, 2008). In the Statue of Liberty in New York City, for example, the signifier of the iconic attraction is freedom and American independence, which is experienced not only by the symbolic visibility of materials (i.e. the torch and chains), but also by visiting its location, as many migrants historically experienced on their arrival to America (UNESCO, 2015) (Box 11.1).

By extensions, iconic in the tourism context refers to the representation, authenticity, mental perceptions, symbolism, brand and image of tourism spaces

---

Box 11.1 The Statue of Liberty

The statue of Liberty in New York Harbor, designed by Frédéric Bartholdi, was a gift to the United States from the people of France. It is a statue of a robed female figure representing Libertas, the Roman goddess of freedom, who bears a torch and a tabula ansata (a tablet evoking the law) upon which is inscribed the date of the American Declaration of Independence, July 4, 1776. A broken chain lies at her feet. This statue, dedicated on October 28, 1886, is an icon of freedom (for many people) and of the United States and is (was) famous as a welcoming signal to immigrants arriving from abroad.

The authenticity of the Statue of Liberty lies partly in its spatio-temporal links to immigration, its location on the immigrants' gateway to the United States and to its explicit representations of freedom. These factors relating to the most prominent aspects of the popular discourse about the foundation of the USA, makes it a classic iconic visitor attraction. The statue of Liberty's iconicity is twofold. At the national level, it symbolizes American values. At the regional scale, it represents the skyline of New York city and is used in marketing the city for tourists. The Statue of Liberty is therefore an iconic attraction because it is a symbolic physical manifestation of ideas, which are communicated through a dialogue and it draws on the pre-existing knowledge of both its visitors and the American people.

Source: UNESCO (2015:http://whc.unesco.org/en/list/307).

---

including visitor attractions (Grayson and Martinec, 2004, Woodside et al., 2005, Tang et al., 2009), which serve as universally (or at least, widely) recognised symbols of their location, and evoke a powerful positive image among both tourists and local residents (Sternberg, 1997, Jenkins, 2003). Other examples include Mount Fuji, Japan, the Eiffel Tower, France, the Great Wall of China and the Taj Mahal, India.

Iconicity refers to a mental template (such as history, fiction or a 'composite picture'), which is used in or through a physical manifestation to represent something perceived as being authentic and significant. It is part of or stimulates a dialogue over history, space and identity, and values between marketers and consumers about authenticity, and is directly affected by social and cultural objectives of its owners or operators and products' marketability (Weidenfeld, 2010, Grayson and Martinec, 2004). For example, a dialogue over history, space and identity has been stimulated by Constitution Hill in Johannesburg, which signifies the new South African national identity as well as a heritage memorialisation and commemoration of a turbulent historical past. Constitutional Hill used to be a prison site during the apartheid years, where Nelson Mandela and Mahatma Gandhi were imprisoned, but has subsequently become the seat of the South African Constitutional Court in the post-1994 South African democracy. The authenticity of this attraction has been questioned by some critics given how the apartheid system is represented, selected and constructed (Ivanovic, 2014), underlining the contested nature of all icons. Iconic attractions may be used for a dialogue and debate on different contrasting values, heritage and religious, such as

Masada (UNESCO, 2015), which is an iconic attraction in the Judean desert in Israel (Box 11.2).

The more that visitor attractions are characterised by higher levels of iconicity than other attractions in their region, the more they can be classified as iconic. Iconicity in most cases is related to the geographical dimensions of the specific location of visitor attractions, but in some cases iconicity has less direct geographical association and more relevance to specific historical or cultural figures or events. These include iconic attractions related to universal values or history. Anne Frank's House and the Auschwitz concentration camp represent the Nazi holocaust and the personal stories of its individual victims rather than relating specifically to Amsterdam or the town of Auschwitz, Poland, respectively. Event attractions such as the Eurovision Song Contest and the Olympics are internationally recognised icons and their iconicity has little relevance to their temporary location or regional image (at least not on a long-term basis). Ayer's Rock/Uluru, for example, symbolises Australian aboriginal culture, as well as the physical landscape of the Australian outback and therefore can be seen as both a cultural and a natural icon.

Iconic attractions are considered to be outstanding landmarks and therefore are often used as a regional brand. They are therefore difficult to replace in terms of importance at the regional, national or international levels. They are often endowed with specific features, which for example can be perceived as architectural beauty. This applies to the majority of the world's most frequently selected landmarks by travellers on the popular TripAdvisor website. The list includes visitor attractions such as Angkor Wat, Cambodia, and Machu Picchu, Peru, which

---

Box 11.2 The icon of the Ancient Jewish Kingdom, Israel

Masada is a rugged natural fortress, in the Judean Desert, Israel, and a symbol of the ancient kingdom of Israel, its violent destruction and the last stand of Jewish patriots in the face of the Roman army in 73 A.D. It was built as a palace complex, in the classic style of the early Roman Empire, by Herod the Great, King of Judaea, (reigned 37–4 B.C.) and remained untouched for more than thirteen centuries after its destruction, including significant archaeological elements, such as the Roman camps and siegeworks. The camps, fortifications and attack ramp that encircle the monument constitute the most complete Roman siege works surviving to the present day. Due to the remoteness from human habitation and its arid climate, the Masada site remained untouched for more than thirteen centuries until its rediscovery in 1828. Therefore very little reconstruction or conservation projects have been required, and there has been little debate over the use of inappropriate materials, or speculative rehabilitation of the site. Visitor interpretation has been undertaken using original and clearly defined archaeological levels. It is used as a heritage and educational site where loyalty, sacrifice, religious piousness, patriotism and humanistic values can be discussed amongst visitors.

Source: UNESCO (2015:http://whc.unesco.org/en/list/1040).

are characterised by exceptional beauty and outstanding visibility in their land-scape (TripAdvisor, 2015). However, sometimes their controversial, extravagant, grotesque, bizarre or even ugly appearances are also regarded as iconic, as long as they are strongly distinctive at the regional, national and/or international scales; for example, *the Basilica de La Sagrada Familia* is one of Barcelona's icons.

Iconic visibility can also portray something which is not only beautiful and sublime, but also something that is ugly or has the apparently banal appearance of mundane 'material life' (Alexander, 2008). The Hiroshima Peace Memorial (Genbaku Dome), for example, is the only structure left standing in the area where the first atomic bomb exploded on 6 August 1945. Subsequently, it has been transformed into a dark iconic visitor attraction (some similarities to the concentration camps such as Auschwitz), which constitutes a powerful symbol of the most destructive force ever created by humankind along with the hope for world peace, epitomised by the surrounding Peace Memorial Park. This received a record number of 200,086 visitors in 2013 (UNESCO, 2015).

Iconic structures are more likely to be considered visibly pleasant and to transform feelings, physical beauty and aesthetics into meaning than non-iconic ones (Alexander, 2008). The Taj Mahal, a UNSECO heritage site since 1983, is not only an impressive enormous and beautiful building; it is regionally iconic because it is inextricably linked to its urban landscape, representing a microcosm of broader aesthetics and symbolic relationships to natural and urban landscapes, including the historical splendour of Agra, the capital city of the Caliphate in which it is located. Symbolically, it has many levels: as the largest mausoleum ever constructed, it represents indisputable love, a semiotic expression of cultural prerogative, as well as an Islamic architectural tradition appropriated for the Indian ethos (Bharne, 2013).

Iconic attractions and events in rural areas are likely to be fewer in number than in urban areas and have greater importance for the regional economy and in terms of appeal to visitors. Iconic natural rural attractions can carry natural as well as cultural and representational images of nations. The iconic White Cliffs of Dover in south east England are a clear symbol of Britain (or perhaps of England) in the way the Statue of Liberty defines America for many. Their cultural and national importance brought the National Trust to appoint a philosopher-in-residence to explore their importance to the nation (Winterma, 2012). The iconic rural event attraction in *Castelluccio di Norcia*, which is a small town located in the *Parco Nazionale dei Monti Sibillini* (*Mount Sibillini National Park*) in Italy takes places between late May and early July each year. The event attraction displays a semi natural and a semi human-made intervention, which creates a colourful plateau from flowers. It provides a strongly distinctive image of its town and symbolic value, attracting domestic and international tourists to the region.

Houses of prayer or worship, including mosques, synagogues, cathedrals and temples, can be considered iconic visitor attractions by tourists because of their religious importance rather than the regional image of a specific destination region, such as the *Kaaba* in Mecca, Saudi Arabia, which is the holiest Islamic site in the world. They may also be considered iconic for their unique physical features and unique architecture, such as Istanbul's mosques, the former Aya Sofia Mosque (previously Hagia Sophia Cathedral and now a museum) and Sultanahmed mosque. It is noteworthy that the role of architecture in the iconicity of visitor attractions and other buildings has been widely acknowledged, not only in religious and heritage sites but also in new buildings such as museums, exhibition halls and skyscrapers (Sklair, 2013, Evans, 2005, Grodach, 2008, Sklair, 2006, Sklair and Gherardi, 2012). The *Auditorio de Tenerife* 'Adán Martín', an auditorium in Santa Cruz de Tenerife, Spain, is considered an emblem and a distinctive symbol of the city and the island as well as being a significant tourist attraction and a symbol of Spanish architecture. Architecture can also enhance the iconicity of visitor attractions in rural areas, such as La Rioja wine region in Spain, which invited major architects to design iconic facilities for wine experiences and creative tourism (Richards and Wilson, 2007).

Some visitor attractions, even iconic ones, are rarely visited, but their importance to the destination image may be larger than that of all other more-visited attractions in their destinations. Entering Big Ben, for example, requires advanced booking for a limited number of visitors, thus most visitors to London never manage to visit its premises. However, its iconic visibility and presence have a unique powerful, meaningful and inspiring impact on London's image.

Iconisation

Iconic attractions are a strongly distinctive regional brand compared to other attractions whether at the regional, national or international scale. They have an overwhelming impact which stems from constituting a direct link with the cultural and/or historical heritage of their destination region or country, or being imbued and iconised by marketing processes. Whereas some visitor attractions were initially built for other purposes and became iconic, e.g. the Eiffel Tower, others have been designed specifically for tourism development. They are an attempt 'to symbolise the changing character of the area and to provide a memorable image that potential visitors will associate with it and to create footfall with attracting visitors' (Maitland and Newman, 2004:16). The process of 'writing' or making of icons is iconography and, in the tourism context, activities and processes which make products saleable by imbuing them with desirable images of persons, cities, regions and cultures (Sternberg, 1997) constitute *iconisation*.

Attractions often become iconised by being used in marketing for destination positioning as a result of a long-term marketing process (Becken, 2005, Sulaiman, 2014). At the end of the process, they project a meaningful and evocative image to draw consumers (Sternberg, 1997), such as the Eiffel Tower, Paris, and the Atomium, Brussels. Iconisation may be reinforced by social and cultural events and practices taking place within attractions such as the coronation of royalty inside St Paul's Cathedral, which carry social meaning and therefore iconic status (Kaika, 2011). Once iconisation is well advanced and high levels of iconicity are reached, the visitor attraction is substantially integrated into the place based image of the destination region. The Berlin Television tower (*The Fernsehturm*), inaugurated in 1969, was planned as a new facility that would serve mainly as a television transmitter for the former German Democratic Republic and as an architectural icon. It is an example of both iconisation and re-iconisation where strong visibility played a major role. Even though it is still perceived by some as an important symbol demonstrating the supposed superiority of socialist societies, it has become an inextricable part of the image of Berlin's skyline, particularly after German reunification in 1990. It is visited annually by more than a million people, including both Berliners and domestic and international tourists (VisitBerlin, 2015, Berlin Fernehturm, 2015).

Iconicity cannot be sustained without constant marketing and branding activities (see Chapter 12), particularly in mature destinations, whose marketing tends to be less icon dependent (Becken, 2005). Miles (2005) argues that the cultural identity of iconic projects evolves and adapts through time, marked by shifting power relationships and is based on the historical identities of people and places. The author advises that researchers should seek out the motivations and expectations that people bring to their interaction with cities in order to ensure the success of iconic projects. This dialogue between history, space, place and cultural memory through time is a part of what may be called the iconisation process. Therefore, 'projects can serve a significant ideological function, at least as far as they play a key role in not simply reflecting a sense of local identity but in actually rearticulating and reconfiguring that identity in complex and paradoxical ways' (Miles, 2005:916).

The iconisation of visitor attractions can be used as a tool to indicate commercial power, achieve political gains and/or boost national pride. The spectacular Burj Khalifa (Burj Dubai) is the tallest building in the world and attracts tourist visitors for its panoramic terrace at a height of 828 metres, as well as international investors in its office space. Its iconisation is not only intertwined with political motives but also with Dubai's quest for a strong and distinctive image, and primacy in the world city hierarchy. It involves all the key players of the Emirate: Sheikh, local government, major stakeholders and transnational capitalist elites (Acuto, 2010, Bagaeen, 2007). The iconisation process of Burj Khalifa is also an attempt to use an iconic skyscraper as a visitor attraction to define the presence of the city on the world stage and reconstitute its identity internationally, as well as amongst its local residents. This process is not unique to Dubai but is a global phenomenon with cities trying to establish an international reputation, and a powerful defining element for a city on behalf of current and past leaders. A similar example is the Petronas Towers in Kuala Lampur. Glorifying current or past leaders is also the political motive behind the Baiterek Monument in Astana, Kazakhstan, and the renovation of Robert Mugabe's former home in the capital Harare, Zimbabwe, and its conversion into a visitor attraction (Maclean, 2012).

Lack of iconicity, de-iconisation and re-iconisation

Attractions that have not managed to draw visitors to destinations may be closed down, re-invented as different attractions or converted to other uses, such as residential areas, commercial complexes and public offices. Unsuccessful iconisation can occur for reasons as disparate as weak thematic linkage between the visitor attraction and its region or locality, corruption, or controversial representation of ideology and political motives. The new 2020 Olympic stadium building was supposed to be an integral element of Tokyo's urban fabric, directly engaging with the surrounding cityscape. However, the plan was harshly criticised by Japanese architects and faced public anger over the stadium's estimated cost, far higher than any previous Olympic stadium. This led to cuts in the scope of the design, which threatened its future iconicity, before the final decision by the Japanese prime minister to cancel the project (Wainwright, 2014, Soble, 2015). Other negative or controversial aspects included environmental impacts and restricted access for local residents, and a reduction in the quality of life for residents due to excessive movements of people or vehicles (see also Jenkins, 2003, Becken, 2005).

Newer visitor attractions might gain an iconic status and diminish that of an 'older' iconic attraction, which may gradually come to be perceived as boring and outdated by both visitors and residents. For example, the BT tower, established in the 1960s as a working icon of technological innovation in London, has lost both its novelty and iconicity (Garside, 2015), which – together with security concerns – brought about its closure to the public two decades later. Its diminishing iconicity can also be explained by the growing iconicity of the London Eye and, more recently, the Shard (opened in 2012). The latter was conceived as being an outstanding architectural mixed use building, allowing daily visits to its viewing gallery and may also be in the initial stage of iconisation.

A natural disaster may also destroy or diminish the levels of iconicity of visitor attractions: for example, the destruction of UN World Heritage Sites in Nepal including the iconic 100-foot Dharahara Tower in the capital, Kathmandu, by the 7.8 magnitude earthquake in 2015 (Holley, 2015). Human activity can also diminish iconicity, such as the damage created by visitors to major attractions including the Great Wall in China, the Caves of Altamira, Spain, and the Angor Wat temple, Cambodia (Veselinovic, 2015). Failure to market effectively a new attraction may also result in low iconicity and a change in function, such as a hotel, a commercial building or a public space. There may be attempts to revitalise its iconicity by various management and marketing efforts, with varying degrees of success. The Sapporo Clock Tower is an example of an attraction which is perceived by its marketers as iconic but less so by its visitors. It is a wooden structure which is a symbol of Sapporo, the largest city on the island of Hokkaidō, Northern Japan, promoted as a must-visit attraction for both domestic and international tourists. Online blogs and visitors' criticisms reveal great disappointment because of its location next to many other taller buildings and its detachment from Japanese culture.

Other attractions may be iconised successfully from the start but lose this status due to both reputational and managerial failures, financial losses and negligence. Heritage USA opened in 1978 in Fort Mill, South Carolina, and offered visitors a distinctive experience of a specific fusion of religious and American national symbols, which was particularly popular amongst those with strongly conservative Protestant beliefs. It managed to combine a very specific brand of Christian devotion and spectacle along with entertaining theme park activities. It had a castle, a tower, a hotel, shops and rides, and attracted millions of visitors annually. After being quite successful both financially and in terms of its appeal to its target markets, a major financial scandal around the founder, followed by management failures, corruption and hurricane damage, resulted in the park's demise in the late 1980s. Attempts to revitalise the park have failed and some of its facilities and buildings were demolished while others were converted to residential and commercial uses (Johnson, 2014). An example of an attempt to create an iconic attraction, which initially failed, for both managerial and design-led reasons, was the Millennium Dome in London. This was a new cultural visitor attraction in south east London, where a dialogue between consumers, producers and other stakeholders, along with poor management, failed to produce the desired outcomes (McGuigan and Gilmore, 2002, McGuigan, 2003). This continued through failed attempts to convert it to a viable and sustainable venue for events until, in 2005, it was rebranded as the O2 arena by a new owner and gradually became a successful entrainment centre and a popular venue for music events. At the time of writing, it could, to some extent, be considered a flagship attraction (Box 11.3).

A conceptualisation of iconic attractions in decline as a result of environmental crises and loss of appeal has been developed by Weaver and Lawton (2007): they proposed the terms *residual attractions* and *attraction residuality* for attractions which have lost their iconicity. The concept of attraction residuality, applicable at a local, regional, national or global scale, entails 'the perpetuation of an attraction in the aftermath of its physical loss' (p. 110). Residual attractions are 'primary and iconic attractions that merit reinvention as residual attractions in the event of a disaster of sufficient magnitude' (Weaver and Lawton, 2007:114). Human-made disasters can also change or diminish the nature and extent of the iconicity of visitor attractions. Recent examples include the physical destruction of world heritage attractions in Syria, Afghanistan and Iraq by the Taliban and the Islamic State.

Iconisation resulting in iconicity is a dynamic process that can be reversed and is therefore best thought of as a cycle (Figure 11.1). *De-iconisation* describes the decline process in terms of loss of iconicity, which remains understudied and deserves further investigation. One of the alternative options for iconic attractions, which have been de-iconised, is to go through a process of *Re-iconisation*, which is an attempt to regain a major attraction's iconicity by re-branding their image in line with that of their destination image. Given a lack of, or diminishing, iconicity, a new place branding strategy – as a part of a marketing strategy – can be implemented. Re-iconisation can be intentional, planned and monitored by authorities and marketers, or can emerge more organically following changes in the political, historical and environmental settings or the development of place attachment over time. The Eiffel Tower, for example, was erected in 1889 as the entrance arch to the 1889 World's Fair and then used as a communication tower. Instead of being torn down, it has gradually become a global cultural icon not only of Paris but also of France, Frenchness and by extension glamour, beauty, romance, modernity and elegance. It attracts 7 million people a year, making it the

Box 11.3 The iconic 'failure' of the New Millennium Experience – 'the disastrous Dome', Greenwich, London, UK

The Millennium Dome is a dome-shaped fibreglass tent located on a south-eastern peninsula of the River Thames at Greenwich, London. It was originally conceived as a major exhibition celebrating the beginning of the third millennium and exploring key issues about contemporary life at the turn of the Millennium. The Dome was the object of immense public controversy in Britain in the run up to 2000 and was subject to strong critical media attention for being a major and escalating drain on public money. It was initially built as both a political and a regional icon, which aimed to symbolise the New Labour Britain nationally and internationally, but ended up being a major political embarrassment.

The Dome attracted over 6 million visitors during its year of operation as opposed to the expected 12 million, which resulted in the New Millennium Experience Company (NMEC) having to receive four additional National Lottery grants from the Millennium Commission, the public body charged with disbursing Lottery revenue to projects to mark the start of the new Millennium in the UK. Its location away from central London, poor accessibility for both domestic and international tourists and unsuccessful marketing attempts to promote it as iconic at the national and international scales all contributed to its relatively low appeal. Additionally, there were design and content issues. The power to design and influence the Dome's themes lay with the sponsors, whose interests did not necessarily coincide with those of the British public. The Millennium Dome experience was the outcome of a complex process of production and representation in which corporate sponsorship was a key ideological factor, rather than being a dialogue amongst people engaged in a debate over their time and place in history. In other words, it failed an essential prerequisite of the iconisation of visitor attractions.

A series of failed attempts were made to sell off the Dome before and after closure, with calls being made for its demolition. For a while, an attempt was made to sell it to developers so as to reduce the losses for the public sector. Eventually, it was given to the Meridian Delta consortium in summer 2002. Thereafter, the Dome was publicly renamed as the O2 on 31 May 2005 after being sold to telecommunications company O2 plc, with further redevelopment to its current use as an entertainment complex by its new owner, the Anschutz Entertainment Group.

The outcome is that the Millennium Dome is an example of a visitor attraction which has been converted into an economically successful flagship entertainment and event attraction for mostly local audiences, but also for some domestic and international tourists when major music concerts take place. Instead of becoming a well-established icon of social democracy with a market focus, the Millennium Dome remains a significant symbol of the problems of contemporary intimate relations between government and corporate power (McGuigan, 2003, McGuigan and Gilmore, 2002). However, the process of iconisation is dynamic, and the Millenium Dome has become iconic, to some extent, for being more recognisable, as well as flagship for drawing large and growing numbers of visitors.

most visited pay to enter monument in the world (Smith and Metcalf, 2015, Sulaiman, 2014).

The largest and the tallest building in Poland, the Palace of Culture and Science at the heart of Warsaw, completed in 1955 was presented as a 'gift' from the Soviet Union to the Polish nation. It is an example of planned iconisation and de-iconisation, followed by unplanned or organic re-iconisation. It is now the home of the Polish Academy of Sciences, libraries, museums, theatres, cinema, congress hall, bars, restaurants and also an observation point. The politically motivated communist iconisation process embedded the palace as a hated symbol of Soviet domination amongst many Poles. However, for others, especially for the younger generation, it has become a trendy and funky symbol of the Polish capital city (Czepczyńskia, 2010).

Iconisation, de-iconisation and re-iconisation processes in relation to flagshipness are described in Figure 11.1. Visitor attractions must sustain their iconicity after successful iconisation. When iconisation processes fail, then a number of alternatives are possible including:

a. Flagship attractions – visitor attractions become popular amongst visitors but not as key elements of the regional image, e.g. Millennium Dome, London, UK.

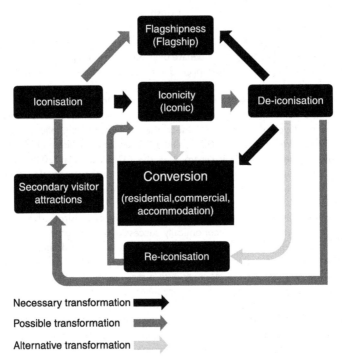

Figure 11.1 Iconisation, de-iconisation, re-iconisation and flagshipness of major visitor attractions

b. Conversion – the visitor attractions close, while their premises may be converted to alternative uses, such as residential, commercial, accommodation or public facilities, e.g. Heritage USA.

c. Secondary attractions – visitor attractions remain un-iconised as secondary (non-major) visitor attractions in their destination regions, e.g. Columbus Lighthouse, Santa Domingo, Dominican Republic.

d. Re-iconisation – an attempt to rebrand visitor attractions as a part of implementing a new place branding strategy, e.g. Berlin Television Tower, Germany.

In this attempt to re-iconise the visitor attraction, it is possible that the four alternative routes of transformation may be selected, i.e. flagship attractions, conversion, secondary attraction or another attempt at re-iconisation.

Organisational approach to the differences between flagship and iconic attractions

The iconic and flagship labels are often used synonymously and interchangeably by scholars and academics, particularly by marketers. There are, however, clear differences between iconic and flagship attractions. Compared to flagships, iconic attractions' images tend to be more integrated with destination images and are perceived as being more authentic and complementary to the tourism features of the destination images by visitors, tourists, managers and local residents. In contrast, flagship attractions are more likely to be less connected, and are sometimes disengaged from the local community. An organisational approach to studying visitor attractions provides a theoretical perspective that helps to distinguish between iconic and flagship attractions. This focuses on the contexts (external environments) that influence the economic impacts on the host area context, tourism industry context and the market context (Dybedal, 1998).

The host area context sets an attraction within a certain area, or a particular destination, for which the attraction is considered a flagship. Some of the key features are the geographical size of the study area, the degree of urbanisation, situation (central or remote area), levels of supply of goods and services other than tourism, accessibility and infrastructure. The proportion of new visitors drawn from beyond their immediate regions/localities is pivotal in differentiating between flagship and iconic attractions. Iconic attractions are likely to be an important regional attractor for new visitors to other attractions and tourism places, whereas a flagship attraction is more likely only to attract visitors to its premises and immediate locality. Both flagships and iconic attractions should be primary attractions for their visitors. However, the very presence of iconic attractions is meaningful, symbolic and representative for both residents and tourists. This is often accompanied by having distinctive external features that make them influential in terms of their regional appeal. Most tourists to Euro Disney, for example, are less interested in its exact local setting and do not consider its location in France as strongly related to the theme park, compared to visitors to the Eiffel Tower which is inextricably linked to Paris and France.

Therefore, the locational context of iconic attractions is stronger than that of flagship attractions.

Major attractions, which cannot relocate because their innate appeal, or nucleus, is dependent on natural or historical human-made objects or both, are more likely to be iconic than flagship, e.g. the Pyramids in Giza, Egypt. The south eastern face of Mount Rushmore in South Dakota's Black Hills National Forest in the US is an example of the dependency of a human-made attraction on natural resources. The site consists of four large carved sculptures depicting the faces of US Presidents George Washington, Thomas Jefferson, Abraham Lincoln and Theodore Roosevelt, and could not be relocated. The appeal of such iconic visitor attractions can also be dependent on their locational settings or destination region if they are associated with a historically significant event, such as dark visitor attractions related to battlefields or burial grounds. The relocation of such attractions would be impossible in terms of authenticity and resources.

In the *Market and tourism context*, a flagship attraction draws various market segments from a relatively large catchment area (regional to international scales) and appeals to wider audiences than its immediate competitors. In the market context, the catchment areas of potential markets is assessed in terms of number of staying visitors, day-trippers, local visitors, tourists, repeat visitors, visitor segments and expenditures. If an attraction is not considered a major attractor of visitors, it is not a flagship attraction but can still be defined as iconic, given that an iconic attraction is not necessarily visited by a large absolute number of visitors. The geographic appeal of flagship attractions can range from regional to international and that of iconic ones from local to international.

The tourism industry context refers to other attractions and the mix of tourism products offered by a destination, including aspects such as synergies of appeal to visitors; compatibility; collaboration; competition; the quality and complementarity of relationships with other neighbouring and/or distant attractions and other tourism products; seasonality and pricing. In the tourism context, there are three main aspects: visual appeal, nature of appeal and the levels of integration of the iconic or flagship attractions with the mix of destination products. A flagship attraction is not iconic if it does not endow itself with a representation of image, including authenticity and/or distinctive mental perceptions. For example, British Airways London Eye is one of the most visited paid attractions in England with more than 3.5 million visitors per year (O'Ceallaigh, 2014), whereas the Houses of Parliament were visited by more than 1 million visitors in 2014 (Association of Leading Visitor Attractions, 2015). The Houses of Parliament are much more representative of British culture and the city of London than the London Eye, which is considered more of a flagship attraction than iconic. It can be argued that the visual appeal of iconic and flagship attractions is important. If the nature of visibility is attached to the place image, iconicity is likely to increase. However, it also possible to argue that unattractive visual features of iconic buildings and sites may also be a part of their iconicity; for example, the Atomic Bomb Dome as noted earlier.

Some of the following differences between iconic and flagship attractions can be contested and examined by further empirical studies. Iconic attractions are necessarily more likely to be more authentic, similar and complementary to the tourism features of the destination image than flagship attractions. In the tourism context, if visitors to flagship attractions constitute a minor proportion of the overall destination visitors, the attraction is likely to be more flagship than iconic. By contrast, if most visitors to a major attraction also stay to visit other places and attractions in the destination region, it is more likely to be classified as iconic.

The suggested distinction between flagship and iconic attractions is summarised in Table 11.1. However, it should be understood that many visitor attractions have features of both iconicity and flagshipness and can be defined as flagship and iconic (Figure 11.2). The Big Ben in London, for example, is visited by a smaller number of visitors than most of London's attractions. However, it is an important element in the city of London's image and represents the city more than most of its other attractions; it is clearly an iconic attraction. The Eiffel Tower is both highly visited and strongly linked to the image of Paris and can be defined as both flagship and iconic. The Millennium Dome is neither, though it could be regarded as more flagship given a growing number of visitors (mainly domestic). A visitor attraction that has strong flagship and iconic elements is the Columbus Lighthouse tomb in Santo Domingo, the capital of the Dominican Republic. It was built as an iconic visitor attraction, which commemorates the continent's

Table 11.1 Differences between iconic and flagship attractions

Context	Elements	Iconic	Flagship
Market context	Catchment area	Local to international	Regional to international
Tourism context	Visibility	High	Low to medium
	Nature of appeal	Authentic, representative, must raise conscious awareness amongst all actors and must-see	'Must-see' and entertainment focus
	Levels of integration with the mix of tourism products offered by a destination	Essentially integrated	Weakly integrated to unintegrated
	Compatibility with neighbouring attractions	High	Low to medium
Host area context	The proportion of destination visitors who are actual visitors to the attraction	Minor to major	Major
	Regional branding and image	Significant	Insignificant
	Perceived authenticity	High	Low

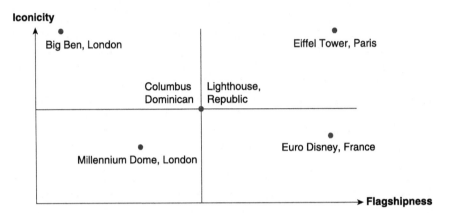

Figure 11.2 Flagshipness and iconicity of visitor attractions

Source: Adapted from Weidenfeld et al. (2015).

discoverer and a national icon given that Columbus was a Dominican ancestor. It is also a symbol of incarnation, modern values and Pan Americanism, i.e. ideology of bringing the Americas closer together into continental cooperation. It has not met expectations as an attraction in terms of visitor numbers (Judd and Fainstein, 1999, Krohn-Hansen, 2001). While it is still considered iconic in its nature and visited by tourists, it has become neither a tourism icon of the city nor one of the most popular attractions amongst tourists in the city and the country.

Museums as flagship and iconic attractions

The role of museums as flagships and icons deserves particular attention because of the tendency by scholars and practitioners to refer to cultural projects in general, and museums in particular, as flagship and/or iconic attractions. Museums are often considered flagship attractions when they become 'a must-see attraction for visitors to the city, by extending their average stay in the city, that results in more money being spent in the city' (Hamnett and Shoval, 2003). For example, Parco Arte Vivente, in Turin, Italy, has been associated with the recovery of the General Market area, while the establishment of the Museu de la Música in Barcelona is associated with the recovery of the area around the Glòries Catalanes square in Barcelona, Spain (Paül Agustí, 2013). Frey (1998) suggests the term 'superstar museums', which can be considered to be a sub-category of flagship and iconic art museums if they meet the following criteria:

a. A 'must' for tourists, feature prominently in guidebooks as not to be missed and perceived to have strong appeal at the international scale, e.g. Louvre in Paris, Hermitage in St Petersburg.
b. A large number of visitors.

c.   Featuring world famous paintings (and other artefacts).

d.   Architectural appeal.

e.   Commercialised impact of ancillary and complementary related and un-related services and products, as well as positive impacts on the local economy, e.g. Guggenheim, Musee du Louvre.

Iconicity and the event–attraction continuum

The event–attraction nexus provides another means to assess the iconicity of event attractions. The event–attraction nexus, which can be used to classify events into different groups (see Chapter 2), identifies whether enterprises or natural phenomena can be considered to be events, attractions or event attractions. This is determined according to the extent to which the core or nucleus of the visitor attraction is thematically and functionally integrated to the particular event's programme or content, as well as by their spatio-temporality, i.e. frequency of occurrence and permanence of location. The greater degree of permanence that there is, both temporally and spatially (that is, in terms of location), then the more likely it is that the enterprises and phenomena should be considered to be attractions rather than events on the continuum. The iconicity of visitor attractions is, above all, about the strong links between specific attractions and their region or locality, and the added value they provide in terms of symbolism and/or representation. Therefore, high levels of iconicity are likely to be strong in event attractions that are located closer to the attraction edge of the continuum. Edinburgh Festival, for example, is held every year in the summer, in broadly the same location (there is only minor relocation amongst venues within the locality) and is iconic to that city.

Events as icons and flagships

Hallmark events are generally strongly associated with, and perhaps inextricably linked to, their region or a community, particularly in the case of recurring events, where they contribute to and benefit from place identity. They have to attract tourists, generate substantial revenues, and be well accepted – and probably be valued – by the destination communities. They are recognised as being 'traditional', are institutionalised and have sustainable appeal and impact on their region to the extent that they may become a symbol of the hosting city, and are prominent in its branding, e.g. the Roskilde music festival in Denmark, Edinburgh Festival, Salzburg music festival (Anttiroiko, 2014, Getz, 2012). Therefore, hallmark events can be considered to be iconic event attractions as well as flagship events drawing a large number of visitors.

By contrast, an infrequent or rare event, which falls closer to the event edge of the continuum, such as a volcanic eruption or a political ceremony, is more likely to be detached from the destination image. However, there is no inevitability or path dependency in the trajectory of such events. In some cases, the event could be followed by the opening of a new attraction which may fix them in time and space, and it may become iconic. This is particularly true of previous Olympic Games' stadia which assume new functions as sports arenas for other events, and over time gain iconic status. In practice, the relationship between the event continuum and iconicity is complex, but the more that event attractions fall on the attraction edge of the continuum, the more likely they are to be classified as iconic.

Conclusions

Major visitor attractions suffer from a lack of definitional clarity, and the terms iconic and flagship are often used interchangeably and loosely to describe them. Discerning between the two is a means not only of providing insights into the nature and impacts of the attractions, but also has significant ramifications for the formation and implementation of development planning policies. Flagshipness is the ability of major visitor attractions to attract a relatively higher number of visitors compared to neighbouring attractions in their locality or region, thereby creating potential for a positive impact on the regional destination economy. Flagship attractions can be perceived as a brand, which may be largely disengaged from its regional context, compared to the regional branding which is more typically associated with iconic attractions. Another key feature of the iconicity of visitor attractions is the use of a mental template within or through which a physical manifestation, such as a building or some other site, is perceived as authentic. It creates a dialogue between and amongst actors including policy makers, marketers, consumers and/or suppliers and visitors. Iconic attractions can be used for improving destination image and place branding, as well as expressions of political and commercial power.

The process of imbuing visitor attractions with desirable images of persons, cities, regions and cultures is iconisation. The time needed for major attractions to gain their iconic status depends on their thematic nature, environmental settings and management and marketing efforts. They can vary between being 'born iconic' (e.g. Statue of Liberty), to being iconised by a long marketing process (and repeated performance), such as the Edinburgh Festival, which may take several years or even decades in some instances. Others may be iconised organically through time such as the Eiffel Tower. Iconicity is also likely to be stronger in event attractions, which have high levels of spatio-temporality and integration with the visitor attraction's nucleus, and in those which sit on the attraction edge of the continuum.

Iconic attractions are visitor attractions, which are perceived as being representative – whether of another object, phenomenon, an important figure or ideas. Their understudied perception by visitors and residents as being iconic is based on pre-existing knowledge or expectations before visiting and/or observing the attraction and remains. They may be perceived differently by various stakeholders and occur at regional, national and/or international levels. However, iconic attractions are generally characterised by outstanding visible features and architectural design ('iconic visibility'), which may range – even for an individual attraction – from being perceived as exceptionally aesthetic to ugly and/or unconventional.

The chapter has drawn in part on the organisational approach of Dybedal's (1998) work. This refers to the range of scales of individual attractions, emphasising their temporal, capacity and geographical aspects (Michael and Page, 2014), to suggest criteria for differentiating between flagship and iconic attractions. Major visitor attractions can be both flagship and iconic. If iconicity characterises a visitor attraction more than flagshipness, or vice versa, then the visitor attraction can be classified accordingly. If, however, a visitor attraction has substantial iconicity and flagshipness characteristics, it can be classified as both iconic and flagship. Such classifications cannot be a priori, but have to be based on an investigation of the specific characteristics of the individual attractions. Such investigations could help practitioners and policy makers to clarify the nature of an attraction and its regional impacts. This may also guide regional policies and inform decisions about how to prioritise the allocation of scarce financial incentives.

It is important to remember that flagship development projects or attractions are not always a panacea for urban decline and regeneration. An important condition for this is that they should be integrated into – or at least be in harmony with – a development plan which addresses the socio-economic challenges of a region, and conditions in specific locations (Ortiz-Moya, 2015). Often, the development of a new flagship project contributes more to the outward image of a city in the short term than to the medium to long-term future (Comunian and Mould, 2014). Iconic attractions can face challenges and fail or may lose their iconicity through time because of a natural or a man-made disaster, or changes within or external to the region. Therefore, maintaining and revitalising iconicity has to be a priority for practitioners and policy makers. No attraction should be taken for granted as an automatic and lasting image maker of any city or region.

Taking into account the previous discussion, a number of planning and policy recommendations can be identified for the development of new major visitor attractions which include:

- There is a need to use the typological differences between visitor attractions to assess their iconicity and flagshipness, as well as their regional economic contribution and impact on other tourism businesses and facilities in general and visitor attractions in particular. Such an assessment can be made based on the nature, content and thematic and functional links between major visitor attractions and their destination region.
- Identifying potential iconisation, de-iconisation or re-iconisation processes of visitor attractions may improve the design and implementation of urban and regional planning processes. Low or declining levels of iconicity and the beginning of de-iconisation can be seen as warning signs and of issues that need to be addressed by marketing and rebranding efforts.
- The provision of subsidies and other forms of support can be prioritised when attractions are identified as having high levels of iconicity, in order to increase regional appeal, visitor numbers and length of stay in tourism destination regions.

Clarifying the similarities and differences between iconic and flagship attractions as well as the iconisation processes involved, and the relevance of iconicity to the event–attraction continuum, are all topics that require further empirical research. It is important to improve understanding of the role of iconic and flagship attractions in urban and regional development processes, how their nature and location are determined in decision-making processes, and how marketing can be used to influence their impact upon the destination regions.

References

Acuto, M. (2010). High-rise Dubai urban entrepreneurialism and the technology of symbolic power. *Cities, 27*, 272–284.

Alexander, J. C. (2008). Iconic consciousness: The material feeling of meaning. *Environment and Planning D: Society and Space, 26*, 782–794.

Andersson, I. (2014). Beyond "Guggenheiming": From flagship buildings to flagship space in Sweden. *Norsk Geografisk Tidsskrift – Norwegian Journal of Geography, 68*, 228–237.

Anttiroiko, A.-V. (2014). *The Political Economy of City Branding*. Oxford: Routledge.

Association of Leading Visitor Attractions (2015). Latest visitor figures. Visits made in 2014 to visitor attractions in membership with ALVA. Retrieved from http://alva.org.uk/details.cfm?p=432 (accessed 15 January 2016).

Bagaeen, S. (2007). Brand Dubai: The instant city; or the instantly recognizable city. *International Planning Studies, 12*, 173–197.

Becken, S. (2005). The role of tourist icons for sustainable tourism. *Journal of Vacation Marketing, 11*, 21–30.

Berliner FernSehturm (2015). www.tv-turm.de/en/geschichte.php (accessed 15 January 2016).

Bharne, V. (2013). The paradise between two worlds: Rereading Taj Mahal and its enviros. In V. Bharne (Ed.), *The emerging Asian city: Concomitant urbanities and urbanisms* (pp. 36–45). London: Routledge.

Comunian, R. and Mould, O. (2014). The weakest link: Creative industries, flagship cultural projects and regeneration. *City, Culture and Society, 5*, 65–74.

Czepczyński, M. (2010). Interpreting post-socialist icons: From pride and hate towards disappearance and/or assimilation. *Human Geographies – Journal of Studies and Research in Human Geography, 4*, 67–78.

Dybedal, P. (1998). Theme parks as flagship attractions in peripheral areas. Bronholm, Denmark Bornholms Forskningscenter (Stenbrudsvej 55, DK-3730, Denmark). Retrieved from http://citeseerx.ist.psu.edu/viewdoc/download?doi=10.1.1.511.620&rep=rep1&type=pdf (accessed 18 January 2016).

Evans, G. (2003). Hard-branding the cultural city – From prado to prada. *International Journal of Urban and Regional Research, 27*, 417–440.

Evans, G. (2005). Measure for measure: Evaluating the evidence of culture's contribution to regeneration. *Urban Studies, 42*, 959–983.

Frey, B. S. (1998). Superstar museums: An economic analysis. *Journal of Cultural Economics, 22*, 113–125.

Garside, J. (2015). Golden opportunity to relive 60s and dine at top of BT Tower. *The Guardian*. Retrieved from www.theguardian.com/uk-news/2015/jun/19/bt-tower-restaurant-to-reopen-to-public (accessed 3 March 2016).

Getz, D. (2012). *Theory, Research and Policy for Planned Events*. Oxford: Routledge.

Grayson, K. and Martinec, R. (2004). Consumer perceptions of iconicity and indexicality and their influence on assessments of authentic market offerings. *Journal of Consumer Research, 31*, 296–312.

Grodach, C. (2008). Museums as urban catalysts: The role of urban design in flagship cultural development. *Journal of Urban Design, 13*, 195–212.

Hamnett, C., and Shoval, N. (2003). Museums as flagships of urban development. In L. M. Hoffmann, S. Fainstein and D. R. Judd (Eds), *Cities and Visitors. Regulating People, Markets and City Space* (pp. 219–236). Oxford: Blackwell.

Hoarau, H. and Kline, C. (2014). Science and industry: Sharing knowledge for innovation. *Annals of Tourism Research, 46*, 44–61.

Holley, P. (2015). Nepal earthquake reduces World Heritage sites to rubble. *The Washington Post*. Retrieved from www.washingtonpost.com/blogs/worldviews/wp/2015/04/25/nepal-earthquake-reduces-world-heritage-sites-to-rubble (accessed 3 March 2016).

Ivanovic, M. (2014). The perceived authenticity of iconic heritage sites in urban tourism: The case of Constitutional Hill, Johannesburg, South Africa. *Urban Forum, 25*, 501–515.

Jenkins, O. (2003). Photography and travel brochures: The circle of representation. *Tourism Geographies, 5*, 305–328.

Johnson, E. (2014). A theme park, a scandal, and the faded ruins of a televangelism empire *Religion and Politics*, 28 October. *Journal of Consumer Research, 31*, 296–312.

Judd, D. R. and Fainstein, S. S. (1999). *The Tourist City*. New Haven, CT: Yale University Press.

Kaika, M (2011). Autistic architecture: The fall of the icon and the rise of the serial object of architecture. In *Working Paper 105*. Milton Keynes, UK: Centre for Research on Socio-Cultural Change.

Kent, T. and Reva, B (2009). *Flagship Marketing: Concepts and Places*. London and New York: Routledge.

Krohn-Hansen, C. (2001). A tomb for Columbus in Santo Domingo. Political cosmology, population and racial frontiers. *Social Anthropology, 9*, 165–192.

Law, C. M. (2002). *Urban Tourism: The Visitor Economy and the Growth of Large Cities*. London: Continuum.

McGuigan, J. (2003). The social construction of a cultural disaster: New Labour's millennium experience. *Cultural Studies, 17*, 669–690.

McGuigan, J. and Gilmore, A. (2002). The millennium dome: Sponsoring, meaning and visiting. *International Journal of Cultural Policy, 8*, 1–20.

Maclean, S. (2012). Zimbabwe outrage over plan to turn Robert Mugabe's home into tourist attraction. *Telegraph*. Retrieved from www.telegraph.co.uk/news/worldnews/africaandindianocean/Zimbabwe/9617667/Zimbabwe-outrage-over-plan-to-turn-Robert-Mugabes-home-into-tourist-attraction.html (accessed 3 March 2016).

Maitland, R. and Newman, P. (2004). Developing metropolitan tourism on the fringe of Central London. *International Journal of Tourism Research, 6*, 339–348.

Michael, C. H. and Page, S. J. (2014). *The Geography of Tourism and Recreation: Environment, Place and Space*. Abingdon: Routledge.

Miles, S. & Paddison, R. 2005. Introduction: The rise and rise of culture-led urban regeneration. *Urban Studies, 42*, 833–839.

Miles, S. (2005). 'Our Tyne': Iconic regeneration and the revitalisation of identity in NewcastleGateshead. *Urban Studies, 42*, 913–926.

O'Ceallaigh, J. (2014, 1 May). London Eye: Complete visitor guide. *The Telegraph.* Retrieved from www.telegraph.co.uk/travel/destinations/europe/united-kingdom/england/london/articles/London-Eye-complete-visitor-guide (accessed 8 March 2016).

Ortiz-Moya, F. (2015). Coping with shrinkage: Rebranding post-industrial Manchester. *Sustainable Cities and Society, 15,* 33–41.

Paül Agustí, D. (2013). Differences in the location of urban museums and their impact on urban areas. *International Journal of Cultural Policy, 20,* 471–495.

Plaza, B. (2008). On some challenges and conditions for the Guggenheim Museum Bilbao to be an effective economic re-activator. *International Journal of Urban and Regional Research, 32,* 506–517.

Richards, G. and Wilson, J. (2007). Tourism development trajectories from culture to creativity? In G. Richards and J. Wilson (Eds), *Tourism, Creativity and Development* (pp. 1–34). London: Routledge.

Sklair, L. (2006). Iconic architecture and capitalist globalization. *City, 10,* 21–47.

Sklair, L. (2010). Iconic architecture and the culture-ideology of consumerism. *Theory, Culture, Society, 27,* 135–159.

Sklair, L. (2013). The role of iconic architecture in globalizing urban megaprojects. In G. D. C. Santamaría (Ed.), *Urban Megaprojects: A Worldwide View (Research in Urban Sociology, Volume 13)* (pp. 161–183). Bingley: Emerald Group Publishing.

Sklair, L. and Gherardi, L. (2012). Iconic architecture as a hegemonic project of the transnational capitalist class. *City, 16,* 57–73.

Smith, O. and Metcalf, T. (2015, 31 March). When did the Eiffel Tower open to the public? *The Telegraph.* Retrieved from www.telegraph.co.uk/travel/destinations/europe/france/parisandaround/11505668/Eiffel-Tower-facts.html (accessed 15 January 2016).

Smyth, H. (1994). *Marketing the City: The Role of Flagship Development in Urban Regeneration.* London: E & FN Spon.

Soble, J. (2015, 17 July). Japan scraps Olympic stadium plan over $2 billion price tag. *The New York Times.* Retrieved from www.nytimes.com/2015/07/18/world/asia/japan-scraps-stadium-plan-for-2020-tokyo-olympics-over-2-billion-price-tag.html?_r=0 (accessed 8 March 2016).

South West Regional Development Agency (2005). *Iconic Tourism Projects in the South West of England, Final Report v4.0.* Bristol: DTZ Pieda Consulting.

Sternberg, E. (1997). The iconography of the tourism experience. *Annals of Tourism Research, 24,* 951–969.

Sulaiman, M. Z. (2014). Translating urban tourist icons across cultures: An English-Malay perspective. *Journal of Language Studies, 14,* 159–173.

Tang, L., Morrison, A. M., Lehto, X. Y., Kline, S. and Pearce, P. L. (2009). Effectiveness criteria for icons as tourist attractions: A comparative study between the United States and China. *Journal of Travel and Tourism Marketing, 26,* 284–302.

Tripadvisor (2015). TRAVELERS' CHOICE LANDMARKS 2015. Retrieved from www.tripadvisor.com/TravelersChoice-Landmarks (accessed 15 January 2016).

UNESCO (2015). The United Nations Educational, Scientific and Cultural Organization, Culture, World Heritage Centre, the List.

Veselinovic, M. (2015). 9 tourist attractions that are dying. *CNN.* Retrieved from http://edition.cnn.com/2015/07/08/travel/9-tourist-attractions-that-are-literally-dying (accessed 8 March 2016).

VisitBerlin (2015). Berlin Television Tower. Retrieved from www.visitberlin.de/en/spot/berlin-television-tower (accessed 15 January 2016).

Wainwright, O. (2014). Zaha Hadid's Tokyo Olympic stadium slammed as a 'monumental mistake' and a 'disgrace to future generations'. *The Guardian*. Retrieved from www.theguardian.com/artanddesign/architecture-design-blog/2014/nov/06/zaha-hadids-tokyo-olympic-stadium-slammed-as-a-monumental-mistake-and-a-disgrace-to-future-generations (accessed 8 March 2016).

Wanhill, S. (2005). The ownership and evaluation of visitor attractions. In J. Aramberri and R. Butler (Eds), *Tourism Development – Issues for a Vulnerable Industry* (pp. 89–120). Clevedon: Channel View Publications.

Weaver, D. B. and Lawton, L. J. (2007). Just because it's gone doesn't mean it isn't there anymore: Planning for attraction residuality. *Tourism Management*, *28*, 108–117.

Weidenfeld, A. (2010). Iconicity and 'flagshipness' of tourist attractions. *Annals of Tourism Research*, *37*, 851–854.

Weidenfeld, A., Ram, Y. and Bjork, P. (2015). The relationships between authenticity and place attachment of visitor attractions in urban place, Integrating City Tourism into the Urban Research Agenda, Gran Sasso Science Institute GSSI, Doctoral Programme in Urban Studies, L'Aquila, Italy.

Winterma, D. (2012). White Cliffs of Dover: Why are they so important to the British? *BBC News Magazine*. Retrieved from www.bbc.com/news/magazine-19343382 (accessed 15 January 2016).

Woodside, A. G., Cruickshank, B. F. and Dehuang, N. (2005). Stories visitors tell about Italian cities as destination icons. *Tourism Management*, *28*, 162–174.

12 Visitor attraction marketing and tourism destination branding

Implications for marketing practices

Peter Björk and Adi Weidenfeld

Introduction

Visitor attractions are key tourism resources, responsible for the existence and survival of tourist destinations and can be considered the 'first power' (Gunn, 1988) in terms of attracting and satisfying visitors (Garrod et al., 2007). They give tourists a reason to travel and are the raison d'être for tourism (Boniface and Cooper, 2001). It has already been argued that visitor attractions can be considered as a separate tourism sub-sector (Chapter 2), which is particularly relevant for tourism destination branding frameworks. Given that the role of visitor attractions is particularly pivotal in visitors' value creating processes, and their interpretation of socio-cultural constructs, this remains surprisingly neglected.

Previous studies of visitor attractions in the context of marketing have addressed issues of tourist behaviour with recommendations for destination management (Litvin, 2007), tourism destination branding (WTO, 2009) and place marketing (Rainisto, 2003), the importance of combining attractions in tourist offerings (Warnaby, 2009), as well as the involvement of stakeholders in tourism marketing (Fyall and Garrod, 2005). However, less attention has been given to the interplay between visitor attractions marketing and destination branding, and the role of perceived authenticity and place attachment in these processes. Other studies examined marketing related aspects from a more geographical perspective, focusing on the regional and local context (Shoval and Raveh, 2004, Weidenfeld et al., 2011). Shoval and Raveh (2004) used a co-plot method to categorise attractions into clusters that are consumed in 'packages' in destinations. In related research, Weidenfeld (2010) examined the relationships between the compatibility and appeal of visitor attractions in the context of product similarity and spatial proximity at the local and regional scales; these issues have been explored in Chapter 5 along with related aspects such as image and elements of attractiveness.

Tourism destinations are, from a cognitive consumer behavior perspective, perceived and evaluated through the lens of consumer associations. Thinking of France, for example, Paris is for some visitors the destination, which stimulates association to the Eiffel Tower as an iconic attraction (see Chapter 11). For other visitors, the association structure can be different. Here, the Eiffel Tower raises associations to Paris and France (cf. Florek and Conejo, 2007). For destination marketing professionals and visitor attraction managers, insight into and understanding of how targeted customers perceive the relationship between destinations and visitor attractions is essential. It can help in identifying the competitive identities of both attractions and destinations, on which their USPs are founded.

The relevance of a range of key concepts in tourism marketing, including perceived authenticity and place attachment, have received scant attention in the context of visitor attractions with the exception of Ivanovic (2014) and Ram et al. (2016). However, these studies have neither linked these concepts to the marketing of attractions nor included frameworks of destination branding. Other studies (see also Chapter 11) have discussed the importance of iconic (Tang et al., 2009) and flagship attractions (Smith and von Krogh Strand, 2011) to destinations. Florek and Conejo (2007), for example, who studied small developing countries – Costa Rica and Moldova – concluded that such countries should focus on flagship products, such as local foods, for destination brand creation and communication.

In the absence of a strong theoretical framework, this chapter is proposing that by framing tourism marketing as value facilitation, and by acknowledging the advent of the experience economy (Pine and Gilmore, 1998), it is possible to merge the theories of service logic and experience marketing into a proposed new model of visitor attraction marketing and destination branding. On an operational level this implies a focus on customer involvement, co-creation of value, network thinking and resource integration. In particular, visitor attraction marketing members of staff need to consider how to involve visitors in processes of experience co-creation.

This chapter suggests a visitor attraction-destination marketing model, which portrays a close interaction between visitor attractions marketing and destination branding strategies, and brings in service logic thinking to the field of tourism marketing. This approach has been used for explaining place product marketing (Warnaby, 2009). The chapter also examines the understudied role of perceived authenticity and place attachment of visitor attractions, which can be used to clarify the interrelationship between attractions, destinations and perceived value (Ram et al., 2016) in the context of the suggested new model. At the end, this chapter examines three suggested practices for visitor attraction and destination marketing actors to follow.

A visitor attraction marketing and destination branding model

Tourism destination branding is about stakeholder involvement, resource integration and value proposition development for image formation (Warnaby, 2009, Qu et al., 2011). In this complex and lengthy process, the marketing of attractions is pivotal, bringing added magnetism to destinations. In attraction marketing, the attraction offering including operand (physical resources, such as visitor centres, signs and souvenirs) and operant resources (processes, e.g. available guide systems, competencies and storytelling skills of the guides) (Vargo and Lusch, 2004, 2006) must be adapted to fit the needs, wants and expectations of visitors. This process, which starts with a strategic analysis linking available resources to the demands of target customers, has three distinct marketing dimensions: internal, external and interactive (Grönroos, 1987). First, *internal attraction marketing* is a process, which identifies the attractions' USPs, explores the current state of development, defines the intentions and elaborates on the profile, that is how the organisation wants the attraction to be perceived. Furthermore, internal marketing is also about how to involve, empower and motivate the staff to be customer oriented. *External attraction marketing*, the second dimension, is about market communication and networking. The essence (brand profile) of the most important attraction features (brand identity) is communicated as 'promises' of experiences to target markets. In tourism systems, it is important to identify the main cooperation partners, network and to define the value constellation structure for possible joint marketing efforts.

In context of this, the third dimension, *interactive marketing*, is about facilitating value creation in processes where the visitor takes on an active role as a co-creator of value. In interactive marketing, resource integration is a keyword. Customers bring to a visit the resources of understanding, knowledge, willingness to participate and, in some cases, even their own equipment. For example, golfers traveling to any major golf course usually bring their own golf equipment, their technical knowledge of the game and an understanding of the social rules that govern behaviour on the fairways and greens (etiquettes). But they also need to integrate these resources with a mix of different interlinked service systems, such as information about courses and reservation systems, catering and retail, which are available for the visitor, as well as often incorporating local knowledge about the specific golf course(s) visited.

Effective marketing and branding require strategic plans which frame operational tactics. Adapting service logic thinking (Grönroos and Voima, 2013) to the context of visitor attractions implies the need for a strategic plan that focuses on value creation in and around the attractions, ensuring authentic value propositions and facilitating resource integration, which takes place in co-created joint spheres of visitors, attractions and other service providers at the destination. The importance of coordinating and merging resources in inter-organisational constellations for tourism marketing is explained by Fyall and Garrod (2005), as well as in Chapter 6. Tourism actors in destinations have to identify who is doing what, and decide on what activities to cooperate on. For destination branding, a coherent brand profile has to be communicated effectively. Marketing efforts can be coordinated in models of joint marketing or co-branding, but there is also an option to bundle attractions in order to achieve an even stronger marketing effect. Many tourism destinations build their destination branding strategies on and around major attractions. Destinations, which lack this possibility, have to find other marketing models. For these destinations, the bundling of attractions, which has become 'more and more common in the tourism industry nowadays, due to the fact that tourists are increasingly looking for tourism experiences rather than tourism products' (Marcoz et al., 2014:6), could be an option.

The bundling of tourist services can take many forms. For example, attractions of the same type found in the same destination (region) can be combined and sold as a single item, such as in diagonal clusters (see Chapter 3). Potential visitors, interested in the World Heritage Site Kvarken Archipelago in Ostrobothnia, West Finland, can also visit Kvarken nature centre Terranova to obtain more information and to learn about the land uplift that has shaped the distinctive terrain. Visitor attractions can be bundled regardless of their spatial proximity. A family tourist package could, for example, consist of a visit to Tivoli in Copenhagen and Legoland in Billund, Denmark. Wine tourists, as another example, could find value in a tourist package consisting of wine-tasting, visits to wine yards, seminars about wine production and eating at restaurants serving local wines. If the attractions are located in different regions, then attention will have to be given to whether, and how, to cobrand the destinations.

Individuals or groups who attend the event attraction of Formula One (F1) motor racing, for example, may travel globally to follow their favourite team or driver, and might combine the Monza Grand Prix motor racing event with a visit to the city of Maranello and the F1 world of Ferrari. The existence of such behavioural tourist patterns could be used to develop a new tourist offering, consisting of two or more attractions with individually strong images. Another form of bundling of visitor attractions involves diagonal clustering. In such clusters, attractions create a bundle of separate products and services with other attractions or with other businesses, which together complement the overall visitor attraction experience. This example can be found in the service package offered to visitors to the World Natural Heritage Site: Kvarken Archipelago (see Box 12.1). In some instances, these may be purchased as a single item, such as Disney theme parks clusters, which are diagonal because they are offered both as a single attraction and as a single bundle of services, including the appropriate theme park, their own hotels and other services (see Chapter 3).

Integrating visitor attraction marketing and tourism destination branding

Drawing on service logic thinking (Grönroos, 2006), visitor attraction marketing is about value proposition offerings. Attractions in the *Tourism actor sphere*, which denotes the tourism sector, become attractions in the mind of the visitors as they evoke associations in the *Joint* and *Visitors' spheres*, the contexts of consumption (Grönroos and Voima, 2013) (Figure 12.1). The Great Barrier Reef of Queensland, Australia, is associated with scuba diving as an attraction, while paragliding activity is associated with Voss in Norway as a destination. Besides activities, attractions can also have a cultural appeal, be of interest for their natural beauty or attractive for their social stimuli. Following Prahalad and Ramaswamy (2004), it can be suggested that visitors often attempt to develop a sense of place attachment with the visitor attractions they visit. They try to be engaged and get involved in activities, interact with other customers and members of staff. They may also seek 'genuineness' in the perceived authenticity of various objects and other physical resources (Ram et al., 2016), such as interior design, and see this as important or even core to their experiences of the destination and attractions

---

Box 12.1 Branding and marketing of a World Natural Heritage Site: Kvarken Archipelago, Ostrobothnia, Finland

The Kvarken Archipelago, in the region of Ostrobothnia, Finland, consists of more than 6,000 islands. It is both iconic for offering a distinctive experience as a World Natural Heritage Site, and flagship for drawing a large number of national and international visitors, particularly families, to experience its flora and fauna and visit archeological points of interest. The shape of the landscape was formed some 20,000 years ago, when the last inland ice sheet started to melt. Eventually, the land was uplifted and made visible to visitors in the form of glacial depositional landforms, which are the De Geer moraines, being one of the main USPs of the archipelago. The moraines provide a strong sense of place attachment and perceived authenticity to visitors of the attraction and the Kvarken region more generally. These two dimensions are key elements for branding purposes.

The branding and marketing of the World Natural Heritage Site, the Kvarken Archipelago, has been ongoing since its inscription in 2006. The fundamentals for tourism development were first put in place before external marketing efforts were initiated. Trails and signage to guide visitors in the fragile area were developed, and nature guides trained as a part of an internal marketing programme. The tourism actors sphere has grown by involving an increasing number of tourism firms, activities, organisations and products. Today there is a large variety of service offerings that visitors can use to experience the area: bikes and canoes can be rented, and guides hired, for example.

Experience value is often created in host-guest interactive processes. Visitors to the Aava Kertun animal farm learn from the information given by the owner and are invited to be active in farm work. The existing service system, which primarily consists of independent service providers, has obtained a new character in terms of actor cooperation and the bundling of services for new service offerings. An example of this is "World Heritage Tours to Molpe hällorna", a service consisting of boat transport to the heritage site, a guided tour in the area and a special world heritage meal offered by the restaurant Strand Mölle. Today, the Kvarken Archipelago is marketed through tourism promotional media such as website, social media, brochures and souvenirs. Additional value is created by offering distinctive world heritage menus, drinks and music to visitors.

Source: www.kvarkenworldheritage.fi/visit-kvarken/

(Pine and Gilmore, 1998). This is taking place in a *Joint sphere*, a space of touch-points, where service providers and visitors meet in physical, social and technological interactions. In tourism destinations, the experience value of the visitor may also be influenced by place attachment and perceived attraction authenticity, a relationship which is moderated by the destination's heritage value and the iconicity of the visitor attraction (Ram et al., 2016) and is further discussed in this chapter.

Visitor attraction marketing assists the visitors in their image and value-creation processes in the visitors' sphere. It starts by introducing the attraction to the

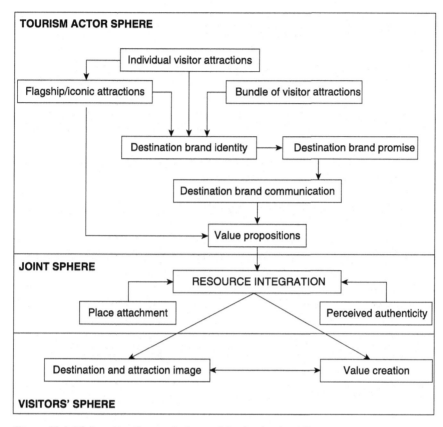

Figure 12.1 Visitor attraction marketing and destination branding

visitors, making the visitors aware of its existence, explaining the uniqueness of the attraction as promises in value propositions, engaging the visitors in co-creating activities in the joint sphere and finally, follows up the visitor experiences, in terms of image and value created. According to Wallace (2000), who developed a marketing guide to Leeds Castle, North England, visitor attraction marketers should collect customer information, focus on the first impression when visitors arrive, invest in staff training, ensure open communication to all actors, regularly challenge assumptions (take nothing for granted) and cooperate with key destination stakeholders and those outside the destination. Cooperation with local stakeholders is especially important in the case of enhancing the value added effect of authenticity.

Following the service marketing approach of Grönroos (1987), the three visitor attraction marketing dimensions – internal, external and interactive – can be linked to destination branding strategies. Internal marketing activities, which take place in the tourism actor sphere, identify destination branding cues. Destination brand promises are communicated by the means of external marketing, and interactive marketing facilitates resource integrations and brand image building in the joint sphere (Figure 12.1).

The task of attraction marketing is aimed at assisting the creation of a positive destination and attraction image and to enhance visitor satisfaction. It also facilitates visitor attraction experiences, which can be linked to one or several attractions on a journey, to meet (or exceed) the expectations of the visitors. Destinations with visitor attractions of major tourism magnetism appeal often use the option to merge destination branding and visitor attraction marketing (WTO, 2009). This implies that attractions become destinations' core brand identity elements (Figure 12.1). The city of Rovaniemi in Finland, for example, harmonises marketing efforts with the promotion of the Santa Claus Village. On their website, Rovaniemi welcomes visitors to 'the official hometown of Santa Claus' (www.visitrovaniemi.fi), and presents a large variety of year-round attractions (service offerings) all with a link to Santa; Santa's springtime, Santa's summer and Elf Taina's skating school.

Destinations with a shortage of flagship and iconic attractions have to use other marketing strategies such as service bundling, as discussed earlier. Researchers have also documented how bundling attractions for marketing purposes can be used for image building (Qu et al., 2011) and to elevate the level of destination competitiveness (Goeldner et al., 2000, Marcoz, et al, 2014). Service bundling, which is the integration of existing initiatives for new service offerings, relies on cooperative relationships between actors in complementary roles (Marcoz, et al., 2014, Alderbert et al., 2011). Another strategy is to redefine an existing tourism form and adapt it locally so as to develop new service offerings and attractions for both national and international tourists. This is illustrated by the 'wellbeing tourism' strategy in Finland, which is based on natural resources, including the archipelagos on the west coast and forests in the eastern part of the country. In comparison to wellbeing tourist offerings in other countries (e.g. Estonia and Poland), which are founded on spa and pampering activities (wellness), the Finnish wellbeing packages are more outdoor oriented and include physical activities, such as trekking and Nordic walking in the nature.

The marketing of visitor attractions and destination branding must be coordinated for the simple reason that attractions and destinations are consumed together by the visitors. The link between visitor attractions and destinations can be discerned in the way tourists discuss and associate with them. Here, associations between visitor attractions and their destinations can go in both directions or be combined. Upstream associations refer to where visitor attractions add or degrade the values of appeal to their destination regions. In contrast, downstream effects refer to how destinations associate with the visitor attractions within their boundaries in terms of adding or decreasing value (Florek and Conejo, 2007). Some tourists think of the Statue of Liberty as a visitor attraction and New York as a destination, whereas others see it differently and may think of New York itself as both an attraction and a destination. The Statue of Liberty brings an added value to New York by having an upstream effect, i.e. positive associations linked to the Statue of Liberty are transferred to New York. Downstream effects are found where a destination adds experience value to a visitor attraction. For example, the city of Vimmerby in the province of Småland, Sweden, where the renowned author Astrid Lindgren (1907–2002) lived and worked, has a special magic, which is reflected on Astrid Lindgren's World, where visitors today can encounter the characters of Pippi Longstockings, That Emil and Karlsson on the Roof, and many more (www.alv.se).

These cases are indicative for how destination branding, the process of creating a positive destination image, demands a holistic approach where visitor attraction and destination marketing processes are linked together. In order to coordinate value facilitating resources, a tourist destination governance model is required which revolves around a central actor or a group of actors as a hub (Björk, 2014). The tasks of this central coordinating actor are to synchronise the destination specific resources that are required to host visitors, identify destination specific identity features, follow up destination brand communication and monitor visitor experiences of the value propositions offered (as measures of destination and attraction image).

Following the discussion of Florek and Conejo (2007:54), destination brand identity is to be sought in those visitor attractions, which 'transfer positive associations' to a destination, as in the case of Santa Claus' Village in Finland. On a country level, flagship attractions 'need to be historically rooted, associated with local culture, currently relevant, functionally adequate and have to enjoy popular support' (ibid.:70). The visitor attractions, which create a particular aura, trigger tourists' perception of authenticity of experience (Rickly-Boyd, 2012) and enhance human-place bonds, an expression of place attachment (Kyle et al., 2004). These perceptions are particularly associated with iconic attractions (see Chapter 11). As noted earlier, the perceived authenticity and place attachment of visitor attractions play an important role in marketing and destination branding, particularly in creating resource integration. However, they remain relatively neglected in the study of the visitor attraction sector and are examined in the following sections.

Perceived authenticity of visitor attractions

Visitor attractions generally, and specifically in relation to authenticity, can generate different perceptions amongst tourists, which vary in relation to their characteristics, such as country of origin and other ethnic, cultural and/or religious backgrounds (Ivanovic, 2014). 'Authentic' is often synonymous to being real, reliable, trustworthy, original, first hand, true in substance and prototypical as opposed to copied, reproduced or done the same way as an original. Authenticity as a concept is highly contested and can be interpreted in different ways (see Molleda, 2010). There has been significant research on stakeholders' perspectives, particularly in the context of perceived authenticity in general (Molleda, 2010) and in tourism in particular. In the context of tourism suppliers, authenticity is perceived as an essential asset of firms that provide services for consumers, who seek 'genuine' experiences (Pine and Gilmore, 2008). This might require tourism

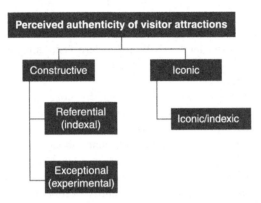

Figure 12.2 Perceived authenticity of visitor attractions

firms to open up or bring their 'back region' to the 'front' (MacCannell, 1973) and invite visitors to be part of the service creation process, which takes part in the joint sphere. In line with this, authenticity can be considered a marketing dimension which brings the three different actor-activity spheres – the tourism actor, the joint and the visitors' – together (Figure 12.1).

The following sub-sections examine three types of perceived authenticity: *exceptional, referential* and *iconic* (Figure 12.2), which are key elements in the model of visitor attraction marketing and destination branding.

Exceptional and referential authenticity

From a constructivist approach, perceived authenticity of visitor attraction genres include *exceptional* and *referential* (experiential or indexal) (Ram et al., 2016, Molleda, 2010). Exceptional authentic refers to the notion that something is perceived as being authentic by virtue of being done exceptionally well and more 'human' rather than contrived or artificially performed (Molleda, 2010, Pine and Gilmore, 2007). The monasteries in Mount Athos, Greece, are exemplars of exceptional authenticity because of the close interactions between monks and visitors, and exposure to their communal way (Andriotis, 2011). Referential authenticity refers to some other context, drawing inspiration from human history with a sense of shared memories and longings rather than being derivative or trivial (Pine and Gilmore, 2007).

Visitor attractions, which are historical sites, fall under this category, as they provide an authentic and thematic physical and mental representation of the past. This applies particularly to situations where objects and exhibits with sacred and historical associations are involved, e.g. artifacts, icons, incense, rosaries, prayer ropes, which provide a direct representation and memory of the place and its history (Andriotis, 2011). Auschwitz concentration camp visitor attraction in Poland would be one such example, and another is Masada, a rugged natural fortress and a symbol of the ancient kingdom of Israel, which has been conserved by the dry and mild weather conditions in the Judean Desert, Israel (Chapter 11).

Non-heritage attractions can also be referentially authentic, if they are designed and manufactured with direct reference to the thematic nature of the attractions. The Biomuseo (Museum of Biodiversity) in Panama, for example, was built on the land bridge known as the Isthmus of Panama, which was formed by underwater volcanoes and the movement of tectonic plates pushed up from the seafloor some 15 million years ago. It is located on the Amador Causeway, a prominent area at the entrance to the Panama Canal in the Pacific Ocean, where visitors can observe, among other points of interest, the Bridge of the Americas. The building was designed to tell the story of uniting two continents, separating a vast ocean in two, and irreversibly changing the planet's biodiversity. The museum includes exhibit galleries and aquariums displaying maritime life in the Pacific and Caribbean (Amador Foundation, 2015). The area provides a referential setting as it has become a region for migration of plants and animals and biodiversity.

Ivanovic (2014) examined the importance of authenticity in the tourists' experience of visiting the sites of Constitution Hill, Johannesburg, South Africa, and confirmed that the distinct properties of urban and historical cultural heritage attractions determine tourists' perceived authenticity and sense of place (see Box 12.2).

Box 12.2 Measuring the perceived authenticity of major visitor attractions: Constitution Hill, South Africa

The perceived authenticity of Constitution Hill, South Africa was evaluated by using the scales and variables of the four main dimensions of authentic tourist experiences: authenticity, attention, outcomes and feelings. The authenticity of the setting (e.g. a prison site in respect of the Constitutional Court) and that of interpretive media and services (e.g. photographs, videos, audio recordings, exhibits and sculptures) were evaluated. The scales pertaining to the attention the tourists pay to activities and demonstrations measure the attentional (how much attention they pay to each of the listed media: audio-visual media, objects, plaques, exhibits and interpretation provided by a site guide) and the perceptual (how important each of the media was in their understanding of the site dimensions of objective authenticity). The outcomes denote the cognitive and affective dimensions of tourist experience. The cognitive dimension is measured by the level of learning or mindfulness (to what extent the site provoked the respondents thoughts), while two variables of affective authenticity related to insightfulness are emotional response (how the experience made them feel) and empathy (how moved they are by the experience). Feelings were measured on a five-point Likert scale which assesses how deep and extraordinary were the feelings which were triggered by visits. The study showed that the constructs tourists' perceived authenticity and sense of place mainly depend on the authentic and distinct properties of urban and historical cultural heritage attractions.

Source: Ivanovic (2014).

Iconic authenticity

Authenticity is communicated through heritage and links with past events, such as by means of storytelling as a value proposition, resulting in the continuance of myths regarding the production processes of certain style icons (Molleda, 2010, Mossberg, 2008). How an icon is promoted is pivotal in the 'dialogue' between marketers and consumers about authenticity, which can be both a social construction and a source of evidence (Grayson and Martinec 2004). The concept of iconicity, which has been already explored in Chapter 11, and has been used in context of the perceived authenticity of visitor attractions, is more relevant in the heritage tourism context (Ram et al., 2016). *Iconicity*, as noted earlier (Chapter 11), refers to a mental template (such as history, fiction or old things or 'composite picture'), which is used in or through a physical manifestation to represent something perceived as being authentic and significant. It creates a dialogue over history, space, identity and values between marketers and consumers about authenticity, and is directly affected by social and cultural objectives and products' marketability (Weidenfeld, 2010, Grayson and Martinec, 2004).

Iconic authenticity is composed of authenticity, which is put in context and is predetermined by added interpretations projected onto objects by customers (Molleda, 2010). It can be classified into two types of authenticity: iconic and indexical (Grayson and Martinec, 2004), and is denoted through physical attributes (indexically), i.e. as a tourism index and brand essence (iconically), i.e. as a tourism icon. In line with Peirce (1998), Grayson and Martinec (2004) note that 'index' refers to cues that have a factual and spatio-temporal link with something else, such as the link between an actor and his handprints. Actors' handprints, a signature and a statue are physical manifestations as they consist of authentic elements of the original figure and therefore are perceived as indexically authentic. To view something as an index, the perceiver must believe in the existence of such a link which requires some kind of verification, which can emerge out of consumers' personal experience (Grayson and Martinec, 2004).

The handprints and stars in the Hollywood Walk of Fame in Los Angeles, California, for example, are physical manifestations, which have a direct and verified link to real human stars who are well known to the visitors (Box 12.3). These links are further reinforced by the coach tour, which takes tourists to stars' homes in Los Angeles. Similarly, the top level of the observation deck of the Baiterek Monument in Astana, Kazakhstan, features a gilded handprint of Kazakh President, Nursultan Nazarbayev, mounted on an ornate pedestal, which strengthens the factual and temporal links between visitors and the president. The index enhances the visitor attraction experience by increasing the emotional bond between the visitor and the elements of the attractions as physical objects.

This indexic authentic facility seems to achieve its goal as visitors place their own hands on the plaque in the imprint and make a wish, or when newlyweds pose for photographs with their hands in the President's print. In this case, as in others, objects are described as 'authentic' when their physical manifestation resembles something that is indexically authentic (Molleda, 2010). In other words, it refers to the use of a mental picture or perception of history, fiction or old things

Box 12.3 Iconic America: The Hollywood Walk of Fame

The Walk is an iconic visitor attraction in Hollywood, California, which stretches along Hollywood Boulevard and Vine Street, which is administered by the Hollywood Chamber of Commerce and maintained by the self-financing Hollywood Historic Trust. It comprises more than 2,500 five-pointed terrazzo and brass stars embedded in the sidewalks. The stars are intended to be permanent and are considered public monuments to achievement in the entertainment industry, bearing the names of a mix of actors, musicians, directors, producers, musical and theatrical groups, fictional characters, and others. Each bronze star embedded into the sidewalk represents one of Hollywood's stars. In addition, in the courtyard of the Chinese Theatre, handprints and footprints of Hollywood's most elite celebrities, such as Marilyn Monroe, Tom Hanks, Morgan Freeman, Clint Eastwood, Meryl Streep, Ron Howard, are immortalised in concrete. Each of the hand or footprints is indexically (physically) authentic, because they are physical manifestations, which have a direct and verified link (index) to the real human stars, who are well known to the visitors. The walk was one of the top tourist attractions in America in 2010 and plays a crucial role in drawing tourists to Los Angeles County, an estimated 10 million visitors annually. The free attraction leads tourists to other local paid attractions and catering businesses.

Source: www.walkoffame.com/

to assess whether a physical object (e.g. statue, building) is similar to another thing and therefore perceived as authentic. The index value contributes to the visitor attraction experience by 'enlivening' its physical objects, creating a significant meaning and by stimulating an emotional bond, which can increase place attachment between visitors and visitor attractions.

Visitors interpret a set of indexical cues, e.g. a cathedral and iconic cues, such as multiple references to an imagined past, e.g. representations of archbishops and saints in the form of arts, statues and personal items. The iconic authenticity of objects is both a social construction of perceptions of people and a source of evidence which fuels and stimulates its construction. Iconic tourist structures including attractions, projects, institutions (terms used synonymously in the literature) have been designed as an attempt 'to symbolise the changing character of the area, to provide a memorable image that potential visitors will associate with it and to create footfall with attracting visitors' (Maitland and Newman, 2004:16). These may be reinforced by social and cultural events and practices taking place within attractions and contribute to its iconisation (Chapter 2), such as the coronation of royalty inside St Paul's Cathedral, which carry social meaning and therefore iconic status (Kaika, 2011).

Place attachment of visitor attractions

'Place attachment' in psychology refers to the emotional link between the self and the place (Gross and Brown, 2006, Gross and Brown, 2008, Hidalgo and

Hernández, 2001, Kyle et al., 2003), which produces a sense of being and feeling in place or at home (Yuksel et al., 2010) and provides a sense of trust and security (Tsai, 2012). This link brings the visitors' sphere into the joint and tourism actor spheres in Figure 12.1 by positioning the visitors in the experience context of attractions and destinations. Place attachment in tourism studies has focused on how its different dimensions influence tourists' perception of environmental and social conditions encountered while on tour (Kyle et al., 2003, Lee and Shen, 2013). It consists of four dimensions: place identity, social bond, affective attachment and place dependence (Kolar and Zabkar, 2010), and is considered as an antecedent of the tourism experience and of tourists seeking genuineness in the context of perceived authenticity of major visitor attractions (see Ram et al., 2016). Therefore, place attachment in visitor attractions, in the context of international tourists to major visitor attractions, refers to visitors' emotional binding to the geographical location of the tourism space of the attraction, but is also influenced by its surrounding environmental settings, i.e. landscape and/or the urban context of where the attraction is located (Ram et al., 2016).

Research on tourists' perspectives of the authenticity of major visitor attractions, as being subjective and experiential (Kolar and Zabkar, 2010), was undertaken by Ram et al. (2016). They examined tourist perception of authenticity by international tourists in terms of an evaluation of the 'genuineness', antecedents and consequences of perceived authenticity by comparing major visitor attractions in Helsinki, Finland, and Jerusalem, Israel. Their study identified the interrelationships between iconicity, place attachment and perceived authenticity of visitor attractions, as well as heritage value and the perceived authenticity of tourism destinations. They concluded that perceived authenticity of visitor attractions increases place attachment but is moderated by two factors: the extent to which a destination provides heritage experience (heritage value), and the extent to which an attraction is perceived as iconic. Therefore, two arguments can be made. The first is that visitor attractions in heritage tourism destinations (e.g. Jerusalem) are perceived as being more authentic than those in non (or less) heritage destinations (e.g. Helsinki). The second is that iconic attractions are perceived as being more authentic than non-iconic (Ram et al., 2016). These arguments may be different for perceived authenticity by domestic tourist and local residents.

Tourism attraction marketing – three practices

In the value constellations of tourism destinations, visitor attractions are important components as they influence travel decisions, can be branded and are an integral part of destination branding. As a destination resource, visitor attractions become offerings for customers to experience and act upon. In tourism systems, resource integration is critical. Therefore, visitor attraction marketing and tourism destination branding should be conceived as a multi-stakeholder effort revolving around a core of central actors offering resources for value creation in what Grönroos and Voima (2013) define as the joint and consumer (visitor) sphere (Figure 12.1). Based on this and the discussion of authenticity and place attachment, three practices for visitor attraction marketing and destination branding can be identified.

Governance model development. The tourism system consists of a large set of stakeholders with different strategic agendas, which need to be synchronised for destination branding purposes. Initially, the destinations' major visitor attractions have to be identified and presented as fundaments in a destinations brand identity structure. Tourism research on iconicity and place attachment can be used as a conceptual guideline on how to link visitor attractions to destination development and branding, emphasising emotional human-place linkages expressed in terms of place attachment and perceived authenticity. The suggested governance model has an open structure. It is built on shared responsibility, and revolves around a creative knowledge environment. With an eye on existing resources, the priority is to develop a holistic, customer-oriented approach focusing on value propositions. Drawing on service logic thinking, visitor attractions – along with other tourism service elements – are considered to be value experience facilitators. It follows that the behaviour, emotions and perceptions of the visitors have to be monitored and interpreted in order to provide insight into the value-creation process. Only then is it possible to understand the customer sphere, which is so important for destination branding.

Bundling of visitor attractions and tourism system thinking. This chapter is arguing for the bundling of visitor attractions in order to enhance perceived value, and looking for cross-sectoral and multi-regional cooperations. However, in this bundling of attraction processes, the distinctive characteristics of tourism must not be forgotten: tourists consume not only attraction services in destinations, but also accommodation, restaurant and other types of services. Especially for destination branding, it is critical that a destination manages to have the appropriate combination of services to meet the expectations of the visitors.

Cultivating a visitor attraction–tourism destination symbiosis. Destination branding and visitor attraction marketing are closely related simply because attractions entice the visitors to the destination. However, in order to increase tourism satisfaction, visitor attractions have to be embedded as key resources in a tourism system which includes other interdependent sub-systems, such as telecommunication, retail and transportation. Internal marketing of visitor attractions, therefore, should focus on the involvement and engagement of the members of staff, external marketing on promises and interactive marketing which composes stories to be told in the visitor attraction experience context. In the setup of a destination specific resource, local residents should not be forgotten. They can be empowered and involved in the destination planning and marketing processes, add to perceived authenticity and stimulate place attachment among tourists. A welcoming attitude is likely to be remembered by tourists.

Conclusions

This chapter argues for the importance of coordination of destination branding and visitor attraction marketing efforts, and emphasises the need for tourism actors to focus on facilitating the value-creating process of the visitors. According to the principles of service dominant logic (Vargo and Lusch, 2004), tourists are value co-creators in service processes. In order to address this issue, a visitor attraction marketing and destination branding model was suggested and a set of marketing practices discussed. At the core of the model, in the joint sphere, resource integration for value creation influenced by visitors' sense of place attachment and perceived authenticity is to be found. The place attachment of visitor attractions is defined as visitors' emotional binding to the tourism space of the visitor attraction and is influenced by its environmental settings.

Among tourists, there is a growing desire to find authentic experiences (Yeoman et al., 2007), a development which challenges all service providers to critically analyse their current identity and how to, in a convincing way, communicate it to the visitors. For attraction marketing this implies in terms of exceptional and referential authenticity an assessment of how genuine and well-designed an attraction service is (exceptional) and the extent to which an attraction provides an authentic, thematic and mental representation of the past (referential). With a focus on iconic authenticity, attraction marketing is about how authenticity as a source of evidence and a social construction is communicated between marketers and consumers, and is relevant to heritage and links with past events. For perceived service quality and service transparency, some service providers might think of if and how to open up their processes and allow the visitors into their back stage, if not entirely, at least partially (MacCannell, 1973).

The perceived authenticity of visitor attractions has been studied among international tourists and was found to be positively influenced by place attachment. This relationship, which is moderated by other factors including the heritage value of the destination, and the extent of the attractions' iconicity, is to be understood by attraction marketers. Not at least because major attractions in heritage destinations are more likely to be perceived by international tourists as authentic compared to those in non-heritage destinations. Further, iconic attractions are more likely to be perceived as more authentic than non-iconic attractions.

Flagship and iconic attractions have a special role in destination branding, being the key identity elements and resources to be communicated as value propositions. In order to effectively interlink destination branding and visitor attraction marketing efforts, a governance model revolving around a destination's key tourism stakeholders has to be developed. For joint marketing efforts, it is crucial that iconic and flagship attractions in the destination regions are willing to participate and cooperate. Otherwise, there is a risk that the destinations will use contrasting or conflicting images that could confuse visitors and may have a negative impact on their travel decision-making. The chapter has also contended that as part of the service development process, new offerings could be developed by means of service bundling, such as diagonal clustering, which would be inclusive of other tourism services and involve a cross-sectoral approach to marketing.

The discussion in this chapter opens up a number of areas for further research including the three following directions. First, there is an urgent need to understand to what degree, when and with which resources visitors want to partake in different types of service processes. Second, further insight is required into how visitor attraction marketing and destination branding can be coordinated. Finally, research on the mechanisms which open up the service processes for perceived authenticity and place attachment, as well as how these concepts apply differently amongst different tourism segments, and between these and local destination communities, should be considered.

References

Alderbert, B., Dang, R. and Longhi, C. (2011). Innovation in the tourism industry: The case of Turismo. *Tourism Management, 32*, 1204–1213.

Amador Foundation (2015). Biomuseo. Retrieved from www.biomuseopanama.org/en (accessed 16 January 2016).

Andriotis, K. (2011). Genres of heritage authenticity: Denotations from a Pilgrimage Landscape. *Annals of Tourism Research, 38*(4), 1613–1633.

Björk, P. (2014). The DNA of tourism service innovation: A quadruple helix approach. *Journal of Knowledge Economy, 5*, 181–202.

Boniface, P. and Cooper, C. (2001). *Worldwide Destinations: The Geography of Travel and Tourism*. Oxford: Butterworth-Heinemann.

Florek, M. and Conejo, F. (2007). Export flagships in branding small developing countries: The cases of Costa Rica and Moldova. *Place Branding and Public Diplomacy, 3*(1), 53–72.

Fyall, A. and Garrod, B. (2005). *Tourism Marketing, A Collaborative Approach*. Clevedon: Channel View Publications.

Garrod, B., Leask, A. and Fyall, A. (2007). An assessment of 'international best practice' in visitor attraction management: Does Scotland really lag behind? *International Journal of Tourism Research, 9*(1), 21–42.

Goeldner, R., Ritchie, B. and MacIntosh, R.W. (2000). *Tourism: Principles, Practices, Philosophies*. 8th edition. New York: John Wiley & Sons, Inc.

Grayson, K. and Martinec, R. (2004). Consumer perceptions of iconicity and indexicality and their influence on assessments of authentic market offerings. *Journal of Consumer Research, 31*, 296–312.

Gross, M. J. and Brown, G. (2006). Tourism experiences in a lifestyle destination setting: The roles of involvement and place attachment. *Journal of Business Research, 59*(6), 696–700.

Gross, M. J. and Brown, G. (2008). An empirical structural model of tourists and places: Progressing involvement and place attachment into tourism. *Tourism Management, 29*(6), 1141–1151.

Grönroos, C. (1987). *Marknadsföring i tjänsteföretag*. Malmö: Liber Eknomi.

Grönroos, C. (2006). Adopting a service logic for marketing. *Marketing Theory, 6*(3), 317–333.

Grönroos, C and Voima, P. (2013). Critical service logic: Making sense of value creation and co-creation. *Journal of the Academy of Marketing Science, 41*(2), 133–150.

Gunn, C. (1988). *Vacationscape: Designing Tourism Regions*. New York: Van Nostrand Reinhold.

Hidalgo, M. C. and Hernández, B. (2001). Place attachment: Conceptual and empirical questions. *Journal of Environmental Psychology, 21*(3), 273–281.

Ivanovic, M. (2014). The perceived authenticity of iconic heritage sites in urban tourism: The case of Constitutional Hill, Johannesburg, South Africa. *Urban Forum, 25*(4), 501–515.

Kaika, M. (2011). *Autistic Architecture: The Fall of the Icon and the Rise of the Serial Object of Architecture.* In Working Paper 105. Milton Keynes, UK: Centre for Research on Socio-Cultural Change.

Kolar, T. and Zabkar, Z. (2010). A consumer-based model of authenticity: An oxymoron or the foundation of cultural heritage marketing? *Tourism Management, 31*(5), 652–664.

Kyle, G., Graefe, A., Manning, R. and Bacon, J. (2003). An examination of the relationship between leisure activity involvement and place attachment among hikers along the Appalachian Trail. *Journal of Leisure Research, 35*(3), 249–273.

Kyle, G., Graefe, A., Manning, R. and Bacon, J. (2004). Effects of place attachment on users' perceptions of social and environmental conditions in a natural setting. *Journal of Environmental Psychology, 24*, 213–225.

Lee, T. H. and Shen, Y. L. (2013). The influence of leisure involvement and place attachment on destination loyalty: Evidence from recreationists walking their dogs in urban parks. *Journal of Environmental Psychology, 33*(0), 76–85.

Litvin, S. W. (2007). Marketing visitor attractions: A segmentation study. *International Journal of Tourism Research, 9*(1), 9–19.

MacCannell, D. (1973). Staged authenticity: Arrangements of social spaces in tourist settings. *The American Journal of Society, 79*(3), 589–603.

Maitland, R. and Newman, P. (2004). Developing metropolitan tourism on the fringe of Central London. *International Journal of Tourism Research, 6*, 339–348.

Marcoz, E., Mauri, C., Maggioni, I. and Cantú, C (2014). Benefits from service bundling in destination branding: The role of trust on enhancing cooperation among operators in the hospitality industry. *International Journal of Tourism Research.* Available at http://onlinelibrary.wiley.com/doi/10.1002/jtr.2002/full (accessed 8 August 2015).

Molleda, J.-C. (2010). Authenticity and the construct's dimensions in public relations and communication research. *Journal of Communication Management, 14*(3), 223–236.

Mossberg, L. (2008). Extraordinary experiences through storytelling. *Scandinavian Journal of Hospitality and Tourism, 8*(3), 195–210.

Peirce, C. S. (1998). *Collected Papers of Charles Sanders, Peirce.* C. Hartshorne, P. Weiss and A. Blank (Eds), 8 vols. Bristol: Thoemmes.

Pine, B. J. and Gilmore, J. H. (1998). Welcome to the experience economy. *Harvard Business Review.* July–August.

Pine, B. J. and Gilmore, J. H. (2007). *Authenticity: What Consumers Really Want.* Boston, MA: Harvard Business School Press.

Pine, B. J. and Gilmore, J. H. (2008). The eight principles of strategic authenticity. *Strategy and Leadership, 36*(3), 35–40.

Prahalad, C. and Ramaswamy, V. (2004). *The Future of Competition, Co-Creating Unique Value with Customers.* Boston, MA: Harvard Business School Press.

Qu, H., Kim, L. and Im, H. (2011). A model of destination branding: Integrating the concepts of the branding and destination image. *Tourism Management, 32*, 465–476.

Rainisto, S. (2003). *Success Factors of Place Marketing: A Study of Place Marketing Practices in Northern Europe and the United States.* Doctoral Dissertation, Helsinki University of Technology, Institute of Strategy and International Business. Espoo.

Ram, Y., Björk, P. and Weidenfeld, A. (2016). Authenticity and place attachment of major visitor attractions. *Tourism Management, 52*, 110–122.

Rickly-Boyd, J. (2012). Authenticity and aura: A Benjaminian approach to tourism. *Annals of Tourism Research, 39*(1), 269–289.

Shoval, N. and Raveh, A. (2004). Categorization of the visitor attractions and the modeling of tourist cities: Based on the co-plot method of multivariate analysis. *Tourism Management, 25*(6), 741–750.

Smith, A. and von Krogh Strand, I. (2011). Oslo's new Opera House: Cultural flagship, regeneration tool or destination icon? *European Urban and Regional Studies, 11*(1), 93–110.

Tang, L., Morrison, A., Lehto, X., Kline, S. and Pearce, P. (2009). Effectiveness criteria for icons as tourist attractions: A comparative study between the United States and China. *Journal of Travel and Tourism Marketing, 26*, 284–302.

Tsai, S.-P. (2012). Place attachment and tourism marketing: Investigating international tourists in Singapore. *International Journal of Tourism Research, 14*(2), 139–152.

Vargo, S. and Lusch, R. (2004). Evolving to a new dominant logic of marketing. *Journal of Marketing, 68*(1), 1–17.

Vargo, S. and Lusch, R. (2006). Service-dominant logic: What it is, what it is not, what it might be. In R. Lusch and S. Vargo (Eds), *The Service Dominant Logic of Marketing: Dialog, Debate, and Directions* (pp. 43–56). Armonk, NY: ME Sharpe.

Wallace, V. (2000). Success guides. Successful visitor experience – getting it right. Association of Independent Museums. Retrieved from www.aim-museums.co.uk/downloads/a4415601-b24a-11e2-b572-001999b209eb.pdf (accessed 13 November 2015).

Warnaby, G. (2009). Towards a service-dominant place marketing logic. *Marketing Theory, 9*(4), 403–423.

Weidenfeld, A. (2010). Iconicity and 'flagshipness' of visitor attractions. *Annals of Tourism Research, 37*(3), 851–854.

Weidenfeld, A., Butler, R. and Williams, A. M. (2011). The role of clustering, cooperation and complementarities in the visitor attraction sector. *Current Issues in Tourism, 14*(7), 595–629.

WTO (2009). Handbook on Tourism Destination Branding, Madrid, Spain. Retrieved from www.imagian.fi/kuvat/etc_unwto_handbook_tourism_destination_branding.pdf (accessed 15 November 2015).

Yeoman, I., Brass, D. and McMahone-Beattie, U. (2007). Current issue in tourism: The authentic tourist. *Tourism Management, 28*(4), 1128–1138.

Yuksel, A., Yuksel, F. and Bilim, Y. (2010). Destination attachment: Effects on customer satisfaction and cognitive, affective and conative loyalty. *Tourism Management, 31*(2), 274–284.

13 Visitor attractions, recent and future trends

A practitioner's perspective

Ken Robinson

Context

This chapter is an overview, from a practitioner's viewpoint, of the development of visitor attractions. The analysis of the future for visitor attractions, worldwide, centres on two aspects associated respectively with the attractions and visitors. There are key contextual influences on the evolution and development of both. This chapter uses the narrower definition of 'visitor attraction' as originally developed by the English Tourist Board. It excludes places or attributes which, while they are aspects that attract visits to a destination, are not owned or cohesively managed for that purpose.

Politics and public policy

This is the most pervasive element for the operation of visitor attractions. Within the framework of global economic conditions, governments set social and financial policy and the taxation structure which affects attractions, businesses and visitors. National and local governments have control or influence over employment legislation that affects leisure time, and the operational budgets of attractions. National governments usually have ownership or control over the most important assets of their country's built and natural heritage, major museums and national parks. They also set the regulatory framework for local government owned assets such as local museums, heritage assets and parks. Governments set policy on admission charges to publically owned attractions, such as national museums and national parks, and local government owned assets such as local museums, which may be accessible free or at subsidised admission charges, which can have very marked effects on the private sector's ability to operate attractions commercially. The resulting disparities in the operational environment for attractions can be exacerbated by public investment funding, such as grant aid, often for developmental or regeneration purposes that are not specifically directed to visitor attractions, but which often stimulates investment in them. Similarly, governments usually influence how the revenues raised by publicly licensed lotteries are usually applied such as the eligibility requirements of public or charity ownership of the Lottery in the UK. The latter has funded major investment in qualifying heritage and cultural attractions, for which private sector attractions are not eligible.

Charitable attractions may also be eligible for valuable taxation reliefs, which in the UK include Gift Aid, which pays a defined contribution to attractions for every qualifying UK taxpayer visitor. In summary, political and public policy has created a very 'un-level playing field' for attraction owners, with two major effects. The economic inequity for private sector attractions of similar style and content to those in the public sector undermines their viability and in the longer term this polarises provision between the two ownerships, so that public policy funding and taxation must continue to support these mainly cultural and heritage assets.

Conversely, as national economies mature and government expenditure rises, there is a tendency for a budgetary-driven policy to seek to reduce public subsidy for publicly owned or fully controlled assets including visitor attractions. This leads them to be restructured from direct state ownership and control, to quasi-autonomous non-governmental agencies, or third sector foundations and charities. This can begin to draw in private sector sponsorship and philanthropic support and even private sector management and alliances that contribute to revenue generation.

Internationally, as the world economy has developed and since the second half of the twentieth century, there has been a strong trend of economic growth in most developed countries. Personal disposable incomes and leisure time have increased. As the amounts and frequency of leisure spending have increased, so governments have sought to impose taxation on such activities, to recycle funds back into public expenditure. In some cases, tourism taxes have been implemented, which may or may not be hypothecated to the management and marketing of tourism, but increase the cost to visitors. The combined impact of such taxes in turn influences and limits visitors' activities. It favours less costly choices; visitors travelling less far, choosing to visit free-access rather than charged attractions, minimising associated expenditure by, for example, taking picnics rather than purchasing food at attractions, and limiting retail spending. In general, the taxation of leisure time activities has increased continuously, and this trend is likely to continue in all economies until it becomes demonstrably unproductive.

Visitors – profile

The most important conditioning factor to predicting future trends for visitor attractions is the source(s) of their visitors: whether they are 'day-trip' visitors, i.e. residents or tourists, staying away from home overnight on the day of their visit. (This differs from the UNWTO definition, for the purpose of describing and analysing attraction visits.) For the purpose of simplicity in this chapter, the word 'residents' is used to mean those travelling from/to home on a day-trip visit; 'tourists' is used for those who are staying away overnight, whether they are domestic residents or inbound (i.e. international) visitors. The main difference in visitation patterns is that most residents can and may return for repeat visits, whilst only a minority of tourist visitors are able to do so. The ability of attractions to achieve repeat visits and the frequency thereof from residents of their catchment area is strongly dependent on the nature of the experience they provide. Attractions with fixed content, providing relatively prescribed experiences, do not usually attract repeat visits. Others, particularly entertainment based attractions and those providing changing content, do. These include leisure parks, zoos and those with seasonal variances such as parks and gardens, and child-focused amusements, which may attract many repeat visits. Where popularity or visitor-sourced revenues are important, attractions will try to vary their content or the experience that visitors derive, to maximise the repeat visit potential. Most attractions draw most visitors and visits from their resident market, even in most popular tourism destinations, other than newly developed resorts. Some attractions are only used by local residents, mostly on repeat occasions. Others may hold little appeal for local residents (such as entertainment and local heritage themed attractions in tourist resort areas). Visits by tourists to some attractions, particularly those located at or near major destinations for international tourism, can be 80 per cent or 90 per cent of the total, with very few repeat visits.

Attractions where income from visitors is important for viability require a suitable density of residents or tourists. Prior to the 1960s, before significant improvements in personal mobility and mass tourism, only small attractions existed outside cities and the few resorts. Previously, since the 1850s, this was the reason for travelling attractions, including fairs and shows which were temporarily located in cities for feast days, saints' days and holidays, staying as long as local demand was sustained. Currently, travelling or re-locatable attractions no longer exist, except for the few remaining circuses and temporary exhibitions, exchanged between museums and galleries. However, a prediction is that they will re-emerge in the future, as it could be more beneficial to move the content of attractions on specialised but popular themes to sites with serviced infrastructure in major conurbations or within new macro-catchment areas for a term of perhaps a year, with relocation during the off-peak season, than to be forced to periodically renew the content at a single location to generate repeat visits. An example could be attractions based on popular sporting topics, such as a 'Hall of Fame', which attract limited visitation in any one location, but could, as an example of a football based exhibition be relocated for periods of time to football stadia sites in different regions, attracting visits from each catchment area.

The key future trend affecting the prospects for all attractions that appeal to the tourist market is the global and inexorable growth of tourism. In most developed nations, domestic tourism far exceeds international tourism, with perhaps 75+ per cent of the volume and value being domestic. The key driver is aspiration. Tourism is an aspirational activity. There is an ever rising awareness of tourism opportunities, products and experiences. Most people who can travel for leisure and tourism will. The principal pre-requirements are available leisure time and disposable income, which are rising everywhere over time, for most people.

The other key element is accessibility. International travel is increasingly seen as a right. International tourism depends on the freedom to travel, which most countries now permit, for most or all citizens. Permission to enter nations and destinations is required, and is usually regulated by visas. This process is being tightened for security purposes but the value of inbound tourism ensures that workable controls evolve. International access is constantly developing, as new aviation, ferry and cruise routes, tunnels and bridges become viable. Despite increasing sensitivity to environmental impacts, these are countered by improvements in fuel economy, emissions controls and similar technological improvements (see Chapter 10). So when people have the freedom, time, money and permission to travel internationally, they will. These are unstoppable growth trends. Overall this means the growth of demand for attractions will sustain product improvements and new developments. It has to be recognised that increased outbound tourism, benefitting attractions at destinations, causes reductions in domestic demand for attractions but in most locations the net effect will still be growth.

Residents, and tourists once within a destination, must be able to reach attractions. Road, rail and to a limited extent domestic aviation must be convenient and affordable. Generally, access for all these modes is improving, although in the most populous destinations, road access at peak times may be unacceptably limited by congestion and delay. Significant traffic delays are frustrating, time consuming and costly, and can make longer distance visits to even the most appealing attractions unattractive. However, in many cases leisure travel can be made to fit comfortably outside peak commuting times. The availability of off-peak packages of attractions' admission and travel, by rail and coach operators, and travel trade intermediaries, is very successful, and will grow.

There are major causes of disruptions to leisure patterns and tourism that attractions cannot influence. Visitors only go to safe, healthy places. Danger, instability and perceived insecurity deter leisure travel and render destinations unattractive or impossible to visit. Terrorism and civil unrest, even when it is localised, impacts demand for whole countries or even regions. Occurrences such as floods, tsunamis and volcanic eruptions, and disasters such as the Japanese nuclear reactor meltdown at Fukushima, stop leisure and tourism activity for variable periods of time. Health problems, such as SARS, Bird Flu and Foot and Mouth Disease, can cause public movement controls and deter leisure visits by the association of unsettling imagery and perceptions, even when in reality visits would be safe. The headline and pictorial content of 24-hour news media, over multiple channels, has widespread effect. Experience over the last 20 years has shown that tourists are increasingly resilient, and short-term disruptions of demand for weeks, months or even a season or two are generally followed by renewed marketing efforts, and price incentives to rebuild visitor demand. Public sector attractions are supported to overcome such disruptions, but the commercial impact on private sector attractions can be much more serious and may destroy viability if not mitigated by operational cutbacks and insurance.

Attractions' characteristics

The key differentiator between types of visitor attractions (see also Chapter 2) is their original purpose. Either they aim to attract and please leisure visitors by being:

- purpose-built or substantially adapted (such as museums, theme parks and most entertainment based attractions, gardens),

- or they have a different original purpose, are largely visited in their original state, but may use acceptable presentation and interpretation techniques to adapt them to visitor attraction use (such as historic houses, religious buildings including cathedrals and churches, workplace attractions, industrial heritage and landmark attractions).

The 'product' of a visit to an attraction can best be defined as the 'visitor experience', albeit that levels of interest and derived pleasure vary widely. By definition, purpose-built and fully adapted attractions are designed to deliver this, and can be modified by structural, content and presentational changes largely without constraint (within development control limitations), to generate visits.

This is usually far harder for non-purpose-built attractions, especially those where the conservation of the status quo (buildings, landscape, thematic probity and relevance) is a legal or moral constraint. Most heritage based attractions (and many museums) are housed in protected historic structures where there are not only severe constraints on modifications, but very high maintenance costs associated with the buildings and installed systems. The affordable creation of a powerful 'visitor experience' of wide appeal is usually much more difficult for these non-purpose-built attractions, but technological innovations are bringing new solutions.

Many heritage attractions have to combine public showing and visitor access with other uses and occupancies: residential, commercial, agricultural, etc. The visitor attraction's 'business' may operate on a semi-detached basis from the over-all site, structures and such different uses. The revenues and costs of the visitor business at museums, historic buildings and similar adapted places are reflected in operational management accounts, but very few ever attempt to evaluate the return on capital employed, nor would they be commercially viable, with full accounting recognition of the underlying asset values.

In most developed countries, heritage based attractions (including museums) account for over two-thirds of all attractions, although in and around tourist resorts the proportion of purpose-built entertainment attractions is higher. The search for local differentiation is a very powerful driver of tourism activity. Tourists seek a sense of local culture, of traditions, of indigenous styles of buildings and local history. Heritage and cultural attractions of all kinds are the embodiment and repository of these facets. They are therefore truly community assets, whether in public or private ownership. This attracts the support and par-ticipation of community leaders, which in turn helps to bring in broader support from local commercial interests and sponsors. They are always at the heart of the destination's tourism appeal and its product.

The fact that most heritage attractions are intrinsic to the history and culture of the locality, area and nation highlights a distinction between them and entertain-ment based purpose-built attractions. Few purpose-built attractions receive any public funding (except for the few eligible for initial development grants) – they are commercially stand-alone enterprises, and as such are very vulnerable to economic conditions. A loss-making operation is likely to trigger product/content change or lead to restructuring, sale or closure. In contrast, the historic and community relevance of heritage attractions gives them the recognition of being 'too important to fail' so, notwithstanding the ownership differentiation described previously, they operate in a generally benevolent policy environment and may receive some public funding on an ongoing basis. This is the case with many local museums, owned by local government as community assets, which may be exempted from, or pay reduced local taxes, or may be helped by the provision of management and operational services. Alternatively, as they are not exclusively 'visitor businesses', cost economies may be sought when necessary by reducing the levels of service or non-essential operating expenditure.

Since the 1970s there has been very fast growth in the number of visitor attractions, fuelled by the growth of disposable income and leisure time, and the other key factors, described above (see also Chapter 5). In some countries the number of attractions has doubled in this time. Social and industrial change has been so rapid over this period that for many potential visitors, nostalgia, an interest in 'the way we were', has prompted demand at heritage centres, industrial archaeological and workplace attractions. This heightened interest in heritage has been sufficient to underpin the creation of new heritage centres, interpreting elements of the past. Nostalgic memories have not only been a strong motivation for visits but have contributed greatly to the 'visit experience' of the whole visitor group of family or friends, giving meaning and creating understanding of the purposes of what is now a heritage attraction. This generational link with the content of many heritage attractions is now fading, as the older generations die. For the future, the challenge for heritage attractions is to maintain demand and deliver satisfaction, without the benefit of nostalgia, to visitors who are simply choosing a heritage attraction for a leisure experience, in many cases without prior affinity with their content.

The now out-dated premises and equipment used in early industrial production processes are in many cases of the lineage of historically well-known names and current brands. Often, they were major employers in local communities and related elements are still recognised in local features and traditions. Early production was of much more human scale, with hands-on craft skills imparted to every product, contrasting with contemporary manufacturing processes that are slick, automated and impersonal – and even outsourced to cheaper production abroad. So the many mills, factories, distilleries, potteries and other industrial places can be very effectively presented as the "heritage of the brand", with related premium retailing opportunities. This can add style and depth to the brands and marketing of products, and provide valuable opportunities for personal contact with consumers (see Chapter 12).

Visitor attractions vary greatly in scale, both in the physical sense (as they may be as small as one or two rooms or extend to many acres) and in terms of the number of visits they attract, although there is an essential correlation between capacity, length of stay and visitor numbers. It is important to differentiate between 'visitors' as individuals, and the number/frequency of 'visits' that they make to an attraction – especially when defining or analysing product content, visit activities, frequency and related marketing. Those outside the visitor attraction sector tend to think that most attractions are 'large', that is attracting (say) in excess of 100,000 visits a year. The reality in most countries is very different, with the great majority of attractions drawing far fewer visitors. Many local museums and heritage attractions may attract only a few thousand visits each year. The average in most countries is probably less than 50,000 visits a year. At this level it is certain that, on a stand-alone basis, they cannot afford professional management. Whatever their asset base, they are in commercial terms no more than 'small and medium size businesses', and many of them fit the description of 'micro businesses'. To exist they require either to be supported by the public sector, or to optimise mixed sources of funding, with simple and flexible staffing, minimised overheads and use of volunteer staff. Often their governance is as charities or community enterprises, which requires the unpaid commitment of senior individuals as trustees and directors.

Free access attractions such as national parks are large in scale and in the number of visits they attract. In most cases, this is because a large proportion of visits are made by a minority of visitors.

Entertainment and amusement based leisure attractions are very different in nature, having evolved from early travelling fairs, to static leisure parks of rides and sideshows. Disney pointed the way to the use of popular awareness created through film, to build high quality, large scale 'themed' parks – these have since burgeoned in some locations worldwide, where the potential market demand from residents and tourists can generate a return on the very high capital, operational, maintenance and re-investment expenditure they require. It should be recognised that the major, internationally known themed attractions (i.e. with annual visits over 2 million) are located in relatively few places, in mature destinations, with high resident populations and inbound tourist numbers: California, Florida, northern Europe, Japan and, more recently, South Korea and China. Themed attractions with annual visits under 2 million are more numerous, but most depend as much on catchment area demand as tourists. It should be recognised that such entertainment attractions are a relatively small proportion of the total attractions in all developed nations.

Themed attractions require the ingenuity of engineers, combined with theatrical skills, and have harnessed continually evolving technological opportunities to create ever more impressive visitor experiences – and crucially a recognisable theme. These are by nature fully commercial ventures, dependant mainly on visitor revenues, supplemented by sponsorship. The perceived pulling power of such large scale leisure parks makes them highly sought after as key elements for development and regeneration, often attracting grants, subsidies, tax breaks and other public sector incentives. The period of rapid growth in such attractions has already peaked, due to the best locations and catchment areas already being served, and the fear of limited, if any additionality on, existing attractions. New international destinations and resorts will continue to provide new opportunities. Over time, there will be problems for many of these resulting from the extremely high cost of major renovations to long-established parks and themes that cannot maintain contemporary appeal (see also Chapter 9). European parks such as Tivoli and EuropaPark have shown that it can be done – but it requires constant attention to high quality, and the all-important visitor experience.

Entertainment attractions can be viable businesses at every scale. Amusement arcades with gaming machines can trade successfully in single street-side retail units. Medium scale, Family Entertainment Centres (FECs) based on activity and soft play, have grown rapidly in popularity, some located in larger ex-retail premises and some in larger more stand-alone premises, often industrial units close to cities and towns. Changes in agricultural profitability have led to a rise of farm attractions, often integrating aspects of adventure play. FECs and farm attractions demonstrate how medium scale attractions can grow from a handful of very unusual ventures, by refining their key elements and taking advantage of new amusement devices, into a successful concept that can be widely replicated, as each attraction only requires a limited market to be profitable. Some attractions are now cloned on a proven theme in multiple locations, such as the Sea Life Centres, Dungeons and Lego parks operated by Merlin Entertainments, and the Ripley's Believe It or Not attractions at multiple locations worldwide. There has also been a global trend, especially among younger experienced tourists, to favour active participation and outdoor quasi-adventure attractions over passive alternatives. So laser battle games, paintballing, bungee jumps, zip wires and similar experiences, requiring low capital investment, have been very successful, needing low capital investment and being relatively easy to change.

Demographic and socio-economic factors are particularly important to attractions, and their appeal and affordability to different age groups. The general trend in all developed nations where attractions are most numerous and attraction-visiting is a popular leisure activity, has been the increase in life expectancy, and the expectations and active participation of mature adults, who have the most free time and often the most money available for leisure. Family groups have constraints on their leisure time, especially education holiday times, they have the highest household expenses and many child related commitments at weekends. Family groups also favour attractions where parents and other adults expect to enjoy their content, so child-centred attractions have reduced potential, relative to those targeted at older audiences.

Development and viability characteristics of visitor attractions

Visitor attractions are either purpose-built and usually commercially run even if owned by charities, or they are adapted from a different original use. As attractions they may be sub-optimal in many respects, such as location, subject, building suitability, capacity limitations and limited evident public appeal. Adapted attractions have always existed for another, non-attraction purpose. If it is decided that they should be retained and be modified to attract and satisfy visitors, there will be inherent numerous limitations on what they can change, quite apart from limitations on the ability to service investment capital from visitor revenues.

Often these are heritage-related and have to be retained as community assets, or are privately owned where visitor revenues are the only practical source of use, and may satisfy requirements to minimise tax liability by provision of public access.

Commercial, and especially entertainment based, attractions are usually the result of optimised business planning. Their promoters choose location, style and content – and where relevant, theme. Being purpose-designed, they should have a stronger chance of success, but in practise they have been shown to be risky, with a much larger ratio of investment capital to net earnings. Even the most experienced operators with the most enviable track record and strongest theme content can miscalculate, of which Euro Disney is a prime example.

The advantages within a catchment from hosting a successful attraction of this type are very well recorded, in terms of economic impact, employment and if their profile is strong enough, for the appeal of the destination (see Chapter 10). The availability of grant aid regeneration and heritage or cultural grant aid, and sponsorship, combined with the challenges of devising dynamic regeneration programmes, have fuelled many hyped proposals for attraction developments. These conceptual projects are often backed by enthusiastic local politicians working with property developers and clients, all too ready to believe high projections of visitation, working with designers and architects whose fees are related to the scale of developments, and where the larger the development, the greater the projected local economic and employment results would be. In the UK this was particularly evident during the first decade of the National Lottery when many unrealistic new and re-development projects were assisted. The flaws in most emerged before completion, for others only the subsequent unsustainable realities forced major compromised adaption or closure.

The number of visitors to attractions is the result of many factors – including those stated above, related to purpose-built or adapted origination. Once open, fluctuations are caused either by macro-economic fluctuations that the attraction cannot control or by public perceptions of the product, compared to its competitors. The perceptions of the product are either intrinsic or the result of marketing activity. Newly opened attractions and those that have been subject to major re-investment will, if effectively promoted, always attract higher demand in the ensuing one to two years. This is known as the 'honeymoon period' and can be related to the wow effect in the Visitor Attraction Life Cycle (see Chapter 4). This is far more pronounced, and short lived from the local catchment area, for single-visit attractions than it is for repeat visits and tourist visits to attractions. Thereafter visits will return to a relatively stable level, affected by catchment area competition and marketing.

For theme parks, the recipe of sequential re-investment in a new major ride, say, every three years, is assumed by some to be essential (see Chapter 10). Yet the assumption of the necessity of regular and substantial re-investment being needed to overcome some inevitable life cycle effect is greatly overstated. It has been asserted that the Kotler 'product life cycle' is evidenced in attractions and that 'most attractions undergo one or more relaunches during their life' (see Chapter 4). Few operators would recognise this as an accurate description – the assertion is true of a few, but an exaggeration of the reality of gradual refurbishment for most.

For the great majority of cultural, heritage, natural attractions and adapted attractions, the concept of a 'life cycle' is irrelevant. What is the life cycle of Colonial Williamsburg, or the Tower of London, or Chatsworth House, or the Taj Mahal, or most museums, or national parks, or cathedrals and churches, or workplace attractions, or heritage railways, or …? The longevity of viable visit numbers for most attractions depends on the frequency of visits and the population within the resident catchment. However, 'single-visit' attractions are so described because few of their visitors would return in the near future unless they are given a strong incentive to do so, such as a financial inducement, or special event, or unless they return to show friends and relatives, even though they have visited previously. There is, in most places, a largely new set of tourist visitors each year from which to generate visits. But residents of the catchment will be disposed to, or can be stimulated to revisit, 'single-visit' attractions over a 10–15-year cycle. Those who came as children may be attracted back as adults and with their own children, then later with grandchildren. Many attractions have relatively timeless content; they are woven into the heritage of communities, regions and nations. Of course they must ensure presentation remains up to date, standards are maintained and improved, and marketing is efficient, but this is mostly routine; their life cycle is related to that of their visitors, not the attraction itself.

The exception where life cycle effects are evident is in the relatively small minority of attractions that are heavily themed and styled to contemporary fashion, or where technological advances make them obsolete attractions in resort areas that are mostly dependent on tourist visits, which will reflect changes in the destinations' popularity and competition from other attractions (see Chapter 7). Entertainment based attractions are the most susceptible to such demand changes, but also at the medium and small scale the easiest to renovate or redevelop.

Admission: free or charged

The attractions sector of leisure and tourism activities is unusual, in that the product – access for visits – is in many instances available without charge to users. This would be unthinkable for other elements of leisure activity, such as transport, accommodation or the provision of food and drink. Most attractions that operate with free entry are in the public sector, where access is provided by public policy as a social or cultural amenity. Often these are major cultural and heritage attractions, and in the UK free access to publicly owned national museums is free, as a matter of political policy. Many others are places where the control of admissions is impractical, such as landscape areas. Many smaller religious buildings, such as churches, wish to encourage free access. A few third sector attractions, and a very few philanthropically funded and sponsored attractions, also provide free access. Attractions may be arranged so that access to some parts is free, with other parts being charged. The UK has over 6,500 attractions which, in the opinion of the author's knowledge of visitor attractions worldwide, is the greatest density of any nation. Just under half of these operate with free access, and more than half of all visits are free. This exacerbates the disparity, and the uneven playing field, for commercial admission-charging attractions, as described earlier.

Attractions have widely differing operational costs in relation to their visitor business, ranging from virtually all costs for entertainment attractions and themed leisure parks which exist solely as commercial visitor businesses, to attractions which incur very low or negligible costs directly related to visits, such as heritage landscape or churches. Where visit-related costs are a high proportion of operational expenditure, the need to generate revenues from visitors is strong. Governments are increasingly seeking to divest attractions from their direct control to reduce the dependence on public funds. In cases where they also require the attraction to maintain free access for all or most visits, there is a need to find permitted ways of generating revenue from visits, often through separately charged special exhibitions and events. These need to be publicised to be commercially successful. This can lead to management and operational resources being focused excessively on these relatively peripheral elements to the detriment of the main permanent features.

Most visitor attractions have high fixed costs and low variable costs, so operational viability is often marginal. Operating expenditure is largely unrelated to the volume of visits – it costs as much to open a museum in terms of staff, energy and most operating costs for ten or 100 visits as it does for 1,000. This makes 'break-even' a critical point, with a very high net contribution from visitors and related revenues (from admission, retailing and catering) from every visit above that point.

Seasonality of demand, primarily conditioned by holiday times and weather, leads many attractions, particularly those dependent on visitor revenues, to close out of season when the costs of opening cannot be covered by anticipated visitor revenues. The simplest criterion for success in visitor attractions is the number of visits, and to a varying degree the resultant income. Commercial attractions tend not to be concerned about the demographics of their visitors except to define and refine marketing programmes. Public and third sector attractions are increasingly concerned with the social aspects of audience development, and outreach activities for those who do not or cannot visit.

Most visitor attractions have been arranged to provide maximum capacity for visitors arriving without pre-booking, which was administratively cumbersome and deterred casual visits. Prior to the Millennium, pre-booking was operated only at a very few attractions that had capacity limits. Generally, potential visitors have expected to be able to visit attractions whenever they choose, and vary their plans at will. The resultant fluctuations of demand, reflecting holiday periods and weather conditions on the day of visit, have created management difficulties over aspects such as variable staffing elements, and supplies for catering, etc. For the small minority of limited-capacity places, and for features such as special exhibitions and events, pre-booking was operated on the style of theatres (by phone, post or via trade intermediaries). Where deemed essential, for example for limited-capacity features and exhibits within attractions, demand has been managed and capacity optimised by issuing timed tickets to ensure a smooth flow and best utilisation of available capacity throughout opening hours.

The unpredictable fluctuation of visitor demand has favoured arrangements for free-flow circulation and interpretation within attractions, which still have to operate acceptably at peak times. How much better the visitor experience could be if the timing and volumes were manageable. Historically this has not been practical. Where admissions are charged, pricing policy has generally been to offer differential prices by age for adults, children, seniors, with very young children being free, and discounts for groups. Some visitors have been given access on special terms; through affinity schemes such as friends, or for visitors with special needs, etc. Most attractions have operated fixed charges, set annually. The earliest variations on this since the 1970s were seasonally adjusted prices to reflect reduced visit content or incentivised off-peak attendance, and promotional offers and vouchers, distributed via area tourism publications, press advertisements and brochures. Prior to the Millennium, however, visitor attractions (not having capacity limits) had not followed the example of airlines, train operators and others where demand was already actively managed and incentivised, and revenue was being optimised, by flexible pricing. In admissions management and in many other aspects of attractions, the internet has rapidly brought major, and continuously evolving, innovative opportunities for the management of visitors and revenue.

Marketing and research

The marketing challenge for visitor attractions depends on whether they are purpose-designed and built, or adapted to visitor use. For the former, the profile of potential and preferred visitors can determine the design and content of the attraction, and the marketing messages and media used to attract them. For most adapted attractions, the challenge is to present the core attraction in ways that support the widest appeal. In both cases, audience related research is essential (see Chapter 12).

While national surveys of tourism and leisure activity can provide general context, the disaggregated information has inadequate sample sizes for use at the level of any specific location or attraction. At established attractions and prior to the 1970s/1980s, research was usually limited to questionnaires among actual visitors, related to their satisfaction with the visit, their opinions of the product and the characteristics of those most satisfied by it. The resultant demographic and lifestyle data was used to plan marketing activities. However, basic visitor research could not be used to analyse the relative cost effectiveness of elements of marketing activity, and tended to simply ensure that the product evolved to match the most attracted elements within the full available market. Attractions with large enough operational budgets then began to additionally conduct awareness research among non-visitors in their source markets among residents and tourists. By analysing their pre-awareness of the product and promotional media, the relative cost effectiveness of differing promotional activity and the potential to attract potential visitors outside the established profile could be evaluated. Awareness surveys also enabled comparative performance alongside competitor attractions to be tracked.

By the 1990s, the semi-automation of research analysis and collectively organised research studies for groups of attractions, arranged by tourist boards, sectoral associations and marketing cooperative organisations, reduced the cost for individual attractions, and so extended their use. Until the 1990s many visitor attractions were reluctant to be openly honest about visitor numbers, as a predominance of annual 'league tables' caught media attention, with a simplistic widespread belief that high visit numbers, i.e. apparent popularity, would stimulate more visits. Rising numbers indicated success and falling numbers indicated failure. As a result many attractions ceased to publish numbers. Many prominent attractions exaggerated admissions, or estimated them in misleading ways – and some still do. It used to be considered potentially disadvantageous to include admission pricing information in promotional literature. These naive practices have largely disappeared, with a more mature approach and a greater sense of openness and trust. As a result, benchmarking schemes are becoming much more widely used, enabling attractions to evaluate their commercial and qualitative performance results with nearby and comparable competitors. This trend will continue – and increasingly the links will be made between performance data and customer choices, both by managers and potential visitors.

The promotional aspects of marketing require the persuasive description of attractions, via marketing media. It is obvious that attractions must deliver the visitor experience that they promise. However, unscrupulous commercial attractions have often hyped the promotional messages and imagery – especially in tourism destinations where commercial attractions are less concerned with possible post-visit criticism than they are with generating visits by tourists who are only briefly in the catchment, and are unlikely to return.

Visitor attractions – standards

Visitors have always recognised and responded to high quality in every aspect of their visit. Equally, attractions' operators have found it possible to track the beneficial effects of investment in improved quality. Most are good and reflecting the rising expectations of visitors, they have been improving. However, the opportunity for unscrupulous operators of low capital investment attractions to over-sell has enabled poor quality attractions to be profitable, especially in tourism resorts, even though local residents are well aware of their inadequacy and would not choose to visit. Misleading selling practices are subject to legal limitations on inaccurate description in many developed countries, but this has been inadequate to limit the use of exaggerated promotional imagery, or drive these poor quality attractions out of business.

As international tourism has become more competitive, governments at the national and local level, and responsible operators, have realised that inadequate products can have a very detrimental and long lasting impact on reputation.

The wish to recognise excellence and drive out the worst has been the motive behind various quality standards schemes for attractions, with 'charters' for visitors, giving assurances of provision and description. An underlying intention was that these would enable visitors to differentiate between good value and inadequate attractions. Some quality schemes have been devised and are managed by attractions' associations and destination organisations, while others are implemented with government backing, on a national basis. These can encompass 'pass/fail' approval systems, and grading symbolised by the award of a graded designation or stars. Generally, 'approval' schemes have been readily accepted by most attractions. 'Grading' schemes are, however, contentious when they supposedly objectively assess and grade attractions by certain criteria – for example, grades of five-star for the best, down to one-star, or 'unapproved'. For visitor attractions, however, grading the core element, i.e. the main reason why people choose to visit, is visitor-centred and cannot be objectively assessed. The intrinsic interest depends on the enthusiasms and level of interest of each visitor, and where admission charges apply, value for money depends on the value derived by each visitor. As a result, attractions' grading schemes tend to focus on the standard of facilities and services, which cannot give an overall guide to prospective visitors such as tourists who are likely to otherwise be unaware of the detail of the product, and what a visit will deliver to them. Additionally, quality standards schemes that have a pre-defined, points based system can lead to attractions pursuing changes that can boost ratings even though they are not of core relevance to visitors. Despite a rapid rise in the application of quality standards schemes, they are unlikely to become much more usable or significantly evolve further, as internet user generated reviews develop. It should be noted that some attractions have to observe statutory and regulatory controls (although these tend to be more related to the content than visitor-related aspects, as in zoos related to animal husbandry and theme park ride regulations); similarly, professional standards which may impact directly on the visitor experience (as in museums).

Enhancing the visitor experience

The essence of successful visitor attractions of all kinds, whether intellectually or entertainment focused, is to create and deliver the best possible experience for visitors. For most, this involves capturing the interest of visitors and imparting knowledge to them, and achieving understanding. What this information is and how it is conveyed varies greatly. Descriptive and contextual information is usually critical, requiring visitors to either read or listen, but rich experiences require the appropriate engagement of all senses.

For many years, displays and static exhibits were enhanced by description; mostly by explanatory captions and display panels. Prior to the 1970s, few had progressed beyond this 'book on the wall' approach, and the involvement of personal interpretation delivered by knowledgeable guides. Interpretive 'storytelling' expertise and techniques were developed. Going beyond this required the implementation of both technological and personal solutions. In heritage attractions, especially within historic buildings and where circulation routes are fixed, the scope for introducing thematic displays is limited, without destroying period authenticity. In these cases, the use of costumed characters and re-enactments of all kinds has literally brought static interiors alive. The use of costumed characters can go beyond acting to direct personal interaction with visitors, which can greatly improve their understanding, engagement and enjoyment of their visits.

Technological progress in presentation techniques was rapidly driven by the potential for consumer products, with variants being available for publicly accessible displays. The evolution of personal, recorded sound devices were adapted for audio description and tours, first from tape, then from digital sources. These installations led to very regimented visit experiences, and often the technology itself was too prominent, almost creating a barrier between visitors and the information to be imparted, and the surroundings. Moving imagery, originally by film, was unreliable and costly in continuous and repeated use. It was superseded by video. Audio visual enhancements of all kinds became affordable and reliable.

Simplistic displays of objects, originally in showcases, have latterly been placed in contextual settings, recreating the ambience of their previous uses. Displays became more theatrical (in scenic settings), more engaging and in many ways more interactive. However, the greater attempt there is to deliver a controlled experience, the less opportunity there is for visitors to experience the content in differing ways, and at differing levels and topics of interest. The challenge becomes how to provide the best varied visitor experience for what is often thought of by the designers of exhibit interpretation as being for 'paddlers, swimmers and divers'. Some visitors seek and are satisfied by fairly shallow experiences, some delve more deeply into the subjects, and some seek really deep interaction with the content.

In leisure, theme parks and entertainment attractions, technology has evolved to provide ever more apparently extreme physical ride experiences. In some cases, such as theme park non-ride features, the intention may be to create a predetermined and fully immersive experience, controlled from start to finish. Often these have been most successfully used to physically create themed presentations based on successful film and television characters and programmes. However, such themed experiences are extremely expensive, and regardless of cost, attempts to replicate solidly and convincingly the fantasy that can be conveyed on screen have frequently been underwhelming and fallen short of hyped expectations (see Chapter 9).

Continuous technological evolution led many to predict that the future potential for visitor attractions would be driven by the opportunities of immersive features, animatronic figures and virtual reality. This beguiling prospect has been pursued with every new development of simulators, three dimensional and multi-sensory imagery and people-moving transport within theatrically constructed sets. However, the extensive application of such techniques and mechanisms has disadvantages. The pace of technical development quite quickly renders installations out-dated. Technical complexity often makes the cost of maintenance high, and this rises as systems age.

The future trend for success will require the exploitation of every opportunity to cost effectively enhance visitor engagement and enjoyment, and to personalise experiences. It is also being recognised by operators that for the vast majority of attractions that offer one single form of access to all or most visitors, there are considerable opportunities to reflect the different levels of interest, and differing disposable wealth of their visitors, by developing enhanced experiences which generate much higher income (and visitor satisfaction). The trend to bespoke visit experiences, alongside general admission, will grow.

The internet and digital data

The extensive public use of the internet only began after the Millennium, and the continuous developments in digital data have impacted on almost every aspect of life. It was not anticipated that the internet and digital data would fundamentally change the relationship between attractions and visitors, nor that they would enable the enhancement and personalisation of visitor experiences. It is now becoming clear that these and many other aspects of the future use of attractions will be affected.

The principal sources of pre-visit information used to be personal recommendation, destination guides, press and television, and brochures distributed in each attraction's catchment area. Already this has been surpassed. The internet has become the primary source. This requires attractions not only to ensure they have an effective website and make efficient use of social media, but that all the evolving uses of data are implemented. The majority of visitors are now informed by, and make decisions based on, digital data via the internet in advance of their visit, as at least one member of each visiting group of family and friends checks details online. Such pervasive pre-visit information and contact was impossible previously. Online commercial transactions have become commonplace and generally trusted by consumers. This combined functionality for information and online transactions has swiftly overcome the formerly administrative complexity of pre-booking.

There has also been a strong tendency for visitors to seek special offers. The reductions of disposable income following the economic crises of recent years have been a contributory factor, but for many the search for a discount or bargain is key to triggering purchase decisions, whether or not they are essential to the buyer. Many attractions offering online pre-booking and an incentive price have seen take-up rise in excess of 50 per cent of visits within two years. This pre-visit contact also provides the opportunity, subject to ticket purchasers not opting out, of attractions contacting visitors before arrival to influence their visit behaviour, inform and modify their expectations and potentially 'up sell' secondary spend during the visit. The visit experience can also be enhanced by emphasising seasonal features, setting quizzes and competitions, offering exclusive benefits and laying the ground for post-visit loyalty activity. This pre-visit personal contact will also in future help make demand management practical, using price and product variations to influence demand.

As part of pre-visit research, most potential visitors consider it essential to consult the rapidly growing volume of 'user generated content' and post-visit feedback recorded on review sites. Users know they are not infallible and following evident abuses, the review organisations are tightening up the detection and removal of false entries. Users are increasingly internet-savvy and form their own opinions after looking at overall rating scores and many comments. As review site systems are improving and the volume of entries is increasing, it is becoming possible for visitors to do what Quality Standards Classification Schemes never could, and use filters to see 'what people like me' think. This makes reviews personally relevant and persuasive, and will render most aspects of official consumer-facing standards schemes obsolete.

Mobile phones have been superseded by multi-function smartphones and apps. The adoption of smartphones has been extraordinarily fast; by 2014 they were owned by the great majority of the adult and teenage population of potential attraction visitors. This is facilitating the next revolution – for enhancing and personalising the visitor experience. 'BYOD' (bring your own device) is becoming not only accepted, but essential in many activities. People keep and use their smartphones at all times. The great advantage for attractions in exploiting this trend is that the equipment is owned by visitors and its usage is second nature to them. It has for several years been technically possible for visitors to use such devices, proactively, using quick response (QR) codes or other contact triggers, to gain extra information about elements of their visit, or in-depth contextual information about displays, but implementation and take up has been limited.

Practicality is now greatly enhanced by the use of Bluetooth Low Energy (BLE) devices, specifically iBeacons, which can be located unobtrusively anywhere within attractions to automatically 'trigger' data display to visitors relevant to that location. The beacons and their associated software are comparatively inexpensive. The system works by interactions between each beacon, the visitor's smartphone and an app loaded onto the phone, which the attraction populates with data. Alternatively, the system can record location and time, therefore facilitating visitor tracking. This opens up many possibilities. Visitors can choose their language. The level of information is selectable (providing personalised experiences for paddlers, swimmers and divers). They are distance-sensitive between 70 metres and close proximity, so can convey differing information at different places. They can give directional guidance. The apps can be populated to make 'gamification' of visits possible. Visitors can retain the details from their visit within their app. The system can also be used for transactional interaction of admission and secondary sales of retailing and catering. By combining the detailed visit activity data, matching this to pre-visit data on customers, it could make possible large scale, in-depth visitor analysis without the usual costs of even small sample consumer research. This is a very big step towards the personalisation of most visitors' experiences – and it has the benefit of being optional for visitors to use it as much or as little as they choose, so those who prefer to can enjoy the attraction without these digitally enabled opportunities.

As international tourism grows, language can be a barrier to understanding and enjoyment. Already language software can provide real-time solutions to translate questions entered on smartphones and tablets. Camera-related software can translate signs without the user physically entering data, and conversational mode translation software (working in real time) can be used between hosts and visitors. Tourists visiting countries who cannot speak the local language are easily able to use this intuitive software. The use of data and the internet evolves rapidly. The opportunities it has so swiftly opened up for visitor attractions were unforeseeable but are almost limitless. Visitor attraction operators and visitors have much to gain, provided operators seize available opportunities as soon as it is practical to do so.

Meanwhile, pervasive use of the internet and the possibilities of 'big data' are enabling internet sellers to respond to users' patterns of activity and preferences. Over time, this has the potential to lead to the selective promotion of potential attractions in an area and of a type that the seller tailors to be persuasive to the potential visitors' known enthusiasms. Whilst this could be useful in matchmaking visitors with individual attractions, and may be appreciated by some, it would limit choice, and potential diversity of experience. At worst, the information could be commercially manipulated to distort preferred behaviour.

There are two leading questions for the future of visitor attractions

a. Reality versus virtual reality?

Will actual visits retain their appeal, as the availability of information, viewing and exploring via the internet and virtual reality become more effective and often freely accessible? Will wearing immersive technology headsets that convey the sights and sounds of a destination be satisfying? As public museums make their collections more available online, and facilitate related research, will it be enough for people to look and learn from a distance? The ability to explore connections and places online is truly amazing. The aspirational nature of tourism and leisure experiences gives a clue to the likely answer and is a strong underlying factor.

In developed countries, research shows that increasingly many people believe that they have all the 'things' that they need. Their principal interests are to improve the quality of their lives and to appreciate new experiences.

The continuing justification for all attractions in public ownership, and for funding support for heritage assets protected by legislation, is that they are important to the nation and community. In most cases, physical access by the public is a requirement.

My judgement is that the power of place, the experience of really 'being there', the intellectual and emotional benefits of discovering a real artefact, or being in historic surroundings, or looking at a great work of art in its place in a gallery, will always be preferable and infinitely more satisfying than any form of recreated virtual reality experience at a distance. Visitor attractions must, and the author believes will, always sustain actual visits.

b. How to progress from marketing to management?

This will be the key challenge for future generations and will require management by governments. The rise of leisure time, disposable income and expectations has fuelled the explosive growth of leisure activities and tourism after the 1960s. Since the 1970s, Jumbo Jets have made international destinations affordable and accessible, and passenger volumes have grown inexorably. The task for most people in the leisure and tourism industries has been to promote and sell more effectively, to stimulate, or win, more visits. Tapping into this rising demand has been relatively easy and the proportion of the world's population that is currently travelling is just the tip of the iceberg of potential demand. Yet already capacity limits are being reached in the most popular places and at peak times. Demand at many natural sites is exceeding tolerable levels with consequent, and in some cases irreversible, environmental degradation (see Chapter 10). The experience of being among crowds of tourism visitors in major tourism destinations can be equally unpleasant for visitors and for residents.

The environmental sustainability of tourism growth is also challenged, but a combination of the demand for revenue by host nations and communities and the reductions of environmental impacts through technological improvements will maintain volume growth. In free markets, the only available means of influencing demand and controlling volumes is by price. In some respects this can be desirable for destinations and attractions, if they can raise more revenue and provide better experiences, from less visitors. However, while rationing by price may be acceptable from the revenue perspective of the destination or attraction, it surely cannot be acceptable from a societal viewpoint for access to be dependent on the wealth of visitors, so that visitors of limited means would be excluded. Cultural attractions are important to the quality of life and the intellectual health of people. Visitor attractions exist to inspire, educate and entertain visitors, and enrich their lives. They must be accessible to future generations. The important question is who will set and regulate the criteria that must in the future determine how visits can remain affordable, and accessible, for all?

14 Conclusions

The spatial context of attractions and events

This book has taken a spatial approach in examining production and consumption of visitor attractions and events, including operational and strategic management factors, locational preferences and visitation patterns relative to their level of clustering, agglomeration and product similarity. The consumption side of tourism includes aspects of appeal and compatibility between visitor attractions, which are interrelated with key aspects of the production side: cooperation, competition, marketing, knowledge transfer and innovation. There are three main reasons for the centrality of the spatial approach in this book. First, there is the importance of the position and relationships of attractions and events with their wider physical, environmental, social and cultural settings, and the varying forms of mutual dependence between attractions and events, and the destination or regional setting. Second, their collective versus individual appeal – not only is the sum of the attractions greater than their individual appeal, but their individual appeal (or at least the translation of this into effective demand) is conditioned by the collective appeal of the attractions and events in an area. Third, the spatiality of the relationships between visitor attractions informs the economic relationships of production; cooperation, competition, knowledge transfers and the diffusion of innovations between visitor attractions are strongly relational. A fuller understanding of their trajectories and strategies requires analysis of these relationships. This is important for both academic knowledge and for the work of planning officers, attraction managers, entrepreneurs, public representatives and other tourism stakeholders. These aspects need to be examined and operationalised at the local and regional scales, which are crucial for understanding the visitor attraction and event sectors.

There are a number of important aspects of the spatial relationships amongst attractions. These include relative proximity, density, central and peripheral location and spatial configuration in terms of different types of clustering and clusters. For example, whether and how firms cooperate or compete, and how they achieve the essential balance in terms of coopetition, is very much shaped by the proximity – both spatial and thematic – between individual firms. In turn, the relationships between these proximate establishments is shaped by whether they are relatively isolated or located in clusters, and if the latter then on the types of agglomeration and external economies that they can draw on. But this does not imply any simplistic spatial determinism, because attractions and events are also engaged – although to varying degrees – in extra-local relationships, which range from the regional to the global. Competition, cooperation, knowledge and innovation flow into and out of particular clusters, destinations or other types of spaces. These are structured by what Urry (2000) terms scapes so that the trajectories of individual attractions and events can be seen as a constant tension between path dependency and path creation (Shaw and Williams, 2004). The persistent challenge for attractions and events is how to balance their own short-term goals (often centred mainly on survival) with the collective and perhaps longer-term requirements of the collective establishments in this particular sector(s) as well as in other related tourism sub-sectors.

Definitions and diversity

Researchers and practitioners have long struggled over how to define attractions and events (for example, Butler, 2015, Leask, 2010). This reflects both their diverse characteristics and the individual perceptions of visitors. What may be an attraction with appeal for one visitor may be a repellent for another, as for example the role of audience participation. Not everyone wants to be part of the performance, as is demanded at some attractions and events. The perceptual approach takes us very close to what constitutes the appeal of an attraction which, as our earlier discussion indicates, is a particularly knotty conceptual and empirical issue (see Chapter 5). Perhaps reflecting this challenge, most definitions have focused on those characteristics which are assumed to be 'objective' or at least can be measured in some relatively simple manner, such as whether they are fee charging, or are of a minimum size.

As noted in the introduction, one 'official' definition of a visitor attraction is that provided by VisitEngland (2013, 2015), which emphasises three main criteria relating to commodification, temporality and function. Commodification emphasises that it is possible to charge for admission; temporality emphasises that it is permanent and open to local residents and visitors; and function stresses that it is principally for entertainment, interest or education, rather than being mainly for retailing, sport, theatre or film experiences. Any such definition is necessarily problematic. What, for example, constitutes permanence and when does sports education become sport? Or does not charging admission at the entrance, but only for individual activities, effectively constitute admission charging if those activities are essential to the overall experience? And the most fundamental question of all is probably about the centrality of payment, a definition which excludes attractions such as beaches, natural parks, city-scapes and free to enter museums.

For a practitioner such as Robinson (Chapter 13), the relatively narrow type of definition outlined above has considerable utility. It provides a relatively clear definition of which attractions should be included in particular associations, and makes it easier to organise the entities thus defined. It also avoids such thorny issues as who would represent a particular beach as an attraction. However, alternative definitions may have greater utility for tourism researchers. For example, they may want to draw on definitions around the notion of appeal, which clearly cuts across all types of commodification or commercialisation/non-commercialisation, and addresses issues such as individual hotels becoming attractions in their own right. In part, the choice of definition is dictated by both purpose and scale. Thus, while commercial operators, or their associations, may prefer to work with a charging definition, destination/resort managers and policy makers may prefer to focus on the totality of the attractions that determine the overall appeal of an area. This may also require taking into account the event–attraction continuum that was discussed in Chapter 2, and could help obviate the simplistic trap of understanding attractions and events as two dichotomous types. Highlighting where particular phenomena or establishments sit on this continuum can help identify differences and similarities between them in terms of their operations, management and impacts.

The principal authors' view is that it is probably a futile pursuit to become over concerned with definitions, especially of the one-size-fits-all type. The first lesson provided by this book is that definitions can and should be contingent, depending on purpose and scales – and that what is important is that we are clear in our thinking, and specific in our writing, about the particular definitions we employ. The second lesson is that definitions should not be seen to imply homogeneity, a point that is discussed in the following section.

Size, ownership, spatial reach and product similarity

There are many sources of differences amongst attractions and events, but this book has noted the importance of size, ownership, spatial reach and product similarity in particular.

There are enormous differences, even in the commercial sector, between attractions and events which attract small versus large or mega-large numbers of visitors. Larger attractions and events are more likely to have the resources to develop long-term strategies, to have specialised divisions dedicated to say tracking and contributing to social media, and various forms of marketing. They are also more likely to be internationalised in terms of their ownership, which has important implications in terms of their access to knowledge, innovation and capital. In contrast, many small firms have limited staff, and very little formal division of labour. All too often, almost the full range of managerial functions falls on a single individual, which makes such firms highly vulnerable to the loss of a key person. Many small firms may also be engrossed in a persistent struggle to survive in the face of competition, and lack of investment for new innovation, so that day-to-day operational needs may crowd out strategic planning, and many forms of marketing and cooperation.

Ownership is another important source of diversity. The attractions and events sub-sectors have an unusually diverse range of ownership types, especially given the neo-liberal tendencies that have tended to lead to increased commodification of many tourism activities (Shaw and Williams, 2004). This diversity of ownership may reflect the way in which attractions and events often engage with community, heritage and cultural issues. The private sector, as noted above, is likely to range from micro businesses to transnational companies, but they are all effectively operating within the logic of a market economy, even if markets are culturally and institutionally differentiated. Owning and operating a commercial Sea Life Centre, for example, poses different challenges in say the US, UK, France and Sweden, in terms of, say, the regulations pertaining to new firm formation, or public attitudes to the involvement of wildlife in educational or entertainment activities. Alongside the private sector, there is often substantial public sector engagement in the sectors. Major events such as, say, New Year's Eve or New Year celebrations are often organised and significantly funded by the public sector. The same applies to many of the large museums and art galleries, as well as historic and heritage sites. In an era of neo-liberal pressures, many of these events and attractions are increasingly subject to an element of market logic, or at least to tougher cost-benefits analyses. However, ultimately, there is still considerable scope for political intervention in the pricing, access, conservation and other practices of such establishment. Finally, in-between the public and the private sector, there are diverse forms of voluntary, charity and/or third sector ownership, ranging from the heavily subsidised to not-for-profit, and from community to large scale national or international owners. They may rely largely on paid staff or on volunteers, or on a changing mixture of these. In any event, this book has demonstrated the need to avoid over-generalisation about the ownership, motives and competition/cooperation strategies of attractions and events.

The third source of diversity lies in their spatial reach. There are considerable differences in the operating environments of attractions and events whose reach is largely local versus national or international. Their reliance on locals versus day visitors versus tourists is likely to be very different, with implications in terms of the probability of return visits, effective word of mouth recommendations, and indeed vulnerability to shifts in demand. Arguably, the more internationalised the demand, or effective demand, for an attraction or event, then the less susceptible it is to the effects of economic shifts and/or other risks. Given that, even in a global downturn, some national economies and/or regions are less affected than others, the broader the scale of the reach of the attraction or event, the more resilient it will be. In contrast, a relatively high degree of reliance on international markets can be problematic in relation to some human-made or natural disasters in the destination region. In the face of a terrorist bomb on an aircraft, for example, inward tourist numbers may collapse temporarily, compared to say domestic tourist numbers.

The fourth dimension is product similarity, particularly in relation to the thematic content of visitor attractions. This is pivotal because it shapes compatibility, knowledge transfer, diffusion of innovation, cooperation and competition (or coopetition) between individual attractions at different scales. This dimension is particularly important in visitor attractions and events as many, perhaps most, tourists are likely to visit a number of attractions/events in a destination region.

The way in which differences and similarities are combined influences both the appeal of a destination, and how it is experienced by visitors. It is a vital focus for innovation and substantially influences the mix of competition and cooperation at different scales.

The dynamism of attractions and events

One theme that runs consistently through the chapters in this book is that of the dynamism that is inherent in both attractions and events. As key elements in a destination's appeal to visitors, it is essential that attractions and events remain attractive to the ever-changing visitor market. Thus, many attractions, regardless of theme, size or location, change their offerings and image several times through their life cycle in order to meet the changing preferences and tastes of their visitors, and in some cases the changing nature and image of the destination in which they are located. Features may be revamped, some removed, some restored and renovated. Some attractions, such as Dreamland (Chapter 4) undergo massive repair and renovation, while their basic appeal remains constant. Other attractions, such as collections, galleries and museums, rearrange their exhibits, offer special temporary exhibitions and introduce new elements and interpretations. Events are equally dynamic, in some cases preserving a constant theme but using new features and a new cast of performers, in other cases changing themes on a regular basis and in some cases changing all elements from one season to another. Innovation remains at the heart of the process of change, and determines the pace and direction of change, as well as the competitiveness of establishments (Chapter 9).

As well as changing the basic components of their offerings, there are also changes in the relationships between attractions and events. Using knowledge from competitors and the industry at large, they may enter into competitive or cooperative arrangements with other attractions and events, both in their host destination and/or in the surrounding region or even beyond. Destinations, of course, also change through the addition and loss of specific attractions and events, resulting in a potentially fluid set of relationships. While some visitors may regret the dynamic element of this aspect of tourism, preferring their destinations and features to remain constant, in reality the resulting differences in offerings and image presented by destinations is generally perceived as positive by many or most visitors. Change is therefore a constant feature of both attractions and events, reflecting the great selling appeal of the 'new' or apparently new and thus bringing added appeal to their host destinations, helping them to retain existing markets and develop new ones. Innovation, therefore, needs to be seen as multi-scalar, with the individual establishment, the network and the local territory (destination) being the key scales.

Impacts through time and across space and sectors

Attractions and events are probably the key influence on the evolution of the tourism sector, and both directly, and through their influence on other tourism activities, are key determinants of tourism impacts. With the continued growth in the number of, and the scale of visitation to, individual attractions, these impacts have and are likely to come under increased scrutiny. The discussion in this book, especially in Chapter 10, has highlighted a number of distinctive aspects of these impacts, three of which are highlighted here.

First, when discussing impacts, it is essential that we are specific about scale. For example, an event may have very few linkages to suppliers or the accommodation sector in the particular locality, because of high levels of income and expenditure leakage. However, if most of those 'leakages' are to establishments in nearby towns, then there may be very high positive economic impacts and low leakage at the regional scale. Similarly, the local environmental impacts on the immediately adjacent community of a well-managed event or attraction may be negligible, but travel to the event may create very high noise and pollution impacts as well as disturbance along particular routes in the wider region. There may also be variations in the cultural impacts of attractions at different scales. Local residents may suffer from a shift to more standardised or internationalised catering in local restaurants, whereas residents of the wider region may benefit from, say, the creation of a heritage attraction that conserves important aspects of the region's culture.

Second, there is a need to take a holistic view of the impacts, that is, of the economic, environmental and socio-cultural impacts. Positive economic impacts, such as job creation, may be undermined by negative environmental or socio-cultural effects. Yet it is often difficult to reach a balanced overview of these effects because of the problems of comparing across such diverse types of impacts. Cost-benefits analysis represents one attempt to provide a unified analytical framework, but the valuations placed on, say, noise pollution, or loss of 'authentic' cultural elements are notoriously difficult to analyse, let alone quantify.

Third, there is a major disjuncture between individual versus collective outcomes, that is what has been characterised as the 'tragedy of the commons' (Hardin, 1968): in other words, individuals acting in terms of their immediate self-interest may destroy the resource base necessary for a successful long-term future. The pressure on firms, struggling to survive in a tough competitive environment, is to deal with problems and challenges now rather than in the future – especially as there is so much risk and uncertainty in respect of the future. However, while individual operators may prosper for a period, ultimately too much traffic, too much parking, too much new building and just too many visitors may destroy the tranquillity or beauty which appeals to visitors. Such pressing issues need to be addressed by regulation or by new forms of governance. But there are still challenges to be resolved, for example, in maintaining cooperation and partnership between different stakeholders beyond the short term, or in terms of managing impacts that are manifest at different scales, or over different time frames. The challenge is multiplied several fold when the scales of the impacts do not match the territorial structures of government and governance. Yet Feeny et al. (1990) caution against understanding the tragedy of the commons as being deterministic, and not open to challenge by effective coalitions of interests (see Chapter 6 on cooperation).

Some future research directions

While this book has provided an overview of some of the recent growth of research on attractions and events, it is evident that a number of gaps remain in both theoretical and empirical knowledge. These range from the more abstract notions of proximities, and the conceptual differentiation between events and attractions, to more practical aspects such as marketing and technological innovations. One of the most significant of these gaps, which we have already discussed above, is the need to understand interrelationships, whether between scales, or between the economic, cultural and environmental impacts. Another is the interrelationships between attractions and events: to what extent are these competing or complementary within a destination? Is there a substitution effect, with one growing at the expense of diverting visitors from the other, or do they appeal to different or overlapping market segments, with positive spillovers of expenditures between sub-sectors?

Most future research will probably build on the emerging corpus of research that we have selectively summarised in this book. For example, there is certainly room for more understanding of the marketing strategies of different types of attractions or events, and of the challenges of maintaining cooperation over the longer term. Similarly, there is scope for more innovative research that, for instance, considers whether attractions and events can be considered to constitute clusters, linked by shared goals, trust and dense knowledge interchange; or whether differences in their temporality, and possibly in their ownership and motivations, undermine the scope for creating such durable interdependencies. Some of this research will be deeply theoretical, and inaccessible or seemingly irrelevant to practitioners, who seek approachable, feasible and effective solutions and suggestions. But both streams of research are important. Poorly conceptualised practical research may have as little impact as deeply abstract research on the real world of events and attractions. The key point is the need to bridge the two approaches, and to produce theoretically informed empirical research, which is not simply responsive to the immediate needs of the industry, or of a particular community. This is essential if researchers are to bring both managerialist and critical social science perspectives to the understanding of events and attractions. For example, it is important to know both what determines successful innovation in attractions, and the distributional consequences of such innovations in terms of, for example, jobs created or lost, income distribution across the community or implications for health and wellbeing.

Visitor attractions play a pivotal role in the creation and trajectory of tourism destinations. If attractions are linked creatively and effectively by a set of complementarities, like book chapters, into a 'story' or a 'play', they could enhance the destination appeal and image through innovation, cooperation and competition. However, although they largely define the appeal of an area, they do not automatically determine effective demand. The realisation of effective demand depends not only on the marketing of attractions, on the roles of events and on the quantity and quality of a range of other tourism services, notably hospitality, but also auxiliary services such as health, and utilities. An important priority for future research is to look beyond the obvious linkages, and at the direction or causality of those linkages. The insights provided may, however, be difficult to implement because of major, and in some instances irresolvable, barriers that stem from the very nature of the attractions and events sub-sectors. In conclusion, a key question remains unanswered: how is effective coordination to be realised in a market largely made up of private capital which is fragmented, often short termist, and mostly just focused on survival?

References

Butler, R.W. (2015). Sustainable tourism: Paradoxes, inconsistencies and a way forward? In M. Hughes, D. Weaver and C. Pforr (Eds), *The Practice of Sustainable Tourism Resolving the paradox* (pp. 66–80). London: Routledge.

Feeny, D., Berkes, F., McCay, B. J. and Acheson, J. M. (1990). The tragedy of the commons: *Twenty-two years later. Human Ecology, 18,* 1–19.

Hardin, G. (1968). The tragedy of the commons. *Science, 162*(3859), 1243–1248.

Leask, A. (2010). Progress in visitor attraction research: *Towards more effective management. Tourism Management, 31,* 155–166.

Shaw, G. and Williams, A. (2004). *Tourism and Tourism Spaces.* London: Sage Publications.

Urry, J. (2000). *Sociology Beyond Societies: Mobilities for the Twenty-First Century.* London: Routledge.

VisitEngland (2013). Visitor attraction trends in England 2013, full report. Retrieved from www.visitengland.com/sites/default/files/downloads/va_2013_trends_in_england-full_report_final_version_for_publication.pdf (accessed 25 November 2015).

VisitEngland (2015). The annual survey of visits to visitor attractions. Retrieved from www.visitengland.com/sites/default/files/annual_visitor_attractions_surveys_-_update_2014.pdf (accessed 25 November 2015).

Index

Printed in the United States
by Baker & Taylor Publisher Services